Personal Psychopathology

By Harry Stack Sullivan, M.D.

CONCEPTIONS OF MODERN PSYCHIATRY

THE INTERPERSONAL THEORY OF PSYCHIATRY

THE PSYCHIATRIC INTERVIEW

CLINICAL STUDIES IN PSYCHIATRY

SCHIZOPHRENIA AS A HUMAN PROCESS

THE FUSION OF PSYCHIATRY AND SOCIAL SCIENCE

PERSONAL PSYCHOPATHOLOGY

Prepared under the auspices of

THE WILLIAM ALANSON WHITE PSYCHIATRIC FOUNDATION
COMMITTEE ON PUBLICATION OF SULLIVAN'S WRITINGS

Mabel Blake Cohen, M.D.   Dexter M. Bullard, M.D.

David McK. Rioch, M.D.   Otto Allen Will, M.D.

Donald L. Burnham, M.D.

HARRY STACK SULLIVAN, M.D.

Personal
Psychopathology

Early Formulations

With Introduction by
HELEN SWICK PERRY

W · W · NORTON & COMPANY

New York · London

COPYRIGHT © 1972, 1965 BY
THE WILLIAM ALANSON WHITE PSYCHIATRIC FOUNDATION

Published simultaneously in Canada by Stoddart,
a subsidiary of General Publishing Co. Ltd.,
Don Mills, Ontario.

First published as a Norton paperback 1984

Library of Congress Cataloging in Publication Data
Sullivan Harry Stack, 1892–1949.
Personal psychopathology.
Prepared under the auspices of the William Alanson
White Psychiatric Foundation, Committee on Publication
of Sullivan's Writings.
Includes bibliographical references.
1. Psychology, Pathological.   2. Personality,
Disorders of.   I. Title.
RC454.4.S94   1972   616.8'9'07   76-152676
ISBN 0-393-30184-2

PRINTED IN THE UNITED STATES OF AMERICA

W. W. Norton & Company, Inc.,
500 Fifth Avenue, New York, N. Y. 10110
W. W. Norton & Company Ltd.,
37 Great Russell Street, London WC1B 3NU

2   3   4   5   6   7   8   9   0

Contents

Preface

THIS MANUSCRIPT, written between 1929 and 1933, antedates most of the Sullivan material now available in book form and is, to a considerable extent, an earlier statement of some of that material. Yet it is of sufficient interest and value that the Committee on Sullivan Publications has decided to make it available in the present form. The manuscript is the product of several painstaking revisions by Sullivan and has been given only a cursory editorial check for mechanical and obvious errors. The bulk of the editing has been done by Mary Ladd Gavell and Gloria H. Parloff. The index was compiled by Marjorie Henry and incorporated a basic working index prepared by Dr. Ralph Crowley. Although we have been unable to identify all of Sullivan's references, most of them have been confirmed and expanded by Katherine Henry.

> Mabel Blake Cohen
> Chairman, Committee on Sullivan Publications

Introduction [†]

For forty years, Sullivan's *Personal Psychopathology* has been finished and consigned to a kind of publication limbo while unnumbered myths have gathered around it like barnacles, even as myths continue to abound about the man himself. One of the myths centers around the title and Sullivan's own description of the book's fate. In a 1940 listing of Sullivan's writings, prepared by him and published in the journal *Psychiatry*, he gives the date 1932 for the completion of the book and notes that it is "Privately Circulated," as if it were prepared for the eyes of a discreet and limited audience. This notation undoubtedly added to the legend that the title had a special meaning—that the book was revelatory of Sullivan's personal life. In point of fact, it is no more autobiographical than any of Sullivan's other writings or lectures. Yet as I have gathered material for a biography of Sullivan, I have come to think that some such *double entendre* existed for Sullivan in the titling of this book, since he often chose to play with words and ideas, numbers and legends, in some derivative of Irish fancy and imagination. It was his first (and only) book, and the title may have suggested the importance of his one-genus postulate, "We are all much more simply human than otherwise. . . ." *My own experience in growing up*, he seems to say, *partakes of the human scene; however unique the individual aspects of the career line that make up my own life, it is part of the human scene. As such it has relevance for science and theory.*

The terms *psychopathology* and *psychopathologist* were widely used in this country in the 1920s and 1930s by those psychiatrists—and some social scientists—who had begun to identify with the new dynamic psychiatry triggered by Freud's writings. After Brill's translation of Freud's *The Psychopathology of Everyday Life* was published by Macmillan in 1917,

† For personal reasons of health, I have been unusually dependent on the encouragement and skills of Susan Tertell Kiehne and Penelope Markle in the preparation of this introduction. I would also like to express my gratitude to Sheila Hart, chief reference librarian at Widener.

the terms became increasingly popular; and a host of articles and books bore the term *psychopathology* in their titles. Two books in particular were undoubtedly of importance to Sullivan in the titling of his book: Edward J. Kempf's *Psychopathology*, published in 1921;[1] and Harold D. Lasswell's *Psychopathology and Politics*, in 1930.[2] Both men were influential to Sullivan's thinking in this period—Kempf as a dynamic clinician in the mental hospital and Lasswell as a bridge person between the social sciences and psychiatry. At this period, Sullivan thought of himself as a psychopathologist, a professional designation that Kempf has continued to use. Later on, probably in the early part of the 1940s, Sullivan preferred to be known as a psychiatrist, and near the end of his life, he sometimes spoke of himself as a social psychologist. Sullivan's foster son, James Inscoe Sullivan, who acted as his secretary for many years, reports that at one point Sullivan said to him, in essence, "I must have been young and in an expansive mood when I called myself a psychopathologist. Psychiatrist is better."[3]

By 1940, Sullivan's writings clearly reflect a differing attitude about psychopathology as his area of interest; he is explicitly concerned with the total society. Yet the term *pathology* was sufficiently entrenched that it survived in his own milieu longer than the concept did. Thus the journal *Psychiatry*, founded largely by Sullivan in 1938, had as its subtitle "Journal of the Biology and the Pathology of Interpersonal Relations"; and this subtitle survived until 1948 when Sullivan changed it to "Journal for the Operational Statement of Interpersonal Relations." The Journal had long since ceased to be concerned with "biology" and "pathology" exclusively, he explained to me, and he had been annoyed for a long time with the inaccuracy of the subtitle. By then I was managing editor of the Journal, and I had been summoned out to his home on Bradley Boulevard in Bethesda, where he then had his office, to spend the afternoon of Christmas Eve, 1947, reviewing the ten-year history of the Journal, what it had been, what it would become, and how the new title would

---

[1] Edward J. Kempf, *Psychopathology*; St. Louis: C. V. Mosby Co., 1921.
[2] Harold D. Lasswell, *Psychopathology and Politics*; University of Chicago, 1930.
[3] Personal communication, date of Sullivan's remark unknown.

look on the cover—it was somewhat offensive to the eye, he feared.

By that time, he saw pathology in the society as ubiquitous; but the possibility for favorable change was also ubiquitous. Pathology, whether at a personal, national, or international level, could be intensified, modified, or nullified by an interpersonal event or events; each significant encounter had an effect. Even the clinician must learn from his patient, if he were to 'help' the patient. Thus in a sense, Sullivan's formulation, *personal psychopathology*, became over time *interpersonal psychopathology*, and finally simply *interpersonal relations*. And *pathology* had become a static term which he largely abandoned.

The Dilemma of Publication

While Sullivan was still officially connected with the Sheppard and Enoch Pratt Hospital in Towson, Maryland, and living at 809 Joppa Road in Towson, he began the first version of this book, probably sometime in 1929. The impetus for beginning a book was undoubtedly his pending move to New York City, for in the fall of that year Sullivan gave a series of five lectures at Sheppard-Pratt which are known as the Farewell Lectures; these five lectures form, in essence, the first two chapters of the first draft of the book. Ultimately parts of the book went through several drafts, and all of it was rewritten about three times. By 1932, the book was finished and there had been some dealings with the University of Chicago Press, which had published Lasswell's book in 1930. But for many reasons, now obscure, the book was delayed and finally withdrawn from publication channels. By 1939, when Sullivan moved to Bethesda, Maryland, he had abandoned the notion of ever publishing the book, noting that he had "changed my mind," supposedly about the theory.[4] But if one reads the book within the progression of theoretical development from the earliest known published paper in 1924 to the time of his death in 1949, there is only a normal development of a theory; and the book is a necessary part of that progression. Historically this book lies between the two posthumous selections of published papers—*Schizophrenia as a Human Process*, which covers the period before New York City, and *The*

[4] Personal communication, James Inscoe Sullivan.

Fusion of Psychiatry and Social Science, which covers the rest of his life. Thus I included an excerpt from *Personal Psychopathology* as an end paper in the *Schizophrenia* book, in an attempt to have some representation of the unpublished book for that historical context; at that time, in 1962, the William Alanson White Psychiatric Foundation had decided against publishing it formally within the foreseeable future, although a mimeographed version of the book was released by the Committee on Publication in 1965.

As I have stated in an earlier commentary,[5] the reluctance to publish *Personal Psychopathology* has been a subject for some speculation among Sullivan's students and colleagues. Initially Sullivan himself contributed considerably to this reluctance. He tended to be restless about his own theory. He discarded and revised from year to year in his lectures given in the Washington School of Psychiatry and the New York branch of the school. He continually expressed impatience with his own earlier formulations. Over time, some of his colleagues came to agree with Sullivan's reluctance, citing various reasons, some of which seem valid to me and some irrational: Sullivan had a perfect right to publish what he wanted to; his style and vocabulary in this book were lamentable (although it seemed to me that there were numerous examples of the same flaws in all his writings); his strength lay in his clinical acumen and he should not be encouraged to continue his interest in the broader social scene; his physical strength was flagging and he should be encouraged to concentrate on his latest and final statement.

Even after his death in 1949, some of these reasons survived, in my opinion, without much reason for their continuance, so that the controversy continued and it was difficult to know what to do. Social process in such situations often seems to survive past rational limits. With this kind of history, the Committee on Publication is to be commended for finally making the decision to publish.

When I began work for Sullivan in 1946, this kind of concern about publication was still operative in connection with the reprinting of the five lectures that he had given in 1939, known as

---

[5] See, for instance, *Schizophrenia as a Human Process,* p. 319, and Index entries for *Personal Psychopathology* in the same book.

Conceptions of Modern Psychiatry. These lectures, originally published in the February 1940 issue of *Psychiatry*, were by 1946 in great demand by students, and the trustees were reluctant to deplete further the stock of that particular issue of the Journal. One of my first official recommendations was for the reprinting of these lectures from standing type, in monograph form, for distribution to students. To my surprise this recommendation was not greeted with much enthusiasm by the colleagues. One colleague voiced the genuine fear to me that the publication of this series of lectures in book form would so please Sullivan that he would rest on his laurels and never go on to write the book that he should; the *Conceptions* were already superseded by later and better theory, this colleague noted. In the end, these 1939 lectures were reprinted from the Journal, commanded immediate attention in the broadest way, and sold thousands of copies in a short time. In the brief period of life remaining to Sullivan, his productivity and cogency seemed to me to improve as a result of this recognition. Lloyd Frankenberg wrote a brilliant and very favorable review in the *New York Times*, and Sullivan was so pleased with this review that he contemplated having a copy of the book prepared for Frankenberg with illuminated initial letters for each chapter, as I remember it—an ambitious plan which he told me about but which never came to fruition.

Although this legend about the danger of premature publication of a full-length statement of Sullivan's theory seemed to follow him throughout his life, the initial decision about *Personal Psychopathology* seems to have had another dimension. Sullivan reports that mimeographed copies of the book were used as a text in the Yale Seminar on the Impact of Culture on Personality in 1932. The cultural anthropologist Edward Sapir was on the Yale faculty at that time, and participated in that Seminar; and it was partly his influence that determined the use of Sullivan's book at Yale. Sapir had already been quite open in his fear that Freud and his followers were in danger of emerging as a cult instead ·of as important innovators in a new and developing science.[6] Yet dynamic psychiatry, as formulated by Freud, was

[6] See, for instance, Sapir's review of Oskar Pfister's "The Psychoanalytic Method," in *Selected Writings of Edward Sapir* (edited by David G. Mandelbaum); Berkeley: University of California Press, 1958; p. 522. The review was originally published in *The Dial* in 1917.

only beginning to come into its own as a major influence in America by the 1930s. Some psychiatrists feared that Sullivan's connection with social scientists in general and Sapir in particular, and his open contesting of some of Freud's tenets would set back some of the necessary changes in American psychiatry.[7] The whole discipline of psychoanalysis in America was still young and tender, dependent on the good will of the stronger group in Europe. While Sullivan refers to Freud and his theory throughout *Personal Psychopathology* (see Index entries for Freud), his praise of Freud's important contribution, particularly Freud's stress on the importance of the unconscious, is tempered by serious attacks on his theory: on Freud's failure to separate early pleasure-seeking in the child from the maturing sex instinct in the preadolescent and adolescent; on Freud's emphasis on the death instinct; and to some extent on the so-called Oedipus and Electra situations, stating that they are "in no sense hereditary endowments," which seems to be implied in some of Freud's work.

Several colleagues—including a social scientist at Yale—thought that Sullivan would "regret" *Personal Psychopathology* once it was in print. And part of this feeling was undoubtedly related to the fear that dynamic psychiatry, just beginning to be an effective force, particularly in the state hospitals in America, might be cast aside in favor of emergent chemical and mechanical procedures for rendering the patient with "dementia praecox" less troublesome. To some extent, some of Sullivan's early formulations were ahead of his time and seemed to forestall the positive influence of Freud's thinking before it had had time to take root.

Retrospectively, Sullivan's decision to set *Personal Psychopathology* aside was probably a crucial one and represented his first major failure. He was already almost forty when the decision was made, and only seventeen years of life remained to him. While he went on lecturing, publishing an astonishing array of papers, elaborately planning his final theory in his various note-

[7] Personal communications, William V. Silverberg, M.D., and Lawrence K. Frank. In 1962, I interviewed Silverberg in New York and Frank in Cambridge on Sullivan's general contributions to the field of social science and psychiatry, in connection with my work on Sullivan's *The Fusion of Psychiatry and Social Science*; New York: Norton, 1964. Both mentioned independently this kind of climate in the psychiatric community in the early 1930s and saw it as a factor in the reluctance to publish *Personal Psychopathology*.

books, another book did not emerge. Aside from the 1939 lectures known as *Conceptions of Modern Psychiatry*, he made no further such formal effort. He gave lecture series in the two schools, and they were well enough organized and thought through so that books could be taken from them after his death; but the drive for a final definitive statement was gone. To some extent his early disappointment in *Personal Psychopathology* must be seen as considerably dampening his spirits. The stimulation of publishing and receiving some reaction to one's early thinking is an important ingredient in the development of a major thinker.

Clinical Background for the Book

While this book moves sharply toward the social scene and its effect on the incidence of mental disorders, Sullivan's actual clinical experience continues to dominate much of the book; thus it stands as a survey of Sullivan's then recent experience at Sheppard-Pratt and his earlier clinical exposure at St. Elizabeths Hospital. While the years at Sheppard-Pratt have been stressed in my commentaries for the posthumous books, I have tended to overlook some of the important earlier influences at St. Elizabeths Hospital. It is difficult to determine the exact year in which Sullivan had his first significant contact there; he became a liaison officer between the U.S. Veterans Bureau and the hospital in 1922, according to his own biographical notes, but he had some encounters there earlier when he was with the Public Health Institute. Sullivan's relationship with William Alanson White, the then superintendent of St. Elizabeths, was of course crucial, and he continued to mention the importance of White's thinking to him throughout his life. Yet the importance of Edward J. Kempf, M.D., another influence from the St. Elizabeths period, has been largely overlooked by myself and others, probably including Sullivan himself. Although Kempf had officially left St. Elizabeths in 1920 and Sullivan did not have an official connection with the hospital until 1922, they probably met at St. Elizabeths during this interim period, Kempf as a brilliant clinician who was already considered a senior person by the staff at St. Elizabeths, and Sullivan as a relative fledgling in psychiatry.

In the 1939 lectures, published as *Conceptions of Modern*

Psychiatry, Sullivan had given the progression of books and/or
papers and people who had been crucial to him in the evolvement
of this theory. Only six people were cited, notably Freud, of
course; one of the six authors was Kempf and Sullivan stated that
Kempf's book *Psychopathology* and its case reports had an
"importance second to none." [8] In other lectures and writings,
including one brief mention in the present book, Sullivan acknowledged his reading of Kempf; in the course of going over
Sullivan's papers for the posthumous books, I have sought out
Kempf's papers as cited by Sullivan and read a good many of
them in old professional journals. Some ten years ago, I made
some effort to locate a copy of *Psychopathology,* but it was out
of print by then and always missing from library shelves, even
when it was listed in the catalog.

In the spring of 1970, I made a trip to see Dr. Kempf in
Wading River on Long Island,* to talk with him about his relationship with Sullivan. In the course of our conversation, I
became aware of the extent to which Dr. Kempf's vocabulary
and ideas were reminiscent of the vocabulary and conceptions
of Sullivan. So it was that I made another attempt to locate
Kempf's *Psychopathology,* and after so many years found a copy
and delved into it. It was published in 1921, before any of Sullivan's articles had begun to appear. The book itself is dedicated
to Willam Alanson White "as an acknowledgment of the opportunities and encouragement for research work in psychopathology
while on the staff at St. Elizabeths Hospital." Thus Sullivan and
Kempf both acknowledged in differing ways their debt to White.
When one reads Sullivan's book, here presented—or in fact any
part of Sullivan's other books—and compares his thought to
even a part of Kempf's long study, one is immediately struck
by many similarities. In fact, Kempf undoubtedly deserves credit
for trying the new dynamic psychiatry on psychotic patients
considerably before Sullivan. In a case reported by Kempf, a
young woman who was in the state hospital where he worked
was cured by him, or at least effected a social recovery. Kempf
relates her recovery to the fact that she was able to make a trans-

---

* Dr. Kempf died in December, 1971.
[8] For Sullivan quote, see *Conceptions of Modern Psychiatry;* New York:
Norton, 1962; pp. 178–179.

ference to him: "This case was worked out in 1911 after reading Freud's Studies of Hysteria. I now feel sure that only the development of this transference made the later grewsome analysis possible." [9]

Kempf's 1921 statement of his theory is in many ways the basis on which Sullivan began his clinical work. Many of Kempf's phrases and conceptualizations were taken over by Sullivan, with only a general idea of his indebtedness to Kempf. Thus Kempf states that "there is no such thing as an undetermined, absurd, or nonsense expression in a psychosis." [10] This theme is considerably enlarged and made central to much of Sullivan's thinking, eventuating in the one-genus postulate, but it is also earlier reflected in the paper "Peculiarity of Thought in Schizophrenia" (1925), in which Sullivan notes that regardless of how peculiar schizophrenic thought is, it is still *thought*. Throughout his book, Kempf uses *social esteem* in the same sense in which Sullivan uses *self-esteem;* in both instances the emphasis is on the interpersonal, although I did not find that term in Kempf's book.

The importance of the *preadolescent era* in Sullivan's theory is obvious to anyone familiar with his work. The term, which does not appear in Hinsie and Campbell's *Psychiatric Dictionary* (third edition), is indeed somewhat inimical to Freudian thought, since it theoretically partitions what is posited by Freud as a somewhat monolithic sexual instinct from infancy onward. Kempf used the term *preadolescence* in his 1921 book, making it a chronologically longer and earlier period than Sullivan did, from 3 to 10 years of age, and adolescence from 10 to 17. But Kempf's differentiation between these two developmental eras and the naming of them must have been crucial to Sullivan's later theory.

Kempf's attitude toward sexual problems in humans predicts much of Sullivan's thinking in this area. Thus Kempf sees much of heterosexual activity for immature men as being "masturbation per vagina," [11] and Sullivan in the present book states: "The psychopathologist encounters innumerable husbands who masturbate through the instrumentality of the wives' vaginas. . . ." [12]

[9] Kempf, work cited; p. 295.
[10] Kempf, work cited; p. 390.
[11] Kempf, work cited; p. 257.
[12] P. 195.

While such formulations are no longer unique, they were unusual at the time of these two books, and Kempf obviously influenced Sullivan here too. Or again, Kempf advises that psychoanalysis is indicated for autoerotic or homosexual men and women before marriage [13]—thus highlighting at a very early period some of the most advanced thinking about such problems; Sullivan later suggested that homosexual problems were often only symptoms of deeper disturbances in the realm of self-esteem, and this was one of Sullivan's important contributions.

A long quotation from Kempf's book may serve to convey to the reader the nature of Sullivan's debt to Kempf:

> One must, therefore, see that, slowly, but incessantly, from infancy, the autonomic apparatus develops a compensatory capacity to act as a *socialized unity* in order to control the segmental cravings, and these compensatory cravings, through their conditioning by associated stimuli, gradually become interwoven into a personality as a *unity* of constantly active wishes. This *unity* responds to the mother's address of "you," or "John." The child begins to think of itself, as "John won over the bad little boy" or bad impulse or spirit or devil. In this manner is slowly developed the *I, Me, Myself* and the *Not-I, Not-me, Not-myself*. When the personality or organism acts as a unity with the hunger cravings, we say, "I am hungry." When the personality wishes to do something and hunger is disconcerting us, we say, "my hunger," or "this hunger." [14]

Some of this could have been written by Sullivan, so closely does the formulation fit. It is clear that Sullivan depended on Kempf early and late, for *not-me* as a central concept did not appear in Sullivan until much later than this book.

In comparing the two men, I do not mean to derogate Sullivan's contribution or to challenge his integrity. He did mention Kempf in his lectures, and he indicated respect for his contribution. But in the history of ideas, it is often difficult to sort out the earliest and most fundamental influences on one's own thinking.[15] Exposure to new ideas in a new discipline—the experience that Sullivan must have had when he first came to St. Elizabeths—

[13] Kempf, work cited; p. 156.
[14] Kempf, work cited; pp. 55–56; italics in original.
[15] I am indebted to Donald Fleming (Jonathan Trumbull Professor of American History, Harvard University) for the formulation of this phenomenon in a lecture given some years ago.

carries with it a certain inability to sort out what one has formulated himself and what has been transmitted from the environment. As time goes on, the theoretician becomes aware of important modifications in his thinking and the locus of these new influences. But the act of 'discovery' of a new way of looking at mental illness, for instance, carries with it the conviction that one has 'observed' for himself what one has been taught to observe through another's approach. Undoubtedly Kempf's approach gave Sullivan new theoretical perspective on his own difficulties in growing up as well as on the difficulties he saw around him in the mental hospital; and the intellectualization of the observation became absorbed at a level so basic that Sullivan never recognized clearly his basic indebtedness to Kempf. Both Kempf and Sullivan took crucial note of White's influence, and this too helped to blur the particular clarification that Kempf offered. But I do not think that White offered the sharp theoretical tools for observing patients that Kempf did; thus any of White's writings that I am familiar with—although they offer an over-all approach that is humane and sensible—do not have the clinical acumen combined with precise formulation offered by Kempf at such an early period.

Other More General Influences

While I have focused here on Kempf, largely because his pervasive clinical influence on Sullivan has been somewhat minimized by me as well as by others, I would like to note here some of the other influences that dominated Sullivan during the same period. It seems to me that he had an extraordinary ability to take the cream off the thought in his own generation and to early recognize a seminal thinker. Thus at this early period, Sullivan was deep into a variety of disciplines, both in the physical and social sciences, and he had predicted to some extent some of the most important thinkers for the next thirty years in America, in that he had cited their early work before the importance of their contributions was recognized: he was conversant with Malinowski at this period, had a fair knowledge of Piaget's findings and praised him for "rather good observational technique," referred to Bridgman's theories and made use of his vector concept in his own field of interpersonal relations—to mention only a few examples. There are over ninety names mentioned in this book, and most of them are obviously more than casual references. Thus Sullivan makes an extensive analysis of Adolf Meyer's classificatory systems as well as systems suggested by others in the field of mental health and illness. Yet his diligence in analyzing the various classifications suggested did not put him into a corner where he might become wedded to intellectual tools merely because he had mastered them. Thus in this particular book, he uses Meyer's term *parergastic* to replace schizophrenic, for instance; but he later put aside most of the Meyerian terminology and thinking, retaining only that part of it that was most central, most cogent, and melding it almost imperceptibly at times into his total theory.

In a more general way, particularly in the last chapter of the book, he shows extensive knowledge of the institutions of the society as they existed and operated at that time, notably courts, police procedures, mental hospitals, organized religion, and so on, with clear recommendations on the nature of the solutions for their failings—for example, the need for adequately trained and properly paid personnel in remedial institutions of whatever kind.

The most important influence throughout the book is the same influence that informed Piaget's work—the use of whatever observational points are available. Like Piaget in his early work in the observation of abnormal children at the Salpetrière hospital in Paris, Sullivan found the beginning answers in observing the most distressed people in the society and then moved on to the broader scene, trying to seek remedial solutions in the larger world. Along the way, he observed animals, children of friends, students, patients, friends, and above all himself—always himself in interaction with each part of the society. Such observation helped to define the need for *change* in the society. At the same time, there was no merit in simply being new. In the first chapter of the book, he defines the intricacy of meaningful social change:

> The conservative attitude, which, to paraphrase Disraeli, perpetuates in us the errors of our grandparents, and the bohemian attitude which tolerates nothing that is not new—both are archaic. The new may well be worse in its effects on us than the old. The fact of *change* throughout the universe is the nuclear conception that must

be grasped. Nothing is timeless, and this is peculiarly true in the most active area of the world, the living.

A Note on the Chapter on Women

In most of Sullivan's writings, he makes no claim at all to understanding female sexuality; in a number of his lectures, he notes that he is only discussing male sexuality, that no definitive study has yet been made of the female. In this book, he has a chapter entitled "Notes on Female Adolescence." The discussion is inadequate, he says, but he does attempt to cover it in some fashion. This chapter has been widely credited to Clara Thompson, M.D., who was a close colleague of Sullivan's, and she told me some years ago that this was true; but some of the wording seems to be Sullivan's. Compared to Sullivan's chapter on male adolescence, Sullivan's or Thompson's notes on the female seem weak and inconsistent with statements made by Sullivan in his own earlier writings.

Thus, in the last part of the chapter, there is a discussion of the 'modern' woman, "whose ambition is to be a 'man among men.'" Such a woman wishes to enter "the more masculine professions—medicine, law, business," according to Sullivan-Thompson. The rest of the discussion of this 'modern' woman displays a good deal of ambivalence about the viability of a woman trying to achieve respect in the larger world. Yet Thompson was by then a successful practicing analyst in New York; and Sullivan had a reputation for encouraging women of his acquaintance to enter the "more masculine professions." Several successful professional women that I have interviewed have credited Sullivan with the impetus for entering their varying professions within the same general period of this book—university teaching, law, psychiatry, and so on. Thus the Sullivan-Thompson discussion of the dangers of being a 'modern' woman seems more related to an attempt to make peace with the then Freudian attitudes toward the place of women than any conviction within their own separate lives and practices. In a footnote in the chapter on male adolescence, Sullivan also makes a rather dubious statement about the place of orgasm in a woman's sexual life, noting that the "female seems to require only occasional incidents of the physiological activity subsumed in orgasm. I doubt, however, *if the prevailing opinion is correct,* which suggests that these orgasms may be missing for years on end. . . ." The italics in the preceding sentence are mine, for they give a clue perhaps to the rather tentative position that the entire discipline was in at that time in regard to the female. There was no body of knowledge, partly because few women of that generation in our society had any consensual validation on the normal progression of sexual feelings in a woman. For this reason, Thompson was probably of little use in helping Sullivan with this particular part of his discussion. Also Thompson had recently traveled to Europe to be analyzed by Ferenczi; and she was probably at that time more self-conscious about her own 'drive' for acceptance in the "male professions," under the prevailing theory of the new psychoanalysis that most women who were eager to make an intellectual contribution were afflicted by "penis envy." By 1941, Thompson had criticized this concept of Freud's; and in a 1943 article, entitled " 'Penis Envy' in Women," [16] she denied any biological basis for penis envy, equating it with cultural forces.

Sullivan's own statement about female sexuality in a 1926 paper seems to be much clearer than anything in the chapter in this book. In the earlier paper he states:

I will say only that I believe we have thrust upon woman altogether too many conclusions derived from the genetic study of the male; in fact, the adolescent developments in the female, as now described, clearly include such artefacts, so that we are expected to believe that the vaginal erogeny is due to a regression! Perhaps, if investigation will follow a path among the facts appertaining to the female child, in some such manner as I have tried to indicate in the other case [male child], we shall come to an entirely satisfactory and self-contained hypothesis which will regard the woman's psychology as no more a caricature of the male's than is the mare's a regressive distortion of the stallion's.[17]

Having often and rather loudly recommended the formal publication of *Personal Psychopathology* for over a decade, I now feel somewhat reflective and sober as I salute it on its initial

[16] See Clara Thompson, "The Role of Women in This Culture," *Psychiatry* (1941) 4:1–8, and " 'Penis Envy' in Women," *Psychiatry* (1943) 6:123–125.

[17] "Erogenous Maturation," *Psychoanalytic Review* (1926) 13:1–15; pp. 11–12.

flight into the wider world. For me, after many readings, extending over a twenty-year period, it still seems fresh and vital on a high percentage of its pages. I find myself enchanted by the influences that crowd it, both formal and informal, personal and scholarly. In my mind's eye, I can summon up the small schoolhouse in Smyrna, New York, which Sullivan attended for ten years; the schoolyard in the recess period, with the farm boy rubbing elbows with the more sophisticated village children; the shock of going away to school in the larger world and living in a big city for the first time; the initial contact with the lonely ones at St. Elizabeths, and the almost overwhelming awe for William Alanson White that lingered throughout Sullivan's life; the years of intense reading and studying late at night, turning the pages of innumerable books, discovering for the first time the stimulating ideas of Whitehead, Pavlov, Freud, Malinowski, and a host of others; the exciting years at Sheppard-Pratt just outside Baltimore, seeing on his ward the effect of the kinds of social values that H. L. Mencken and Sinclair Lewis were writing about, echoing all the crippling loneliness and hypocrisy that marked his own growing-up years and that of his patients.

This book is, I believe, the working notebook of a seminal thinker; and as such I expect that it will interest many students, particularly those concerned with the development of American ideas. Beyond that, I think that it still has much to say about the need for social change in the larger society, the faults of our institutions, the tragedy of our penal institutions and our mental hospitals. As such it should amaze many of the dedicated young people in our midst today who will discover for themselves that forty years ago someone walked almost the same roads of hope and despair as he contemplated the American scene.

H.S.P.

Cambridge, Mass.
September 18, 1971

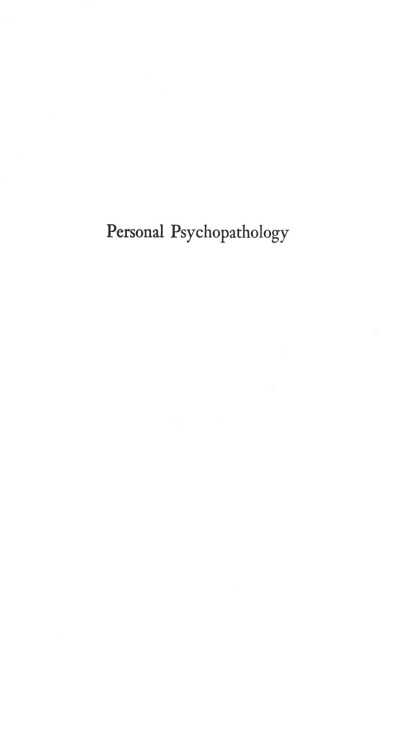

Personal Psychopathology

CHAPTER
I

The Totality of
Organism and Situation

IT HAS BECOME conventional to regard "the mind" * as a dubious
field for investigation. Devotion either to an outworn materialis-
tic tradition or to an even older and more threadbare spiritualistic
metaphysics has eventuated in two groups of crudities in this
field. Thus there are more or less competent "natural" scientists
without number who react to "the mental" as to something necessarily erroneous. And there are sad folk far more utterly without number who demand of "the mental" nothing short of the
truly miraculous. For readers ingrained in either of these traditions, the following pages can bring but disappointment. Psychopathology is neither a form of brain physiology, a system of
speculations about the physicochemistry of nerve colloids, nor a
subvariety of consoling spiritism, exciting pornography, or ele-
vating philosophizing.

Psychopathology is a field of thought in which processes of
living, of actual, mundane *persons*, in and within more or less

---

* *Editors' note*: Sullivan used an abundance of both single and double
quotation marks, originally reserving double quotes for material actually
quoted and using single quotes to call attention to special, often ironic
meanings of words. Helen Perry's introduction follows this policy meticu-
lously. The surviving Sullivan manuscript, however, is highly inconsistent
and has obviously been the victim of successive generations of typing errors.
We have therefore used double quotation marks almost exclusively—and in
most cases the words involved are, in a sense, quotations from common
usage in the field of psychiatry or in society in general. In a very few cases,
where the usage has been closely identified with Sullivan, we have allowed
the single quotation marks to remain.

commonplace *social situations* are studied with some considerable emphasis on the side of the inefficient and harmful. It is thus a division of psychobiology, the division concerned with the evil rather than the good of human life.

As we are all much more simply human than otherwise, so psychopathology deals chiefly with matters of common experience, but with matters the *personal significance* of which is in each case veiled from the person concerned in each unfortunate complex of social living. It does not deal with diseases in the sense of medical entities like scarlet fever, but instead with processes of living that are unusually inefficient, productive of strain and unhappiness, and contributory to failures of the individual as a self-respecting unit.

While there are few indeed who have no self-esteem, and many whose self-regard is pathologically exaggerated, there are numbers of our contemporaries in the case of whom the maintenance of some measure of self-respect is a never-ending task, and one entailing great cost not only in personal effort but also in interferences with the comfort and success of others. It may be said that whenever the maintenance of self-esteem becomes an end instead of a consequent of life, the individual concerned is mentally sick and a subject for psychopathological study, finally to be understood by the same formulae that we must work out for understanding the "neurotic" and the "insane." [1]

That creatures so endowed with abilities to understand and manipulate themselves, their like, and the circumambient world should have spent the first hundred thousand years of their history in getting started is credible. That they should thereafter make a series of not quite successful essays in group living follows easily. That their earlier civilizations were so limited in intrinsic organization that they did not survive seems but natural. That even the current Western European civilization may at times

[1] Neurotic is a word of ill-defined meaning used generally to refer to those suffering the milder mental disorders, such as hysteria and the anxiety states. Insanity is a legal term frequently misused to refer to the grave mental disorders, properly called *major psychoses*—for example, paranoid states, parergasia, and the thymergastic illnesses. Morbid personalities, neither definitely in neurosis nor psychosis, are numerically and socially very much more important than are those ordinarily referred for treatment for mental disorder.

show stress within itself is made possible if by nothing else than by its artificial frontiers of language and politics. But that our people, peculiarly favored by natural resources, possessed of linguistic and political solidarity, and wealthy indeed in technologies in a great many lines; that this offshoot of the Occidental civilization should be almost primitive in many of its current practices regarding interpersonal relations; such a situation is surely unnecessary. The current culture [2] adaptive of man to man is sadly deficient, far indeed behind the development of our technologies and the accumulation of material advantages.

One may surmise that it is by misdirected application of some of his abilities that man has continued in a rather primitive interpersonal adaptive culture. Our unique tool of communication, language, has not proven an unmixed blessing. Verbal behavior can communicate many sorts of things, things fictitious quite as readily as things simply true; and at its best, it can never quite bridge the unique singularity of the creatures that it links. Always an activity using symbols—in this case sounds standing for something else—the verbal operations that include symbols standing for *inner* activities, thoughts, feelings, desires, have ever been equivocal, and man's growth in skill at the task of intercommunicating his inner life with other men has been pathetically slow. Moreover, he has been handicapped in this connection by witting and unwitting interference on the part of the relatively few who came to be particularly apt at verbal performances, some of whom turn their relative advantage to the pursuit of shortsighted personal gain, while others function unfavorably not so much by direct self-seeking as by resistance to man's emancipation from error.

Before he reached the threshold of history, man had found for himself sundry and varied normative formulae referring

[2] Culture is made up of and includes all those entities of the world which are wholly or partly products of the human mind. *Material culture* includes inventions, constructions, wealth, and the like. *Substantive culture* includes language, mores, customs, folkways, law, religion, and other institutions, and the like. The folkways are conventional "ways of doing things" and of thinking. The *mores* are those of the folkways that have become invested with considerable emotional value. (Term derived from the Latin *mos*. See W. G. Sumner, *Folkways*; Boston: Ginn and Co., 1907). We shall presently come to distinguish two types of substantive culture: the *adaptive* and the *normative*.

certain events to transcendental influences, usually with the elevation of some of his fellows to more or less definitely theocratic power. To this day, we have not completed an escape from the theocrats, and the less fortunate live still in a world fogged with ancient verbal entities that have been perpetrated on generation after generation in unwarranted interference with human progress. We shall come presently to some insight into a factor tributory to the ubiquitous belief in a supermundane power. To understand, however, the source of the impulses that make some men claim transcendental authority, and to comprehend the tendencies that cause others to yield unthinking faith to the words of these alleged ministers of God—this double problem will finally be seen to comprise most of the psychopathology, and to be close indeed to the ancient philosophical paradox as to the nature of Evil.

We shall hold, provisionally, that Evil is the unwarranted interference with life. The tracing of the warranty for each interference that one man thrusts on another is a task that should constantly confront the worker of welfare and the physician. The psychopathologist is especially concerned with the interferences with life which are not only thrust upon, but, in fact, built into the individual in his growth among men and their institutions, customs, and fashions. Given an understanding of that which is really warranted in social control and individual self-control, and freed from certain archaic entanglements, Western civilization might proceed in a few generations to a cultural height at which its members would be justified in thinking about God and the universal Purpose, on the basis of real utilization of their marvelously evolved psychophysical organization. Until that time, the religious impulses of man would seem to have abundant outlet in the use of our talents in elucidating individual-social welfare. In this more than abundant meanwhile, any other seems an unsuited vocation, at least for the intelligent and fortunate.

Psychopathology has a peculiar urgency in this field. If one wished to generalize, one might refer this to the passing of the agrarian culture. When man was young, the Gods were near him everywhere. When man became a farmer, They moved off into the heavens and the earth. Now that man has become a tech-

nologist, They have moved very close again, and have taken up residence in other men. The unhappy still pursue Gods over the horizon, but, in the great urban areas, the horizon is one that separates them from an earthly Elsewhere, not one that marks the gulf between Earth and Heaven. This seems, on the whole, to be a healthy progress. It should culminate finally in our coming to know one another, and thus give substance to "the fullness of life." But we must gain and hold to a novel appreciation that this knowledge is not to be obtained except by an investigative process by which we constantly safeguard ourselves from premature conclusions as we go about stripping off the almost infinite superficial fictions, superstitions, prejudices, and delusions that have accumulated as husks around the only entity that we may ever hope to know fairly well—the human personality.

There is an essential inaccessibility about any personality other than one's own. Years of intimacy with another does not put the most devoted friend in a position such that he can predict every act of the other one. No amount of effort at self-revelation conveys the whole unique totality of one's personality. There is always an ample residuum that escapes analysis and communication. There is usually a good deal that seems to have been communicated in the best of faith, which, none the less, is fictitious. The attempt has been valid, but the result is not only incomplete but inexact. No one can hope fully to *understand* another. One is very fortunate if he approaches an understanding of himself.

On the other hand, for the greater part of life, the individual activities of any one of us are very like indeed to well-known, widely-spread human acts. One's way of doing any particular thing is apt to be very well precedented, including but little that is novel. The great body of one's information and belief approaches the content of one's fellows in that particular culture. The great part of one's "explanations" of one's acts is stereotyped and accorded almost automatic responses. Friends accept them unquestioningly and enemies present alternate stereotyped formulae just as widespread and widely accepted. There is no particular indwelling truth in these matters. The two sets of explanations are quite often contradictory, yet equally convincing to selected recipients. Neither set is apt to survive an appeal to impersonal facts, or even a consideration in a time perspective. Our most validly intended act, on which we today stake our reputation, is often so significantly at variance with a related act of three months ago, or one of next year, as to put us to shame. So true is this that, for a fairly large group of our fellows, we have but to ask and receive an explanation of any behavior to be misinformed. And personal appraisals of one's self are well known seldom to merit even qualified acceptance. They are always illuminating, but only the most naive presumes them to be simply related to the facts.

The word that recurs monotonously in most discussions of personal behavior and thought is *reason*. Among some score of dictionary meanings that are attached to this word is its function as a term with which to refer to the abstraction that psychologists call *general intelligence*. Thus, Michael Faraday's reason applied to certain rather well-known phenomena ensued in the formulation of a fundamental insight into the relation of magnetism to electric currents. Human reason is superior to the endowment of other animals. So far, so good. But the "reason" that is most used in conversation is of quite another order. A reasonable statement is frequently no more than a *plausible* reference to some mutually accepted principle or belief. "Reasoning" then becomes the finding of a mutually accepted belief with which to justify one's action, or to convince another. This process, by which almost anything that anyone may do on any occasion can always be "explained" in a self-congratulatory fashion, we technically call rationalizing. The phenomena of rationalization are the principal ingredients of most explanations of one's behavior; the extreme ease with which a commendatory principle is found for any action is the outstanding handicap to self-understanding and to the objective appraisal of other people who stand in an emotionally-toned relationship to one. The behavior of one's friends is always to be explained by reference to the currently approved conventions; that of one's enemies, to the more prevalent unfavorable prejudices. And irrational and frequently inconsistent personal prejudices, likes, and dislikes are an almost ubiquitous characteristic of man. They provide the levers by which propaganda carries its victims before it. So greatly do they expose their carriers to emotional manipulation by crafty folk that a mutuality of prejudice comes often to be a strong bond of affection; and many a disintegrating association of people has been given new solidarity by the discovery of something or someone to defend or to oppose.

As prejudices stand to the individual, so the mores, the submerging prejudices of the group, stand to each social unit. The mores are generally irrational. They include glaring inconsistencies. They are almost universal within the group. They are all but indomitable. Their influence is not to be questioned by reason. They are accepted as innate, "right" ways of doing and thinking. The man who questions one of them finds himself suspect by all "good people." He is judged to be perverse, irreligious, or insane. In some cases, his depravity offends; in others, infuriates. There is no need for giving him answer; "everyone knows" the correctness of that which—for reason of personal Devil, malicious mischief, or disease—he has the temerity to question.

The prejudices of an individual and the mores of a group have each a history. Each has an origin, a differentiation from something else, and a course of evolution to the particular manifestation currently encountered. Each has originated in some necessity, which has been somewhat mitigated as a result. This is a general formula of life to which we know no exception: mental acts have always some measure of validity; they do not occur to no purpose whatever. But, if the prejudice or the custom has been crystallized in a behavioral formula—for example, speech or ritual—it generally outlives any vestige of its initiating purpose and is used long after it has become an obstruction, rather than some measure of facilitation, to the life of the carrier organism. It does not remain just what it was in the beginning. It changes rather than remains static. But the velocity of change is apt to be so low that it escapes any notice of the carrier, and correspondingly obscures his observation of the changes in his necessities.

The mores manifest themselves in the doing of people, and their changes are similarly manifest. If the transitions are insidious, their manifestations are apt to come gradually and all but universally among the group. If the change is rapid, the manifestations in individuals are apt to be much less uniform, and some continue for a time quite unaffected. If these latter be numerous, the "resistance" to those "in step with the times" may easily burst out in such violent opposition as to palsy the progress— occasionally, to reverse the movement. It behooves the man on the progressive fringe of social change to go circumspectly, lest he be thrown to the lions, lest he be placed on trial before the bar of "what has been tested and tried by a thousand years of human achievement, the precipitated wisdom of the ages." But the mores change, regardless; and to hold today to some things which everyone knew were right two hundred years ago might well lead to one's permanent confinement in a mental hospital; even as some things which everyone knows are good and proper cause for penal servitude today may come to be civic virtues two hundred years hence.

At least for a time in the span of each, the crystallized prejudices of a person and the mores of a group serve a purpose. For that period each is to be regarded as a valuable if imperfect formulation of experience. There could scarcely be social living without a large body of customs of behavior, thought, and valuation. The time and energy necessary for dealing with novel situations could scarcely be found if one had to reach good formulations for most of his interpersonal experience. Within limits, the more of life that is stereotyped, the greater the freedom of the individual. That this paradox has decidedly real limits has been evidenced repeatedly in the historic period. But any notion that wholesale destruction of prejudices and mores, were it feasible, would in itself represent a great progress, is everywhere contradicted in the current situation. Thus, failure of the individual to find a group to support him by adhesion to some novel course of behavior, thought, and valuation to which his participation in life has carried him, appears to be an important tributary to the increasing disability from mental disorders.

It is the magical power of the formulated mores that must be called in question. Just as the unthinking acceptance of personal prejudice has to be broken down before a man can be led toward self-appreciation, so also the inviolate durability of emotionally-toned customs has to be shattered before the group can advance rapidly to new levels of achievement by way of a clearer understanding of its problems. Hallowed beliefs, enshrined prejudices, and sanctified customs are more apt to be chains fixing people

to their barbarous ancestors than distinctions that elevate them
to something possessed of fairly human value. The durability
of a custom is a function of the necessity that gave it birth; but
it is also—in so far as it implies a low velocity of change—an
index of its potentialities for evil. Some primitive folk ascribe the
lightning to an angry god, while many of our contemporaries
confuse antiquity with venerability, if not with transcendental
origin.

The conservative attitude, which, to paraphrase Disraeli, per-
petuates in us the errors of our grandparents, and the bohemian
attitude which tolerates nothing that is not new—both are
archaic. The new may well be worse in its effects on us than
the old. The fact of *change* throughout the universe is the nuclear
conception that must be grasped. Nothing is timeless, and this
is peculiarly true in the most active area of the world, the living.
Everything human changes inevitably. Change has to be accepted
as one of the given characteristics of reality. Attitudes intolerant
to the new or to the old are morbid, and only a broad tolerance
fits one to deal with people as they are. Man has enough inherent
distaste for any marked novelty to insure him from disastrous
innovation—except when he is rendered mentally sick by artificial stabilities to which he is required to conform. Our growing
appreciation of the nature of man and the social processes manifesting in and through him must make us ever more skeptical
toward any finality in human formulations, and increasingly
cautious about emotional extravagance in regard to beliefs and
customs.

The American culture shows an enormous lag [3] in the sense
that the accumulation of material culture is proceeding at a high
rate while the achievement of substantive culture, particularly
culture adaptive to the pyramiding material advantages, is proceeding but very slowly. In this situation, we must school ourselves to true tolerance for inventions in adaptive culture, something utterly new to the majority. Such tolerance requires a
novel appreciation of the intrinsic value of knowledge concerning
the underlying realities of man and of group life. This is no open-
mindedness toward philosophical realities, toward ultimates of

[3] See William F. Ogburn, *Social Change*; New York: Viking Press, 1922,
for a good presentation of the conception of cultural lag.

human nature and culture, whatever, if anything, these may be. It implies a warmly receptive attitude to the discovery of the actual processes going to make up, firstly, the conversion of the newborn, marvelously adaptive human creature into a product of family and school culture, and secondly, the adjustment of this individually cultured youth to life as a person among the complex personal and superpersonal entities making up our modern world. These processes, now but dimly adumbrated, must be essentially simple and within the grasp of the reasonably well endowed. Their discovery, however, requires a wholly unprecedented variety of open-minded investigation and experimentation. No one may any longer expect much discovery to follow automatically from living. If it did, there would be no social problems, interpersonal relations would be our "most natural" success, instead of our most universal failure, and self-respect would be so integral and uniform a human characteristic that we would probably have no verbal expression for it. The discoveries which we must seek require a new orientation to the material of investigation—interpersonal relations.

Life begins in the primary group. The child is born into a world composed principally of materials and two people. He includes within the physical confines of his body individual cells aggregating a number between two and three followed by thirteen ciphers. He has something like twelve thousand million nerve cells. In his first eighteen months, he develops a marvelous relationship to the materials of his world. At the same time, he is developing facilities for *communication* with his people. Soon after birth, he responds to emotional conditions in the mother. We may say that he prehends [4] the signs made up of facial postures, gestures, and the like. How this prehension comes about need not concern us; we have not yet secured the factual material from which to make the processes clear. To this primitive interchange or intercommunication of emotional tones between par-

---

[4] To *prehend* is to be understood as a step toward conscious apprehension, in the sense of having at least *capability* of verbal formulation. In other words, the initial *sentience* poured into the person, as a result of involvement in a particular stream of events, is elaborated usefully—but not to the point of being communicable by speech, writing, or the graphic techniques. It is conceived that many prehensions occur without any "knowledge" of the individual.

ent and child we apply the term *empathy*.[5] In empathy, we have a factor of great importance throughout life. No matter how far one comes to see "as if through a glass, darkly" as a result of cultivating the scientific technique, every one of us "knows" about some other ones who are really of importance to us, a body of fact the communication of which has been quite exterior to our knowledge. When questioned about any particular manifestation of this knowledge, either we appeal to our "faculty" for giving plausible "explanations"; or we read into these situations the manifestation of an inexplicable process of *identification*. It seems decidedly simpler to accept the one mystery of empathy clearly manifest very early in infancy and continuing as a factor of extreme importance in its effects throughout life.

Not very long after joining this world, the young one begins to acquire the great tool of *primary* communication, the spoken language of his people. Already he has acquired a great many of the deep unconscious man-ways. He now begins a long education in the mores, the customs, the fashions, as they are represented in his primary group.

With the acquisition of ability in reading, the confines of the primary group begin to expand. He now receives intelligence from people not directly present to his senses. To this extent, he is capable of entering into secondary group relationships, and of receiving information from the great world. As soon as he has learned to write, he is equipped with the basic tools for our fullest type of group living. He needs nothing more except knowledge and skills in various technologies.

If it were not for the unyielding primacy of the experience that he has received by empathy, the child would profit greatly

[5] That I ignore any physical medium and any definite end-organ in the statement of the term *empathy*, need not disconcert the student. The "obvious reality" of vision and hearing, for example, rests in a considerable measure on two series of events: on the one hand, the impressive force of utility of comparatively simple functions of the organism together with our study of the histology and physiology of the parts concerned; and, on the other hand, an appeal to the *exact measurement* of phenomena of nature which had been clearly perceived to have an immediate relationship to the subjectively observed sensory phenomena. Empathy phenomena—because they are not by any means so simple, nor once verbal communication and visual interpretation are acquired, so continually impressive—have been permitted to remain chiefly exterior to careful investigation.

from novel experience coming toward him in the secondary group interchanges of reading. If it were not for this primacy, the defects and deficiencies of the home group would slough off in subsequent education in the school. But the emotional processes are more anciently established than are the intellectual. The nerve cells that require the years of infancy and early childhood for their functional maturity are phylogenetically recent. The old brain that mediates emotional life learns its lessons in early infancy. Growth of the nice discriminations by which one comes to apprehend the novel in the manifold of the accustomed tends to be almost as rare as genius. The emotional stereotypes exterminate budding tendencies to originality step by step throughout the course of personality growth. No one can guess the range of individual differences in potential abilities of the newborn. There are good grounds, however, for assuming that the proportion of these abilities that reach some degree of fruition in adulthood is exceedingly small.[6]

The foetus in the womb of its mother lives in communal existence with her. However carefully the anatomist may figure out that which is foetus and that which is mother's body, we know that there is no real disjuncture. There is an unending interchange from mother to foetus and from foetus to mother. Just this *communal* existence, without disjuncture, is one of the three major categories of the factors that are encountered in the scientific analysis of life. Not alone the foetus, but everything that lives, does so in communal existence with its medium, its environment. The organism once actually separated from a certain necessary environment ceases to live. There is no such thing as an organism living *out* of its medium. Neither is it possible for us at any time to differentiate completely the organism from its environment. The two are indissolubly mingled, regardless of the degree of organized integrity that the organism may possess.

The fertilized egg, safely ensconced in its suitable medium, proceeds by cell-division to grow into a member of its biological

[6] It is hoped that these comments will not be regarded as justification for one of the current, or recently current, educational doctrines—that of "self-expression." The facilitation of bizarrerie during childhood or in the course of the juvenile era, after the greater and entirely irrational part of the human cultural heritage has been built into every personality, is an unexcelled instance of our social tinkering in lieu of social melioration.

species. Its proliferation of cells, their differentiation, their arrangement—all the processes which miraculously produce from two confluent cells a fully developed creature—all these may be subsumed as factors of *organization.*

Certain parts of each organism are arranged in such manner as to facilitate the communal existence in and within the environment. To these regions we refer as *zones of interaction:* for example, the respiratory apparatus of man, the lung cells being the zone of interaction for the gaseous interchange. We speak of *functional activity* within the organism-environment complex as making up the processes of life, and thus complete the rudimentary sketch of the fundamental categories of biological factors.

Processes and the interrelations of processes; of these the world is composed, and with these psychobiology and psychopathology are concerned. Throughout, as in general biology, the three groups of factors mentioned above have constantly to be kept in mind: communal existence, now not alone in and within an environment physicochemical in nature, as ordinarily conceived, but in and within an environment including, as important elements, other people and those monuments and ghosts of other selves, the institutions, traditions, mores, and economic and social situations, that go to make up culture, however simple. And secondly, organization, now not alone of the physicochemical universe, but also of the entities of this expanded world including other selves and culture. And lastly, functional activity, again inclusive of the incredibly complex groups of processes making up other people, and the interwoven suspending and enmeshing fabric of culture. The zones of interaction to which we must give chief attention are not simple—and none the less marvelous —cellular membranes that maintain a wonderful one-way traffic. They are such complex psychophysical appurtenances, for example, as the organs of the special senses, the apparatus of speech, and the syncretistic-analytic dynamisms making up the prehension and intelligent perception of the "outer" world.

The person, then, is an extremely complex bundle of processes and their relations, organized from units of the physicochemical, the social, and the cultural worlds, in communal existence through functional activity in and within these three spheres.

We make use of the term *mind* to subsume those aspects of the life-process that represent total actions of the person in and within the total situations in which he has his being. The mental life is composed of total activities, in contradistinction to local action; of manifestations of the individual as a person in communal relationship in and within total situations, rather than of events in which but a part of his organism is affected by the impinging on it of some externally or internally conditioned circumstance. As the individual is but a bundle of processes and their relations, it might be thought that any event impinging upon him must extend its 'effects' throughout. To revert to the universe of physics, a magnet may be said to radiate stress the theoretical limits of which are wide-flung. The practical limits of these stresses, however, are close to the magnet. The attenuation of influence from the magnet is very rapid, so that, while there may be an intense "field" between its poles, the field intensity fades to an infinitesimal value at a finite distance, and we look for effects of the magnet only in the neighborhood of its poles. So, likewise, we look for the 'effects' of an event impinging on an individual to manifest themselves either as an activity of the person—mental phenomena—or as localized phenomena in close relation to the area of contact only. We distinguish events which expend themselves on a limited aspect of the organism as *local action.*

A hot cinder falling into one's eye exerts marked effect upon certain conjunctival cells. It exerts noticeable effect on certain nerve endings. These effects may properly be called local action. If one is studying the life of conjunctival cells, one must regard these phenomena as of total activity—they represent the whole gamut from healthy life to utter destruction and dissipation of life. But from the standpoint of the person, we have, so far, only local action. However, we also have total activity because, due to the irritation of the nerve endings, the organism as a whole is made aware of pain, and of the location of the injury, and there ensues certain behavior for the relief of pain. In so far as the person is aware of pain and thereupon suspends everything else he is doing to make some movements toward relieving the pain or removing the cause of it, to that extent we have total activity in and within a situation including the cinder-falling-in-the-eye event.

Needless to say, there is a borderline where one cannot, except by definition, establish that a particular event leads to total activity or to local action. I wish to discuss two aspects of this uncertainty, some consideration of which is essential for clear thinking in psychopathology. One I have touched upon; it is the point of view with which one approaches the situation. To a student of cytology, the injury of a conjunctival cell is perhaps as broad a field of study as one could wish; such injury is total activity in a total situation concerning a conjunctival cell. As a physiologist, one may be concerned in such a situation with the way in which the related nerve endings act, how the body fluids act, how the neighboring cells act, and so on and so forth, both in getting rid of the cinder and the destroyed cells, and in repairing the wound in the conjunctiva. To a physiologist, leaving out pain in its larger aspect, leaving out the interruption of talking or whatever else one might be doing when the cinder made its presence felt, there is still plenty of total activity in the total situation to be studied. As a psychologist, or a psychopathologist, however, one is interested in the eye only in so far as it is the special place of impinging of an event and to that extent conditions the succeeding phenomena. It is chiefly that which happens to the thought and behavior of the individual, the manifestations in a total situation, that one studies. As a student of larger than personal units, one may become concerned as to a whole stream of social phenomena arising within an organization of which the affected individual happened to be a significant unit. One can conceive instances, for example, where the eye concerned is that of a railroad-yard switch control man on the point of clearing a through-express around a stalled freight. Being distracted by pain, he may have delayed the necessary movements a little too long, in which case everything that happened to him as a result of his eye injury may well be considered to be local action, from the standpoint of the public concerned. The total activity occurs in a wide group of people of which he can be considered to have been the essential center at the moment of the cinder-in-the-eye event.

There is, then, an objective consideration of the course of events concerning an individual, which may distinguish local action in and within the organism from total activity of the person. There is also a subjective aspect to this dichotomy, and a borderland in which such a two-part classification has its difficulty. Certain events impinge upon the individual and produce definite sequences clearly total in character; a matter "given" focal attention within the individual's consciousness is obviously in this category. Even in the case when attention is but marginal, it is still marginal attention of the total organism, total activity rather than local action. There remain two cases to be considered, the event in either case causing no occupation of attention and no subsequent alteration of the behavior and thought of the individual, *so far as his subjective appraisal is concerned*. Called to his attention, such events must be viewed by the individual as events of local action if of anything at all. Turning, however, from the subjective appraisal (or lack of appraisal) to the objective, we find that *some* of these unnoted events are clearly reflected in an altered subsequent course of the individual, are events of total activity, although their prehension has been extraconscious or unconscious. Of these we shall have a great deal more to say. Others of the subjectively unappraised events that the observer notes as impinging upon the subject-person have to be regarded as actually nonexistent—from the standpoint of the personality primarily concerned. They are artifacts *projected* into the siutation from the personality of the observer, and are irrelevant to the subject-personality's total situation.

While all *total situations* combine to form *the* total siutation, the universe, only some certain factors in the momentary situation of a person are relevant to the course of events concerning him. Of these relevant events, many are practically universal and unchanging over relatively very long periods of his life. The latter are therefore of but limited relevance in delineating the factors entering into the total activity in which he is engaged. We may, then, define the total situation of any person as that complex made up of his "own" organization, the relevant environmental factors, and the relation existing between these (somewhat indistinguishable) two elements, including particularly the changes in the complex which are being brought about by his activity.

A complication is introduced into this explanation of the mental as the total activity occurring in a total situation by the necessity of including the conception of *potentiality* of action. The vast stores of memory are obviously contributory to each total situation. The "surviving past" is in part relevant, and some of the relevant "past" enters into most total actions, yet we need not concern ourselves with a theory of memory. The conception of potential energy in physics has found a degree of realistic explanation, but it served quite efficiently long before. So likewise with much that is recondite in the life processes; we need not concern ourselves primarily with the ultimate nature of the matter, but only with its effects as we encounter them. Thus we can scarcely hope to state the nature of *thought*, considered as an implicit or inner process. Yet everyone knows that such processes occur. Everyone knows that each thought is in our terms a total activity; it is *his* thought, not an affair of his brain, or his endocrines. And there are but few who encounter any great intellectual difficulty in adding "inner" processes without immediate "outer" manifestations to the conception of total activity in and within total situations.[7] It will presently appear that some of these implicit total activities go on quite without representation in consciousness; in other words, that just as there is explicit total activity that is unknown to the individual concerned, so also he is given to subconscious or unconscious "thought." Since the total situation concerns all the actually relevant factors, and since these unwitting processes may at times possess extreme relevance, the analysis of a total situation is not by any means a matter simply of objective inspection.

Total activity refers, then, to that which the whole person does. Our next concern becomes the matter of the way in which even the more concrete individual part of the person, itself of great complexity and engaged in most complex functional activity in communal existence, can enter into any one thing as a total activity. We thus come to the conception of *integration*. In passing from the unicellular type of organism to the highest one, one finds in the phylogenesis of life increasing specialization of dynamism [8] for keeping the complex aggregation of morpho-

[7] This is offered notwithstanding the Watsonian "behaviorist" preoccupation, with its peculiar restriction to that which it can call "objective." For the rest of us, the "private history of great events" often includes some particular "streams of thought."

[8] The writer objects to the term *mechanism*, because of its wholly gratuitous implication of substantial engines. The term *dynamism*, implying a complex of energy, however manifested, seems much more alignable with the current hypotheses as to the fine structure of the universe. Moreover,

logic tissue-systems and the varieties of functional activity tied together. At the level of the mammals, there are three clearly distinguishable dynamisms used for that purpose. The earliest evolved is one which depends on fluid circulation for its effectiveness in functioning. This one, perhaps foreshadowed in the general protoplasmic properties of irritability and conductivity, is shown in the activity of autacoids—complex substances elaborated by the endocrine (ductless) glands. In keeping with the type of total-organism–total-situation complex which permitted evolution of the early multicellular organism, the adjustive facilities provided by the autacoid dynamism of integration are suitable only for low-velocity, relatively massive, changes in process.

The second integrator is much more specific in its fields of effect, and, both relatively independently and by the way of its intimate tie-up with the autacoid dynamism, can produce change in processes with much greater speed. This specialization of functional activity and morphology—including the palaeoencephalon (old brain) and the involuntary or vegetative "nervous system"—permits a decidedly more complex type of communal existence than did the autacoid dynamism alone. The relative number and the variety of factors which can enter relevantly into a total situation centering in an organism possessed of this higher type of integrator dynamism are greater by far than in the case of one dependent on the autacoid dynamism alone.

It is essential that the student take care always to view integration as a process occurring in and within a complex organism-environment situation more or less definitely 'held together' by the integrator dynamism concerned.[9] The autacoid dynamism

it avoids too close an ideational association of known function to unknown structure. The adoption of the writer's suggestion in this connection in so valuable a treatise as *The Structure and Meaning of Psychoanalysis as Related to Personality and Behavior,* by William Healy, Augusta F. Bronner, and Anna Mae Bowers; New York: Knopf, 1930, may mark the scientific popularization of the usage.

[9] Error arises as soon as the psychobiologist or psychopathologist permits his thinking to take the form of "considering the effect of the basal ganglia on the expression mechanism," or otherwise artificially to disconnect these integrator-dynamisms from the organism-environment totality in which they are functionally meaningful. It is perfectly right and proper to emulate C. S. Sherrington, for example, and study the integrative action of the central nervous system, as a matter of physiology. Our concern, however, as students of human nature and the processes making up human life, excludes preoccupation with these part-aspects of the organism.

suffices to integrate situations of a certain complexity as to the factors concerned; the palaeoencephalic dynamism (including the whole 'involuntary nervous system') functions to integrate situations of a much greater complexity. But the integration of these organism-environment situations of one sort or another is not something done by the organism in identical situations. This is the old view of the organism as a separate entity, as not in communal existence. The integrating of a situational complex differently from another integration means that the *situation* in its totality is different—different environmental factors and different organismic factors are brought together functionally.

The first of the integrator dynamisms, the autacoid system, was for a long time overlooked—and is now receiving frequently quite fantastic attention. The phenomena in which its activity is most clearly manifested are those of the more forceful emotional states. In other situations its activity is overlaid by the more discriminative neural (nerve) systems. The autacoid dynamism functions with peculiar reference to factors in the immediate environment of the organism, in fashions perhaps most clearly to be analyzed by comparative biological procedures applied to the reactions of much simpler creatures. The old nervous system, on the other hand, even from its appearance, had very significant relation to situational factors existing well beyond the spatial limits of that which is obviously the organism. It included specialized receptors for effectively connecting the organism with certain external factors. Thus the line organ of fishes— which probably has a great deal to to with the ability of the fish to maintain a vertical course through its medium—is perhaps the evolutionary parent of these. This initial system has been well elaborated until we have many different groups of processes, the referent of which, one might say, is clearly outside the spatial limits of the organism.

We have, then, devices for keeping track of processes going on outside of the clearly organic processes but having great importance for success of the organic processes. On the basis of this 'remote control' the third system has made its appearance and exercised its very great influence on the course of evolution that has culminated in man.

Not only does the neoencephalic dynamism permit the integration of extremely complex situations *existing* in the ordinary sense of the word, but it also develops a prompt and specific connection of past experience of the organism with activity concerning the particular 'diagram' of the situation in which the organism is existing at any moment. In other words, the third integrator system, the new brain, seems to be largely a device by which all the previous experience of the organism, of relevant events that have impinged upon the organism, is made accessible, that is, readily usable, in 'directing' the total activity which any particular situation demands for its resolution.[10]

Life processes are series of events inseparably interwoven with events of other sorts: with 'inorganic' events, with events of subhuman living things, and, particularly in the mental field, with events of other human lives, contemporary or existing from the historic period. It appears that the situation that includes each individual and everything else relevant to him at a particular time has implicit in it a 'demand,' so to say, for certain processes in and within the situation. This demand of the total complex is a demand in much the same sense that a magnet demands movement of its armature—demands certain processes. These 'demanded' (and forthcoming) processes are the processes of living which, in the mental field, we call *actions toward adjustment* (biological adaptation).

Action toward adjustment is to be taken to refer to specific activity in a particular total situation, and not to an enduring condition. It is necessary to distinguish this specificity from such usages as "maladjusted children," "good home adjustment," and the like, which imply statistical norms or averages, derived or alleged to be derived from series of total situations involving many individuals. In this text, the three terms *adjustment, mal-*

[10] These remarks concerning total activity in total situations are not wholly without relationship to current psychological thought. They are probably nearest to the viewpoint of the *Struktur Psychologies*. See, in particular:

Kurt Koffka, *The Growth of the Mind: An Introduction to Child Psychology;* New York: Harcourt Brace, 1924.

Wolfgang Kohler, *The Mentality of Apes;* New York: Harcourt Brace, 1925; *Gestalt Psychology;* New York: H. Liveright, 1929.

F. Krueger, *Uber Entwicklungspsychologie;* Leipzig: Engelmann, 1914.

E. Spranger, *Types of Men;* Halle: Max Niemeyer Verlag, 1928.

L. William Stern, *Psychology of Early Childhood up to Sixth Year of Age;* New York: Henry Holt, 1924.

adjustment, and *nonadjustive situation* never arise from inference imparted to a statistical treatment of the individual's acts, or of acts customary in the group in which he has his being. If the particular action *actually in progress* in the total situation at the moment involving a particular individual (and other individuals as important factors in the situation) is proceeding in a manner such that the situation is being changed in the direction of resolution, we regard the person as showing more or less fully adjustive processes. If the particular action is continuing the situation without material change, we say that the individual is engaged in nonadjustive processes. Almost any form of activity may be more or less adjustive in most situations, and there is little to be gained from classifying forms of activity on the basis of the frequency with which they are used adjustively. Despite this, there are two kinds in particular, depressive ruminations and worry, which but very rarely accomplish much besides the extension of a total situation in time, and which therefore, are quite generally nonadjustive. They seem, at first glance, to violate the principle that all mental activity is directed toward the achievement of an at least dimly foreshadowed goal. The goal, however, of the nonadjustive activity—a bundle of processes—is the neutralization of other processes making for change in the situation. They are directed toward a preservation of the status quo, toward a stabilization in the shifting flux of life which is as truly impossible as its achievement would be undesirable to mankind at large. The nonadjustive situation includes then a distinguishing *impossibility,* in contrast to all other situations.

Actions toward adjustment, then, do not include the preservation but always the change of a situation. The utility of the distinction between processes as adjustive and as maladjustive in particular situations arises not from consideration of possibility as against impossibility of achievement of the implied goal, but rather from considerations of ease and difficulty, of directness and indirectness, of simplicity and complexity. Maladjustive processes occur in unduly complex situations and are in themselves unduly complex processes. The undue complexity refers not to a statistical norm, but to the abilities of the individual concerned, as they chance to be correlated with and to constitute significant factors in the given total situation. A situation that is relatively simple for one person might well be very complex for another, depending on the previous experience, native endowments, and so on, of the individuals concerned. Statistical considerations, to be relevant to this conception, become so specialized as to be useless. The conception of maladjustment is thus seen to refer to the momentary (even if relatively persisting) life situation, and to imply a complexity which prevents a characterizable satisfactory progression—a progression the absence of which is accompanied by certain objectively detectable phenomena. Thus, the individual may become "tense," he may suffer "emotional disturbances," or he may "have difficulty concentrating." In other words, he is uncomfortable either subjectively or as a person among other persons. As long as one's progression does not cause suffering or discomfort to one's self or to environing people, or to both, the total activities being manifested are to be considered to be of a decidedly adjustive character.

If, now, factors "in him" from his past experience, native endowment, or both, or factors "in the external situation," conspire to demand two or more sorts of resolution of the existing situation, then there appear complex processes that are definitely painful to the person, to environing persons, or to both. A crude example may be helpful in elucidating this view. A mentally defective person may be required to "understand" a complicated algebraic formula well beyond the grasp of his intelligence; this may constitute a situation in which adjustive, maladjustive, or nonadjustive processes make their appearance. If the "requiring" is of such a character that no factors of prestige or status as a person are included, the individual, after some effort, resolves the situation by "giving it up" and passing on to something else. In such a case, there is no suffering. If, however, he has been made to feel that other people will think less of him if he fails, if he has been taught to anticipate scoffing following a demonstration of his inability to handle certain problems of this kind, then his situation will include not alone the demand for understanding of the algebraic formula, but also a demand—a powerful demand —for preservation of his status and his self-respect. As he comes to a realization of the hopelessness of his grasping the formula, he is required to act in such fashion as both to abandon the problem and to seem not to have failed. In such a case, he suffers.

If, in the presentation of the situation, he is caused to perceive that failure will entail the loss of some, to him, extremely desirable factor, then the realization of his impending defeat may be attended by a blocking of activity such that he merely frets or grieves, doing nothing about the problem—a nonadjustive situation. It is perhaps more often the case, under this type of circumstance, that he shows, instead of the "self-contained" distress, random activity or rage behavior, thus exteriorizing his suffering and actively involving others. Finally, particularly if this situation has followed on a long series of rebuffs, he may disintegrate the complex situation, "ignore" the complex demands, and involve himself in a simple apathetic self-absorption, or a "childish" amusement, in the course of which the environing other people and their activity cease to be relevant to him, and if they have any effect, reach him only by way of subordinate processes more or less completely exterior to his awareness.

Were the integration of total situations a matter of cold intellectual appraisal of all the factors concerned, the occurrence of a too complex situation would be singular, indeed. The general rule would be somewhat the sort of action which the skilled mechanic shows in dealing with a mechanical difficulty that he is competent to understand. But instead of this, almost from the moment of birth onward the factors of prime significance in the integrated total situations are other people, and other people go on being rather beyond the grasp of intellectual processes, as does the self. Fortunately our marvelous adjustive potentialities come to be realized for the greater part exterior to awareness, and thus we are left more or less free to attack the complexities of the material world, and of schematized society, with at least the possibility of unemotional, rational analysis. Notwithstanding the necessarily "automatic" character of the great body of our total activity, which thus permits us to progress into situations of increasing complexity, it is all too nearly the rule that we make but little unemotional, rational analysis of our difficulties in adjustment.

For reasons that shall presently concern us, it comes about that people depend at the wrong time, or *in the wrong situation*, on the extraconscious dynamisms and, when they should be making use of the best analytic tools that they have, are actually in the grip of emotional upheavals—the discomfort that signals a maladjustive response to the demands of their momentary situation. It is more often the rule than not that the person concerned is not deficient in abilities to deal with his situation, and when maladjustive or nonadjustive situations arise, the psychopathologist is generally required to discover extraconscious processes underlying the complex situation that is baffling or tending to baffle the individual. In elucidating these subconscious or unconscious processes, it is almost always necessary to study the growth of the personality, in the course of which these *personally* unrecognized extraconscious processes had their origin.

In brief recapitulation, it should now be clear that one who would be useful to those whose life course is bringing them and their associates a measure of unhappiness and dissatisfaction is called upon to achieve a practical understanding of human individuals functioning as persons among persons. The fact that there are limitations in the possible completeness of this achievement no more justifies him in oversimplifying his conceptions of himself or his fellows than it justifies a pessimistic solipsism that does violence to the common-sense observation that people *do* carry on a considerable measure of understanding coöperation. On the other hand, the persons concerned in each situation possess each some measure of uniqueness which may or may not require his appreciation. He must school himself from the beginning never to seek in the individual alone the explanation of a psychobiological phenomenon. In this realm, all effective understanding is to be sought in a relevant complex including the individual principally concerned, and having practical limits. Understanding comes neither from the conventionally far too narrow field of exploration nor from a schizophrenically [11] universal search. The measure of success and of one's potentialities for usefulness to others is to a great extent dependent on one's being neither overly preoccupied with surface appearances nor lost in the almost infinite diversification of the individual personalities that one encounters. The education of the psychopathologist is thus

---

[11] The reference here is to *parergasia* (schizophrenia), a grave mental disorder classed as a psychosis, in which the limits of the relevant universe are greatly extended, and everything is apt to take on an intimate personal meaning.

primarily a matter of learning the limits of relevance in things human by the study of the factors entering into growth of personality from birth onward. This sort of information can never be excogitated; it must itself come as personality growth.

The Growth of Personality

WHEN one has habituated himself to seeking the explanation of each psychobiological phenomenon in an integrated complex of events including not only the person individually concerned but also the environmental factors at the moment relevant to him, one has mastered the first great explanatory principle of human nature. The actual understanding of a particular group of psychobiological or psychopathological phenomena, however, requires the discovery of certain frequently abundant relevant factors that are more or less completely unrecognized by the person primarily concerned in each complex. The clues to these factors are often obscure and, when found, may be anything but easy to follow.

The unrecognized factors that have importance in each personal situation arise generally in close relation to *past* experience of the individual concerned, and the most useful procedure for their elucidation consists in a search of this past, *as it continues to exist* in the personality. This search, however, is rather to be desired than to be accomplished, for it entails not only a very warmly coöperative attitude on the part of the subject-person, but also an amount of time and effort that can scarcely be expected in any but the most favorable circumstances. Thus, it is not uncommon to find that five hundred hours have been consumed in a moderately efficient inquiry into the developmental history of a personality, without one's having reached the end of the story, whereas the student of human nature has often to content himself with an attempt at assaying a total situation on the basis of from one to five hours of conversation.

It would obviously be very useful to have available a schematization of personality genesis and growth in general. Uniformities in human nature seem to be fairly abundant, as are also similarities in a great many types of experiences. I would not wish to discourage such an enthusiasm for generalizations on personality growth, but I must warn the student against the popular error of assuming that, because the momentary situations of two people *seem* to be alike, the experience each is undergoing need even resemble each other. The factor of past experience enters into every total situation, and enters so effectively that on occasion the true character of the situation may actually be quite beyond the power of the observer to conceive. Only the individual who has come to reduce his interpersonal relations to the minimum can be complacent in a conviction that he "understands" other people. To the rest of us each personal contact, if it is permitted to become even a rudimentary interpersonal situation, is certain to present to us at least a modicum that is new, that is novel and additional to our previous insight into personality. A general schematization of personality growth is therefore of but very limited utility, and must be made up of the broadest terms, applying in turn to the least complex of personality factors.

Yet, if one is ever to learn anything of the universe, one must start with some notion as to that which one is to study. Something of crude generalization is a necessary point of departure for our reasoning processes. We must proceed by analytic steps in finding order in the infinitely interrelated, syncretistically prehended world of things and people. We must have generalizations, and, having them, we must ever be alert in learning the qualifications to which they must be subjected in each application to any series of events that becomes a datum of investigation. To the extent that our attention is almost reverently applied to the *discrepancies* between each personality and our generalizations about personality—to that extent do we permit ourselves both to grow wise in the world of interpersonal relations, and to develop better and better generalizations.

The psychopathologist, finding the world of persons almost as variegated in significant details as it is in individuals with whom he permits himself to be involved, none the less grows more and more facile in discovering essential characteristics in the total situations that concern him. He comes to have some fairly comprehensive schematizations of personality and of total situations, in turn of considerable service to him in the prompt identification of some factors relevant in new total situations. These schematizations are always synthesized from abstracts out of the concrete experiential data that have flowed through his own personality. The have generally reached a measure of verbal formulation, which he can "call to mind" and "express" to another. But the verbal formulae are but a rationalistic superstructure built on the effective but only partly recognized buttresses of his success in appraising total situations. In the case of his work, as in many another form of interpersonal relations, that which the psychopathologist does in a given total situation involving a problematic person is apt to be much more simply related to the truths that he has come to know, than is that which he, in the best of faith, undertakes to communicate about it to his pupil.

Verbal formulations about total situations function best in communications between persons of closely parallel experience. In other cases a great deal of preliminary statement is necessary to provide a background experience against which the central formulation can be expected to assume somewhat of the intended meaning. If one can begin this preliminary formulation from a basis of actual experiential equivalence, so much the better. If not, then the expounder has frequently to decide between a long course of all but academic instruction by which the student is brought to an appropriate status, or a rapid excursion by impressionistic techniques calculated to succeed by virtue of fortunately restricted 'analogical' mental processes. It is to this latter method that I shall now have recourse, offering a body of dubious analogical schemata that are useful only to create a "mental set" suitable for more exact thinking about a systematic psychopathology. If these schemata are taken too seriously, the results will be anything but desirable. For that matter, the student must postpone to the utmost the growth in him of a conviction that he knows "all about" anything in the field of interpersonal relations. The best that he can hope to obtain from textual study can never be more than a reference-frame useful to him in making first approximations to an understanding of the various total situations of which he may become cognizant. There are, in the universe of psychobiology, no static entities, no "states" that continue fairly true to any labelling definition. There are not to be found typical personalities, consistent syndromes, and particular diseases and disorders. Roughly typical courses of events are the most that one is entitled to expect, and even this expectation should not be permitted to become oversanguine.

The world of biology contains three classes of living organisms: the unicellular, the higher plants, and the multicellular animals. The first mentioned of these, protophyta and protozoa, exists in a relatively simple medium, maintaining functional activity with and within a relatively very simple environment, yet manifesting a group of total activities of much interest to us.[1] Not only are all higher organisms at one stage in their individual history unicellular organisms, but, if I mistake not, throughout their life cycle they show recurrences of behavior which is significantly related to the type of behavior that one finds in the aggregation consisting of the unicellular organism and its environment. One could say that the uniform state of the higher or lower organism when showing behavior of this type is related generically to the state which in ourselves we identify as "sleep." In sleep, certain vegetative (or prevegetative) behavior is manifest. The most complex organism—man—shows not only the relative inertia and loss of "touch with the environment" that one is taught traditionally to regard as characteristic of sleep, but likewise can easily be caused to show slow, purposive activity, suggestive of the state of maximum activity in much lower forms of life. In the state of aggregation shown prevailingly in plant life, one finds a rather high degree of activity. Without digression into any of the attractive implications here, I will point out that even in man we see a parallel of this, in a great many nonspecific phenomena that occur in the borderline conditions which we speak of variously as "light sleep," sleep with dreams, panic states, night terrors, and the like. Somnambulism and the hyp-

[1] See H. S. Jennings, *Behavior of the Lower Organisms;* New York: Columbia Univ. Press, 1906. This is an unexcelled presentation of the way in which the "simple" complexes consisting of unicellular organisms and their necessary environment include phenomena entirely parallel to that which we call "behavior."

notic phenomena constitute a bridge between these and the next level of aggregation. Animals are characterized in general by their relative freedom from spatial limitations. They can move about—leave, for example, arid areas of their environment and go to fertile. They are emancipated to a considerable extent from the static condition in which plants live. We may say that the animal state is characterized by the evolution of distance receptors as a highly specialized part of the organism for use in adjustive effort which has no gross spatial limitation. That to which we refer as "consciousness" or "awareness" accompanies and is a part of these peculiarly comprehensive integrations of the organism in and within its complex. I would complete this schematization by offering, as the last division, "self-consciousness"—that state of activity in which there is a clear-cut, prepotent formulation within, or accessible to, awareness of the organism's own part in the complex; a situation in which activities occur that are the resultants of a very complex group of factors, including an approving reference-system called the self.

The point of origin of this last division may be taken to lie in the evolution of tools of intercommunication prevailingly symbolic in type. A new form of discrimination of total situations here appears, such that one thing can stand in the relation of consciously perceived meaning to one or many other things. A great context of experience is subsumed in a verbal symbol "me," and the whole more or less integrated context—at least, a great body of relevant material of the integrated context—is activated by conscious manipulations of the symbolic verbal term "myself." From this evolution there comes not only a great change in "environmental," principally "outer"—as against "individual," chiefly "inner"—factors, but a whole new and tremendously important body of environmental factors, the human culture, made up of the symbolic products—schematizations, embodiments of schemes and systems of living, and variously expressed generalizations—of other *persons*, living and "historically surviving" (represented in monuments of art, institutions, books, laws, traditions, and the like).

Even in presenting so fantastic a quasi-biological summary as Scheme I, I must warn the student against assuming that it can be "read both ways." The customary implicit total activity of man decidedly is *not* creative thought. Statistically considered, having due regard for the time partitioned to sleep, the most common form of implicit activity may be that to which we refer as the *primitive*. Certainly, people spend the greater part of their waking life in fantasy; periods characterized by adjustive thinking are fairly frequent, though often brief; and actual incidents of creative-inductive thinking are a decided rarity.

In our study of total situations as manifested by any given personality, we must not neglect to consider each instance with some reference to the type or class of behavior state in which we find the person. There is a great deal to be learned by a minute study of a person's sleep, or rather of the personal-environment complexes in which the type of his activity is pre-

SCHEME I

Analogical Division of the Living on the Basis of Factors Entering Into the Organism-Environment Complexes

TYPE	CHARACTERISTIC OVERT ACTIVITY	CHARACTERISTIC IMPLICIT ACTIVITY	"RELEVANT ENVIRONMENT"
Protista	Sleep	Primitive "Mental" Processes	Physicochemical Colloidal
Plants	Twilight Activity	Fantasy	Molar Physical
Animals	Consciously Conditioned Acts	Adjustive Thinking	Molar Biological Social
Man	Self-conscious Acts	Creative Thinking	Cultural

vailingly that of sleep. Certain phenomena of so-called waking life are understandable only when the total situation is recognized to be not of the type that we call consciousness, but rather that of a state of reduced consciousness, approaching or actually constituting a 'twilight state.' I have come to the belief that by the elucidation of sleep, and by thoroughgoing work on animal consciousness (or animal psychology)—these both proceeding from the proper postulates—we shall secure much greater insight, for example, into the problems of the already-mentioned schizophrenic changes, the most extraordinary of which seem to pertain to the type to which I have referred as 'twilight phenomena.'

Simple aggregations are simple because the total situation needed for maintenance of this variety of life requires little organization. The activity-type that we call sleep, and the total situations existing when organisms fall within that class of activity, pertain similarly to a relatively simple body of factors. In the same fashion, the total situations existing when dream-states are the prevailing activity-type are relatively far more simple than those attending full consciousness. Thus, I have come finally to believe that the "environmental" facts in the schizophrenic situation are decidedly simpler than we might be inclined to assume from reviewing our feeling of how we would be, and what would matter to us, if we were involved in what we conceive the schizophrenic situation to be. This restriction on too facile conception also assists us in formulating the mental state of the defective, of people who are fatigued, and of those who are, so to speak, intellectually slovenly. A variety of pseudo-problems arises from overlooking the fact that the activity-type in the given total situations is not that of a self-conscious organism, but instead is that of an organism that is merely conscious —one in the case of which consideration of the highest elaboration of activity is not relevant, because the more complex processes arising in the more complexly integrated situations are in abeyance. In other words, it is important to study the activity-type as a clue to the sort of total situation that one is dealing with. Techniques peculiarly suited to the self-conscious individual produce absurd or meaningless results when applied to a total situation of the activity-type of sleep. I stress "activity-type" because it is our objective clue to the type of existing total situation.

SCHEME II

Division on the Basis of Complexity of Process Required in the Resolution of the Organism-Environment Complex

ACTS EXPLICIT	"MENTAL PROCESSES" IMPLICIT
(1) Reflex	(1) Primitive
(2) Impulsive 　　Innate (instinctive) 　　Learned (habitual)	(2) Fantastic 　　High-grade intuition
(3) Consciously Chosen	(3) "Reality Controlled" 　　(a) Adjustive 　　(b) Creative

The influences of heredity in the life of the individual are chiefly manifested in the determination of characteristic tissue organizations, some of which make for familial differentiations, but most of which are characteristic of the species. Among the latter are the peculiar combinations forming neuromuscular units by which are effected a great variety of local actions, from massive chain reflex phenomena, like swallowing, to the sort of reflex presented by the protective blink of the eyelid. While most of these automatic responses of parts of the body to impinging events are clearly local actions, there is at times, particularly very early in extrauterine life, some reflex activity that approaches the total character of behavior. In the human young, however, the lability of the neuromuscular network is so great that habit formation rapidly overlays the innately determined performances, and the possibility of isolating purely reflex behavioral units disappears early in infancy.

There is a body of inferential evidence in support of the hypothesis of primitive implicit processes, the exclusive "mental content" of early infancy. While we have two kinds of evidence of the existence of the other forms of implicit processes—namely, our personal experiences of revery and thought, and our inferences of similar experiences in others from consideration of the courses of events including them—the direct experience of primitive implicit processes is rare after early childhood. Excepting for the occasional dream of cosmic participation, and some related semiwaking experiences of religious mystics, such a content seems to be the rule only in panic states and during the most profound schizophrenic disturbances. Implicit processes are far more labile than behavioral units, and the overlaying by reality-differentiation progresses rapidly in infancy to such effect that we develop very early an acquired unfamiliarity with the primitive implicit processes. Their later appearance in vivid awareness produces the impression of a vague but extremely important something like a transcendental experience, difficult indeed to relate to the self.

The innate impulsive acts, "total reflexes," are mostly of a highly plastic character, very readily modifiable by experience. They are rather easily pressed into conformity with the particular needs of the individual and tend to disappear among the rapidly increasing learned or habitual impulsive acts, in so far as they pertain to the skeletal musculature. Their manifestations in the activities of the unstriped "involuntary" muscles, however, continue clear-cut much longer, and, particularly in those personalities that have encountered serious warp in the earlier stages of development, may persist conspicuously throughout life.

The fantasy or revery processes are most easily described as including all those lying between the primitive and the highest type of implicit process, which I shall presently discuss under the rubric "externally controlled." In the field of fantastic implicit activity we have a great variety of mental processes. At the "lower" end of this broad band we find those barely distinguished from the primitive, and at the "upper," the intuitive products that are fully adjustive. The former are fantastic rather than primitive in that they show some evidence of the *organism-reality disjunction* that begins to be learned in the first hours of extrauterine life. This 'reality experience' character is wholly lacking in the primitive processes. Throughout the broad and important band of implicit processes that we observe in revery— the results of which are very frequently evident in the course of events—we find a gamut from the rudimentary, through the quasi-adjustive, to the more fully adjustive products (for example, Kekule's "benzene ring") which function with extensive reality references. These latter, like the other implicit processes presently to be discussed as "reality controlled," include features of the organism-environment complex prehended as of a particular sort of impersonal validity.[2]

---

[2] I must at this point refer briefly to *reduplicative memory*, a group of processes by which, the organism having come upon certain factors, there is a rather prompt "reproduction" by 'mental representation' of the situation in which such factors had previously been experienced. This group of processes, I suppose, first appears with the coming of clear consciousness. How elaborate it becomes, how few become the factors of previous situations necessary to lead a reduplicative experience of the past, is probably the measure of evolution of consciousness. Reduplicative processes occur in fantasy; for that matter, some investigators, like Rignano, regard these processes as the essence of the mental, if not of life itself. In this connection, I may refer to the work of Richard Semon, *Mnemic Psychology;* New York: Macmillan, 1923, and perhaps to H. L. Hollingworth, who has the notion that "reintegration" explains "thought." I doubt, however, if such broad generalizations will prove particularly helpful to the student, and urge a fundamental schematic distinction between implicit mental processes on

The universe includes two kinds of information: the personally valid and the consensually or interpersonally valid. A particular coin may have, because of its mint date, the occasion of its being secured, or other fact, a peculiar, distinctive meaning-value for some one individual. This peculiar distinction of that particular coin represents its peculiar relationship to him, himself—in fact, to his self. It is a unique relationship; it is not inhering in the coin, and could scarcely be communicated by any means to another person. The owner might distinguish the coin among similar coins by discussing it with another person, but it will not even then be to that other person anything like what it is to him. Its potential purchasing power will be *consensually* valid— so with its mass, and so on. The peculiar value to him, its *autistic* valuation by the owner, is of an entirely different kind, a personal matter, not an interpersonal one. The total situation including him and his particular coin may be extremely complex in its ramifications, in the factors entering into it; the total situation including him and other similar coins lacks many of these factors of meaning-context-around-a-coin, and approximates very much more closely "the average" total situation of a person with such a coin. The latter is relatively easy to communicate to another person.

Consensually or impersonally valid information is the result of a *conscious* eduction[3] of relations discriminated on multiple bases of experience with other people and things. It is the derivation that makes up our third division of implicit processes. Thus, in scientific research, data are accumulated under the inspiration or direction of some particular notion that the worker has evolved; when these data have become fairly abundant, they are classified on the basis of some alleged characteristic that seems to be conspicuous throughout them, and the individual then attempts to deduce certain incipient relations. If he is relatively competent, having deduced a few of these, he tries to introduce some novel notion, and having introduced this, he formulates a series of experiments with which to find whether it is correct or

the basis of their *potential consensual validity*. By this locution, I refer to a criterion by which the 'externally controlled' implicit processes are clearly distinguished from revery.

[3] Charles Spearman, *The Nature of 'Intelligence' and the Principles of Cognition*; London: Macmillan, 1923.

false. If it proves to be correct, he presumably has discovered a consensually or impersonally valid insight into a body of data to which he had been "applying his mind"—with which he had been occupied in a total situation demanding an adjustment in and within similar situations.

We must now pause to consider the thus far neglected relationship of these conscious eductions of consensually valid information, the 'rational process,' to the fully adjustive revery processes. It may have appeared that the two are widely separated; that, for example, we rationally formulate intelligent behavior in striking contradistinction to the higher beasts who are denied this valuable assistance, and have to adjust their acts to their necessities by intuition (revery processes). There is much evidence in favor of the view that the *conscious* rational processes rest invariably on an extensive series of revery processes; that, in other words, the eduction of consensually valid information is the next step that occurs in some few fully adjustive revery series, without which it could not have existed. The above account of scientific research, therefore, needs a very considerable revision before it becomes really illuminating. The selection of the problem for investigation, the recognition of the relevant data, the discrimination of the characteristic used as a basis for their classification, and a wealth of unnoted processes concerned in the deduction of the "incipient relations"—all these are chiefly fantasy or revery processes. So, likewise, the novel notion, from which comes the series of experiments. Most of the mental work done by the scientist goes entirely unnoticed. The innumerable trains of fantasy that were started here and there in the course of his investigation, and "run into the ground" by following them until they were found obviously unsuited to the world as he had experienced it—all these are quickly forgotten. All the instances of *successful* "inspiration," of good "hunches," are likewise obscured by the splendid verbal formulae that finally stood forth. The last member of our evolutionary series, the externally controlled implicit processes, is not a great novelty completely overshadowing the functional utility of the less evolved forms, but merely a final improvement by which *correct information* can be subjected to preparation for consensual validation. The importance of the latter for the cultural progress of humanity is not to be minimized, but the role of these highly evolved processes in the life of individual persons must not be unduly exaggerated.

There are three potent factors that hamper the widespread application of these "rational" processes in our dealing with the world. Our experience with people and things begins in *sentience*, the "crude material" presented as a result of the impinging upon our sense organs of particular series of events. Sentience is strictly limited by the inherent functional characteristics of the sense organs themselves,[4] and, as we shall come presently to consider, previous experience exercises a powerful influence on the educting or "knowing" process, itself. Thirdly, the rational processes function under certain optimum conditions only, and these are rarely encountered in "thinking about" the self or about other persons for any reason particularly significant to the self. The sources of the latter two limitations will become apparent as we study the general course of growth of the personality.

The experience of life and the individual personality begins in primitive processes. These evolve and are overlaid by a great development of the second type, impulsive acts and fantasy thinking. The latter are sprinkled over by consciously chosen acts and "rational" implicit processes. Total situations of great simplicity continue to call out in adjustment primitive and rudimentary revery processes. Customary life situations require but the impulsive, habitual, and fantasy processes. "New" and complex total situations require the best that the individual has evolved in the way of consciously chosen activities, implicit and explicit; that these are not forthcoming is one obvious antecedent to maladjustment and nonadjustment. I hope that no one of my readers will be so naive as to see a remedy for these situations in "telling the patient" what he ought to think and do.

The growth by which innate impulsive action-systems and primitive inner processes are converted, through experience, into more

---

[4] The student may most profitably peruse in this connection A. S. Eddington, *The Nature of the Physical World*; New York: Macmillan, 1929; and P. W. Bridgman, *The Logic of Modern Physics;* New York: Macmillan, 1927. The latter includes a clear argument as to the inutility of other than "operational concepts" in scientific descriptions of reality. Once we leave the realm of exact measurements, we are almost certain to be confused by our verbiage and given to meaningless conclusions.

or less fully adjustive processes is one important manifestation of *growth in personality*.[5] As a biologist, one may consider the foetus as a parasitic organism. Psychobiologically, the intrauterine state may be taken to be the first period of growth in personality. Particularly in the last six weeks before birth, there is ample evidence that we are dealing with total activity of an organism in a total situation; like all other total activity, this leaves traces. I believe it is safe to assume that most of intrauterine life shows total activity of the type to which we have referred as sleep, and that, in the last six weeks, there occur events of the type that we have called 'twilight phenomena,' which implies that there are implicit activities of the nature of primitive and lower-grade fantastic thought, and activity of the explicit sort classifiable as the lower impulsive acts.

Not solely because one loves a comprehensive theory, but because it sheds much light on so-called panic states, one may consider particularly the great change in the total situation that marks the preliminaries of birth. It seems absurd to argue that such an interference with the food supply, coupled with changes in the postural situation, and the subjecting of the organism to entirely new stresses, can go without providing experience. It pleases me to think that the preliminaries of birth do provide experience, which can be called, if one must call it something, not, I hope, "birth trauma," but the initial experiences of a series, manifestations of which can be discovered throughout later life. Thus I would express my belief that each organism shows throughout its life discoverable evidences of primitive experience connected with the transition from the relatively parasitic intrauterine situation to the more or less independent postnatal situation.[6]

[5] I shall now present a scheme of steps in personality growth. There are no dividing lines in reality, and I can but hope that this schematization will be used by the student solely as an aid to organizing thought about personality.

[6] The theoretical considerations touched upon at this point include a general theory of experience, itself. The current text is scarcely suited to carry any extended discussion of so purely philosophical an issue. I must be content with a statement that facts and speculation seem to ensue in the notion of experience as in each case a nexus "containing" at least two dynamic components, namely, the *previous* relevant general tendency of the organism, passing over into the *resultant* of a vector addition representing

In *infancy*, besides breathing, the prevailing activity is sleep. Thereafter, in the order of importance, are the taking of nourishment; that group of events which is connected with relieving forms of distress not primarily hunger; then, and growing in importance day by day after birth, that group of activities and local action, which we call "play" and which represents in part an inherent tendency to exercise the parts of the organism as they are elaborated—in other words, to give a sort of "trial run" to each new neuro-musculo-glandular apparatus of the organism.

One must note, however, that some play is not to be explained in this fashion, but is to be referred to already organized needs. I can perhaps best illustrate this class of situational demand by considering the urgent requirements of the body for oxygen. If there is interference with the supply of oxygen, there ensues a situation of intense distress. We say that the organism has an oxygen need which can, under certain circumstances, completely dominate the total activity. Similarly there is a nourishment need connected with the satisfaction of which we find an elaborate

---

the effect of the impinging event, this together with a configuration (underlying reduplicative memory) of certain unknown elements of the vital processes. This nexus continues in a fashion *to exist*, being capable of reecphoriation by recourse to the apparent mnemic "reversibility" of tendency systems. Actually irreversible, owing to extension in the time-dimension, this memorial retraceability is none the less shown prominently in living organisms as bundles of processes. My conception of the "preconcept" is a formulation of the *initial* nexus in the case of each important tendency system of the organism. It is rather vaguely delineated in "The Oral Complex," *Psychoanalytic Review* (1925) 12:31–38. See also "The Importance of a Study of Symbols in Psychiatry," *Psyche* (1926) 8(1)81–93. Read, in the latter, as the heading on page 90, "The Individual Series." Both of these papers are now of but suggestive value, as also the notes in *Amer. J. Psychiatry* (1924) 81:77–91 ("Schizophrenia: Its Conservative and Malignant Features").

The primitive experience arising in the preliminaries of birth, I consider to constitute (with preexisting tendency systems, as stated) the Death-Evil Preconcept; this to imply that it is this experience which constitutes the first stage, or the background, if you please, of a considerable part of those implicit processes of later life pertaining on the one hand to death, and on the other to evil. This does not seem the place to discuss the Preconcept of Cosmos, by which term I have referred to the elaboration of experience of the parasitic uterine existence antecedent to the preliminaries of birth; nor to the more specialized preconceptual experiences concerning the upper and the lower ends of the alimentary tract, the urethra, and the kinesthetic apparatus.

neuro-musculo-glandular apparatus. Not only is the nourishment need in case of privation capable of dominating the total activity, but the elaborate apparatus evolved for its satisfaction requires at all times the discharge of the energy partitioned to it. We therefore find the infant with a 'secondary' need for activity of the nutriment-securing apparatus, one that may perhaps be called a desire to suckle. "Play" activity satisfying this desire to suckle is not the exercise of evolving neuro-muscular-glandular apparatus, but is behavior under the domination of full-blown "psychological necessity"—need, desire, or what one will. As such, it might better be called oral activity, or oral behavior, for it is a total activity—and ultimately to be an extremely important form of total activity.

The infant progresses in the use of the voice apparatus to the point at which differentiation of vocalization rather abruptly takes place—probably in part owing to the completion of the appropriate part of the central nervous system—and crying gives over at least occasionally to a new sort of vocal activity, babbling and cooing, which rapidly develops into articulate speech. The appearance of articulate speech leads to so great an acceleration in the velocity of change in the organism that we should regard it as marking an epoch in personality growth, ending infancy and initiating childhood.

The principal partition of activity in *childhood* continues to be to sleep, but its importance is diminishing and its character showing some change. All the other activities characteristic of infancy are undergoing important modification by the appearance of new sorts of total activity. In childhood, consciousness has progressed in character to the point where certain entities of the type of ideals and ambitions can be inculcated into the organism. In other words, an obviously cultural type of environmental factor is making itself felt—that is, becoming relevant in total situations.

I must pause to remark the dearth of information as to the "content" of the infantile mind. We have as yet no method for investigating the primitive implicit processes of the neonate, and can but infer something of the reveries of late infancy and early childhood from study of the course of subsequent events.[7] With-

---

[7] In this connection, reference may be made to the works of Jean Piaget, now available in translation under the titles *Language and Thought of the*

out, however, some appreciation of the distinctive characteristics and limitations of early implicit processes, no approximation to an understanding of personality growth can be obtained. Until one has refreshed his memories of the rich fantasy life of the first six years, the unique character and the peculiar effects of childhood inhibitions and ideal-formations escape him.

It is in the months of infancy and the years of childhood that the principal changes are wrought by which an animal with an ultraelaborate apparatus for communal existence in and within extremely complex situations is caused to take on the peculiar features subsumed in man as a creature of culture—in the human individual as a *person.* How great these changes may be is but beginning to concern us.[8] As the writer some time since predicted, the hypothecation of such abstractions as the "racial unconscious" no longer finds justification; infancy and childhood of the human young are characterized by the acquisition of a great body of culture, transmitted in a variety of ways most important as matters for scientific study.

There comes a time when the child develops a definite need for other children as playmates. When playmates are not available, the appearance of this group of phenomena is indicated by the childish elaboration of imaginary playmates that are specifically children. Previous to the outcropping of this need, the imaginary constructs of the child have had all sorts of marvelous

---

Child, Judgment and Reasoning in the Child, and *The Child's Conception of the World;* New York: Harcourt Brace, 1926, 1928, and 1929. While these studies may be criticized as an overintellectualization of child psychology, they are an outcome of rather good observational technique, and should be read by the student.

[8] The student might impress himself with one aspect of the matter by visiting a suitable institution and considering the life-process of an idiot; thereafter discover the relative simplicity of the interests of a low-grade imbecile; and finally familiarize himself with some biographical data on genius. Thus, for example, see the trilogy concerning Leonardo da Vinci, Peter the Great, and Julian the Apostate, by Dmitri Merejkowski (Merezhousky), *The Death of The Gods, The Forerunner: The Romance of Leonardo da Vinci (The Resurrection of the Gods),* and *Peter and Alexis: The Romance of Peter the Great* (translated by Herbert French); New York: Putman's, 1901, 1902. There is another aspect more germane to our study that cannot be discovered so readily; there is but a beginning of the study of average infants and children, by the methods of Arnold Gesell, by the institutes for child study, by the techniques of Dorothy Swaine Thomas, and by way of the experimental school.

patterns. From this time on, however, the child has playmates, real or imaginary, and playmates that are like himself. His implicit processes are beginning to take on an objectivity, so that he shows a rather rapid development of appreciation, not only of his own wishes, his own abilities, but also of the "other fellow's" wishes and abilities. We thus come to the beginning of socialization—socialization in a true sense in contradistinction to the preceding quasi-social adjustment to authority and parental prejudices, which has been the condition in later childhood. With the appearance of true social tendencies, the total situations change very fundamentally in character. I choose to call that which follows *the juvenile era*. It is the period of growth of egocentric sociality and of the elaboration of social personality—including marked additions to that which we later shall discuss as the *self*.

The clearness with which these stages of personality growth may be distinguished diminishes as we proceed from the intra-uterine condition onward. For obvious reasons, individuals in each succeeding stage show more or less striking differentiation because of dissimilar experience, and each individual becomes progressively more individuated. For this reason the application of any schematization of individuals in the juvenile era, and thereafter, is anything but all-encompassing—which is perhaps not too bad, after all. As the stage during which there is developed appreciation of the general importance of other people of comparable status, it is an era of great importance—not by any means to be dismissed as a "latency period." Events move swiftly in the juvenile era, and the recall of the experience undergone in its course is no mean task. This is rendered all the more the case because, at the close of this era, there appears a new and 'intensely personal' accent on interpersonal relations.

Sooner or later, in the play and social life of the juvenile, one sees a beginning of genuine attachment of a unique type to some other individual. Love, one might say, has made its appearance. The individual now begins to organize his experiences, real and fantastic, occurring in the total situations including the other person, in such a way that the other person becomes signally important to him. No sooner has this change appeared than it brings about a rapid modification in the type of total situation. Being an important organizing factor late in its appearance, this love factor changes the fundamental character of the individual, brings about

a "need" for interindividual affection or love, and results in an
alteration of the fundamental character of social situations which
the individual seeks. The egocentric sociality of the juvenile
passes, and there is ushered in the *earliest phase of adolescence*.
With the appearance of this unique type of interest in some one
companion, the personality has proceeded into its ultraimportant
phase of growth, in that from henceforth, unless there be grave
miscarriage, there will always be one or more persons of great
importance in the total situations through which the individual
passes. True personality is born, and intimate interpersonal adjustment now becomes the great problem of life. Before we are done
with this aspect of our subject, we shall perhaps see that it is not
strange that but few individuals are capable of more than two of
these attachments at any one time. Perhaps from the general
social tendency of the juvenile era, blending with the new tendency making for close interpersonal relations, it comes about
that numbers of boys who have passed over into early adolescence
tend to constitute themselves into more or less highly organized
groups to which we apply the term "gang." [9]

With the appearance of frank sexual impulses, we have another
alteration in the character of total situations, and an exceedingly
important one in our "best of possible" cultures. In any primitive
culture, this change is taken rather seriously by suitable adults,
and so is stripped somewhat of the tragic movement that often
attaches to it among us "enlightened" ones. The appearance of
frank ("genital") sexual impulses marks the transition from early
or preadolescence to "true" or *midadolescence*. I will pass on
without discussing the characteristics of this period, to the point
where habituation is established as to the relief of the sexual necessities, remarking that the acceptance of a habitual form of activity more or less directly adjustive to the sexual urges is taken
to mark the beginning of *late adolescence*.[10]

[9] The parallelism in personality growth of the male and the female ceases
usually in later childhood. While the current social change in the status of
women is bringing about a great modification in this connection, I feel that
any simple transposition of the terms of male adolescence to that of girls is
still misleading. Divergences and parallelisms will presently concern us in
Chapter VIII.

[10] The coincidence of frank sexual motivation with the appearance of
processes making for intimacy between persons should not be accepted
either as a cause-and-effect relationship or as a substantial identity. The intensive study of adolescent personalities continues to be one of the urgent

As the last step in this schematization of personality development, I offer *adulthood*, a phase the inception of which is marked by the occurrence of a unique experience—to wit, a total situation including another person (conceivably, two other people) in a total activity, prevailingly sexual in character, the resolution of which is complete, in the sense that it does not proceed into disturbing situations which in turn require resolution. In other words, one becomes adult, according to this schematization of personality growth, when finally, after having successfully passed through the previous stages and having found himself in a total situation containing at least one other person, in which situation sexual drives, desires, or needs are the conspicuously effective force within him, he resolves the situation in a fashion which leaves no derivative new desires, needs, or what not—such particularly as those we ordinarily call regrets, recriminations, and the like—yet to be resolved. It will appear in the subsequent pages that the proportion of our fellows who have completed the evolution to the state of adulthood is not very great.

From this conspectus, we see the person as a nexus of processes in communal existence with a physicochemical, a social, and a cultural world. He integrates total situations of various complexities in part on the basis of his previous experience with appropriately related series of events. He *learns*, shows some measure of profit from the experiences of life. By the maturation of his integrative equipment and the accumulation of experience, he progresses along a more or less definable path from a wholly nonrational parasiticism to some large measure of understanding adjustment in and within an extremely complex world. That peo-

---

needs in personality research. A great deal of information, the ultimate implications of which no one can foretell, remains to be discovered. The role of the sexual motivations in the evolution of personality in a culture-situation very different from ours would be greatly changed. Many if not all of the statements hereinafter presented would need modification if they were to apply to the young, for example, of a society such as that studied by Malinowski in Melanesia. As we develop factual data by the application of the total-situation conception to our own young, we will progress to the point at which an anthropology of personality differentials will be our most valuable means of control in hypothesis formulation and experiment. So great is the present ignorance of the factors entering into personality evolution that the broad pseudo-anthropological statements so often heard concerning personality disorder and "mental disease" in disparate cultures are feebly amusing.

ple, as products of this progression, are of very various degrees of success seems to need no argument. That the numerous cases of relative failure are more often the results of experience-deviation than are they the inevitable outcome of deficiencies in biological heritage is still somewhat moot. I believe there is no denying that a great many of our fellows have fallen short of their innate potentialities for personality evolution. It is the work of the psychopathologist to identify and then, so far as possible, to remedy the individual's handicap in this evolution. It is the work of the social engineer to identify and take effective steps to remove the all too nearly ubiquitous factors in our culture which bring about the widespread handicap of individuals in their personality evolution. I trust that the student will appreciate that these troublesome factors are not solely or even chiefly identical with sex. The all too general coincidence of personality disaster with the stages of adolescence is by no means merely a phenomenon of the sexual life processes.

CHAPTER III

Dynamisms of Difficulty

WE HAVE BEEN considering the growth of the configurations that are created by the organism, its relevant environment, their relations, and the activities or processes going on in the complex. We shall now discuss terms that may be applied to these total situations, with a view to classifying them with reference to their bearing on the outcome of the individual's life course. We know that some people progress to old age with what seems to be a considerable measure of success. We know that there are infants who encounter insurmountable difficulties early in life. And we know that there are all sorts of gradations between success and failure that go to make up what one might call successful existence.

From the standpoint of the psychobiologist, the successful life is one that is principally characterized by a series of adjustments in the organism-environment complexes as the individual progresses in time from conception to death. Successful living, or the *state of mental health,* may be said to consist in the continued resolution of total situations to such effect that the growth of personality is neither arrested nor materially deviated as reflected in ensuing sequent situations. As such, it is distinguished from maladjustive situations and from nonadjustive situations. The term *adjustment* may thus be seen to refer to the type of resolution of a particular situational complex, to the total activity that occurs in the organism-environment configuration under consideration, viewed from the standpoint of the sequent total situation. In other words, adjustment resolves the situation so that it is no longer existent, other than as experience of the organism.

The maladjustive group of processes, on the other hand, while they may resolve the situation, do so with wastage of energy, increased complexity of processes, and unwonted extension of the situation in time. Considered subjectively, the individual in maladjustment undergoes stress and "feels" varying degrees of unpleasantness.

Thus far we have made use of the term *personality* without particular attention to its context of meaning, *as if* there were a something in the human being that was not merely a moving locus of processes, a manifestation of the total organism in and within its series of total situations. I will now attempt something of a definition. Personality is to be taken to refer to that relatively enduring pattern of life-processes which comes to characterize each human individual. This characterization is in itself temporal and dynamic; it is but a relatively enduring group of consistent manifestations found in the series of total situations of which the particular individual is a part. These manifestations are in an important degree the "reactions of other individuals" to the subject-individual. By this locution, I wish, through an appeal to conventional speech, to stress the factors of other persons that enter importantly into the formation of the dynamic pattern to which we refer as *personality*.[1]

Personality is the relatively enduring configuration of life-processes characterizing all of the person's total activity pertaining to such other persons, real or fantastic, as become from time to time relevant factors in his total situations. The "other ones" may be presented to the senses, in which case we speak of processes within primary group relations, or they may be exterior to sensual contact—effective by virtue only of the individual's faith in their past or present existence elsewhere—in which case we speak of processes within secondary groups. The characterizing bundle of processes making up the personality includes relatively static (low velocity) qualities of the individual, such as his physical build, visage, and so on. It includes qualities that

---

[1] The meaning of this expression will become more evident after a perusal of Chapter IV. Needless to say, the personality *is not* the factors of other persons; personality is not composed of other people's reactions to one. As we shall presently discover, it is the *self* which comes nearest to being such a composite of the "reactions" of others; and the self is by no means coterminous with the personality.

change but slowly, such as those which we shall later discuss as the individual's life-plan and his hierarchy of values. And it includes some qualities capable of rapid change that actually show persistent patterning over comparatively long periods of time (as judged by the life span), such as qualities pertaining to the functional activity of the expressive apparatus—his vocabulary, intonation, play of facial postural tensions, and so on.

Besides having an historic evolution reflecting some of the hereditary factors of organization, with which experience has entered into functional combinations, and besides being susceptible of more or less clearly justified divisions into epochs of growth, personality may also be said to manifest itself in typical processes pertaining to the progress of the organism—to his evolving course through adjustments and maladjustments, or his nonadjustive arrest in some total situation.

As long as adjustment characterizes a life-course, the individual progresses in time from total situations in which the relevant factors are less complex to those in which there is greater complexity. Put rather loosely, his field of interests grows more or less rapidly in spread, or depth, or both. There is an infinity of individual processes that may appear in and contribute to such a course of adjustment. Maladjustment and nonadjustive states, on the other hand, being restrictive of this theoretically infinite freedom of growth, lend themselves somewhat more definitely to classification. By schematization in these latter fields, we at the same time organize thought in regard to adjustive processes, for there is nothing unique in the unsuccessful ones. In other words, in the scheme I am about to submit, I am giving a classification of types of processes that make their appearance alike in success and in partial or total failure of adjustment. Uncommon adjustive ability is apt to be manifested in considerable measure in an invariably well-directed application of processes which in other cases form persisting patterns of less fortunate outcome. The recurrent manifestation of certain unsuccessful processes by any given individual is generally to be understood by reference to some warping influences brought to bear on him at some stage in the course of his evolution. The student must appreciate, however, that each significant experience is a point of radiation for interlocking consequents, and that any important ramification of them is directly dependent on the subsequent role of the affected tendency in the totality of the personality concerned.[2]

The schematization of human dynamics herewith presented is a gross classification of total actions considered abstractly, *as if* they were not highly individuated phenomena representing the functional interaction of unique personalities in more or less singular total situations, but instead were typical patterns of machinelike regularity. Something of a defining meaning is attached to the term, *as if* one could eliminate consideration of the historic evolution entering into each and every total action. Neither of these "as ifs" has any other than expository justification.

SCHEME III

Human Dynamics *

Scheme of classification of total activity
on the basis of the degree of resolution brought about in
an organism-environment situation.

(I) Adjustment: Total resolution of the configuration so that there is no remaining stress, but only results, including experience.

(II) Partial Adjustment: By which stress in the organism-environment situation is more or less reduced, but the configuration is not resolved directly.

---

* This table is slightly modified from one appearing in "Research in Schizophrenia," *Amer. J. Psychiatry* (1929) 86:553–567.

[2] The awe-inspiring Grand Canyon of the Colorado River is only a very remote resultant of the exact location of confluence of the Green and the Grand Rivers. Had their joining been determined at some other point, the course of the resulting Colorado River would probably have been other than it is. But this also would have been the case if factors manifested as geological characteristics along its course had differed at some important point. And the Canyon itself would be very different indeed if there had been no weathering, or if the stream had been a stream of mercury, or if the wind had been incandescent gas. The point I wish to make seems incapable of overemphasis—every personality is the resultant of many factors, from innately determined assets and liabilities, up to and including the significant experience of yesterday. No series of geophysical events is even remotely analogous in *complexity* of significant processes. Personality exceeds in this respect every subhuman series, for social and cultural factors are potent in it. Clearly, a "psychical trauma" occurring to one when two years old is not a *direct antecedent* in any particular sense to anything manifested at the age of thirty. *Per contra*, the remote resultants of the event may have an important place in the thirty-year-old personality.

(A) *Compensation:* By which simpler activities and implicit processes are substituted in lieu of resolutions of the configuration, which is more or less disintegrated by changes in the tendencies concerned.

(1) Daydreaming in lieu of constructive thought or action.
(2) Sport, theatre, reading, and the like instead of effort.
(3) Seeking and preying on sympathy.
(4) Unsocial lying, pathological lying of idealizing type, and so on.

(B) *Sublimation:* By which more complex activities and implicit processes which are in conformity to systems of ideals, social or derived, are unconsciously substituted for more direct adjustive processes which, if carried out, will create new organism-environment situations because of the disapproval of others.

(1) Altruistic activities.
(2) Religious practices.
(3) Other ritualistic behavior of positive social value.

(C) *Defense Reactions:* By which more complex activities and implicit processes, often without close conformity with the systems of social and derived ideals, are unconsciously substituted for more direct adjustive processes which are blocked by *conflict* within the personality, the stress of the conflict being avoided or reduced thereby.

(1) In which the "inner" aspect of the situation is the more impressive:
　　(a) Forgetting.
　　　　(i) Suppression
　　　　(ii) Repression (*vide infra*)
　　(b) Rationalization.
　　　　(i) Elaborative
　　　　(ii) Retrograde falsification
　　　　(iii) Detractive
　　(c) Transfer of blame.
　　　　(i) Impersonal—luck, fate, and so on
　　　　(ii) Personal—"my sickness," "my views," and so on
　　　　(iii) Paranoid—suspicion—blame—persecution
(2) In which the "outer" aspect is the more impressive:
　　(a) Negativism.
　　　　(i) Passive
　　　　(ii) Active
　　(b) Incapacitation.
　　　　(i) Special
　　　　(ii) General

(D) *Dissociation:* By which some of the systems of experience and some of the somatic apparatus are disintegrated from the rest of the personality and engaged in overt and implicit quasi-adjustive processes not in harmony with those of the rest of the personality.

(1) "Psychogenic" tics, mannerisms, and stereotyped movements.

(2) Automatisms, including automatic writing, crystal gazing, and so on.

(3) Mediumship, and so on.

(4) Hallucinosis.

(5) Multiple personality and the like.

(E) *Regression:* By which more recent experience, and the resulting elaboration of complexes, sentiments, and tendencies, are disintegrated in such fashion as to remove them as factors in the organism-environment situation; this resulting in the reappearance of adjustive efforts of a chronologically earlier state of personality.

(III) Nonadjustive Processes: By which stress in the organism-environment situation is not reduced and no resolution of the configuration is brought about.

(A) *Panic:* In which the acts are reflex and of a primitive impulsive order, and the implicit processes are primitive. An uneven regression most striking in the awakening of primordial fear.

(B) *Anxiety:* Varying from more or less frank attacks of fear to extremely obscure "physical" illnesses, more or less episodic in character.

(C) *Excitement:* Including many "abnormal sublimations," the work of reformers, and so on.

(D) *Obsessive Preoccupations:* Including morbit doubts and scruples and pessimistic worrying.

(E) *Morbid Grieving.*

(F) *Depression.*

The classical example of compensatory substitution is shown by the boy who starts out bright and early to look for a job, meets some rebuffs, and presently wends his way to the theatre, there to pass some hours enjoying the performance. Before he "gave up," he was pursuing a course of activity to resolve a situation integrated by a tendency not yet fundamental in his personality, but rather an acquired means to far more fundamental ends. He "had to do" something only indirectly satisfying to the powerful tendency-system characterizing his personality. The "having to do," however, is a genuine tendency, integrating a real situation in turn "demanding" a real resolution. It cannot be made nonexistent without action of some sort. As long as attention is not occupied by something else, the boy "is conscious of his duty"—to look for a job until he finds one (or *until the passage of time has made it officially futile* to continue this activity today). One of the ends to which working is a means is the experiencing of novel features of living. The theatre is another means to this end. True, in the latter one experiences only a vivid fantasy of participation, while working might provide one with means to enjoy directly. But the latter is a remote goal, a long time away; and if one "puts off" the now tedious and dispiriting actual pursuit of the job and enjoys the theatre (as if one had found the job—and could really afford the money and time—and everything was lovely), then one or more of the more powerful, less evolved, tendency-systems from which the duty-to-work tendency has been elaborated becomes active and the latter disappears from consciousness, for the time being. The more purely the dynamics are those of compensation, the less clearly conscious will be the appreciation of the steps delineated above. If our boy does not succeed in draining off most of the energy from the duty-to-work tendency, the duty to pursue a job continues to harass him during his attempt at enjoyment, and he suffers a minor variety of the state later to be discussed as conflict. If he avoids this by "finding a formula" that "justifies" the recreation, he is showing the more elaborate dynamism of rationalization.

If instead of the above example, we had taken that of the high-pressure executive who, in the face of a complex problem, feels that he must go to the links for eighteen holes of golf, we would have found ourselves concerned with a somewhat more complex situation. This good man is scarcely to be taxed with evading an unpleasant task by simple compensatory activity. In the face of such an interpretation, he would react indignantly or with justified amusement. He has an excellent rationalization—he must "keep fit" for his difficult labors. Beyond this, he has discovered that an interruption of conscious preoccupation with a problem can in some cases facilitate its solution.

Athletic performances enjoy such good standing among us that their inclusion under compensatory activity must be defended.

Not only is the pursuit of physical fitness a very good formula, but some part of the general esteem accorded sport arises from its multiplex service in the interest, for example, of sublimation processes. A man in an angry mood may engage in bowling, thereby substituting a simple performance for the difficult task of directly resolving his antisocial tendencies. At the same time, in throwing a ball at the pins, he may be substituting a socially approved, *more* complexly motivated performance for behavior such as flinging stones at an enemy. "Taking it out on the cat" can thus be seen to fall somewhat under at least two rubrics in our scheme, and, by this token, to emphasize the shortcomings of this and similar catalogings of life processes. An act, as we shall presently discover, is often a sort of compromise between two or more tendencies.[3] Before discussing the relationship of various levels of fantasy to the classificatory problems arising in the objective study of behavior, I wish to offer a word about the misuse of terms in this connection.

We find that certain athletic performances serve both as compensatory and as sublimatory substitutions, often synchronously. To call a particular example of this duplicate service either a compensatory or a sublimatory process is incorrect. For that matter, there is no particular virtue in "calling" anything by its generic name, so far as the relationship of the psychopathologist and his subject-individual is concerned. The less of labels and the more of factually substantiated formulation of actual processes that enter into such a relationship, the better. The utility of generic categories in abstract thought depends largely on the virtue of their definition. The "meaning" sometimes assigned to compensation is so broad or diffuse that the one category can subsume almost all human activity except sleep. Thus, some of our colleagues are given to interpreting almost everything but behavior in accordance with their own prevailing interests as "compensation for a feeling of inferiority." This type of general interpretation is itself an excellent illustration of maladjustive compensatory processes in interpersonal relations, in the narrower sense of our scheme. By recourse to the ubiquitous "compensation for feelings of inferiority" one substitutes a verbal gymnastic for the much

---

[3] The neurological doctrine of domination of the "final common path" is decidedly more simple than are these facts of total activity.

more difficult task of coming to understand the total situation with which one happens to be confronted. But as in the case of athletic behavior, so also as this particular "snap" interpretation occurs in nature, it too often serves a double purpose, being both a compensatory process and a defensive substitution. Used in a critical sense, this interpretation is frequently a rationalization by which one plausibly appeals to the alleged principle of compensation for justification of one's own socially undeveloped urges, at the same time detracting from the prestige of the (unadmitted) antagonist by covert reference to his personal suspicion of inferiority. This particular "interpretation" comes to be one of the most vicious of the inadequate interpersonal processes in that it tends to degrade socially approved behavior, including a great body of useful sublimations, and this at the hands of the socially inadequate.[4]

The unwitting combination of a pursuit of social approval with that of a more individualistic goal—sublimation—is frequently the most nearly adjustive activity in which one can engage. It functions satisfactorily for a great many in the case of whom a direct satisfaction with social disapproval would be either intolerable to self-esteem or economically disastrous. It is the goal of almost all good plans for handling the social problem of the mentally deficient. As far as it goes, it is an excellent dynamism. That it is somewhat less than adequate, particularly in resolving situations including strong sexual drives, must be realized. It may, as for example in the practice of surgery, serve very "profitably" as adequate resolution of most situations, including the personality-characterizing sadistic tendencies directly satisfied by inflicting pain on others. It may, in the cultivation of begonias or chow dogs, resolve situations demanding parenthood. But when called upon to handle the sexual integrations, it is liable either to lamentable failure or to such exuberance of pro-

[4] Interpretation that uses as its material some glib phrases that are activated in a variety of situations of which one does not approve has no place in practical psychopathology. The student may secure for himself some status as an intellectual superior by a judicious use of this device among the stupid. The parallel status to which the sensitive will exhalt him is a sad one. He will be regarded by them as a heavy-footed fool who has deceived the elect, whence they come to a measure of despair, feeling that the world is indeed delivered over to the noisy pundits who find in "the extraverted" the "normal" of humankind.

cess as to be best classified as nonadjustive excitement. If a man discovers within himself a strong desire to take from his neighbors their wives and daughters, passes on the problem in the region of unconscious mental processes, and sublimates by becoming a minister of the Gospel, he needs at least a word of caution: his marriage should be early, and his wife one who will not be "sexually frigid." And if a man finds, whether from "unduly prolonged continence" or other specious reason, that he is having trouble because of the "imperfect sexual differentiation" of boys from women, shrugs his shoulders, and discovers unwittingly that he has great aptitude as secretary for a boys' club—to this man it should be recommended that he avoid "accidentally" spending a night under the same covers with one of his charges. *Per contra*, the post-schizophrenic discharge of sexual tendencies in sublimatory persecution of the sexually promiscuous is even less of a social blessing, at least in its indirect effect on the spread of venereal disease by way of clandestine prostitution. [Such crusading zeal thus minimizes the possibility of adequate public health supervision.]

It is in alleged social reform as a sublimatory solution of one's life situation that the great strength and serious weakness of these dynamics are made obvious. Sublimatory processes being unwitting and essentially unconscious, "reform" movements originating in them are characterized by unreasonable and illogical features. The "vice" to be remedied is not subjected to a rigorous analysis; no careful estimation of the facts is engaged in; no inquiry is made into the virtues of the opposition. The "movement" is highly emotional. The formulation of the "cause" is such that it is propaganda, an appeal to prejudice. Facts are transmuted to suit the purpose, and anyone not readily converted is subjected to the darkest suspicions—the least that he can be is an enemy of progress. Mere social reality as a bundle of processes in which one cannot meddle recklessly without incurring the possibility of evil consequents is given a subordinate role, the "vision" of the reformer taking full precedence. Anyone who pauses to question is a weakling, a tool of the wicked, or an object for prayer. The weakness of personal adjustment by such processes appears with the increasing pressure of social reality. Since they are processes in the region exterior to awareness, any scrutiny of the total situation is impossible, and the divorcement of the reformer from the commonplace satisfactions of life increases to the point that sublimation fails, and excitement or a defense reaction makes an appearance.

We may say that sublimation is effective in adjustment only so long as the components are in a certain relationship. If the augmentation of self-esteem by the accrual of social approval is definitely subordinate to satisfaction derived from direct action of the sublimated tendency, the sublimation is unstable and prone to fail, either *in toto* or partially, at intervals. If the reverse is the case, the sublimation is relatively stable. In general, the degree of success achieved in socializing the personality is a measure of the energy partition available toward successful sublimation.

It seems probable that there exist in each of us a great many fantasy processes dealing with the direct satisfaction of each tendency that we have developed in the course of life. In the socialized personality, only such of these processes as are in agreement with the accepted social code are permitted to receive focal attention. This selective attention does not obliterate the unacceptable fantasy processes but does facilitate the sublimatory resolution of situations. Thus a well-socialized man may be angered by a situation in which "unfair" advantage has been taken of one of his weaknesses. Direct resolution of the ensuing situation would violate his social code. He is in a situation so urgent, however, by reason of its relation to his self-esteem, that the unsatisfied tendency "causes" in him an angry *mood*. He sublimates this by going to a bowling alley and playing a series of games. The success of the maneuver is indicated by the disappearance of the angry mood and the becoming irrelevant of most of the details of the anger-provoking situation. The "ten-strikes" that he has made have perhaps defeated the competitor with whom he put himself in primary relationship at the alley. Occasionally, perhaps after a bad shot, there may have been a marginal awareness of his secondary relationship to the person responsible for the mood. At still lower a level, quite exterior to awareness, the successful projection of the ball and the fall of the pins may well have served as the projection of the player's virility and the overthrow of the offender. The substitution of a pleasant gaming companion for the offender is a sort of semiconscious make-believe. The substitution of the pins for the offender is magic. But every one of us has come through a period in which make-believe was an approved way of life, and every infant is a magician of parts.[5]

If one has no difficulty in securing his sleep and food, and if he makes some fairly successful resolution of his sexual needs, there is no great difficulty in securing the rest of his personality needs by compensatory substitution. It is true that his self-esteem *may* be uncertain, so that he is somewhat tense and inclined to defensive operations; but, whether by tennis championship, big-game hunting, world travelling, by the less glorious methods of tale spinning, movie patronage, or even the ignoble course of keeping himself an object of sympathy—in any or all of these cases, he struggles through, rather to the envy of his fellows. If, however, he includes the sexual drives in those to be solved by compensatory processes, then he is the envy of very few; he is a much harassed man.

[5] It is not wholly accidental that many people, otherwise proud of their kindliness, are fond of observing dog- or cock-fights. The newspapers that inform the populace of every little detail connected with the latest crime of violence may be contributing to the deterioration of society, may even on occasion provoke outbreaks of mob barbarism; but quite as probably, they may be preserving a considerable number of us from untimely demise at the hands of our neglected mates. Devotees to the reading of criminal publicity are thereby provided with socially tolerable satisfaction for criminal tendencies, by way of multiple identifications, chiefly unwitting, with the notorious figures paraded in the news.

The reading of mystery novels, while chiefly a compensatory process, has its sublimatory aspects—the fact that "right" triumphs with such unearthly regularity is a response to the demand of the "social conscience." The writing of bloody mystery yarns is a most fortunate sublimation; the number of people preserved from untimely extermination must be very considerable. It sometimes comes to pass that a potential uxoricide, either of his own volition or on the advice of the doctor, decides to write a story "as a relief" from the homicidal desires. If this estimable labor is conducted at the conscious level, the story is either a very inferior literary product or a stillbirth. Quite often, however, while engaged in the voluntary effort, the author succeeds in sublimation, whereupon he is "inspired" and the creative struggle eventuates in a meritorious performance, both as to the criminal tendency, and as to the story—in the latter of which the reader could find the family romance but slightly disguised, with a solution initially agreeable to the murder impulse, and later, to the tendency to secure social approval. The fact that two people, the criminal and the clever detective, have been used to carry the two "meanings" need not deceive us; if the author is clumsy, the traits of the two will be singularly alike, and necessarily familiar to their creator.

The limits of possibility are rather less sharply drawn with the sublimatory processes, but few are those who can depend solely on sublimation for their sexual satisfaction. In persons of a certain type of personality, when too great a burden has been placed on sublimatory processes, a breakdown appears in the form of excitement.[6] The fantasy directly related to the tendency-system to which an underlying complex resolution involving social approval has unwittingly been attempted makes appearance at least in the fringes of consciousness. There then appears a very complex situation, part of which I shall shortly discuss as threat of conflict and part of which we identify as anxiety, which drives the victim to an almost uninterrupted series of screen activities that keeps the awareness of the disturbing fantasy at a minimum, and tends more or less to avoid anxiety. By plunging rapidly through acts and ideas, one prevents, as it were, the development of situations to the point of consciously activating the negatively evaluated tendencies, and also escapes a measure of anxiety. Excitement is a sort of random occupation in which *anything but* the really essential factors are given relevance. The social results of such a process, entirely aside from the wear and tear on the individual organism concerned, are thoroughly unfortunate. The constant flight renders any constructive thought impossible; the acts constituting the excitement are so conspicuously characterized by lack of judgment and glaring disregard of consequence as to render the sufferer a menace to himself and to others; and the fully developed process is one of the major psychoses for which custodial attention is required.

In some of those who are susceptible to this morbid excitement, there may be prolonged periods of life characterized by a low-grade excitement to which we refer as *hypomania*. In some cases, where, for example, sexual gratifications are sufficiently uncomplicated so that this drive does not contribute an important

---

[6] The difficulties of classification and of formal exposition in this field are well illustrated at this point. I formerly classed *excitement* with the defense reactions, agreeing in this particular with the outline of T. V. Moore's *Dynamic Psychology*; Philadelphia: Lippincott, 1924. For reasons that will have begun to be evident by the end of this chapter, I now regard the excitements as nonadjustive processes, but prefer to discuss the subject at this point because of the frequent resemblance of excitement to a "wild" sublimation.

share to the threat of conflict,[7] this state may not progress; while in others, it is a prelude to psychotic excitement. The hypomanic individual may be an extreme social nuisance, engaging in unreasonable performances of almost any kind. When one of the reformers to whom reference has been made, having unwittingly included too powerful a group of tendencies in his sublimatory substitutes, passes into the hypomanic state, we see "high-pressure uplift" at its worst. He becomes a complacent demagogue, appealing in an unprincipled fashion to the lowest prejudices in alleged furtherance of his elevated aims.[8]

The fully *manic* development of excitement is characterized by extraordinary distractibility and exaggerated activity; attention shifts rapidly from object to object, and there is "flight of ideas" and "pressure of (behavioral) activity." The individual attends to something new as frequently as possible, seizing upon every triviality that comes within the range of any sense organ. He leaves each train of thought as quickly as possible by way of outer distraction or inner transition by rhyming, punning, distortions of word-syllables, "clang associations," and the like. His behavior is redirected as often as may be; there is great volubility and a considerable display of emotional signs. The mood is more or less persistently elevated, the elation continuing in spite of showers of tears at more or less suitable occasions. The attention and response of others is demanded, being literally fought for if otherwise unobtainable. At the same time, the integration of any intimacy has to be avoided, and the most frequent manifestation of manic interpersonal relations takes the shape of more or less malicious mischief. Action in primary group relations is generally augmented by a fervid activation of our instruments for intercommunication, the manic individual going into action like a nation at war. The picture is one of turmoil increasing towards fury. The acts and ideas that one can notice are individually rather simple and direct, but hopelessly truncated; the

[7] In some of these, however, the anxiety seems to arise from tendencies closely identified with the sexual impulses in the satisfaction of which the hypomanic is engaging. See also the discussion of the *superego*, and its relation to "sense of guilt."

[8] See, in this connection, "The Agitator" in an important treatment of the political aspects of human relations, by Harold D. Lasswell: *Psychopathology and Politics*; Chicago: Univ. of Chicago Press, 1930.

total pattern is lacking in any other than accidental meaning excepting in so far as it suspends activity in any significant total
situation.[9] Even the activity that we call sleep has to be reduced
or temporarily abolished in the manic state.

It is from the study of individuals who show excitement as a
part of their activity that we can obtain insight into the "inner"
aspects of distressing situations that call out the defense reactions.
The more "pure" a picture of excitement one sees in an individual, the more certain one can be that it will presently give
place to the nonadjustive situation called depression. But frequently one encounters an *unhappy excitement;* even while the
individual is shouting his joy in song, the facial postures are seen
to be those of sorrowful longing or of fear. One can sometimes
establish enough genuine contact, become intimately enough
related in the situational context of such a one, to learn that the
overactivity of behavior, attention, and emotion is a *relief* either
from anxiety or from "fear of oneself." In the latter case, there
is experienced some strong impulse that is recognized to be so

[9] There are some none too well delineated elements in this nonadjustive
dynamism to be found in the field of the somatic accompaniments. The
persistent elation is to be explained in part as (1) the "uplifting" mood
accompanying superego gratifications (*vide infra*), (2) preserved by in-
attention to (or rather, very truncated apperception of) the responses of
others, and (3) expanded by a euphoria that is partly the result of the
release of sensory fields from conative control and concentration—in the
service of distraction they manifest their whole range of acuity, and the
sufferer seems to himself to be endowed with previously unexperienced
power of vision, hearing, and so on—partly an accompaniment of a rather
specific change in the integrator balance. The autacoid dynamism seems to
be most effective in the nonadjustive situations. One often observes a sort of
caricature of the integrator situation in that the discriminative functions are
so nearly suspended that only the more massive skeletal movements are used,
and the delicate play of the prehensile equipment is submerged—the manic
waves his arms about when forearm or hand movements would appear to
suffice (and in depression, these "large joint" movements are suppressed by a
similarly distributed inhibitory rigidity). The physiology of the organism is
so adjusted that fatigue phenomena are slow in appearing, and the catabolic
processes and the accompanying emunctory activity proceed at an astonishing rate.

In more ways than one, excitement is a "scoptomizing" activity (convert-
ing to feces), and if there comes a time when, by reason, for example, of
solitary confinement, the sufferer has no persons and their values in primary
relations with him, he usually continues this transmutation by crude cop-
rographic delineations on as much as possible of the physical surroundings.
Vide infra, visceral representations in the self.

highly repugnant to the self, or so completely inconsistent with the life-plan, that conflict supervenes.

The concept of conflict is a most important one. A rather precise meaning must be attached to it; otherwise, like "compensation," it can come to "mean" anything. In one of the broader senses, everything else might be said to conflict with the primitive tendency to sleep, and everyone, when awake, might be said to be in conflict in that connection. A person undecided as to going to the opera or to a prizefight might also be said to be in conflict. In the sense intended in this book, however, conflict is *a total situation so integrated that two or more disparate resolutions tend synchronously to occur*. Put loosely, a situation, in order to evoke conflict, must imply two or more mutually exclusive, highly desirable goals, one of which cannot be secured except by relinquishing any hope of the other. From this standpoint, it should be evident that tendencies that can be satisfied, seriatim, will scarcely enter into a state of conflict. The "postponement" of resolution of one situation while resolving a more urgent, intercurrent one, is a commonplace of life. The putting off of many things for a hoped-for time of affluence and leisure may be a form of compensation or of adjustive processes. It is not conflict. The pursuit of parental satisfaction by nursing instead of by parenthood is not a conflict situation, but one of sublimation. Anything that "works" is *not* conflict.

It is difficult to formulate the "state of mind" of a person in conflict, for the traditional unity of the consciousness is wanting; concentration is destroyed by the continual shifting of attention from one to another content. At one moment, the individual is acutely aware of the ultimate necessity of conforming to some certain one of the mores, a violation of which would greatly reduce his self-esteem, perhaps by leading to an immediate unfavorable valuation by the other person involved in the situation. At another moment, he is filled with acute desire to engage in the action the inevitable consequence of which he has just considered, and is a prey to fantasy of such a course. His state is anything but enviable. He is acutely and often terribly unhappy. The baffling of one integrative tendency by the other leads to a piling up of tension in his organism. Such a state, endangering as it does the very maintenance of life, is invariably of brief duration.

A maladjustive process representing a substitute for resolution of the tendencies that are in conflict may make its appearance. Or one of the tendencies may be split off from access to consciousness, the personality thereafter being incomplete. Or panic may supervene, and, out of its extremity, grave maladjustive processes such as regression or suicide take their course.

The *defense reactions* are the most frequent solution of conflict. They are so often encountered that the student, once past the danger of generalizing everything as a "compensation for a feeling of inferiority," now finds himself liable to envisage almost everything as a "defense" against something or other—for example, the same ubiquitous "feeling of inferiority" which is so glib a formula for threatened diminutions in self-esteem. There is a certain ease not only in universalizing the defense reactions as a genus, but likewise in the case of certain of its species. Thus repression (called by W. H. R. Rivers, suppression) is widely quoted as a sort of universal formula in the etiology of mental disorder; all the intelligent are suspected of paranoid states; and the least relaxation from one's habitual social form is construed as an evidence of regressive tendencies.

The avoidance of conflict by recourse to the processes of forgetting is widely important. A certain facility possessed by many to avoid giving any offense by accepting any and all invitations, thereafter "forgetting" the least desirable appointments, is widely quoted as an instance of repression in everyday life. It is not necessary to refer to the defensive processes to account for the disappearance from the content of consciousness of those minor irrelevant matters, the retention of which would actually be a nuisance. From birth onward, we show ample evidence of a native talent for forgetting. A variety of chiefly verbal procedures comes to be the social armament of most of us. Such of our promises as possess validity because of the importance to us of the other person concerned do not escape us. Unless one has so organized himself that "his word is his bond," the others leave scarcely an impression. Even in the case of the paragon to whom every one of his verbal acts is given extraordinary importance by reason of principle, there is plentiful evidence that the natural forgetting talent has not disappeared.

There are certain events, however, to which the native forget-

ting process does not apply in spite of a great conscious willing-
ness on the part of the person concerned to be rid of the unpleasant recollection. These recollections are retained because they
are relevant in a perduring total situation. They are unpleasant
by reason of the inadequacy of the personality concerned to
"accept" the reality and the personal significance of the incident.
This unpleasantness and the persistence of the recollection to
which it is attached may be so troublesome that a defensive
process, *suppression*, is applied to the situation concerned. The
self-esteeming tendencies integrate a situation in which the avoidance of any reduplicative recall of the central unpleasantness is
primary. This is achieved by a negative activity by which perception is suppressed and by positive action in the shape of unwitting alertness for and avoidance of factors apt to be relevant
to the suppressed situation. The individual in whom suppression
is active shows a combination of a specific alert nervousness,
coupled with a facility for slurring over some matters, that is
pathognomonic. If the suppression pertains to a situation including
one of the major tendencies of the personality, the danger of
failure is ever present in the fringes of awareness, and the individual is constantly fearful, the more in that the suppressed tendency
persistently escapes and integrates at least abortive relevant situations, through "accidental occurrences," "slips of the tongue,"
awkward entanglements, and so on and so on. Moreover, in
such cases, while the consciousness of the victim may be fairly
clear of the suppressed tendency, his expressive mechanism and
even his behavior may give the lie to his mental content, and advertise the "missing" tendency, thus acting to integrate the relevant situation.

When, however, there has occurred an event that "awakened"
a tendency in the individual, manifestations of which he regards
with loathing or horror, when, in other words, a previously all
but unsuspected tendency has created an intense conflict in connection with some situational complex, some individuals are able
to *repress* the memorial elements concerned in the occurrence, and
thus the awareness of the tendency. It seems that in this process
there is something like a divestiture of reality from the incidents
and their subsequent association with content of the "never
happened" or mythological kind. They are not rendered null

and void; their effect in a modification of some related tendency
is evidenced. But recollection of the events themselves is manifested neither by continuing effort of suppression nor by recurrence to the mind. The memory cannot be recalled, excepting
by special procedure. Presentation of the actual factual context
of the occurrence is apt to be met with an entirely honest denial
that such was the case. At most, the individual, thus taxed with
the facts, may develop a vague uncertainty, in turn readily
"forgotten." Repression may be effective excepting for its social
effects. Others are not given to acceptance of the repression of
factors concerning them; they take it as weird, or fraudulent.
They distrust the individual from whom actual facts can so
miraculously, and conveniently, disappear. This social reaction
is the more certain in that the vanished experience often leaves
rather conspicuous marks in the shape of changes in the tendency
system characterizing the personality; the social reaction itself
also repercusses on the self concerned and leads to a deterioration
of self-assurance. Aside from these none too desirable consequences, there is but one grave disadvantage to repression. The
latter is a quantitative matter. If too much is repressed, or if the
tendencies repressed are powerful components of the personality,
the success of this defensive process disappears, either as frank
failure with a flooding of consciousness with the "forgotten"
material, or as the appearance of a very dangerous kind of process, dissociation. Before taking up this complex and often destructive group of processes, I shall discuss some defensive reactions rather closely related to suppression and repression, and
even more commonly manifested.

We observe that repression is presumed to associate certain
experience with contexts of a mythological order. We shall now,
in considering *rationalization,* secure some insight into the rationale of this process when it occurs in the field of awareness. Each
of us constructs from the perceived reactions of others to us a
body of beliefs as to our personality, this going to make up the
self.[10] In this body of beliefs are many of the nature of principles
of goodness, virtue, and so on. These are "right" opinions as to
thought and behavior, decorum, attitudes, and so on. We "pride"

[10] The conception of the self will be expanded considerably in the next
chapter.

ourselves on some of them. The dispassionate observer may note not only that we are decidedly emotional about these particular individual sources of pride, but also that we are expert in referring to them in "explaining" actions rather woefully out of keeping with them. Asked why we have done a certain thing, or expressed a certain opinion, self-esteem demands that we produce a plausible "reason," and one calculated to cast no unfavorable light on the self. That a great many of our acts and the great body of our opinions are not to be "explained" by any ordinary inspection of awareness is a truth readily accessible to the thoughtful. The plausible pseudo-explanation by a facile appeal to principle we call rationalization. Good or bad behavior, vicious or indifferent opinion, all comes out beautifully "in our favor." Moreover, when "caught" at a contemptible act, and given a chance to spin a neat rationalization of it, many people many times succeed in losing the reality of the act, and have remaining a transmuted precipitate suited more to the angels than to denizens of this mundane plane. This sort of a process can also—and often does—work retroactively on memorial elements, so that not only is a speciously exalted motivation found for past doings, but the actual placing of these events in the time dimension is wonderfully falsified, so that, by their "new" order, any evidence of the unworthy course of one's life is completely destroyed. This is retrograde falsification. In the rationalizing processes, current or retrograde, it often occurs that the "other fellow" suffers a considerable depreciation. At times, perhaps chiefly when the direct rationalization is all but impossible of success, an indirect rationalization by direct detraction from the esteem of the other one is attempted. The appeal to a principle in this case approaches somewhat to the use of the paranoid dynamism. The difference is one both of degree and of personal awareness. In the detractive rationalization, one has done an unworthy act "because they are the low sort of people that understand only abuse," "one has to fight fire with fire," or something of the kind. As in the case of sublimation, so in that of suppression, if very powerful tendencies of the personality are involved, the effort to keep the tendency inactive is apt to fail and grave phenomea to appear, frequently in *excitement*.

Remotely like the rationalization by detraction, the person

undergoing a *paranoid* development finds his escape from conflict in the "fault" of something outside himself. Here too, the outcome depends in great measure on the importance of the tendencies involved in the threatening conflict. If only the secondary tendencies—for example, the socially approved drives for self-respect are involved, then some individuals achieve a measure of complacency by blaming failure of their "luck," on unfortunate interventions of Fate, or on disastrous coincidences. This procedure is a sort of "exterior rationalization" and is usually accompanied by rationalistic procedures and compensatory appeals for sympathy. If the latter is a conspicuous element, we often find blame for personal inadequacies and failures passed over to a more or less real sickness, a more or less unnecessary identification with some "lost cause," or something else that is both personal in its application and yet allegedly beyond control by the individual. These processes are fairly successful in bolstering up a limited self-regard, if, and only if, the situation concerned does not include a powerful tendency.

Even in the case of threatened conflict including a powerful tendency, a *transference of blame* to one particular impersonal object may go far to save the self-respect. I refer here to the blaming of "heredity." Some very remarkable distortions are "rationalized" in the dangerous paranoid fashion by virtue of the alleged inevitability of a fate called Heredity, the success of this maneuver being to a considerable part a result of an unwitting blame of the parents, and through them, in a son-parent fashion, humanity at large. The unfortunate-progeny-of-a-degenerate-stock formula may be quite a neat way out, as long as it works— as long as the people of importance to the subject-individual give satisfactory responses through its instrumentality.

The transference of blame processes, called upon to deal with the drives really powerful in interpersonal relations, tends generally to an extremely unfortunate outcome. The self, that construct to the honor of which so much of social life is directed, arises chiefly through our delicate evaluation of the opinions of us held by the significant people with whom we have come in contact. We are always on the alert for the approving and disapproving reaction of others to our acts and expressed opinions. A great many of us are extremely sensitive to this sort of critical appraisal. It therefore comes about that, when any tendency central in interpersonal relations—such, for example, as the sexual drives—comes to be involved in conflict, the factor of other people's opinion takes on extreme importance. If now the prevailing type of action toward adjustment in the person concerned has not reflected a fairly exact appraisal of the situations through which he has moved (if, for example, he has progressed toward his present state of personality growth by way of sublimatory and minor defensive processes), now, confronted by a siutation prehended as including ignoble tendencies that would greatly reduce the esteem in which he is held if revealed to the other person concerned, such a one may attempt the resolution of the situation and the escape from conflict by a massive transfer of blame for the unworthy tendency upon the other person.

We enter into innumerable actions because of real or fancied factors nucleating more or less definitely in the other person with whom we are momentarily involved in a total situation. The more competently socialized person recognizes that his actions are a result of himself and the other one, scarcely to be credited as to causality to either person. But the individual who has grown to depend greatly on favorable appraisals has usually also developed a marked concern with techniques for "pleasing" the other person, and this attitude implies a great emphasis on "what the other one wants." If his conscious preoccupations with the desires and wishes of others are not distorted by reason of serious deviation in the evolution of his own personality, then the course of events in life will gradually reassure him. He will come to a measure of unwitting appraisal of others, and to automatic adjustment. This will make him a success in interpersonal contacts, at least at the customary superficial level, and, be his (private) love-life ever so troublesome, he will be "successful" outside of the real intimacies. Given some measure of genuine satisfaction of the sleep, the nutritive, and the sexual needs, such a person usually progresses through life, a delight to business associates, an economic success, and a good citizen. As a salesman, he may be phenomenal. As a politician, he may be one of the least vicious. He may encounter various rebuffs in interpersonal relations, but once assured of his general efficiency in these situations, he comes rather readily to dispose of the failures by minor defensive processes, often detractive rationalization.

But we find many inadequately developed personalities in

whom there has been inculcated this same overdependence on the reaction of others, together with ideals inhibitory to any direct satisfaction of the primal interpersonal drives, such as the sexual. After the fashion later to be elucidated, many youths come to possess considerable unwitting social technique without having acquired any processes making for real sexual satisfaction, without any ability for action toward adjustment in intimate interpersonal situations demanding sexual behavior. This deficiency generally includes at least two factors: a lack of development of certain aspects of the personality, and a more causal morbid development of other aspects inhibitory to behavior. Put loosely, these folk have been taught to overvalue favorable personal appraisal, and to regard sexual behavior as in general uncouth, vulgar, or frankly sinful—at any rate, the sort of thing that "nice" people would not expect them to do.

When such a morbidly virtuous person encounters another person of the personality organization that tends to form with him a situation in which sexual drives are the most potent integrator; when, in other words, such a one meets, under suitable circumstances, a person who "exerts a strong sexual attraction on him"; then conflict manifests itself, and a train of undesirable consequents makes appearance. It may be that the individual's sexual desires are not strong, in which case he is able to handle the situation before conflict appears. There seems to be an hereditarily determined individual variation in the "strength" of the sexual impulses. Also, many people become accustomed to an unwitting drainage of the sexual drives by way of unrecognized fantastic satisfactions and other quasi-personal devices. To these, acute interpersonal situations integrated around sexual motivations may not be of serious moment. But when, for reasons in part already presented, and in part yet to concern us, conflict in a sexual situation does arise, the relative mental health of the individual concerned is always imperiled.

The outcome is generally a grave defense reaction, or, for reason yet to appear, an even more serious dissociation or regression. Whether a defensive process will take the form of a "paranoid state" or manifest as a negativistic or disablement reaction is dependent chiefly on the previous experience of the individual in regard of the relations in which he stands "to" other people.

I refer here to my surmise that the whole body of defensive processes, paranoid and negativistic reactions in particular, are the fruit of an unnecessary artificial disjuncture of people as separate units. In other words, the individual schooled in the true interrelation of himself and significant others can scarcely come to the morbid appraisal of his situation necessary for the appearance of these maladjustments.

To the potentially paranoid, the appearance of conflict in any interpersonal situation leads to a suspicion that all is not good in the attitude of the other person to him, that "something is wrong," exterior to himself. The other person is suspected of exactly those features which go to make up his own conscious appraisal of the tendencies in conflict with self-esteem. In other words, the paranoid process begins with the *projecting,* into one's appraisal of another, of those features of himself for which, if he accepted them as of unqualifiedly personal origin, he would be much ashamed. We might say that, while much of his self-satisfaction has been obtained by way of the perception of approval on the part of other persons, in projection, he reverses the process and "finds" in the perceived aspects of some other persons evidences of undesirable traits of which he has begun to suspect himself. If they have such traits, they will probably suspect him of having them. It would certainly be best to avoid such people, if one is to remain unsmirched. But such people are always showing up. It seems almost as if there must be something about him that attracts them—either that, or there is some fatality, or perhaps even a plot.

As some powerful factor in his personality, usually the sex drive, is responsible for the becoming relevant of the particular persons that interest him, the carrier of this projection process can scarcely escape entanglements. No matter how many individuals he has shunned or driven away by his suspiciousness and peculiarity, no matter to what lengths he has cultivated an austere and forbidding manner, no matter, in fact, if he has actually become so repellent that even casual strangers automatically avoid him, there is no escaping the drive that integrates him into new situations, frequently including utterly unsuspecting people. Not only is the suspicion of another the antithesis of a satisfactory resolution of a sexual situation, but probably quite exterior to the sexual factors, this attitude of suspicion interferes with the satisfactory resolution of the general gregarious need, existent since the beginning of the juvenile era.

In common with the need for air, for food, and for sleep, the requirement for sexual satisfaction, unsatisfied, can become all-pervading. The extremely poor adjustment to it provided by the paranoid dynamism is therefore pushed more and more wildly. The individual may be driven into such a state of tension that overt acts of hostility make their appearance and he is recognized to be "insane." Or, still maintaining some measure of ability to conform with the conventions, he may engage in legal and similar offensives against his "enemies." It is much more frequently the case, however, that, along with the growth of hostility to unfortunately attractive people, coupled with increasing tensions for unsatisfied desires, the sufferer becomes so clearly conscious of the conflict that another maladjustive process is added to the picture. The self-regarding tendencies, confronted not only with universalized suspicion of some unadmitted, intolerable cravings of the personality, but also with dawning awareness of the factitious nature of the projection—in other words, unable to disregard the personal source of the trouble—*dissociate* the abominated features of personality, which now become *as if* they were autonomous, and "persecute" the victim in the guise of devilish thoughts "forced on his mind," hallucinated voices, and the like.

This presentation of the severe paranoid states and their complication by dissociation may tend to deflect attention from the numerically and socially far more important instances of a paranoid attitude without complete maladjustment in interpersonal relations. A key to this type of situation may be given by reference to the individual who is "unwillingly led into" the resolution of his sexual situations. There are a great many people who can get on quite well in resolving all sorts of situations in which conflict is threatened, if and only if they can lead the other person concerned into making the first moves. The "guilt" of the action is thus taken over by the "other one," who can then be blamed for real and fantastic sequelae. One finds a great many who, once thus protected, do not need to go on to the actual blaming of the other; it is sufficient that they "know" that it is his fault. There are, however, a somewhat smaller but still great number who, regardless of the satisfaction secured by resolving a situation, must thereafter complete the resolution by discharging an actual hostility to the other one, punishing him for his coöperation. A fairly common type situation of this sort is seen in the psychopathic man who experiences an intense "love" for one loose woman after another, cultivates each in such fashion that she is led to make the first overt move toward intercourse, engages in the sexual act, and immediately loathes the woman, lets her feel his "disgust with her," and usually advertises her "immorality" during the brief interval before he finds another. To such a one, once is enough with each woman, for a second intimacy would not be so clearly "her fault." Related devices for distributing blame are so widespread and so greatly diversified that a monograph could be devoted to this subject alone. To some, sex satisfactions are always the result of "unexpected accident"; to some, any incident of drunkenness is the result of "unsuspectedly bad" companions; others are "led into" a variety of antisocial acts, from the making of slanderous statements to the doing of homicide.

If it is all someone else's fault, the processes are paranoid; if it is partly one's own fault, but mitigated by the depravity or defect of others, the processes are rationalistic, of the detractive variety; if it is not a fault at all, but looks enough like one to need "explanation," then we are dealing with processes of the type of elaborative rationalization. So much, then, for the transfer of blame. We come now to situations in which not a feeling of guilt but a feeling of privation of the self-esteem is the energizing component in the personality. The genetic history of some people includes the bases for the transfer of blame as a satisfactory device for the maintenance of self-respect. In others, there has been a long historic development of an attitude that may be described as one in which one's importance as an independent person is always being minimized. People are always overlooking one's importance, ignoring one's rights and prerogatives, demanding things to which one is solely entitled, or expecting returns from acts insufficient in payment for one's coöperation. Such a one must protect himself by resisting these inroads into his self. He must defend himself from demands by interposing *negativism.*

He must become automatic in refusing coöperation, until the situation shall have been so changed that it is his "will" that the action transpires.

Of the negativistic organization of defenses against actions that threaten conflict, there are many grades. In one case, it may suffice if every "demand" is converted into a polite request. In another, the demand must take the form of a subservient plea. In yet others, there must never appear anything of demand, but only an opportunity for one to "choose" a course. In still others, there must not even be a suggestion of any alternatives; "the data" must be laid before them with obvious lack of any expectancy of action on their part. Only by such ritualistic performances is their *importance* protected from fancied slight, with ensuing action toward its demonstration. In these individuals, there is not a projection of tendencies valued as unworthy upon the other person who is relevant to their satisfaction, a sort of reversal of the reflections from which the self is constructed. Instead, there is a generalized valuation of the self as a source of reflections of any sort, and much less of a valuing of individual impulses. Negativistic phenomena do not appear in any simple relation to ethical valuation of acts, to acquired inhibitory ideals, or to ideals of "right" behavior and thought. They appear in a decidedly more primitive, less abstractly differentiated, context: the crude relation of the self to others, regardless of specific integrative tendencies. Unfortunate experience in childhood has taught these individuals that status among others is more easily acquired if one is an obstacle than if one is compliant. They have been made to feel that domination is a great virtue intimately associated with man's estate, and have profited most from experience in which they were successful in "not being run over." Along with this emphasis on the side of the subordination and superordination of selves, there has been a corresponding failure of valuation of other sorts of experience, and the self has come to be composed in such fashion that it must secure these reflections of its importance in order to have respect. Any interpersonal situation is thus prone to stir conflict between the drive to reaffirm the importance of the self, and some other drive for satisfaction by way of coöperation.

The negativistic person is peculiarly difficult in relations with superiors and tends to seek his satisfactions among people definitely inferior to him. The degree and kind of inferiority which guarantees self-respect may be almost anything—intellectual, economic, social, physical, or merely constructive-fantastic. The degree of appreciation which the individual can possess as to his need for respect varies from utter misapprehension to intellectual appreciation of his complete intolerance of suggestions from others. If he is conscious of his maladjustive tendencies in this connection, and otherwise competent, he may build himself a world that permits him great achievements despite his negativism. If he is quite unaware of these processes, or if he has real or fancied intellectual or other deficiencies, he may be so driven by sexual or other powerful integrating tendencies that he becomes *actively negativistic*, compelled to do the acts conceived to be the opposite of those expected by the other person involved in his momentary situation. In this case, barring most exceptionally fortunate circumstances, the personality is seriously disorganized by the unsatisfied impulses, dissociation ensuing, as in the case of the severe paranoid states. The systems rendered autonomous by dissociation because of negativistic blocking of the life-processes are not particularly "persecutory" in the sense of hallucinated abuse, injuries, and so on. They take the form of misinterpretation as to the wishes active in the people, real or fantastic, to whom the dissociated tendencies attach and involve the subject-individual in distressing "misunderstandings" of a specific kind.

Before taking up dissociation, it is necessary that we consider a defensive dynamism in many ways the opposite of negativism. In the *defenses by incapacitation*, the threat of conflict between self-regarding impulses and some other tendency is dealt with by the development of a "physical" illness that provides a convenient "way out." One may be so enfeebled in this fashion that interpersonal relations are greatly simplified and most tendencies are worked out by compensatory preying on sympathy, while the major tendencies, like the sexual, are so distorted by suffering that their otherwise "highly immoral" character is lost in the "intense suffering" they occasion. Much more commonly, the incapacitation defense eliminates from the sex act any physical sensations making for pleasure, the individual thus becoming, as it were, a passive and rather martyred vehicle for the satisfaction of the mate. Occasionally, this process is used in securing convenient lapses of consciousness, during which the disapproved tendency is satisfied. A subvariety, showing even greater superficial affiliation to transference of blame, is the utilization of states of alcoholic intoxication, and of light sleep, as a device for relieving the self-regarding tendencies of complicity in "sin." The differentiation of such performances from devices for the transfer of blame is made on the basis of the subsequent attitude of the self toward the partner.

In some superficially similar cases, we find that there has been a *dissociation* such that the individual as a self-conscious personality has been "missing" during the prohibited act. Some behavior, perhaps as extensive in its somatic processes as is the sex act, has occurred while the self was not functioning, while it was asleep or unconscious. Our first impulse is to assume that the ensuing blank in this individual's memory is false, that he is making a specious report. Investigation, however, shows that this is not the case. He goes on without showing the telltale alterations in the course of events, until the same sort of thing occurs again. Again, the self has been missing, and his data on this occurrence consist in hearsay report of the details. This is a case of major dissociation, bordering on multiple personality. The individual is at one moment a self-conscious person, at another, a quite different person engaged in activity intolerable to the self. We "explain" this by saying that some unsatisfied tendency system has been able to dissociate the self, so that the individual functions *as if* the self were not any part of him. He has undergone the experience of his action, but did not incorporate it in the memorial series going to make up the accessible history of the self; the results of the previous experience will ordinarily be clearly evident only in a subsequent similar episode. It is sometimes the case that, *after* the act, the individual "comes to" and recalls the behavior. As he was not there "himself," the recollection shows characteristics like those of a recollected dream; there is not the same absolute validity of the recollection that attaches to those of the waking life. If the previously dissociated self is strong and the action highly repugnant, the recollection may fade quite rapidly, being again detached from the self and becoming "unreal," repressed.

These extraordinary integrations of total situations in which the self is not a part, or toward which the self stands as an unwilling and detached observer, include phenomena of the whole organism—somnambulism, some trance phenomena, some hysterical behavior; of extensive neuromuscular units—automatic writing, mediumistic speech; of the projection field of one or more special senses—hallucinosis, crystal gazing, shell hearing, and so on; and of more or less limited parts of the expressive apparatus—the tics and stereotyped movements. They are rather astounding in that the traditionally unitary organism becomes the moving locus of two (or conceivably more) streams of total activity, integrating and being integrated into two (or conceivably more) coexisting and mutually exclusive total situations.

Situations in which the projection field of a special sense, rather than the whole somatic apparatus, is at the disposal of dissociated tendencies go to make up the various hallucinoses—the auditory "hearing of voices," the tactile, the olfactory, the visual, and the gustatory. In these, the special sense affected functions toward the self-conscious personality as if it were in the service of another personality, the embodiment of the dissociated tendencies. Besides the "persecution" experienced following dissociation in a paranoid state and the amazing hallucinatory phenomena occurring in schizophrenics, such dissociation of a sensory field may be the unwitting aim of mystical or religious effort. A good deal that may seem not of this earth is thus brought about in automatic scripts and in the visions of scryers and seers. In the mediumistic trance phenomena, of similar origin, there sometimes occur phenomena of seemingly definitely transcendental character. The most extraordinary phenomenology that I have observed, however, seems to include nothing beyond explanation on the basis of empathic exchange, coupled with relaxation of the self-conscious pursuit of consensually valid information. The trance acuity of a medium may seem incredibly superior to her talents in the "normal" state. Similarly, however, the psychopathologist finds the dreamer often much more competent at formulating his total situation than is the same individual when awake. The very process of dissociation indicates that the "normal personality" is but a part of the whole. The systems dissociated during periods of "normality" generally include some of those

making for interpersonal intimacies. It is not strange then that
the "normal" person should be stupid in dealing with people, or
that the dissociated systems, once in the physiological saddle,
freed also from a personal tradition—the self—by the assumption
of a fantastic trance self, should be shrewd in accomplishing interpersonal adjustments in certain limited fields. Children enjoy
good repute as artisans in similar connection, not to mention
horses and dogs. We shall secure a better understanding of dissociative maladjustments after we have studied the chronology of
difficulties, the subject of the next chapter.

The last grand division of the maladjustive processes is subsumed under the term *regression,* a difficult psychopathological
conception, only to be understood by reconsideration of the processes by which personality is evolved. We know that as one
evolves along the path of personality growth there is an elaboration in the processes at the disposal of the organism. And we
know that when the organism encounters certain unfortunate
situations, such as those produced by some toxic substances or
by conditions of starvation (due to lack of certain chemical
necessities), or again from the intricate thing we call fatigue,
then the more recently elaborated adjustive processes of the organism tend to disappear and chronologically earlier processes
to take their place. One sees this clearly manifested in the shifts
of consciousness in young children, in which they awaken, go
about certain things, pass into what might be described as their
maximum consciousness and most complex types of activity, go
on for a time, develop what appears to be fatigue, then show for
a little while some much earlier habits, and fall asleep. Thumb-
sucking, for example, is often resumed before a child falls asleep,
although it has long ago been abandoned as a principal activity.
Not only do we see this sort of thing, but in certain complex life
situations one discovers that the personality is itself regressing;
and as the type of total activity goes backward in the history of
evolution of the particular organism, one sees that recent experience—or at least I think one sees that recent experience—tends to
become *as if it were not.* In other words, not only does the type
of processes suffer a retrograde historical regressive simplification,
but experiences of the organism, the precipitate of events in
which the more complex, "long-circuited," newly acquired ten-

dencies were included, seem to go entirely out of evidence as if they had not been undergone.[11]

If the theory of repression is correct, it is useless in dealing with a regressive situation to appeal to experience which is no longer manifested, the "meaning" of which depended on tendencies no longer evident. It seems that this conception is in keeping with that which one encounters in many schizophrenic situations, and if so, we must parallel it in simplifying our attempts at entering into total situations calculated to be useful to such patients.

It may be thought that in regression one is dealing with the dissociation from the self-conscious element of the personality of a great part of the recent experience. This is theoretically untenable because actually dissociated tendencies, including the organization of relevant experience, manifest the quasi-autonomous activity described when they are activated by situational factors. It would be necessary to assume that the individual suffering a marked regression never encountered situational factors such as those with which we customarily deal. Any such massive dissociation would in fact bring about the inverse of the regressive picture, in that the self-conscious individual would be more or less constantly in abeyance because of the multitude of factors relevant to the dissociated systems which would maintain them in activity. This is clearly in line with observations concerning the whole cadre of dissociation phenomena. Where the tendency thrown out of integration with the self is a minor one, we see the appearance of a tic or stereotyped movement when situational factors relevant to the dissociated tendency crop up in the course of life. For instance, because of a series of unpleasant experiences in connection with a particular process, an individual may have dissociated that process and may have developed feelings of disgust at crude language commonly used to describe it. He will then be seen to perform the telltale "sniffing" that constitutes its dissociated expression when he encounters the appropriate feature in his contact with another. Where the dissociation has included the powerful group of sexual tendencies and they remain

[11] The student may be interested in consulting an earlier study by the writer, "Regression: A Consideration of Reversive Mental Processes," *State Hospital Quart.* (1926) 11:208–217, 387–394, and 651–668. See also an interesting treatment of regression in *Tannhäuser: A Psychoanalytic Study of the Wagnerian Opera*, by William V. Silverberg.

unsatisfied, we find either a total automatism of the individual in a hysteric fugue, or the more or less constant harassment by hallucinosis. In the victim of regression, however, the whole interest system has shriveled to a historically earlier stage in his growth and there are no evidences that factors formerly "interesting" to him as a more adult personality retain any validity. They are simply unnoted or treated as uninteresting nuisances.

We come now to consideration of processes by which the individual accomplishes little or nothing toward resolving his total situation. Before discussing the classical, widely demonstrated, nonadjustive dynamics, I wish to devote some considerable attention to a relatively uncommon but exceedingly important nonadjustive situation, *panic*. In panic the individual shows little other than primitive processes, implicit and overt. Its first manifestation may be conceived to occur *in utero* at the beginning of the birth processes. In later life it is a relatively brief event occurring in certain uncommon situations gravely imperiling the individual either as a living organism or as a person. Thus, we may consider a man who has walked perhaps three hundred days a year over a certain sidewalk, only one day to experience its collapse. To such a one, in the interval between the moment of collapse of this something which in a long experience he has never had any occasion to doubt, and the moment of arrival at a new level which is presumably trustworthy, the total situation is that of panic—a very ghastly business not to be cultivated as sport. It appears that in all too many life situations something not as material as the sidewalk, but something of far greater importance, fails with similar utter unexpectedness and contrary to what might be called one's implicit assumption about the universe. That which fails in these dramatic situations is the self. Utterly unexpectedly, contrary to all of a long series of experiences that has ensued in an implicit belief in one's competence, the self proves to be woefully inadequate for a stress to which the individual has subjected himself with what might be called a warranty of struggling through. There follows upon such an event a state of panic.

Nearly everyone has had the experience of being in a more or less public situation in which some personal inadequacy is pointed out in a most unpleasant and embarrassing fashion. Brief maladjustive processes in this sort of situation are the rule, but more or less successful resolution generally follows. Even if it is but the thinking of a bright retort several hours too late, at least one does something which saves self-regard. But sometimes a person caught in such a situation reverts immediately to the primitive reaction of panic. Nearly anyone can recall an occasion on which there was an easy progression into a situation the denouement of which came as a sudden and very embarrassing surprise, the withdrawal from which remains none too gratifying a recollection. Sometimes, when the facilitation of the unwitting involvement is the result of powerful dissociated tendencies, the shock of belated discovery as to "what one has let oneself in for" includes the reintegration of the previously dissociated system and the appearance of violent conflict. In such cases, panic is particularly apt to supervene. Once one has undergone this experience, the paralysis of behavior and thought while one is a prey of utter, formless terror, followed by collapse or by blind random action, one is not what one was before the experience. In some, there is a gradual recovery from the shock, and the development of adjustive processes tending to insure the personality from a recurrence of the horror. In all too many, however, the panic episode is prelude to an immediate outcropping of schizophrenic processes amounting to an acute psychosis, while others go on for a considerable time thereafter, always less certain of themselves or of anything else until another blow ushers in the frank psychosis. A good many of the latter are obviously eccentric and morbid from the initial episode of panic. Some of them so simplify their situation, often by adopting the life of a recluse, that they are able to escape severe mental disorder.[12]

[12] Panic is a brief phenomenon. It is probably impossible to remain in panic for long. The organism is not benefited in any way by the experience, nor is anything accomplished toward resolving the total situation.

Speculation relating panic to the immobilization reactions of certain lower forms of life is vicious. Such "reasoning by analogies" is justifiable only when used as a point of departure from scientific investigation. In psychiatry and related disciplines, its exuberant overgrowth is all too rarely recognized for what it is—entertaining fantasy.

In the case in point, W. H. R. Rivers, in *Instinct and the Unconscious;* Cambridge Univ. Press, 1920, has said succinctly, concerning the "reaction by immobilization" and panic, "I suppose them to be poles apart so far as the accompanying affect is concerned." Panic is wholly destructive, even in the event itself.

Panic may be said to be primordial fear. There are two more adult forms of this emotion that are of great psychopathological import—namely, the anxiety states and equivalents, and the phobias. Both are conditions of morbid fear in the sense that the object feared is unknown or irrational, respectively. The *phobia* is to be understood as an obsessional substitution of one object of fear for another. The latter, the proper object of the fear, is often very difficult to discover. While it is thus apparent that in both, the real object is unknown, there is otherwise little in common in the two states. We shall leave the subject of phobia with the comment that each specific instance is to be regarded as a "formula" substituted obsessionally (*vide infra*) in lieu of action in a total situation.

The *anxiety* states are among the most frequently encountered of the nonadjustive processes. In major anxiety one finds that the individual either, apropos of no very evident cause, undergoes attacks of intense fear—often fear of immediate death—with all the well-known signs and symptoms—tachycardia, tremor, blanching, perspiration with subjective feelings of cold, disturbances of the breathing rhythm, tending to relaxation of the sphincters, and so on—or, in the even more important group of conditions called *anxiety equivalents*, with equally recondite cause, undergoes a seizure with some one or more (usually the same in each seizure) of these signs and symptoms of fear. It is not unusual for patients suffering certain of the anxiety equivalents to seek and secure extended medical treatment for alleged morbidity—for example, paroxysmal tachycardia. On the other hand, some individuals experience mild anxiety equivalents so frequently that they are taken to be peculiarities of the physiology, personal idiosyncrasies that are only to be endured—and perhaps outgrown. An especially common example of this category is an excessive perspiration of the hands whenever one is confronted with a "difficult" interpersonal situation. In the middle distance are a number of the so-called hysterical conversion symptoms, such as the peculiar choking sensation called *globus hystericus*, transient impediments of speech such that one cannot make a sound, this with or without sudden dryness of the mouth, and pains, especially in the region of the heart or "in the head." The student will notice here that the delineations of the disablement reactions, of the autonomous manifestation of dissociated systems, and of nonadjustive attacks of fear of an unknown cause, are overlapping. This difficulty of delineation is by no means accidental, for the three categories of phenomena are but aspects of a nuclear process—namely, that called *conversion*. When an autonomous system takes over a major skeletal unit, the individual suffers a symptom which may or may not function as a specific disablement. When some part of the expressive apparatus is affected, we must question whether the more appropriate formula is one of unwitting expressions of a dissociated content, of interference by tensional modifications required to suppress an expressive impulse, or of the complete or partial expression of fear of known or of unknown origin. When some part of the deeper visceral apparatus is affected, we have generally to deal with anxiety, but again may be encountering a hysterical compromise—a specific or general disablement. The point of reference by the use of which some progress in abstract classification of these phenomena can be made lies in the consciousness of the individual concerned. The defense reactions avoid conflict that has been at least vaguely threatened. They have, therefore, a sort of "right" to exist and are not ordinarily offered for "treatment." The anxiety attacks are unalloyedly troublesome, the sufferer *not* having experienced any unpleasantness that they have eliminated. The victim would be delighted to be rid of them. The tics and stereotyped movements, mannerisms, automatisms, hallucinations, and other phenomena attending dissociation are *peculiarly nonpersonal* in their subjective interpretation—"neurological," "hereditary," "spiritualistic," the machinations of enemies, and so on. Their remedy is an especially ticklish problem, progress toward which not infrequently *brings about anxiety attacks*.

In this peculiar relationship between the three categories of processes, we find a clue as to the nature of the anxiety attack. It is of the nature of a threat, but one never attended by a context of meaning in terms of interpersonal relations. It is an expression in consciousness, mediated by the affected somatic apparatus, of incomprehensible danger to the self. I shall presently touch upon the peculiar characteristics of tendency-systems that customarily manifest themselves in this fashion.

We have already discussed the nonadjustive state called *excite-*

ment, which we conceive to be a more or less random activity to avoid conflict or anxiety. In adolescents, a morbid excitement showing objective manifestations of great (and frequently fear-ridden) tension may precede the onset of panic and subsequent schizophrenic disorder. But in others, the structure of whose personality is quite different, excitement of a "pure" type grows and wanes, and gives over to depression in the curious alternation making up the nosological entity of the manic-depressive psychosis. These individuals are of the group who show a "cyclic" swing of the mood, being at times unduly high in mood, somewhat exalted, then—with or without fairly clear "cause"—being unduly "blue."

In *depression*, there is a preoccupation of consciousness with a small group of grief-provoking ideas which recur again and again.[13] It is conventional to point out the singular reversal of the clinical picture in passing from the manic excitement to the often chronologically related state, depression. The actual difference, however, between excitement and depression is perhaps not one of kind, but one of direction and autacoid integration. Distractibility is wholly lacking, but the same "purpose" seems now to be served by a resolute concentration of attention on a formula, preoccupation with which is as unproductive as was the excited preoccupation with distractions. Activity is greatly diminished; the "inner" processes, like the behavioral acts, are few and slow. But there seems often to be a marked and facile flow of inhibitory impulses *opposed* to any intrusions of sentience, change of the ideational content, or behavioral act. The mood is as persistent as that of excitement. The more massive skeletal movements are especially inhibited. And the physiology seems to be so adjusted that anabolic processes are at a minimum and the emunctory activities greatly handicapped.[14] While depression is generally a

[13] A classical example is the patient who thinks and (if he can be led to express his thoughts) says: "It is terrible—all is lost—God has forsaken me— I have committed the unpardonable sin—it is terrible"—and thus starts over again, going on indefinitely.

[14] To parallel the note on excitement, we may consider depression as a scoptomizing activity applied now to the subject-individual. In those of the *involutional illnesses* that are most nearly related in form to the manic-depressive psychoses, manipulation of feces with reference to the environing people is all too conspicuously a central theme. And in another of these "late-life depressions," the *agitated* depression, distress about uncleanliness

phase of the manic-depressive psychosis, there are also schizo-phrenic illnesses the initial phenomena of which give the impression of a rather "pure" depression. There are some young patients in whom the gloomy preoccupations mask for a time the serious distortion of thought, "queer" beliefs, and delusions of the schizophrenic.

Another by no means uncommon group of the nonadjustive processes is that to which we may apply the term *obsessional substitution*. It is peculiarly the disorder of the "thinker," a state without parallel in the subhuman phyla. Varying from low-grade ruminative preoccupation, a considerable part of which is derived from the revery subordinate to adjustive thinking in connection with some fairly complex situation, to a preoccupation of awareness by logical, or pseudo-logical, formulations so intense that adjustive thinking appears only in crisis situations, the obsessional dynamics cover a broad field of processes. Dreads, phobic fears, doubts, and unending scruples—of such are the more severe obsessional preoccupations made up in conscious representation. The corresponding explicit activity includes socially useless rituals without number, time-destroying habits of complexity, speech disorders of the type of stuttering and stammering, and an awesome array of systems, procedures, and precedence—all with some relevant historic justification, almost invariably grown meaningless with the passage of time.[15]

Before concluding this hasty survey of nonadjustive processes, a word may be offered as to the emotional situation called grief.

sometimes shows itself in incidents to be a resymbolization of a desire to soil oneself and others.

[15] There is room for serious question as to the propriety of classifying the obsessional processes as nonadjustive. It may well be urged that obsessional preoccupations seem often to serve as defense reactions. And it may be mentioned that certain personalities are principally characterized by a *compulsion to think*, yet clearly progress from situation to situation, and are not arrested in a nonadjustive pause. Likewise, some people become depressed yet carry on a measure of adjustive activity, sometimes through rather deep depression. And people who suffer anxiety attacks are often quite "efficient" in their chosen employment. There is nothing holy about the classification that I have given, and there is nothing of our systematic presentation that hangs on the acceptance of its rubrics. Consideration of *the* total situation concerned in each manifestation of the processes mentioned will, I believe, give ample confirmation of their actually nonadjustive character. As to the compulsive thinking, we shall have more to offer in Chapter X.

Whenever, in the course of a total situation, a person relevant in it becomes either literally or practically disintegrated, before the resolution of the total situation is complete—at that time there always appears an emotional state of the subject-individual. Thus, for example, when an individual integrated in an intimate situation with another is removed by death or similar accident, there is left a total situation including powerful processes now without a real object of application. It seems to be an inherent necessity of the organism that certain phenomena be experienced in the course of dissolution of the now meaningless sentiment. These emotional processes take the shape of grief. In the course of their manifestation there is reorganization of the tendencies concerned. The processes of grief may be said to apply to a fantastic construct of the lost person, which as it gradually disintegrates releases the tendencies concerned from the preceding configuration and makes them again available for interpersonal adjustment. There are some individuals whose grief does not seem to serve this purpose. They grieve and grieve over the lost object, seeming in various ways to protect the substitute sentiment of grief from disintegration by augmenting interest in its fantastic object. This deviated functioning, morbid grief, is a nonadjustive process, accomplishing an abnormal extension in time of the disadjustment involved in the privation of the love-object. This sometimes comes about because of an unwonted sweetness in the sympathy given to the bereaved one. It is then a particular form of compensation. In other cases its extension can be envisaged as a defense against a new interpersonal situation.

Depression, also, can often be seen to be a sort of false sublimation for destructive tendencies integrated into a sentiment of hatred. The object of the powerful negative sentiment is made to suffer by the continued depression of the subject-individual. Even self-destruction may be "used" in finally circumventing the escape of the hated object; the suicide occurs under circumstances so arranged that it shall leave a permanently painful scar in the object-personality. From this standpoint, these nonadjustive processes are seen to be motivated toward the accomplishment of something other than mere time-extension in interpersonal relations. This "purposiveness" becomes even more impressive when one considers the condition of the significant people environing an obsessional neurotic. Not uncommonly, they are ground under a tyranny that could scarcely be enforced by a technique other than that of "illness." The case occurs to me of a thoroughly underpaid draftsman by whose effort his employers were enabled to profit greatly, while requiring of him a modified serfdom approximating the role of an office boy. By an obsessional fear of flinging himself from any stairway he might attempt to travel, he easily eliminated many disagreeable features of his work, and secured for himself through the instrumentality of his wife an almost Oriental emancipation. Having finally become arrested by his illness while on the second floor of his residence, his work had thereafter to be delivered by his wife, his meals had to be brought up to him, and so on.

That there are important positive functions of the nonadjustive processes in the interpersonal relations of the individual is not to be ignored. In this respect, they but manifest the invariable rule [16] that there is nothing haphazard or meaningless, inutile or foreign, in the "mental life." Any and all total action, explicit or implicit, has a valid place in the personality concerned. It is never *de novo;* it is never without consequents. The meaning of the term *nonadjustive* may then require further scrutiny. These processes must, in "merely extending a configuration in the time dimension," be serving the personality just as really as does adjustment or maladjustment.[17] We shall perhaps further our understanding by recurring to the definition of mental health, our hypothetic prehension of a continued growth of personality

[16] There is no greater truth underlying the progress of psychopathology, psychotherapy, and social engineering than this one; credit for its establishment is due almost solely to the genius of Sigmund Freud. For that matter, that type of opposition to "The Psychoanalytic Doctrine of the Unconscious" which has the form of vigorous arguments about purely verbal considerations, is, in itself, a convincing demonstration of the actuality of extraconscious dynamisms.

[17] Appeal to the life-profile does not clear the situation. Futile lives, from the objective standpoint, are often explicable by reference to a too compulsive discharge of tendencies by compensatory processes. Negativistic activity has stood in the way of success in innumerable cases. The grave eventuality of schizophrenia—comparatively free from processes included under our nonadjustive rubric—is frequently far more nearly a complete arrest of useful living than is the manic-depressive psychosis—chiefly composed of processes classed as nonadjustive—with its frequently extended periods of relative mental health and comparatively efficient living.

through total situations of increasing complexity. The significant complexity is to be sought in the interpersonal relations of the individual. The whole group of maladjustive processes, even though most of them represent an excessive complexity not in the direction of personality growth, none the less represent activity toward interpersonal relationships that contribute to self-esteem, and that are along the line of that which is regarded by the self as *good*. The effort is still for personally estimable behavior and thought—for an approximation to ideals acquired by interpersonal interchange.

The nonadjustive processes, even excitement with its augmented intereference with other people, are all opposed to interpersonal relationships. They are activities toward the resolution of situations integrated by tendencies which, if recognized, would be estimated as clearly antisocial and *bad*. The effort is really in the direction of destruction of interpersonal relations or of actual persons significant in one's total situation, but awareness of this motivation is *never* developed. The beginning of insight into the actual goal of a nonadjustive activity is the end of the process. Ordinarily, however, their beginning and ending are matters concerning which the individual is wholly unable to find intelligible explanation. That he has been hyperactive, or had an attack of fear, or worried about some ghastly eventuality, or was profoundly depressed—all this he knows. He may consult the physician because he is unable to "clear his mind" of some phobia or some necessity to do a meaningless ritual. His best-intended efforts, however, never bring him more than a *probable* explanation of the underlying interpersonal realities, in complete contradistinction to the type of insight obtainable into other than nonadjustive dynamics.

If, in working with the physician, a permanent "cure" is effected, or if, relatively unassisted, the personality "outgrows" the malady constituted by the nonadjustive situations, in either case, the verbal formulation of change which the individual can give is incomplete and frequently irrelevant. Even if the "cure" is forced by the studied use of situational factors, interpretations or other, the "favorable effect" cannot be "believed" by the patient—it does not assume meaningful relations with his available experience. In brief, the dynamics of nonadjustive situations pertain to tendencies that are presocial, to processes lacking any of the characteristics of selfhood as a reflection from significant others. They date from late infancy and early childhood, before self-consciousness and the growth of an experiential context differentiates oneself and others. Their later manifestation in the form of the nonadjustive states is indicative of their nonincorporation into the self in the stages of childhood and the juvenile era. They have not developed from a primitive and low-level fantasy type of content, and an impulsive character of action.[18] If they had been incorporated into the self-conscious personality, no matter how severely they might ultimately have been suppressed or how completely dissociated, they would have acquired at least a personal reality, and would have undergone some favorable modification by application in interpersonal relations either in higher-level fantasy or constructive thinking,[19] or both. The implications of these considerations should become more evident in the course of the next chapter.

[18] The depressive and the obsessional "neurotic" manifest this feature, in the one case by a preoccupation with an entirely ungratifying *megalomania* coupled with notions of *divine* retribution for the unpardonable sin; in the other, by an "omnipotence of thought" such, for example, that it is not uncommon to be told by such a patient that he "cannot say *anything* that comes to my mind, *lest it be wrong.*"

[19] I have suggested that depression is often in the service of hate. The paranoid is another case in which sentiments of hate are in evidence. A comparison of (1) a self-consciously hateful person deliberately injuring his enemy, (2) the conduct of a paranoid individual in drinking with a significant person, and (3) a depressed person punishing the world that is in contact with him, should illuminate three general types (degrees) of social elaboration of hateful tendencies within the personality.

CHAPTER IV

The Chronology of Difficulty

THE STAGES OF personality growth must be retraced with attention now directed to the morbid deviations that may come to characterize them. Recalling that the distinction between adjustive and maladjustive processes is not one of essential nature but only one of degree and consequents, we may now attempt to clarify the sequence of events that establishes success or partial failure in the personal utilization of the human dynamic equipment. At the same time, some light may be expected as to the gap that separates the nonadjustive processes from those that aid in maintaining or partially approximating the state of mental health.

One must first consider the determining power of heredity. Inborn factors of organization fix the limits of life opportunity in certain ways. Gene arrangement which gives one unusually short fingers precludes great virtuosity as a pianist; and an inherited stubby thumb may be the finger of Destiny for the youth who "must" bowl if he is to be "one of the boys." Similarly, injuries inflicted in the brain tissue during the birth process may lead to internal bleeding which has an unfortunate determining effect on the individual, for the blood may permanently obstruct passages concerned in the drainage of fluid from the brain and thus produce a condition called hydrocephalus, which interferes gravely with the growth of various parts of the brain. In the first few weeks of extrauterine life, previously latent inherited determiners make their appearance at increasingly uncertain chronological periods. This phenomenon occurs with rapidly diminishing frequency up to perhaps the twenty-fifth year of life. There is little of this sort of predetermined change from the latter part of infancy to puberty, at which time there is a very considerable change due to inborn factors which have required from six to eighteen years to mature to the point of functional manifestation. One is justified, also, in accepting an hereditary determination as anterior to the appearance of the socializing impulse which I use as the landmark at the end of childhood. This, too, is the case with the intimacy-impulses initiating the earliest stage of adolescence (frequently prepubertal). These may be taken to be the first manifestations of the sexual determiners concerned in the appearance of the genital functions proper.

While I do not regard it as sound theory or practice to "see" manifestations of "sex instincts" from birth onward, as in the original formulation of Freud, I find it even more difficult to entertain the "predestination psychology" which sees everything as a matter of hereditary factors—for example, Rosanoff's "theory which explains the recoveries [from, for example, 'dementia praecox'] by a special relative order of ontogenetic development of the different temperamental elements of personality." What we *cannot* develop because there are no suitable organizatory factors in our inherited make-up, I am quite willing to accept as determined. Anyone with a mind open to experience, however, must come to see that experience has a tremendous influence on the development of the individual, an influence, for that matter, that can be studied well down the subhuman phyla. I prefer to believe that post-natal experience exerts a marked influence on the time interval required for the appearance of latent determining influences, and in some cases an absolute control over their maturation. A particularly deviated environment may delay the socializing tendency until the age of eight, and the appearance of the genital sexual impulses until after seventeen. Given, then, the limiting factor of innate determiners, let us take up consideration of the processes at work, the more common experiences, and the resulting alterations in tendencies, that may be observed or assumed in the course of personality growth.

The mental life of the infant is a baffling field of exploration. There is a beginning of method for this study and we may hope finally for a good measure of exact information as to the implicit and the behavioral processes occurring in the first fifteen months of extrauterine life. Work with schizophrenic patients, however, has compelled me to construct for myself a body of assumptions concerning the infantile personality—this, in considerable advance of direct factual material. While these constructs are not to be taken too seriously, they are not quite purely fanciful.[1] Heretofore, they have stood the test of subsequently discovered facts, and may still have some definite predictive value.

There are no grounds for assuming that the neonate has anything even remotely like a notion of his own individuality. But there is, I have reason to suppose, much in his mental state that pertains to himself. This constitutes the rudimentary basis of the later elaborated self-consciousness. It is, however, a mental state without any suggestion of boundaries of the self. It is a state which is approximated in later life only in certain dreams and in the sort of experience which some of the religious mystics undergo—one that recurs, in addition, in the experience of certain individuals progressing into acute mental disorder. The mystics call this contact with the primitive content *universal participation* —participation in the infinite—and I suppose that that is about as good a combination of words as one can find with which to refer to it.

Against such a background, needs are felt and lead to extensive disturbance of the organism; expression is given to these needs in the use of the cry and in alterations of the facial expressive postures. We touch here on the highly elaborated oral apparatus (as I choose to call it) consisting of the motor equipment of the lips, the tongue, palate, swallowing mechanism, the glottis, the salivary glands, and so on, together with the sensory apparatus including that by which stimuli applied to the face and the lips are effectively correlated with activity. All this is ready at birth. It is the principal point of contact with the environment that is in a condition of high efficiency from the very start. It is used frequently. The mother puts the infant to the nipple, or the nurse

---

[1] They have rather more in their favor than have hypothecations concerning a racial or a universal unconscious, theories of the inheritance of archaic symbols, and a variety of related fantasies to be found here and there in the literature.

gives the infant a bottle with a nipple on it, and activity ensues in the case of all those that are to survive. In early infancy, the particular total situations including contact with the nipple constitute extremely important experience, in considerable part because in this situation there is the satisfaction of chemical necessities arising in the body.

The growth of life-techniques arises in the successful escape from pain, unpleasure, and the felt needs of the organism. The vital first breath is poorly represented in the memorial series, as it occurs in the midst of neurophysiological recovery from the cataclysm of birth. The maintenance of peripheral temperature by covering the body is similarly fogged. Excepting for chilling and warming of the face, exposure of the body continues for some time to be a protopathic rather than an epicritic matter.[2] But the coincidence of suckling and the disappearance of hunger-discomfort is clear, as is the sensory input from the facial and the trigeminal nerve areas concerned in the act. From a syncretistic prehension of primitive hunger, the nipple, the complex kinesthetic sentience arising in oral activity, the gustatory input from the milk; out of these data vividly contrasted on a background of death-evil, the coenesthesis disordered by chemical needs, there comes experience that is central in the conscious series of the individual.[3] The roots of many categories of reality are included in this "hunger-nipple-lips-satisfaction" syncretism: serial order in events; sensation and feeling; pleasure definitely conditioned as a reality by the rapid changes from discomfort associated with sentience; matter, as manipulated and as recurrently encountered, unchanged; motion; and values, power to assuage need.

---

[2] It is unfortunate that this one of several important series of events still lacks investigative attention. The fate of tendencies developed in the escape of discomfort associated with the dermal periphery remains to be explored for psychobiology. The role of this factor in the personality is poorly represented by the present dubious synthesis under the rubric *exhibitionism*.

[3] We may accept the consciousness of the first few weeks of infancy as containing nothing whatsoever which would distinguish the nipple from the infant. The nipple cannot be conceived of by the infant as anything but a more or less independent and uncontrollable part of its own more or less cosmic life. I think that there is good evidence for the notion that there is such a consciousness of it, that there is, in fact, much more of 'mental content' than is commonly assumed.

Quite early in postnatal life, the nipple and its attributes (which may be those of a bottle or of a breast or whatever) take on distinguishing marks—these distinguishing marks being the first of the long series of marks by which we recognize "external reality." We might say that this growth includes the analytic segregation as an "external" phenomenon of some factors intimately associated with this nipple. Throughout infancy there are plentiful signs of the continued elaboration and functional improvement of the distance receptors. In other words, the infant is becoming more and more capable of noticing phenomena which occur outside of its own body and in that region that comes gradually to be recognized as an outer world. The comings and the goings of the nipple are the first of those building blocks with which we are compelled to structuralize our conceptions of the world. Particular functional relations of the nipple to the infant in the shape of the *unification or separation* of the nourishment-satisfaction and the activity-satisfaction (of the sucking dynamism, itself), almost entirely dependent on the rate of flow of the milk, have a conspicuous role in later development.[4] The intimate relation of *expressed need* to suckling has probably been powerfully influential in buttressing the unconscious dependence on *verbal magic;* the remote effects in this connection of the modern pediatric practices in regard of regular feedings and parental avoidance of undue response to crying may be stupendous.

From the appearance of the first rudimentary prehension of the person associated with the more or less unmanageable doings of the nipple—which I shall call *mother-recognition*—we have proceeding in the infant a variety of experience which is of the first importance in the development of every personality. The gradually more and more realistically prehended person, the "mother," is the source of practically all the satisfactions that there are, other than satisfactions from play. All the needs which arise that are not simply a call for the exercise of neuromusculo-

[4] See, for this aspect of too great ease of securing nourishment, the work of David Levy on the etiology of thumb-sucking. The reverse case, in which the sucking dynamism is exhausted before the food-need is fully discharged, must not be ignored on the basis of "obvious" relationship to malnutrition. For all we know, it too may have a long and thoroughly important role, even though fairly promptly remedied by the pediatrician.

glandular apparatus require in the human young some activity on the part of the environment. The environment concerned is generally consistent in the sense that it is usually the same person. There is nothing on which to base a "rational" appraisal of this person—the only thing which can constitute infantile experience of the mother is the data which the infant's receptor apparatus is capable of giving him. This combines to form a primitive syncretistic conception of a more or less vast omnipotent creature who engages at times in activity pleasant and satisfactory to the infant. The activity of this satisfactory piece of the world is more or less responsive to certain activities of the infant, but has a none too simple relation to such activity. This conception is quite like the fundamental conception which nearly everyone has of God. I do not doubt but that the primitive mother sentiment—the infantile mother-experience-grouping built around most of the strong impulses of the infant—is the *fons et origo* of the conception of God, of the beliefs in mysterious transcendental interventions in nature, and of faith in the efficacy of prayer and other ritualistic procedures.

The primitive mother sentiment, which is thus a product of early infancy, in late infancy and throughout childhood undergoes much differentiating experience. Inhibitions have to be taught the infant; the infant's constantly growing needs and specialization of needs have to be curtailed here and there as to satisfactions—as in the case in which the youngster cries for the moon, even the most absurd mother being somewhat handicapped in satisfying such a demand. Thus, in the universal experience of human beings there develops an inadequacy in experience secondary to that which was elaborated and "recorded" in the past. Unlike the primary inadequacy, never very fully represented in consciousness—by which one is driven from the Nirvana of sleep into the satisfying of needs, finally to resume peace—this secondary inadequacy, once prehended, continues, unhealed. There was once a time when the primitive mother satisfied everything, and now the mother of childhood—even though she has grown insidiously out of the primitive mother—is not only inadequate in some situations but is definitely troublesome in others, and gives rise to pleasure *or* pain. There comes from this the first great body of disappointments. One never has a clear recollection of the collapse of the mother as a figure ideally good, ideally powerful, and ideally satisfactory, since that would require an abstract view of a series of very early events of an intrinsically syncretistic character precluding analysis. It seems none the less certain, however, that it is from infancy that there comes the conception of God, a more or less anthropomorphic universal power; and it is in childhood that the disappointments of life begin potently to redirect the personality, by the formation of that which we shall come later to study as the "superego" aspects of "the mind." [5]

The greater part of the infant's time is spent in sleep. One must recognize in the state of sleep a group of processes, a considerable number of activities, rather than merely quiescence and central inhibition.[6] It is often in sleep that there appears the first objective evidence of processes that are not producing a satisfactory resolution in the organism-environment complex. Crying, fretting, and other manifestations occurring while the infant is awake may well indicate unsatisfied needs, may mark ineffective activity in the infantile total situation; these, however, may or may not pertain to factors that are sources of important experience. Quite often such signs of discomfort are related to matters of no great ultimate importance. In fact, owing to various mismanagements to which the infant has been subjected, crying and fretting often come to function almost as local action—they are then perhaps of the character of "conditioned reflexes," and do not interfere gravely with the elaboration of total activities that will later be required by changing situations. The expressed distress may be regarded as of grave moment only when it interferes materially with some important activity of the infant. With dis-

[5] I can but hope that the student will avoid a glib assumption to the effect that we have now elucidated the "roots of the Mother-Complex." *Mother*, as a term in the current presentation, is generic; it refers to *the one who mothers*, by no means necessarily the blood-mother. (In the case of some Trobriand Islanders, for example, it might quite possibly be the blood-father—if these "savages" use nursing-bottles.) Only the empathized factors of the personality actually doing the early infantile mothering enter as potent agents into the infantile personality growth. Entirely analogous developments occur over a biological range more extensive than is the mammalian order. Relative elaborations of relevant experience in each species are a function of the relative evolution of the integrative dynamisms.

[6] This topic will be considered *in extenso* in Chapter IX, in which a somewhat 'new' theory of sleep and dreams will be presented.

turbances of sleep, on the other hand, the contrary is rather the case.

It is not strange that sleep disturbance should in some cases be related to adenoid growths and the like, for interferences with the respiratory apparatus certainly produce at birth and at any time thereafter a very great disturbance of the total organism. Asphyxia, I presume, is the most acute and terrible hunger mortal is capable of experiencing. But one must not assume that night terror is a direct local effect of interference with the oxygen supply. Instead, it must be regarded as a total activity of the organism, and, as such, a mental phenomenon to be understood not by considering brain cells or lung cells or any organ, but instead by considering that the organism *in toto* in its relation with the absolutely necessary environment is suffering as a result of insufficient functional activity, an inadequacy in the interchange of oxygen and waste products. The local action which might be related to oxygen deprivation is entirely different from night terror or from the experience of asphyxiation. As one would expect, the latter makes appearances only when the organism is no longer safe. When the organized neuromuscular activity to avoid oxygen hunger has failed, then comes total activity, behavior, for its relief—restlessness and excitement.

Sleep disturbance in infancy is more apt to be due to difficulties which can be formulated in biochemical terms than to anything else. This accent on what might be called physicochemical causation shifts rather rapidly, however, and we find sleep disturbances in childhood are much more apt to be due to 'mental' causes than to physical. Crude physicochemical necessities—while always of final importance and always ultimately capable of suspending everything except action for their satisfaction—shrink steadily in temporal importance as we grow. In other words, we become more and more competent in escaping the physicochemical crises and have more time to devote to the growth of other interest-systems or traits. Sleep disturbances in the second year of life are often due to grave maladjustments of the infant-mother situation in which not the satisfaction of physicochemical needs but instead another group of factors is of primary importance.

It happens as a result of the geometric function of the bones— coupled with the growth of myelin in the nervous system, and the functional completion of muscles and glands—that the play activity of the hands tends often to localize itself in proximity to the genitals. These appurtenances are discovered to be peculiarly useful in play.[7] Perhaps from similar personal experience, for some reason regardless, in many cases parents look on any manipulation of the genitals by the infant or child as "awful." Some mothers, and doubtless some fathers, find in this accidental anatomical arrangement, coupled with the play impulses of infancy, a door opened to all that is horrifying. To handle one's penis is to some mothers equivalent to something at least as bad as "original sin"; to others, it is in very truth Original Sin; to others, it is a portent of excessive sexuality in later life, whatever that may be; and so on. I have remarked on empathy, the marked emotional linkage between the infant and the adults who habitually deal with it, by which, for example, any emotion strongly felt by the mother while the infant is nursing is prone to interfere with the nursing, and a sudden fright of the mother while she is fondling the infant to lead to marked, almost instant, modification of the infant's activity—a sort of direct contagion of emotion. When so-called infantile masturbation makes its appearance within a home where the genitals carry an extreme curse, there is a great emotional upheaval in the parents. This emotional upheaval is conveyed by empathy to the infant. At least in part because of the amazing speed with which the integrating apparatus is being completed, the activities going to make up "infantile masturbation" become "conditioned" by the incorporation into the activity pattern of a powerful unpleasant feeling. The occurrence of these processes—to later manifestations of which I have applied the term *primitive genital phobia*—invariably represents a serious distortion of personality, and often leads to night terror.[8]

[7] See, for an earlier and more extensive discussion of the subject, "Erogenous Maturation," *Psychoanalytic Review* (1926) 13:1–15. The relevant material begins with the first paragraph on page 4 of that article.

[8] The use of the term *phobia* in this connection is not to be construed as indicating an identity with those obsessional fears often encountered later in life. This, instead, is a profound primitive formation not represented in consciousness excepting in the indirect reecphoriation of primitive terror in sleep.

It can pass over into a more mature sort of formation. If the infant, for reasons which we cannot always explain, in spite of this inhibition or

In like manner, in infancy, generally because there is not enough oral work connected with the securing of nourishment, thumbs, toes, and the like are sucked in order to permit the apparatus to secure its satisfaction, discharge its energy (so that the subordinate configuration involving the mouth is completed). Many parents have more or less information to the effect that years of thumb-sucking are apt to result in protrusion of the incisor teeth. Others fear that "the habit" may continue and lead to subsequent embarrassment of their child. To yet others, for more obscure reasons, it is considered to be a "nasty habit." The parents seem seldom to wonder why there is thumb-sucking; I judge that the devil's intervention is rather to be expected in the early years of life, when "original human nature" is still "unregenerated." Whether for cosmetic or ethical reasons, something has to be done about the thumb-sucking, and the parents attempt to do something about it. They consult the family physician (nay, even sometimes the expert pediatrician), and he in too many cases prescribes aloes, iodine, quinine, and I know not what else, for destroying the pleasure of the sucking. When these have failed for the sufficient reason that the oral apparatus *will* discharge its energy, recourse is had to remarkable orthopedic devices, wristlets, metal braces that interfere with the flexion of the elbow, and the like. The result of effective interference is a deviation from mental health; sleep disturbance is a not uncommon manifestation.[9]

In their order of importance in infancy, we may list sleep, feeding, and play. To these are added in childhood the activities connected with articulate speech, followed in turn by those

---

"conditioning" by unpleasant feelings, continues genital manipulation, the parents often have recourse to tools—mittens and other devices—and thus finally succeed in interfering with an intrinsically unimportant matter which their interest has converted into a rather important tendency. Such a successful interference with an artificially enhanced play tendency is followed by marked maladjustive processes.

[9] Until there is some other outlet for the unexpended sucking impulse, there is nothing safely to be done about the infant's "bad habits." As speech makes its appearance, the excess oral energy has a useful outlet. If thumb-sucking or a related infantile discharge *is resumed on a large scale* after its abandonment, then there is being manifested a serious deviation from mental health for which remedy should be sought. Such recrudescence of earlier behavior is a regression that can drain off energy necessary in personality elaboration.

connected with locomotion and with sphincter control. The factors that enter into the determination of which of the principal activities are to show signs of mental disorder might well concern us. In general, the less the partition of time to a particular activity, the less ultrasignificant is the disturbance of the activity; the less serious is a mental disorder principally manifested by its disorder. Thus, when sleep is disturbed, there is present, without exception, a serious mental disorder. It is not quite correct, however, to apply this rule in the reverse order. In other words, there may be serious interference with the life processes without disorder of sleep. We touch here upon an almost unexplored field of life processes, the understanding of which awaits extensive research. I must dismiss the subject, for the moment, with the remark that individuals seem to show fundamental differences in *the scope of the integration process* called into action in falling asleep. As a result, there are fundamental differences of at least two types in regard to the bundle of processes concerned in maintaining sleep. In one sort of person, an undue partition of time to sleep may in itself be the presenting sign of serious mental disorder.

One looks on disorder of sleep in infancy as a sign of grave disturbance in the organism-environment complex; so, later, with disturbance in the feeding performances; and later still, disturbances in articulation—perhaps as a preliminary to these, peculiarity in the appeal mechanism, interference with crying. Whenever we find a history of this sort we must realize that everything that has followed is deviated from a simple relation to the normal development of personality. Anything that we have to study in an individual who has had *pavor nocturnus* in early childhood should be studied with a clear understanding that this individual's experience has not been entirely the average experience at any time subsequent to the appearance of the "night terror." The fact that an infant had adenoids, the resulting interference with breathing and, therefore, periods in which his communal existence was endangered—this historic fact may not seem of much import some ten years after the successful removal of the polyps. I wish to emphasize, however, that this very fact, excepting only the case of an individual who has also undergone extraordinary experience reorganization, is and continues always to be of import for an understanding of the personality concerned. Incidents of panic—of which *pavor nocturnus* is a close relative—are never insignificant. No one is ever "the same" after any experience, and he is particularly "different" after an incident of panic. The earlier the incident, the more fundamental are the effects of the related events in determining specific deviation in the course of subsequent development.

In the case of the infant of the type in which sleep is peculiarly safeguarded from disturbance, and to a lesser extent in all infants, disturbances of the feeding function are of great import. Without repeating the comment concerning thumb-sucking and other eccentric discharges of the sucking-dynamism, let me remark on the relation of feeding peculiarities of infancy to distortions in the subsequent acquisition of speech. However unwilling the student may be to accept the determining role of infantile experience in other fields, I presume that he will agree—if he has fraternized at all intimately with someone given to stammering or stuttering—that speech disorder is at least sometimes associated with decided personality warp. As a matter of fact, any material feeding difficulty in infancy is followed by an important series of distortions, of which speech disorder is but one of the most spectacular. Deviations in the character of the 'self' often arise in this region, and these underlying deviations are more antecedents than consequents of the speech disorder. Speech is a *social* tool of the first importance, but by no means the first of them to be acquired.

It is necessary to repeat that clear indication of maladustment at any genetic stage—whether by appearance or by nonappearance of activity—means not merely a situation then existent, but means also a determining influence of importance in the related processes occurring subsequently. It is therefore not by any means sufficient to know that a person as an infant had *pavor nocturnus* or that as a child he was slow in learning to talk, or that as a schoolboy he stuttered. It is necessary also to consider in what fashion, from the very time at which each of these things appeared—and in every case from that time and in every significant way from that time—he deviated in character of personality growth and was, in significant ways, a personality different from the more usual patterns.

At this point, we may pause from discussing the significance of early mental disorder to reiterate the ultimate significance of certain aspects of infancy and childhood, and to develop certain conceptions for further study of personality growth. It is by no means improbable that the fullest differentiation of the newborn is opposed by the environmental factors with which most infants are surrounded. In other words, it seems quite possible that infants at birth are very much less stereotyped than are the situations which are provided for their first years of postnatal life. The time may come when, for example, by such extensive investigation as that directed by Gesell of Yale, we may identify important groups of differentials in the newborn and adjust subsequent training in a fashion so as to make the most of them for the common good. At present, the psychopathologist must rest content with assembling all the data that he can secure bearing upon any individuality in the course of his subject's infancy, remembering always that he is investigating into the determination of some of the most permanent, the least changeable, features of the personality concerned.

There is a conception of traditional psychology which may well merit our consideration at this time—namely, the notion of the *sentiment*. A sentiment is definable as an "emotionally toned group of experiences about some particular object." In the evolution of personality, various tendencies are evolved which may be regarded as vectors—that is, as forces having as an essential characteristic a direction of manifestation. A sentiment may be conceived to be an accumulation of experience that is determined by the application of such a vector to some particular person entering into one's total situation. Taking for example the traditional sentiment of love, we might say that in the case of A being in love with B, we have in the A part of the situation powerful factors arising from the sex impulses and from the group tendencies that can be called self-assertion, sometimes with powerful factors from submissive, acquisitive, and parental tendencies (the latter being those that bring about interest in the bearing and rearing of young), acting as a vector-addition or vector-sum, holding together, modifying and being modified by all the experience, real and fantastic, which A has of B. The particular utility of the conception of sentiment arises from the fact that to a striking degree such a system of experience and

tendencies acts in a unitary way as a highly elaborated acquired tendency possessed of a specific "object," another person.

A large part of life experience entering as evolutionary history into the tendencies involved in such a sentiment is not readily accessible to consciousness. We are inclined to call this inaccessible part of experience unconscious.[10] In the case of a sentiment-formation of any kind, much of the relevant experience and almost all of the understandable data as to the tendencies involved are exterior to the awareness of its holder. To this extent the sentiment is in traditional terms a "complex." A complex, one might say, is an extraconscious sentiment. The distinction, however, of complexes and sentiments is much more apparent than real. All alleged complexes have some measure of representation in consciousness and all sentiments have extensive and important foundations which are markedly inaccessible to awareness.

Expressed somewhat paradoxically, there is in each person a sentiment largely unconscious, yet very frequently manifested and usually in evidence near the very focus of awareness. It is distinguished from other sentiments in that its object is not another person, but, instead, the person himself. This we call the *sentiment of self*. Of this conception, I must say that it has its difficulties. I shall attempt to elucidate it by dealing with it rather too abstractly, adding, in partial justification, that this sentiment, like any other, is at times manifested in the total situation in the way of a unitary acquired tendency (or bundle of tendencies—vector-sum). Keeping in mind the artificial simplification of this consideration, we can study the origin and growth of the sentiment of self, and, in so doing, can discover a good deal concerning the object of this sentiment, the *ego*. In discussing its growth, I shall touch not only on matters of genesis but also on considerations pointing toward one possible classification of personality, for this sentiment is so important that the

[10] I do not wish to discuss at this point the psychoanalytic notion of The Unconscious. I wish merely to point out that the explanation of most mental phenomena requires the inclusion of a great deal of the past, which is by no means readily accessible to recall. I do not believe that there is anything that occurs as thought or behavior that can be explained solely by appeal to the "conscious content of the mind" of the person concerned; there are always plentiful sequents of each such antecedent which not only do not "occur to" the person, but some of which are actually all but impossible for him to bring to awareness.

characterizing interrelations among its tendencies determine a characteristic group of tendencies in the organism-environment adjustments, which latter are commonly said to be typical of the personality concerned.

We have given brief consideration to the personality of the infant. We have touched upon the growth experience with reality. I wish now to emphasize in this connection the activity of the oral zone as a part of the organism entering into especially close relations with the relevant environment. In the growth of experience with reality, not only does the mouth-nipple combination provide the root experience for a separation of the 'me' and the 'not me,' but also the oral play provides the first or root experience of that which we call autoerotism.[11] Furthermore, the activity of the vocalizing equipment, which is indistinguishable from the mouth (in infantile consciousness, at least) is the basis of what Ferenczi calls omnipotence by magic cries. As McDougall puts it, it is the principal instrument of the "instinct of appeal." It is the tool of domination most generally effective for the organism in its complex relation with another personality, until such time as the individual learns to enter into what we have called secondary group relations—and even thereafter, so great is the relationship of the oral apparatus to thought, even to written expression of thought, that it might still be said to be the principal intrument of domination. By this I refer to the fact that in writing and in otherwise communicating with persons who are not present in the immediate environment, we are still doing the same sort of thing that we would be doing in talking to them, excepting that we have to fantasy more extensively or to rationally elaborate their reaction to our words.

[11] Autoerotism, homoerotism, and heteroerotism may be taken to refer to modes of securing satisfactory sensations, pleasurable sensory contents within awareness, by manipulatory procedures including, respectively, parts of one's own body, parts of a body like one's own, and parts of a body in peculiarly significant fashion unlike one's own. An attempt should be made to maintain a distinction between erotism and the more specific sexual satisfactions, the latter having the relation to the former of a part to the whole. Pleasure-seeking is evidenced from birth onward; not so, the seeking of sexual pleasure. I do not find any virtue in clinging to the generalization by which all pleasure is identified as a part of a libidinal input, as expressed by Freud. The doctrine of partial impulses expressed in the *Drei Abhandlungen* has been of great value in the evolution of our understanding of personality. I believe that we can now dispense with it.

This instrumentality of the oral zone, beginning at the very beginnings of conscious life and being of such extreme importance in the consciousness of the organism, may be regarded as fundamentally distinctive in the elaboration of tendency groups within the personality. The sentiment of self might be said to take its origin in experiences connected with oral activity. For that matter, the manifestations of the sentiment of self may be studied most effectively throughout childhood by considering the growth of verbalizations about the self—how the child talks about itself, what fantasies it can be gotten to express about itself. As we study this aspect of the sentiment of self throughout the juvenile era, we observe the juvenile picking up the expressions of others about him, incorporating them, fitting them into what Cooley has so cleverly called the "reflected self." We observe the growth in every individual of that which I choose to call the fundamental *oral type of personality*, and we see in some cases the growth of deviations from it. I stress the overweening importance of the oral zone of interaction in the organism-environment complex; the student must consider how much of the sum-total of adjustive activity, functional activity in and within the environment, biophysical to psychobiological, takes place with special relation to this oral-buccal-pharyngeal-laryngeal apparatus. There can be no personality not very greatly warped, in which the oral zone does not continue to be the prepotent zone of interaction.[12] Even in the infant free from exaggerated oral experience (from cultivation of crying, disjuncture of suckling and nourishment, and the like), the eruption of teeth, locally, and the major phenomenon of weaning, generally, confirm its importance.[13] Yet we find among our fellows some

[12] I regret that considerations of mere brevity compel me to depend on the student's collateral reading *and thought* to inform him of such potent factors in personality evolution during mid-infancy as those constituted by *experience of nipple withdrawal*, changes from the breast to the bottle, and the like.

[13] Karl Abraham, whose untimely death lost to the psychoanalytic branch of dynamic psychopathology one of its really brilliant minds, worked out a classification of genetic steps, in which he isolated an oral sucking as initial, and a following oral chewing stage. The latter, he called the *oral sadistic*. I am particularly sympathetic to this generalization, for reasons that will later appear. The intimate relation of the oral zone and the primitive rage-anger action should be developed *not only* as a universal generalization *but significantly* as an individual resultant of experience. The actual exper-

in whom the determining influences of fundamental personality type are distortions, if not overshadowings, of the oral zone by some other zone of interaction.

We find, for example, some individuals for whom the psycho-analysts have devised the formulation of "anal erotism"; on which see in particular the studies by Ernest Jones.[14] Jones has included in his earlier formulations a number of things which are not in any sense specifically anal erotic. He has included certain traits which, if they "belong" anywhere, belong at the other end of the alimentary tract, and are a part of the funda-mental oral personality type. His studies none the less confirm our belief that there is a distinctive group of people in whom experience has resulted in attitudes toward other people that can be traced genetically to an early attention to the sphincter functions, especially those of the anal sphincters. I am inclined to believe that what one might call sphincter-and-feces conscious-ness normally appears rather late in the course of the second year of the human extrauterine life. Many parents, however, have very keen sphincter consciousness and feel that it would be a great mistake to let any child of theirs live two years without becoming clearly aware of the misfortune subsumed in careless-ness about defecation. It is easy to train the human young during the second year of extrauterine life to conditioned relaxations of the sphincters—for example, by use of automatic procedures connected with the toilet chair. This sort of training is not attended by any peculiarly vivid experience. It is the same sort of learning as that connected with successful acquisition of walk-ing. There is no particular valuation which fixes sphincter activity and feces as important matters in the rudimentary consciousness of self. As I have mentioned in discussing primitive genital phobia, overzealous and emotion-driven parents are able, however, to build into the personality of the child an abnormal valuation of successful sphincter control, and correspondingly, a distinct interest in sphincter relaxation and feces.

It also happens that in the young the olfactory and gustatory

_____

ience undergone during weaning, *including previous oral experience enter-ing into it*, may have a great deal to do with the evolution of a subsequent aggressive hostility; but, again, it may not.

[14] Ernest Jones, *Papers on Psychoanalysis* (3rd Ed.); New York: William Wood, 1923.

senses may be playfully tried out with the excrement. This, like a great many other things which go to make up the experimental curiosity, the neuromusculo-glandular activity that constitutes late infantile and childhood play, is not from the very nature of things calculated to continue very long to be an interesting pastime. But it likewise is often the case that this play with excrement is an extremely exciting thing to the parents; it calls out in them powerful emotional disturbances which can scarcely be explained by simple reasoning about excrement or infants. In such cases, as in the case of hyperreaction to "infantile masturbation," interest is excited and attached at an extraordinarily early age to matters of which the ordinarily evolved consciousness would be minimal for a considerable time thereafter. These two sorts of abnormal experience arising from the parental part of the organism-environment complex—premature sphincter consciousness and excrement consciousness—effect a considerable alteration in the prepotency of the oral zone of interaction and seem to lead to the elaboration of what Jones and others have called the *anal erotic "character type."*

To a lesser extent one can sometimes observe deviations in the prepotency of the zone of interaction toward the micturition apparatus and the urine. With this there comes an excessive interest investiture in the urethrogenital apparatus, and we find a deviation somewhat in the direction of adult sexuality, appearing a considerable time before the later awakening of the sexual apparatus that ordinarily takes a share from the prepotency of the oral zone. The coincidence of primitive genital phobia and the *urethral deviation* of interaction zone prepotency is an interesting matter on which I can offer no final opinion. The role of the two factors in the etiology of morbid enuresis also awaits elucidation. Some enuretics remain prevailingly oral in type, but the evolution of their genital sexuality is considerably distorted; from consideration of the data of a few of these, I am inclined to believe that primitive genital phobia is frequently antecedent to urethral deviations of personality, but that its effects are by no means encompassed in any delineation of "the urethral character" at present extant.

In this fashion, I attempt to delineate not absolute types of human beings, but again merely a scheme useful in the growth of thought about personality. Under one rubric the natural predominance of oral interaction is outstanding throughout life; under another we find an abnormal interest or tendency deviation centering around the lower end of the alimentary tract and the excrement; and under a dubious third there is unusually early deviation of interest and activity tendencies in the direction of the prostatic urethra, often with coincident morbid interest in the genitalia. These might be taken to be three vector directions of the important tendencies organized in the sentiment of self, shown under many guises as the individual "makes contact" with the world.

Not only are the tendencies derived from inborn growth potencies and experience, in some cases greatly distorted; but some of them, duly activated in early infancy, are so deviated by experience undergone in early childhood that their further elaboration is very slight, and they do not come to be represented in the self-conscious personality. If, by reason of extraordinary circumstance, they manifest themselves in the waking life, the phenomena are unnoted by the subject, or regarded as a wholly mysterious physiological "accident." [15] This shunting of some tendencies evident in infancy out of the channel of personality evolution is probably accomplished through the instrumentality of empathy. Its important results are twofold: the "richness" of personality is diminished, and there is continued in the affected individual a dangerous substratum of absolutely unconscious integrative tendencies wholly unsuited to socialized living, or even to anything but early childhood behavior. These results are entirely different from those of repression and dissociation, processes occurring within the self-conscious personality, and con-

[15] This conception of tendency-systems of an extremely inaccessible kind (owing to their nonincorporation into even the earliest *self*, their relatively undeveloped, infantile character, and the utter foreignness of their manifestation) is both difficult and important. Some innate growth potentialities are never activated: they are of no moment to the psychopathologist. Some are manifested for a time, cease to have any utility (owing to maturation of neurological and similar structures) and disappear—perhaps to reappear in case of some extraordinary accident. Most of them, however, undergo a progressive elaboration from birth onward. Those under discussion belong in this most inclusive category but are elaborated slowly only outside of the current of personality growth, and with relatively little effect on its course. Note, presently, the discussion of 'extravert' and 'introvert' organization in this connection.

cerning experience and tendency-system modifications that have or have had reality value and meaning to the self. The wholly unfamiliar substratum thus formed in late infancy and early childhood I conceive to be the immediate source of the impulses that are manifested in nonadjustive processes.

The relationship of panic to this thoroughly unconscious substratum of personality is obvious. This is not so clearly the case with *anxiety*, the discussion of which may now be carried somewhat further. We find ourselves again delineating a crude classification of personality, an abstraction that we may call the three primary emotional types—again with a caution lest actual existent entities be hypothesized out of theoretical formulation. It has been fairly well demonstrated by Margaret Grey Blanton and others that the infant manifests three gross sorts of emotional behavior—those, namely, of fear, of rage, and of satisfaction. Cannon has shown that extensive modifications of somatic tension and physiological function are correlated at least with the first two of these generic states.[16] Probably chiefly because of infantile and early childhood experience, the interrelation of these three patterns of organismic response undergoes very great individual differentiation and comes finally to characterize personalities as: (1) those readily manifesting differentiations of any of the three primitive states; (2) those in whom rage impulses have been partly relegated to the primitive unconscious substratum; (3) those in whom rage and "satisfaction" impulses have been thus sidetracked. Before this formulation can become particularly meaningful, it will be necessary to reconsider the general formula of personality growth.

The *growth by experience* that has culminated in any personality must be conceived of as having been a "long-circuiting" of primitive tendencies. Experience functions in growth by adding components of two general kinds to the primitive vector qualities—namely, increasing specificity in the integration of situations that will not lead to pain or discomfort after the more primary satisfaction, and situations that will lead to new opportunities for the securing of future satisfactions. With this in mind, we have now to reconsider the integrator dynamisms

[16] Walter Bradford Cannon, *Bodily Changes in Pain, Hunger, Fear and Rage*; New York: Appleton, 1915.

PERSONAL PSYCHOPATHOLOGY

mentioned in Chapter I. The primitive tendencies that are modified through experience-growth manifest through activities of
these dynamisms. Their modifications must include modified
patterns in the manifestation of the dynamisms. This, in turn,
may—and probably always does—imply modification of the
somatic organization of the integrators.[17]

The primitive emotional phenomena may be taken to arise
chiefly from the autacoid and paleoencephalic dynamisms. In
rather loose language, that which we in ourselves recognize
as an emotion is fundamentally a function of the paleoencephalic
integrator, plus coenesthetic sentience referable to somatic
changes wrought by way of the autacoid integrator. The growth
of personality shows in this field as an increasing graduation and
combination of emotional tones, in turn to be considered the
results of inhibitory and of discriminative functions of the neoencephalic dynamism integrating the past and expectations of
the future into the various situations that might once have called
out one or more of the primitive tendencies. One way of elaborating experience may then be a long-circuiting of this neoencephalic sort.

We know that infancy includes a vast development in personality. We can be sure that much of the growth is of the sort
just described. It is probable, however, that there is also a considerable growth of the paleoencephalic dynamism, per se, and
perhaps also of the autacoid. We may surmise, provisionally, that
the sidetracking of primitive tendencies is a manifestation of
paleoencephalic integrator modification, rather than of changes
in the "new brain" dynamism. Besides its convenience as an

[17] Thus, in the guinea pig, in which the myelinization of the nerves is
largely finished by the time of expulsion from the parasitic intrauterine existence, the *possibilities* of extensive modification of the neonatal or primitive
tendencies are very much less than is the case in a species born with the
neural apparatus in a highly plastic state, such as man. Other things being
equal, the first type of animal has relatively very little capacity for learning;
the second, enormous. This gives a hint as to factors responsible for human
civilization. Regardless of other factors, the extreme plasticity of the neoencephalic integrator at birth and the long period of life spent in its completion—from birth to perhaps twenty-seven years of age—express in
organic terms the opportunity for incorporating into the personality the
vast cultural experience that brings about the almost incredibly complex redirection of tendencies, from the primitive equipment of the neonate to
those of the fully adult, "highly civilized" man.

"explanation" of the extreme inaccessibility in later life of the processes fundamental in the nonadjustive phenomena, this hypothesis suggests a meaning to be attached to a body of rather obscure events—epileptic fury, violence in states of severe alcoholic intoxication, in cocaine poisoning, after cerebral trauma, and so on; some of the more recondite phenomena of so-called deterioration; and, finally, panic and anxiety.[18]

Regardless of the imponderable influence of heredity, the personal influences bearing upon the infant are largely responsible for the deflection of primitive tendencies away from a coherent parallel development in part into the nonconscious substratum. It is easily seen that primitive reactions are continued in some children by the failure of the culture-carrying parents to provide the experience necessary to secure fortunate modifications in line with the social demands later to be encountered—for example, in those in whom "temper tantrums" are not discouraged, but are permitted to accomplish the ends for which the individual should be learning much more socially acceptable techniques, or again, in those in whom speech or locomotion is delayed because the infant is continued in a state in which most of his needs are satisfied before unpleasant degrees of desire arise and drive him to acquire increasingly complex behavior patterns. It is rather more difficult to envisage the parental influences working to split off some of the tendency-systems from those integrated into the self-conscious personality. The unwelcome child of parents one or both of whom is "sensitive" to rage behavior, can suffer such summarily repressive reaction to his manifestations of primitive rage that the greater part of this growing tendency-system is displaced, and frank outbursts of rage behavior tend wholly to disappear. In part, thenceforth, this vector manifests in overelaborated behavior, and in part *it manifests as anxiety*. In situations that tend to "call out" the emotion of rage,

[18] Much of the data subsumed in the Watsonian modification of the Pavlovian conception of the "conditioned reflex" probably belongs here. The notion that "conditioning a reflex"—in the sense of Pavlov—is a simple matter of sensorimotor neurology, however, may well be avoided. "Conditioning" the paleoencephalic dynamism may be one of the most recondite of earthly matters, for all I know. The atomistic addition of "conditioned reflexes" that is rather the fashion today is by no means unlike the atomistic "association" of "ideas" that was popular some years since.

there is either a modified and perhaps heavily disguised anger, or only anxiety, or both disguised anger *and* anxiety.

The anxious child is not to be confused with the bullied or browbeaten child, the product of indiscriminative abuse without specific repressive reactions directed against some particular tendency. Both may be timorous; both show evidences of insecurity. But the anxious child does not "look ill-natured" and does not take his grievances out on the dog. He suffers an "inner" insecurity that is not much benefited by later uninterrupted kindness, while the other one's distrust of people can be extinguished by a sympathetic environment, with a fairly well-rounded personality growth thenceforth. On the other hand, it is not to be supposed that the anxious child cannot show anger. I doubt if it is possible to sidetrack the tendencies evolved from primitive rage so completely that the personality has no tendencies to show anger, but only anxiety.[19] The difference between the anxious personality and that in which there is a major dissociation will presently concern us.

Before leaving the era of infancy and early childhood, we must consider in somewhat greater detail the evolution of the sentiment of self, from which the tendencies manifesting as anxiety have been excluded. As stated, the disjuncture of the organism from "external" reality is conceived to receive its first impetus from events connected with nursing. The earliest experiences that are attended by that peculiar characteristic to which we refer as self-consciousness likewise emanate from the oral zone. This is insured by the recurrent *rapid dissipation* of discomfort synchronously with the activity of nursing. The syncretistic prehensions of this situation are neither suddenly nor completely elevated into a new kind of awareness.[20] Most of them continue

[19] Of the primitive emotional tendencies and their evolutions during infancy and early childhood, fear is never sidetracked. The group pertaining to rage is the most frequently affected by this distortion; the root-tendency to which I refer as "satisfaction" is sometimes partly deflected.

The student will note that this discussion of anxiety and of the deeply unconscious substratum of personality, manifestations of impulses from which take the general form of nonadjustive processes, is confined here to infancy and early childhood. We shall presently reencounter the subject.

[20] Quite to the contrary, a considerable part of the nursing behavior-complex is not ordinarily incorporated into the readily accessible content, but remains exterior to awareness. See, in this connection, the work of

as extraconscious experience, organized, however, as the sentiment is formed, and coming to constitute a part of it. The particular event which happens to be the first that is prehended as of
a *personal* nature is capable neither of prediction nor, ordinarily,
of being detected. Once having transpired, however, there is
something new in the more or less cosmic consciousness of the
infant, and a something that grows rapidly and reduces the primitive consciousness to a thoroughly secondary role.

The parents, and particularly the mother or her equivalent,
treat the infant as a person, even if a sadly rudimentary one.
They provide sentience at first by empathic linkage, but increasingly by manipulations that impinge on the maturing sensory
receptors. Some of this is colored with pain, and some with
pleasure. More and more of it comes to be meaningful in the
sense that it includes enough of previous experience to stir memorial recall. At the same time, more and more of it becomes
personal to the infant, becomes integrated into the sentiment
of self. Thwartings of impulse, either with empathic disapproval
or with the more complex sentience arising from quasi or actually
sadistic play; facilitations of impulse, similarly simply or complexly colored; and specific zone stimulations—all these and a
great many other sorts of experience pour in and add to the self-
conscious prehension of the world. By the third year of life,
the average child has elaborated from these experiences a schematization of the self that is to a considerable extent *somatic*, in
the sense of being representations of interaction zones and related
phenomena. This somatic schematization of the self is at first
extremely crude and ingenuous. It is rapidly sophisticated in
later childhood, and thereafter, coming to be a more or less realistic ideology about the body. Early stages in its evolution, however, are frequently active in fantasy processes, especially in the
service of dissociated systems.

The important role of earlier somatic schematizations of the
"formation" of neurotic symptoms, the determination of "physical" manifestations of anxiety, and even in the localization of
organic disease processes, has been neglected. The morbid mother

---

David M. Levy. He shows the origin of many mannerisms and characterizing
movements to be relatively unmodified survivals of postures assumed by
the infant at the mother's breasts.

who, under rationalization of "the necessity of keeping the penis scrupulously clean to avoid irritation and masturbation," devotes herself month in and month out to an obscure way of exciting the child's genital zone is contributing exaggerated genital representations to the "somatic self" and making the genital zone prepotent "in response to" interpersonal situations marked by positive tendencies. When the morbid maternal drive works itself out in scrubbing the anal zone, this region and its functional activity are exaggerated in representation, and a body of "manifestations of anal erotism" appears in later interpersonal relations.[21]

The area of later childhood is the stage on which is played the Oedipus drama, so extensively discussed in the psychoanalytic literature. The primitive mother sentiment, evolved in midinfancy, has generally by now ceased to pertain directly to any person actually in contact with the child. Disappointments of various kinds have been experienced, and again and again pain has had its educative effect. There are manifest a variety of maladjustive phenomena aroused by the privations enforced by life. Some of them, unfortunately, are apt to be encouraged by distressed and shortsighted parents, and may thus come to be important deviations of personality growth.[22] The fading, if not full evanishment, of the "mother of infancy," and the succession of flesh-and-blood embodiments of authority contribute much of the reality underlying the so-called *castration fear* often used as an explanatory principle of various states prehended as personal insecurity. The loss of the primitive mother is a necessary step

[21] With these fleeting references, I must both leave this important topic and pass on from consideration of personality growth in infancy and early childhood. The relative rate of growth seems to increase rapidly from birth to some point near the middle of childhood, then beginning a slow decline, to rise abruptly once more. The increments of personality obviously parallel this rate. The importance for the understanding of a personality of an assay of the late infantile and early childhood experience is, then, clearly very great. This field of investigation is finally receiving belated attention.

[22] I must depend on collateral reading to familiarize the student with outstanding features of this era. See, for a bibliography, Appendix C, *Proceedings of the Second Colloquim on Personality Investigation*; Baltimore: Johns Hopkins Press, 1930.

To present here anything even remotely adequate to the era under discusion would expand this already too large volume entirely beyond reason. There are excellent data already available which should be studied with the orientation of the first seven chapters of this text.

in personality growth, and the longer it is postponed into childhood by reason of maternal (or related) oversolicitude, the greater a handicap there is imposed on the growth of the child's personality.[23]

The growth of personality in the era of childhood includes the incorporation of stereotypes of the general character of dominant and submissive individuality.[24] There are much obedience to authority, attempts to evade it, and seeking of ways to escape and relieve thwarting. In other words, tendencies have to be long-circuited in agreement with the cultural entities imposed by their embodiments in the parents on the growing personality of the child. The disappointments enforced by the parents and elder siblings are often passed on in some form by the child to its younger siblings, its pets, or accidentally encountered animate and inanimate objects. Unless the personality growth of all those intimately relevant to the subject-child has been relatively unwarped, there will be a good deal of this vicariously displaced pleasure and discomfort incorporated into his personality. He is all too apt to be a plaything of the unsocialized tendencies of both parents and his elder siblings; and sometimes of those of one or more grandparents, and a miscellany of aunts and uncles, elder nephews and nieces, and so on. *Each and every individual habitually or frequently incorporated in the family group has an inevitable part in the child's evolution of personality*, but the role of each significant person often requires for its elucidation insight, in turn, into the courses of his personality.[25] I shall now

[23] See, in this connection, a forthcoming study by David M. Levy.

[24] The *stereotype* is to be understood as a particular component or subcomplex (subsentiment) entering into the formation of the sentiment of self. It is, as it were, the *self-centered* complement of an "externally" conditioned sentiment—of one the object of which is another person—but of one that is quite subordinate in its manifestations to those of the stereotype. A stereotype remains, built into the sentiment of self, on the frustration or dissolution for other cause (*vide*, grief, *supra*) of any sentiment. The conception may become clearer if we express it more loosely as the emotionally toned pattern of experienced reflections to the self associated with a particular person who was once important to the self. Major or even minor (even really irrelevant) attributes of the person incorporated in the stereotype, when reencountered in another, tend to stir mnemic recall of the emotional and other tendencies embodied in the stereotype.

[25] Relevance fortunately intervenes in this dilemma, so that personality study intended for therapy or even for psychobiological research does not need to be an eternally regressing series back to the founders of a culture. *Sympathy* (and its negative form, antipathy)—broadly, the easy integration

give thumbnail outlines to suggest, rather than to reveal, the significant content of childhood experience in this connection.

The only child, particularly the only surviving child, or a child whose birth has been long deferred and greatly desired, is almost always pampered and protected in such fashion that he is restrained from development of realistic self-appraisal, and goes on into the era of socialization with characteristics potent against his acceptance by other children. It thus comes to be a very real misfortune to live even for a few years as the only child. The possibility of full development of personality under these circumstances is thereby rendered rather remote. A degree of the same handicap extends to a great many first-born children. It is escaped only in case there is an interfamily group so expanded that others of comparable age, with or without blood relationship, are more or less constantly present as environing factors. Even the parents' experience may to some extent be remedied by this situation.[26] Otherwise, there is but a minority of parents capable of avoiding the evils discussed, for example, by Brill in "The Only or Favorite Child in Adult Life," [27] and I venture that no

---

of a person into one's total situation—is evident in childhood. *Personal discrimination*, however, is not yet much developed. As a result, people much older than the child are parental in role if they are important, otherwise all but irrelevant, often merely the *embodiment of mythology* the effective content of which is determined by its creator. Thus, the much older brother paraded by the parents as the embodiment of all the virtues is so lost as anything but the carrier of the parental myth, that it is but occasionally that his personality organization becomes directly relevant in understanding one of the much younger children. The much older brother who assists his widowed mother in raising several younger children, on the other hand, becomes a parent even if one significantly distinguished from the "average father."

[26] It seems almost to be the case that, in this "best of possible" cultures, many of the potentialities of at least one child have largely to be sacrificed, to provide parents with belated training. In the final chapter of this book, I shall expatiate on remedial measures conceivably applicable to this situation. At present, if one must be an only child, one might well choose to be born of very poor but honest parents who *do not* provide a home for any of their [adult] relatives.

[27] A. A. Brill, *Psychoanalysis*; Philadelphia: Saunders, 1922. This renowned authority, the leader of American psychoanalysts, was at that time rather more optimistic than I have come to be; for example: "We find that only those [only children] who have been brought up in the manner described develop into abnormal beings, those who are not pampered and coddled have the same chance as other children." I would not wish the task of being a good parent to a single child. Once we have perfected a general under-

two parents living can do as well by a lone child as could they with two or more, nor bring their child—separated for the first six years from habitual contact with anyone near his age—to a well-rounded adult personality.

Families including no sons tend to show in some of the daughters reflections of the disappointment of the parents. The eldest daughter is quite apt to incorporate powerful antipathetic tendencies due to the unwitting—and increasing—feeling of injustice of Fate, of which she is the embodiment to the father. Her difficulties in situations including him are eluded by the next younger, whose techniques in resolving situations involving him show much unconscious profit from the elder sister's failures.

Families including no daughter tend to show in one of the sons the disappointment of the mother's wish for "an heir," in the shape of excessive exaggeration of feminine tendencies—finally augmented by the unwitting hostility of the father to this victim of the mother.

Almost always, in three sons serially born, the eldest and the youngest are more or less affectionate, and the middle son is hostile to the other two, and to the father—the eldest is his heir, and the victim of his inexperience and his thwarted ambitions; the youngest profits from the conflict between the first two for the greater favor within the family.

To illustrate, in a family group comprised of a domineering and none too successful father, deeply attached to his mother—who lived in the immediate neighborhood—and a gentle, rather incompetent mother (the only girl in a fairly large family, herself gradually progressing into a condition of chronic anxiety as her children grew around her), there were born three sons in succession and then a daughter. The eldest was frequently in conflict with the father and grew into adolescence so warped that he underwent a schizophrenic illness; the middle son came to a markedly paranoid attitude; the youngest became a politic but markedly

standing *not only* of the evil factors operative in personality growth, but also of the constructive factors, then, and not until then, can two intelligent people possessed of ample facilities undertake to provide a better-than-natural environment for a lone child. In the abundant meanwhile, however, no small number of individuals handicapped by a lone childhood will continue to make important contributions to human welfare, thereby making up somewhat for their relative detachment from the common give-and-take.

unsocial sort of unconscious homosexual; and the daughter grew into a remarkably good approximation of mental health.

In almost every parent-child situation there is found a factor extremely vicious in its possible ramifications. I refer here to the parents' reference of many peculiarities of the child's behavior to the "explanatory" principle of *heredity*. If some resemblance can be recalled or surmised of outstanding characteristics of the child's behavior to this or that one individual in the line of forebears, that behavioral characteristic is removed from contemplation as a resultant of experience, and, moreover, fixated by the parental expectancy of the stereotype. This factor may be of so much influence that the parents react with astonishment and disappointment on the appearance of growth-phenomena tending to extinguish an *undesirable* tendency-system. This heredity-mythology is so generally inculcated in the young that it crops up later in life in all sorts of unexpected contexts. *It is not, however, a factor in early childhood experience;* this perhaps underlies the singular absurdity by which even those parents who "explain" everything by heredity none the less continue to distribute *personal* praise and blame. No matter how thoroughly the mother may explain to herself and anyone else suspected of interest that Johnny's aggressive tendencies to destroy and injure are the result of his "taking after" her eldest brother, Johnny's little brother, the victim of his aggression, comes to know that there are hateful people in the world and that they are to be distrusted, avoided, and circumvented, and, if fortuitous occasion arises, repaid in their own coin, with or without refinement of method. This younger brother does not appreciate how real physical resemblance may be, nor how near an actuality the "taking after" is made by recondite factors of the mother-uncle antipathy and resulting sensitivity of the mother in regard of certain behavior of Johnny. All this is beyond the period of early childhood. But he may be led presently to identify Johnny and the particular uncle after whom he "takes"; and this confluence may be so powerful as to prevent any growth of appreciation of favorable aspects of the uncle's personality. To that extent, the mother's antipathy to her brother is transmitted to the child by the creation in the self-organization of the younger child of a stereotype including characteristics of the uncle, of Johnny, of the mother's mythology, and of *antipathetic tendencies variously evolved* in regard to the father and others, dynamically coupled with presenting physical traits, statements of like and dislike, and habits of expression, intonation, and so on. Such a stereotype includes a tendency-organization that makes the probable outcome of subsequent integrations with "that sort of a person" an unpleasant experience; this very expectancy itself continues to keep the younger child relatively segregated from series of events that might contribute negative—that is, counteracting—experience, and thus destroy the stereotype as an effective factor in the sentiment of self.

Childhood, then, is peculiarly characterized as the era of tendency-systems integrating the individual as an organically feeble, easily "punished" (impotent) entity, with other individuals prehended not as comparable entities but as embodiments of pleasurable and discomforting activities. It passes over into the juvenile era, in which an effort must be made to bring compeers among these entities into pleasurable coöperative activities, and some measure of success initiated in dealing with other individuals who deviate in various measures from the childhood stereotypes of similar, more or less adult entities. We may glance at this transition and then consider two major deviations in the childhood personality growth.

Children do not enter into relations with their compeers, other children, on anything like a uniform basis. Even in gross activity in social contact, Dorothy Swaine Thomas, working in the Columbia Child Study Institute, observed three prevailing types: (1) "children who consistently show certain patterns of behavior; who consistently talk in certain terms, say, who consistently use nouns that refer to objects or consistently are playing with material objects rather than persons"; (2) "other children who will spend say 90 per cent of their time consistently in groups where groups are forming, whose language will, to a predominant extent concern other persons"; and (3) "others who are disproportionately withdrawn from these overt forms of activity. . . . they are neither concerned with material objects to any extent as shown by these techniques, nor with other persons, but their activities seem to center around their inner life." [28]

28 "Proceedings, Second Colloquium on Personality Investigation," *Amer.*

Before proceeding to discussion of the juvenile era, I wish to sketch two major directions of growth that occur in the era of childhood, with sequent profound modification of the course of personality.

As the growth of reality-prehension might be taken to be the principal of many accessions to personality during early infancy; and the prehension of interpersonal necessities of the type of submission to authority, by which a great body of the parental culture-complexes is incorporated, that of late infancy and childhood; so in the following juvenile era will be the acquisition of social techniques. Each stage of development must prepare the personality at least for the principal development of the next era. The grave disorders of growth in childhood will then be failures that tend to disqualify him for the juvenile socialization. There are principally two: (1) the so-called psychopathic personality, and (2) the obsessional personality.

Stage by stage, the growth of personality includes an increasing prehension of the superiority of certain situational demands to anything experienced as an immediate personal need (or wish, if consciously formulated). *The field of the future interpenetrates more and more the momentary situation of the personality.* The long-circuiting of tendencies is more and more in the interest of remote and immediate consequents. From the primary unmanageability of the hunger-and-sucking-satisfying nipple to the stupid interference of a suffering world to the healing formula of the philosopher—all is an urge to the elaboration of more and more indirect and inclusive manipulation, if one is to be free from discomfort, much less occasionally occupied with joy. The greater the realistic prehension of the world, the less

J. *Psychiatry* (1930) 86:892–895, p. 895, and *loc. cit. supra.*

Any student inclined by previous experience to wish for *quantitative* data in the field of psychopathology should peruse this eminent social statistician's "The Methodology of Experimental Sociology," the introductory chapter in *Some New Techniques for Studying Social Behavior,* by Dorothy Swaine Thomas and Associates; Child Development Monograph No. 1, Teachers College, Columbia Univ., 1929. Her contribution to the solution of the quantification problem in so far as it refers to "controlled experiments" in human behavior may be indicated by quoting: "We want to find means of [necessarily] uncontrolled environment to which a given individual, at a given moment, reacts overtly—what consistency is observable in his selective responses over a period of time and what variability is shown among different individuals."

unreasonable—even if irrational—this demand for elaborate process tends to impress the individual. The further he grows as a
personality, the easier it becomes to adapt himself to these demands of the world-situation.

The world of the child is often nucleated in the same people
as was his infantile world. This sometimes implies a serious disadvantage to the growing personality. If the mother was quick
to respond to the infant's cry, and now the child finds that oral
procedures are efficacious in securing all satisfaction, his growth
of manipulative techniques is apt to be arrested at the level of
verbal behavior. He continues at the stage at which certain combinations of words, expressive postures, and gestures possess
magical power in securing pleasure and avoiding pain. All that
his situation demands is the production of the necessary formulae. The way by which we acquire dexterity at logical
(verbal) thinking is by the intricacies of learning to validate
propositions consensually. It is, then, always the case that words
as such are very late in losing magical investiture and standing
forth as merely peculiarly facile symbols for abstract thinking, and rather efficient aids for intercommunication of intelligence. If the people significant in the childhood milieu have
preternatural respect for verbal techniques, and permit them to
take precedent over less symbolic behavioral acts, the child naturally does not long-circuit his tendencies further in this particular.[29]

The growth of the sentiment of self, like all other growth of
personality, is largely through the increasing spread of factors
relevant in the series of total situations through which the person
lives. If now, in the learning of adjustment to parental authority
and the assimilations of the parental culture, the emphasis is
placed on the acquisition of chiefly verbal techniques which pre-

[29] People overimpressed with the role of verbal propositions are no great
novelty, and this disorder of childhood growth—the consequences of which
are now to be developed—is therefore not by any means rare.

The ease with which a great many people can be deceived by verbal
techniques is all too apparent. It seems reasonably evident that there is
here something of a problem for education. Without desiring in any way
to encourage a revival of scholasticism, I cannot but recommend to those
to whom verbal propositions are sacrosanct a study of *The Meaning of
Meaning*, by C. K. Ogden and I. A. Richards; New York: Harcourt Brace,
1923.

vail over other aspects of interpersonal reality, then the growth
of the self is severely affected. The acquisition of fairly realistic
stereotypes does not proceed to anything like the usual extent,
and, instead, there are incorporated fantastic patterns of people
as foci for verbal and other expressive gestures useful in "having
one's own way."

The child under discussion shows a failure to profit from experience, but—unlike the so-called mental defective, who has an
inherent or early-acquired inability to undergo a fully human
experience because of deficiency of the neoencephalic dynamism
—the failure of the *psychopathic child* applies only to factors
of interpersonal events. He learns in an average fashion to appreciate the stubborn complexity of inanimate nature. He may even
grow competent in adjusting his behavior to the demands of his
pets, being quite reasonable in his expectancies regarding their
coöperation in play. But in dealing with people he continues
largely in the late infantile and early childhood stage of applying expressive techniques to distressing aspects of reality, and
thus shows increasingly *an incapacity to be personally real in
interpersonal situations.*[30] It is as if he lived in a world in which
people are significant from moment to moment only in the
course of his pursuit of pleasure, and then only in so far as they
momentarily demand prompt expressive gestures. They are appraised neither in terms of avoiding unpleasant consequents to
action, nor with regard to the enhancement of opportunity for
future gratifications.

As the integrator dynamisms mature and function normally,
these psychopathic individuals undergo the average flow of sentience, including that arising in their contacts with other people.
The great part of this, however, is in their particular case irrelevant, because of the restricted meaning that people continue
to exhibit in the psychopathic *modus vivendi.* The elaboration
of interpersonal experience is split into a restricted growth of
personal prehensions within the self and a fairly large growth of
rather syncretistic complexes. These latter manifest as peculiarly
irrational positive and negative emotional tendencies toward

[30] See, in this connection, the discussion of "growth of the sense of
reality" in Ferenczi's *Contributions to Psychoanalysis* (translated by Ernest
Jones); Boston: Badger, 1916.

others. The growth within the self shows chiefly in the form of improved technique of expressive (mostly verbal) gesturing. Fantasy processes thus continue to predominate in interpersonal situations, there never having been learning of the technique for consensual validation of information in this field. In later life the psychopath often comes to be considered a great liar, although this judgment can scarcely survive a close study of his statements. There is little or no clearly conscious determination to deceive to be found behind his apparently fraudulent utterances; *if* past performances and probably future circumstances can be ignored, the statements of the psychopath are for the most part remarkably well adapted to the immediate interpersonal situation in which he happens to be. Even in the case of the psychopath who cannot be brought to give an authentic account of any of his doings—the so-called *pathological liar*—the intention to deceive is not as conspicuous as is his inability to believe the facts that he has experienced.

The psychopathic self continues to be of an astonishing simplicity, and the reality that can be awarded to other selves and their doings is correspondingly limited. Whenever his motivation of an interpersonal situation miscarries, the "set" is usually dissipated by grief or anger, and the impression of the inexplicable unpleasantness is replaced by a fantasied success. If, subsequently, one insists on hearing about the event, the recall takes the form of a retrograde falsification. If pressure is applied with a view to securing greater accuracy of recall, anger is generally elicited, but it is not so much anger at being disbelieved, as it is anger at aggression; the inquisitor is treated as if he were hostile and attempting to injure the psychopathic individual. The handicap to socialization presented by these deviations of personality growth is obviously enormous, and their first evidences appear in the beginning of the juvenile era. Very soon after beginning coöperative behavior with their compeers, these juveniles begin to sense a difference from others, and this is emphasized from thence onward by the lengthening series of failures in their social efforts. Because, however, of the singular deficiency of their self-formulation, they are incapable of correcting erroneous actions which apply to other people, and their unpleasant experiences tend to be repeated without any evidence of profit on their part.

Some of them, finally, thoroughly embittered, go about offending exactly the people with whom they should be on good terms. Some of them, perhaps fortunately a minority, become such masters of verbal techniques as to profit greatly from the gullibility of others. But always, when any one of them encounters the need for really intimate interpersonal relations, his difficulties become acute. No psychopathic personality is capable of a sound sexual adjustment, and in this field their efforts are an unfailing source of trouble to themselves and their very temporary mates. In situations requiring their submission to authority—excepting only in regimented groups such as the armed forces—the psychopathic individuals are generally inadaptable. I surmise that no other personality deviation approximates this one in importance as a source of general social nuisance and disorder.[31]

We are dealing in the psychopathic child with a peculiarly truncated self with so many of his interpersonal tendency-systems functioning extraconsciously that he is, as it were, an uncomprehending victim of inevitably recurring disappointments that contribute but very little to his adjustive improvement. He stumbles on through the years, often evolving a cocksureness of attitude to others that acts but to speed the unpleasant denouement of each new contact.

Let us now consider another of the childhood deviations resulting from morbid parental interests and tending to a similarly lifelong series of failures in interpersonal relations, but of a strikingly different sort. The *obsessional personality* is characterized superficially by an excess of personal uncertainty and scrupulosity. These children tend to express doubts and uncertainties about everything. This is not to be mistaken for a timorous uncertainty or insecurity; for example, these folk are usually tenacious and stubborn to a degree—especially in doubting. To some children the world has become an unfriendly place always to be distrusted; fear has become for them the

[31] See, for a good résumé on this subject, George E. Partridge, "Current Conceptions of Psychopathic Personality," *Amer. J. Psychiatry* (1930) 87:53–99. Drs. William Healy and Augusta Bronner, Directors of the Judge Baker Foundation, have made excellent contributions to this subject. The usage of the term *psychopathic personality*, as here restricted, corresponds roughly to the Healy-Bronner Unstable-Egocentric Personality, and to the Partridge Delinquent-Incompatible type. I continue its use in the interval awaiting the adoption of a more rational social-psychiatric classification.

customary emotional tone in approaching situations. To some, rage or anger has proven efficacious in brushing aside troublesome obstacles to satisfaction. The obsessional child shows neither signs of fear nor tendencies to resort to tantrums. His peculiar device is *thought*. Apt to be of superior native intelligence, the obsessional youngster has no difficulty with actually adjustive implicit processes; he learns easily, shows excellent ability to profit from all experience *except* that pertaining to other people significant in his total situations. About these, and about any and all of his actions *and thoughts* in connection with them, he seems superficially to have a really bad time. Even as a young child, he has found innumerable *estimable* considerations with which to perplex himself and his parents. His "delicate sensibilities" connect him with so many "problems," especially about right and wrong, good and bad, that those briefly in contact with him are either impressed favorably or moved to compassionate—and thoroughly disappointing—assistance. The "anxiety" of the obsessional child to do, say, and think just *the* right thing, the many problems found to be relevant to selecting the right thing, the punctilious, overcareful scrupulosity of every act, the undeviating thoroughness of every preoccupation—all these features combine to make the life of those constantly in contact with him something rather less than paradisiacal. Younger members of his immediate family may escape the full weight of the obsessional goodness; the parents, however, pay and pay for their share in such a child's personality deviation.

Loveless marriages complicated by hypocrisy and imposture are the prime sources of this deviation. The suppressed contempt and hatred in one or both parents (its reflection, if originally lacking in the partner) renders the growth of antipathetic tendencies in the child an extreme trial to the parents. Empathy phenomena sidetrack these inevitable tendencies out of the current of personality-growth, and they continue to function *wholly unconsciously* in a complaisant martyrdom in search of Truth, the paradigm of which is the "love" of the child so emphatically protested by the parents—and so unreliably manifested in their inconsistent behavior to him.[32] The child of parents of this sort

[32] I pause again to emphasize the danger inhering in our analytic simplification of the family situation to a matter of three terms—mother, father, and child. This is not only artificially simple in the sense mentioned above

undergoes a thorough disintegration of the primitive mother sentiment very early. Both the father and the mother make efforts
to play the mother role to him. Neither of them sustains the
role. The child is their most effective tool for malicious efforts,
and the exaggeration of his importance in this connection is conditioned chiefly by the parental uncertainty of his allegiance. As
long as he shows positive response to one parent, the other strives
to secure his affection. At times when he is not manifesting positive behavior, he is of little interest to either. He is taught to be
"uncertain," to stretch out the period of suspense, and to make
problems of the most commonplace situations. He finds himself
most interesting to others when he is hesitating, and he develops
a facility for doubts and scruples that make a thought-ridden
hesitation his outstanding characteristic. The prompt integration
of interpersonal situations gradually disappears; the manifestation
of emotionally colored behavior becomes obscure; and the obsessional child comes chiefly to be distinguished by a specious
thoughtfulness that turns all the virtues into instrumentalities of
aggression and aggrandizement of his self. His acts, his thoughts,
his beliefs and judgments—all are enhanced into matters of preternatural gravity. He needs reassurance, even in matters on
which he was reassured but a few hours ago. He has to "explain"
his acts, to avoid the least probable of misinterpretations. The
very absurdity of his self-important uncertainties has to be "explained" and reassurances about it secured. The environing persons are thus hoist by their own petards, being punished for the
intolerance of the child by the child's great concern lest he do
the wrong thing.

The obsessional child is one in whom rage and anger tendencies have been sidetracked. Their satisfaction in the obsessional
aggression is often so complete that these children become singularly free of fear. The misutilization of thought, and particularly
beneficent thoughtfulness, in this fashion continues the earlier
developmental state in which the cosmically unbounded self is
everything. These children are thus preternaturally apt at the

---

in the discussion of stereotypes, but also in that the *actual* three-member
family has an *only child* problem. Obsessional children are fairly frequently,
at least for a significant period, the only child. This is not invariable, nor
is it the rule that an only child is always obsessional.

emotionally toned "satisfaction" responses; their self never sheds its original omnipotence *anlage;* they are not of the common lot, but behave and think as if the environing people were but shadowy selves definitely tributary to the unconsciously-driven obsessional self. Secured reassurance is the unwitting right of these children. If it is refused, the expression of uncertainty and hesitation is redoubled. When it is secured, the giver is of no further importance in that connection. Either a new "problem" has to be presented to him, or another source of reassurance on the old problem secured.

The personality grows during infancy and childhood from the intrauterine state to one characterized by a clear-cut self-organization. The stereotypes that go to make up this self are generally prepotent thenceforth throughout life. They may be classified as the personal inclusion of culture-entities imposed on the growing personality *from above,* therefore wholly irrationally and involuntarily. They include the important group that manifest thenceforth as the *superego* aspects of personality.

The Juvenile Era

FROM THE subjective cosmic participation, through the growth of awareness of limits and sad limitations in infancy, to the real beginning in childhood of formulation around the verbal symbol "me," the self as a factor in mental life has had little objective import. In the course of childhood the self is chiefly evidenced in the interactions pertaining to domination by and submission to older people. Most of the energy of the child continues to be utilized in quasi-realistic activity, and there is little that approaches implicit processes of the fully adjustive type. Configurations that include other persons customarily ensue in one of three outcomes, these carrying respectively three valuations of the other person concerned, and contributing in one of three ways to the growth of the self.

In one, the impulses of the child progress easily to complete satisfaction; the adult is compliant and is pleased by the child; and the feeling-tone of the child's related self-consciousness is pleasant. There is no great difference between these situations and similar experiences in infancy, except for the increasing clearness of self-reference.

In another sort of situation, the impulses of the child are directly thwarted; the adult is disapproving or displeased with the child; and the feeling-tone is either a hateful feeling appearing as a tendency to primitive rage, or one of antagonism originating by differentiation from the primitive rage. In the latter case, there is an increasing approximation to adult self-reference.

In the third typical situation, the impulses of the child meet neither compliant facilitation nor direct thwarting, but instead are met by accidental or by studied indifference on the part of the adult. The total situation, which has been integrated to include this adult, thus tends to fail of resolution. Neither is it dissolved into emotional implicit processes, as in the case of active thwarting. The situation persists and its persistence, as in the case of all persisting motivations, is accompanied by a felt interest, in this case in the other self. At the same time, there is a new measure of awareness of the child's self and of its needs for response by the other. It is in such situations that there arises in the self-consciousness the need later to be manifested as the seeking of *status*, an enduring organization of the self and its appurtenances such that at least indifference will not be the outcome of situations including other persons, and preferably that the outcome will be favorable appraisal and approbation.

The development of the drive for status is one of the clearest manifestations of beginning socialization. Up to this time the "principle" of the child's life might be said to be a sort of crude hedonism, but from this time onward evidences of favorable attention must be a part of the successful resolution of interpersonal situations. It happens in some cases that the status that is pursued has a negative social value, but that makes it none the less urgently necessary. It is in the case of children whose impulses have evoked disapproval much more frequently or effectively than compliance that the pursuit of status by hateful or antagonistic activities is almost to be expected. To them, being "bad" is at least being something.

To elucidate the social importance of status-seeking, I must discuss the *exteriorization of the self*. Not only does the sentiment of self grow along the paths of assertion, domination, and submission, and a variety of perhaps subordinate factors, from all the experience in which an appraisal by another person has made its appearance in a social situation, but also it grows by a peculiar extravasation of selfhood upon material and immaterial objects in varying degrees attached to or associated with the individual. The clothing worn by a person is usually intimately related to his self. His home, his parents, the family car—all these are represented in a self-context. Any contribution of a positive or negative valuation to any of these objects also contributes to the self, and to the satisfaction, or the reverse, of the status-seeking. It is only a matter of time until verbal expressions of opinions by the juvenile, too, come to be precious parts of the self, and their good or bad reception a contribution to positive or negative self-feeling. This factor often becomes so important that an individual will go to great lengths in defending his expressed opinion long after he has become convinced of its falsity.

It is all but inevitable that the juvenile will be confronted not only by the home situation and the situation with compeers, but also by situations in which family or nonfamily adults (such as teachers) are relevant in the same situational context with other juveniles; thus, this status-seeking involving not only the nuclear but also the augmented self will often present itself in the shape of very complex situations. The intelligent schoolboy who must secure good marks and yet avoid suspicion of "standing in" with the appreciative teacher has a sort of complex situation to maintain quite different from that of the boy to whom being "teacher's pet" is the "highest good," his classmates being but subordinate nuisances whose open hostility alone he needs to avoid. And difficult as these achievements may be, they are as nothing to the difficulty of the really dull boy who must secure the esteem of the teacher in order to "get by" and likewise have the good will of most of his compeers in order to preserve his self-respect.

Every juvenile experiences much that is of but transient relevance which passes rapidly into oblivion. He encounters, also, innumerable relevant factors the integration of which has to be suppressed in the interest of more satisfactory performances. Even from midinfancy each organically average individual has exercised some selection of factors in the integration of each total situation, chiefly by suppressing rudimentary awareness of "distracting" factors. Consider, for example, the common occurrence in reading when one's eyes "inform" one of a symbol such as "teh"—a symbol of a complex kind, in that its meaning includes "the," an error by the compositor, and errors of omission by the proofreader and the author. Yet there is no ensuing consciousness of these meanings, other than that of the implied "the." The collateral processes which might and should be activated in another total situation—such as the reading of this section as proof—are suppressed. They may make their presence felt, even objectively, as when we are observing the "rate" of reading of a subject, and note that there is an interruption or slowing of the rhythmical eye-movements in "covering" the line including the typographical error. This objectively demonstrable "delay" incident to the suppression of sentience whose growth would disorder the total activity, may or may not be attended by processes in the fringe of awareness. The reader may "interrupt" his prevailing activity at the end of the paragraph, and "look over" the text, more or less consciously "looking for" something—perhaps even, now that the determined activity-system is in brief abeyance, "looking for a typographical error." The facility with which the irrelevant processes gain such marginal awareness is a resultant of at least two factors—namely, the reader's *interest* in securing the meaning of the text, and his habituation (another interest) in regard of perceiving typographical errors. If the "set" had been in the latter connection, the author's meaning would not have been perceived, excepting as an irrelevant process, while attention to the "teh" would have been focal. If, however, in the activity determined by the proof-reading set, a context is encountered that connects importantly with one of the reader's interest-systems, sentiments, or tendencies of the self, this "connection" may disorder the proofing "set," and lead to reading for meaning. It must be obvious from this example not only that suppression is a very necessary type of process, but also that the success or ease of suppression of irrelevant factors impinging upon a total situation is a variable determined in part by a characteristic of the irrelevant processes stirred in the organism part of the complex. This significant characteristic is the energy partition to the process in question— in the end, a matter of the innate endowment and subsequent experience that are combined in the evolutionary growth of the particular process.

A great number of adjustive suppressions are required in the school situation. In warped children, some of the tendencies that must be suppressed are very powerful. Their suppression, if accomplished, is done at the cost of so great a state of stress within the personality that but little else can occupy the child. Moreover, one of two complications usually appears. Either the frustration releases a more or less directed antagonism to the embodiment of the demand for suppression—this in children in whom the evolution of primitive hateful-destructive tendencies has not been sidetracked from the personality synthesis—or it reactivates relatively primitive tendency-systems that have been excluded from the conscious experience-series, and the child manifests signs and symptoms of anxiety.

Besides encountering the demands from the school situation proper, the enforced limitations connected with which are modified by a growing *social conformity* in which the common practice of all the children encourages a modification of the various suppressed tendencies in the directions of sublimation and conforming compensatory satisfactions, the juvenile is subjected to interpersonal demands originating in situations "more private" than is that of the classroom. Especially for the shielded "only" child, but in some measure for all, there is a widening acquaintance with various vicious and discomforting aspects of one's fellows—such as the sadistic bully and the sexually precocious individual, to mention two important subvarieties. Sadism, the securing of pleasure by inflicting pain, has its great inning in the juvenile era, so much so that some authorities seem to regard sadism as a universal feature of human nature. I am not convinced of this ubiquity of sadism, either pure or with its "opposite," masochism—the enjoyment of inflicted pain—but I am certain that there is a great deal of it and that the time of its most frank manifestation is in the juvenile era. Whether it is entirely acquired, or whether it is in part an hereditarily determined tendency—as it may be thought to be in members of the cat family —will remain a question until we know much more about the experience of the young.[1]

[1] If I mistake not, sadistic tendencies are chiefly manifested by juveniles who have been subjected to much irrational and/or malicious thwartings by one of the parents; and such tendencies are not manifested by other juveniles. However that may prove to be on full investigation, there is wide individual variation in the tendency to enjoy the inflicting of pain, and in the complexly—but closely—related enjoyment of suffered injury (personally or quasi-personally inflicted).

I am indebted to William V. Silverberg for a comment in this connection to the effect that much that appears in the current literature in reference to sadism, masochism, and sadomasochism seems to refer to nothing as specific as is my meaning, but merely to refer to activity versus passivity, or to "aggressiveness" as opposed to "submissiveness." While sadism and masochism contain elements of these, they are much more specific containing the

There is a curious interrelation in many individuals between these sadistic, masochistic, or sadomasochistic tendencies and the later acquired sexual impulses. Individually and socially, this combination is of no small moment as it seems that a large part of the sexual drive can be dissipated through the channel of cruelty or the undergoing of abuse. One might well pause, therefore, to consider this particular phase of the juvenile personality, on which, unfortunately, we have all but no data.

Some juveniles react to bullying by the incapacitation defense. Those are recruited, for the most part, from the homes where one of the parents has used the defense of incapacitation and the child has not been so fortunate as to grow up in rough-and-tumble with brothers and sisters of approximate age. When such a one comes in contact with the school bully and has an entirely unexpected, very bad time, he may show a facile recourse to incapacitation reactions and incorporate an unwitting attitude somewhat to the effect that in certain interpersonal relations one's reaction is that of becoming sick, feeling faint, or whatever. Thus, even in the kindergarten one can see the building of the hysteric or hysteroid way of dealing with interpersonal difficulties. I shall not elaborate the more or less obvious steps by which certain of these people go on into major hysterical illnesses, nor point out the particular influences in our present culture which make hysterical manifestations much less the mode for men than for women. Even when the prevailing maladaptive tendency in the earlier years is an hysterical one, the attitude of the boy's fellows usually deflects this in the course of preadolescence to some different kind of morbidity—for example, hypochondriacal interests. In some number of cases there is established a combination of hypochondriacal preoccupations irregularly alternating with paranoid states.

To the majority of juveniles, the hysteroid incapacitation is repugnant to the self. When, therefore, they are discomforted by the aggression or sadism—including scorn—of a school-fellow, and the unsatisfactory tendencies concerned are not susceptible of suppression, a recourse occurs to repression, often with ensuing dissociation. This comes about because each in-

---

additional element of definite pleasure returns. I would regard the more general usage as contributing to confusion and unwarranted generalization.

stance of the suppression of activity motivated by any powerful tendency requires the activity of a still more powerful tendency. Thus, if in a given interpersonal situation one is motivated both to anger and to conciliation, the anger behavior cannot be suppressed unless the tendency to conciliation represents a vector addition of tendencies distinctly more powerful in their sum than is the system tending to anger.[2] In many children, outbursts of rage, anger, or "irritation" have been fixed by experience as effective in situations threatening them with frustration. Despite the necessity for conciliative behavior having been enforced by recent experience, this utilization of anger can scarcely be suppressed. The juvenile experience often effects teaching of conciliation and abnegation, by the instrumentality of those very powerful tendencies stirred by danger and accompanied generally by fear. Recall of the first few experiences in which the childish tantrum, the "bad temper," or the show of annoyance brought as a consequent a fear-provoking event is usually highly repugnant to self-esteem. These experiences are therefore generally repressed. There is little profiting from experience the tendency components of which are repressed. Recurrences of the particular anger-provoking situations therefore continue, but must tend to identical unpleasant outcome. Repression cannot function in a frequently recurrent situation. The repression of one instance of a total situation attended by a repugnant total activity is perhaps fairly easy. Another instance of closely related total activity, particularly if not far removed in time, makes repression difficult. The repression of a whole series of incidents of related activity is impossible.[3] The recurring situations must re-

[2] If the balance is nearly even, the resultant action, both systems continuing effective, would be neither conciliating nor satisyfing to the impulses to anger; it would appear as "blocking," a disintegration of both situations, a regressive phenomenon peculiarly apt to manifest itself in negativistic situations.

[3] An animal that converted recurrent experience with particular threatening aspects of reality into a never-happened insubstantiality would in all probability come to an early end.

From the broader biological viewpoint the consideration of repression as an actual process of living receives such limited support that I must deny it much importance in human life, even entertain chronic doubt as to the validity of the conception. It is retained in this treatise solely because (1) there *seems to be* a gap between manifest suppression and manifest dissociation, which it fills, and (2) actual human manifestations of *regression*

sult either in healthy growth of tendencies or in dissociation of
the tendencies manifesting disastrously.

The related stereotype may be dissociated from the systems
operative as the conscious self. While one may continue to show
anger in various situations, the anger-tendencies previously
evoked by the situation in point cease to appear in consciousness,
and find expression instead in some unrecognized alterations in
postural tensions of the skeletal muscles or the viscera, or in unnoted symptomatic acts. If the dissociated system is frequently
energized by situational factors, its expressions may appear as
tensions in the muscular equipment that tend to persist excepting in deep sleep. The expressive apparatus centered in the face
is often concerned in this, "lines" in characteristic patterns appearing as evidence of the chronically recurring tensions. The
facial movements develop characteristic peculiarities that are
manifest whenever the complex situation including activity of
the dissociated system arises. Interferences with the freedom of
the cheek muscles and the movement of the jaw and with the
freedom of movement of the lips, as well as interferences with
tension-changes in the larynx and even in the diaphragm, may
manifest the dissociated system in characteristic alterations of the
voice. Quality, intonation, emphasis, rate and precision of syllabic
articulation, and several other elements of speech may undergo
both persisting change and this sort of automatic activation. In
the latter connection, the changes may or may not be consciously
"heard" by the speaker, this in turn depending on the power of
the systems concerned in the dissociation.

The enlargement of personal interaction in the juvenile era
augments greatly the importance of the social tools, primarily
the expressive apparatus. Not only do daily contacts with many
now take the place of hourly contacts with a particular few, but
the zones of interaction tend to become more strictly those of
the visage, the voice, and the posture and carriage. The importance of the *face* thus grows rapidly, the more in that sentience arising from other faces is chiefly visual, of the type peculiarly easy to elaborate in the direction of consensual valida-

---

so *greatly* exceed anything apt to happen in the subhuman phyla without
prompt death of the animal concerned that one cannot reason too surely
about human limitations from mere *lethality* of a process.

tion. This is not so much the case with the voice. Sentience of voices is mediated by the phyletically much older auditory system, consensual validation of information from the sentience of which is by no means as frequent (and probably essentially much more difficult). The *eyes* come to be of such nuclear importance in the primary appraisal of personal factors that they often take on a preternatural personal import, the more in that parents and teachers advertise their own superstition in this connection by demanding that they be stared at when attempting to assess the truth or falsity of verbal reports by the juvenile.[4]

The visage, the voice, and the posture and carriage of the body —in fact, all the interpersonal expressive equipment—are subject from midchildhood onward, increasingly, to molding influences of two major categories. The one is that of the self-esteemed tendency-systems, including the idealizations of the self. The other is that of the tendency-systems chronically dissociated from the self. The changes that are wrought by these latter tend to become conspicuous and persistently characteristic in the course of the adolescent epoch.[5] Before going forward with this

[4] The notion of the eyes as the "windows of the soul" must be a survival from primitive culture, for neither the eyes themselves—relatively unchanging excepting to evidence interest—nor their extrinsic movements— shifting and so on—nor yet again the circum-ocular postural tensions, are any or all especially illuminating in personality appraisal. A "shifting gaze" is telltale; but the tale it tells is the story of personal discomfort coupled with a previous ingrained superstition about the revealing character of the eyes.

Close visual observation of a comparative stranger is apt to disconcert him, both by reason of his window-of-the-soul superstitions and because everyone is at least dimly aware of the remarkably expressive character of the face. It would be interesting to know what proportion of uncomfortable people could undergo scrutiny with entire calm if the lower half of their faces were concealed. It is in the circum-oral tensions and in the play of the cheek musculature that a very great part of the actual facial expression of personality takes place. *Vide infra*, Chapter II.

[5] The lability of the expressive apparatus generally remains intact throughout the juvenile era, and the relief of personality difficulties during this stage of growth generally brings with it a marked improvement in face, voice, posture, and skeletal movements. The favorable alterations in this connection that are wrought by timely remedy of adolescent problems are often startling. Some few teachers of the expressive arts attempt more or less crude psychotherapy as a part of their technique. Perhaps a day may come when parents otherwise unenthusiastic as to the aid of psychopathology in the rearing of their young will look to it for a "beautician" technique for increasing the surface value of their children! I marvel that there is not

consideration of maladjustive phenomena peculiarly associated with the juvenile era, I must present more fully certain aspects of the first of these categories.

Besides the augmentation of the self by more direct accessions of status, there occurs, in this and all subsequent periods, an increment in the spread of relevance, the horizon of the significant world being greatly expanded by the growth of secondary group relationships. These arise in part in the more formal education. Their initially most important source, however, lies in the expansion of direct primary relationships. "They," the people outside of past, present, or immediate future direct sensory experience, take on various measures of reality and relevance. Whether "they" be the semimythological parents of the playmates, or other children of whom the teacher tells, or yet even more remote folk about whom stories are read, "they" become more or less significant in a fashion quite distinct from the objects of direct action. Much that is new and exciting is presented in consciousness. Inadequacies appear in the family-group stereotypes. Discrepancies among absolutes are accented by minor differences in the principles and parental prejudices governing the young representatives of the various families. Questioning becomes a major business. Everything is liable to investigation. In those still possessing comparative mental health, the more accessible aspects of the stereotypes undergo extensive differentiation and resymbolization, with distinct if gradual change in the related tendencies.

Favorable aspects of the kindly teacher, coinciding with less clear-cut appreciations of the mother and father, may receive focal attention. A new sentiment grows rapidly, in which are

---

already a supply of quack "psychologists" busy in this doubtless lucrative field.

The protection of physical health by the enactment and enforcement of laws calculated to reduce the menace of quackery to operatives possessing medical or osteopathic degrees, while it continues to be legal for anyone to entrap the populace for almost any sort of tinkering or tampering with mental health and human personality, must ultimately concern us. It is another manifestation of the underlying politics that insists that the children of the underprivileged shall be saved from death and physical disease and given enough of the tools of culture to make them easy victims of propaganda, while leaving to the more promising of these children the alternatives of a career in crime or a life in the mental hospital.

incorporated some of the sympathetic tendencies toward each of the parents. Or unfavorable aspects of the teacher, coinciding with unpleasant aspects of one or both parents, may permit the growth of a new sentiment including much more frankly anti-pathetic tendencies than could function in a unitary fashion in the earlier stereotype. The process of weaning from the child role is thus initiated, being augmented by failures of the members of the family-group to survive as absolutes in the face of secondary relations with the teachings, prejudices, acts, and omissions of the parents of playmates. *Conscious comparisons* arise from dissatisfactions previously dealt with in lower-level fantasy, but none the less powerfully motivated. A beginning of active emancipation is made, often by questioning the central prejudice of the parent—"Jimmy's mother lets him play with Johnny ['a bad boy']," "Walter's father lets him play marbles for keeps," "Pete doesn't have to go to Sunday School," and the like. To this quo warranto procedure many parents react in unwholesome fashions, to which the child must then adapt his efforts. *Their* injunctions, rules, and regulations, being exteriorizations of their none too adequate personality, often the more treasured in that they represent sacred hereditaments of sainted parents "minded" all too late by the offspring, are degraded by comparison with the degenerate mismanagements of contemporary upstarts. Insecurities, private miseries from concrete disappointments in status pursuit, defensive stereotypes, a great body of parental deviations that have sought perhaps unwitting satisfaction in *their* child as an extravasation of personalities—all these are activated as the juvenile shows signs of coming under external influences inimical to a continued identification with the parental stereotype. The parental reaction may be violent.

In the family group where the maturation and final emancipation of the offspring are most bitterly opposed—always "unconsciously"—and the juvenile for that very reason, if he is not already whipped into submission, is the more anxious to secure experience that will help him, we find a situation that is prone to eventuate either in active hostility or in the cultivation of fraudulent behavior toward the parents. If the latter is the tendency, since the juvenile seldom possesses capacities for conscious

hypocrisy that will function to deceive the emotionally stimulated parents, there is almost always a dissociation in its morbid
form, and unwitting use is made of the somatic expressive equipment in the interest of motivations that are not consistent with
the major integration of personality. Such juveniles effect a striking and wholly unwitting metamorphosis as they enter into the
zone of influence of the parental environment, remaining for the
parents what the latter desire, yet manifesting in the school, play-
ground, and elsewhere a fair approximation to an average growth
of personality.

If the juvenile is thwarted in all attempts at emancipation from
the child role, and continues in it without material growth, all
further experience with authority must either fall exactly into
the parent-child pattern or occur exterior to self-consciousness,
tributary to the tendency-systems dissociated as a result of the
submission to the continuing immature role. These personalities
continue to be juvenile. They do not become socialized in the
ordinary sense and, were it not for the supply of inadequate
elders to whom their veneration is sweet, would almost certainly
progress into grave mental disorder at the time that others enter
adolescence.[6]

The juvenile who engages in frank hostility to the parental
codes and valuations, even if successful, still suffers considerable
damage to personality growth. There still clings to the father and
mother much of the aura from the time when they were God.
Parents who are inadequate enough to desire the continued complete subordination of their offspring are scarcely likely to
achieve a good-natured benevolence as an outcome of a losing
struggle. The issues are joined again and again. Appeals to sympathy, vituperations, threats, and gloomy forebodings—these are
a few of the devices used against the rebellious juvenile. He
comes early to prehend that there is no going back to a friendly
status for him. Whenever he tries it he discovers that he is im-

[6] Many of these chronic juveniles, however, do find themselves a series
of foster-parents, from whom they secure encouragement and the necessary
adjusted opportunity—excepting always such opportunity as might permit
an overshadowing of the patron. The complicated situations integrated by
the adolescent intimacy-need and the sexual motivations will presently concern us.

mediately imposed upon. Like the quasi-hypocritical juvenile, he has usually to have recourse to morbid dissociation.[7]

The dissociation processes by which these juvenile maladjustments to the parents are brought about apply at the level of (sentiment and) complex formation. Certain complexes and the related acquired tendencies are thrown "out of gear" with the increasing experience, and continue to function without much relation to the general evolution of tendencies. One or another of these groups becomes relatively unelaborated as time passes, and we refer to this part of the personality as "the dissociated system." [8] The ultimate outcome of such situations is determined by two factors: the partition of energy to the two systems, and the measure of awareness of the dissociated system that the individual retains or develops. As long as the system within the self that "attends to" the reality of one's activity in relation to another person is so characterized by its evolutionary history that it insures a considerable measure of recognition of the dissociated activity as of personal origin and due to unknown but real factors in the total situation, the necessary synthesis of the self is secure from grave dissociation. If, however, the self-consciousness is not only unaware of the situational factors leading to the dissociated activity, but also without evidences of the activity itself, then the way is open for most unfortunate developments. This state of the self reflects the early sidetracking of important tendencies, such that there are in the personality profoundly unconscious powerful emotional tendencies of which the individual "knows" nothing.[9] In any case of major dissociation the individual is at the mercy of motives that can carry him toward consummations with other people—not only without his

[7] I need scarcely remark the entanglement of parent and child appearing at this stage in homes where psychopathic and obsessional deviation date from childhood. For that matter, lying, stealing, truancy, even arson and mayhem, are among the "conduct disorders" commonly encountered among those who have failed at this juncture. The whole child-guidance movement might be said to concern the juvenile era. Its literature is voluminous.

[8] Consideration of the actual tendencies that are incorporated in the dissociated system gives an important insight into the probable outcome of the personality. This is implied in the next statement in the text. The energy partition is a function of the particular tendencies involved, coordinate with the situational factors to which the personality is subjected.

[9] *Vide supra*, the discussion of the subtrate from which rise the nonadjustive processes.

wish, but distinctly in opposition to his ideals and conventions—and he can never be sure when he will be threatened with conflict. However, the individuals in whom the dissociated systems are associated with deeply unconscious tendencies are even more unfortunate in that they come often to suffer anxiety whose sources are impossible for the self to discover. In any case, the more of the personality there is in a state of dissociation, the greater the probability that it will "take over" the somatic apparatus when it is activated by a suitable situation, and the more deeply uncertain the individual must become as to all interpersonal situations.

It is chiefly in the juvenile era that this division of the tendencies in interpersonal relations takes place into those susceptible of awareness and those denied conscious appreciation. The rationale of the division, however, is rather a matter of the growth of the self, than one of a positive exclusion from consciousness. For example, if the influences at work on the individual are such that he comes to find it easy to "forget" "disgraceful" submissions to the school bully, or "shameful" coöperation in genital play with one of the older boys, then submissive tendencies in the one case, and tendencies to be involved in the sexual motivations in the other, tend to be developed exterior to the appreciated self—in the region of unconscious processes—that is, as dissociated systems. The role of the parent and other moral censors in this connection is very important. For example, if a juvenile knows that he is in many of his performances and most of his expressed beliefs a hypocrite, it is too bad, but it is still far better than if he comes to be wholly unconscious of the fraudulent in his thought and behavior. If one must be "bad," it is a very good thing to know that one is being bad.

The individual, for all that I have presented thus far, might well be taken to be a bundle of processes innately ordained but otherwise wholly susceptible to directing and redirecting into an infinity of more or less accidental patterns. This conception is not without approximation to the facts of the eras of infancy and childhood. The factors limiting the freedom of outcome in personality growth, prior to school entrance, are chiefly of two classes: the innately determined potentialities, and the prepotency of certain vector patterns, once these are formed. The prepotency of the latter is again predetermined by virtue of biological facilitation of the related total-situation integrations. Once these more properly human configurations of tendencies have been permitted by postnatal experience, it is only as a result of most extraordinary circumstances that they are extinguished. I wish now to discuss one of these prepotent vector patterns or configurations, the time of probable formation of which is certainly past before the end of childhood, the manifestations of which, when present, become increasingly significant in the juvenile and subsequent stages of growth. Showing chiefly in the motivation of the self, this deeply unconscious configuration or major stereotype, to the evidences of which we refer as *character,* controls the freedom of personality growth, limiting the fields of relevance and determining, for example, a coherent pursuit of status in which only certain situational factors are permitted to become relevant and only certain ones of the extensive possibilities of interpersonal adjustment, acceptable.

    This factor of character is none too fully elucidated at the present time, perhaps chiefly because the juvenile era has been neglected by students of personality. It seems to be missing in obsessional and in psychopathic juveniles; and its manifestations may be faint indeed in many others. I surmise, none the less, that it is a normal evolution in the growth of personality, and that only in the case in which it is well developed is mental health to be presumed. From observation of its absence, we may venture that it depends fundamentally upon a rather normal evolution of the primitive mother sentiment, after the fashion of an implicit assumption of the essential unity (and goodness) of the universe. The functional activity of the character factor seems to depend on a fairly comprehensive grasp on the reality both of the self and of other selves. Further than this I go with extreme hesitancy, for the ramifications of our submerging culture tend inevitably to deceive one as to what is essential and what accidental in this field. If I mistake not, character is a stereotype founded in the first differentiation from the primitive mother sentiment, and integrating in it the subsequent *experience of consistent manifestations of enduring constructive attitudes toward the child* on the part of either or both parents and others relevant in the early situations. All that is fully adjustive in the relationships of the individual during infancy and early childhood with significant others, and only that which is fully adjustive, is experience tributary to character. That character is frequently vestigial is thus seen as an automatic resultant of maladjustive and nonadjustive processes in one or both parents, in their own interpersonal relations, and in their individual and combined interpersonal relations with their child or children.[10] My surmise is that character is founded on that part of the cultural heritage embodied in the parents that has continued to function smoothly in their individual-social synthesis, in the series of interpersonal situations through which they have progressed. Unfortunately, the study of culture and the study of personality have proceeded with little regard one for the other, and the processes of ac-

[10] It seems that foresight—not as an intellectual gymnastic for verbal display, but as a situational factor making relevant to each given complex probable events still more or less remote in the future—so completely lacking, for example, in the psychopath, is found only in those in whom the character factor is conspicuous.

I doubt the utility of moral valuations in this field. Some authors measure character by the "goodness" of the life it "inspires." At least one such finds "no character in the insane"—getting "character" being thus *la grande* mental hygiene. Some authors include as manifestations of character a body of processes which I have already included in the schematization of maladjustments—for example, "high capacity for sublimation." Some others seem to feel that character is a conscious formulation to which the individual holds himself unwaveringly. And all of these views are certainly incorrect, even as they all, to paraphrase Henshaw Ward, have a good bit in them. Character may be conspicuously associated with a life history singularly devoid of any claims for "goodness" as currently defined, although this might well be rare. No combination of maladjustive or nonadjustive dynamics is character, even though its influence may, in unfortunate life-situations, interfere with regression to lower-level "adjustments," and continue difficult integrations amounting to acute mental illness. Neither does a rigidity of formulation of life-goal that interferes with the growth of total situations imply anything of character, other than its unfortunate rationalization. Character, if it is present at all, antecedes in its appearance any such formulations. Opportunism is not a manifestation of the character factor— quite the contrary; on the other hand, a strong character factor implies no extreme stability, but often makes itself manifest in resisting the tendency to stabilization so conspicuous in certain cultures. Perhaps character is only the "delusion of the great mission" born in the early fantasy, but *successfully* applied to a world of processes some of which can be foretold and some of which must be turned to whatever use their unexpected occurrence permits, but always in line with one's "duty of greatness." [*Editors' note:* Sullivan here appears to be using the word *character* in a literary sense rather than in terms of its current psychological usage—that is, he seems to be using it to describe persons of "strong moral fiber" and self-discipline.]

culturation—aside from the relatively late, and comparatively insignificant, acculturation by education—have been neglected by both.

The chief import of the character factor arises from its effect in limiting the growth of tendency-systems exterior to the self. The less effective it is, the more the total situations (and quasi-total situations integrated by dissociated systems) contribute to a polymorphous growth of the personality, and to the appearance of the various maladjustive processes that are engaging our attention. We must now turn to attend briefly to another controlling factor of much less useful effect.

As character seems to me to be that of the cultural heritage which "worked" in the lives of the parents, so another major stereotype that contributes largely to the self and its vicissitudes, and thus to the ability of the personality to progress in growth, seems to embody that of the cultural heritage transmitted in the late infancy and childhood that did not function wholly adjustively in the parents. I refer here to the *superego*, or *conscience*. Successful man-ways begin to be incorporated in the first days of infancy, and the integration of the character-stereotype is all but finished by the time that unsuccessful, biologically subversive, and incoherently contradictory tendencies can be inculcated. Character therefore roots in the deep unconscious, while conscience is much nearer the level of late childhood. The manifestations of the character stereotype limit the growth of destructive conscience, but, strong or weak, they readily "take on" attributes of later experience and may be mistaken for phenomena of the same order as conscience. The distinction is thus ordinarily masked, for conspicuous manifestations of character often require rationalization and this is provided by appeal either to the ideals of the self or to the more accessible parts of conscience. The fundamental difference in functional activity of the character and the conscience factors appears in the powerful control of relevance by the earlier stereotype and the feeble control of relevance by the later one. Conscience is a differentiation in the self, composed of self-conscious experiences in which the parents (and analogues) function as theocrats, as agents of transcendental power, and one by which a self-tendency is created to function theocratically. Its explicit mani-

festations take the form of inhibitory tendencies, failure of which
is attended by the appearance in consciousness of a *feeling of
guilt*, peculiarly antithetic to self-esteem. Threatened loss of
status among others is so potent in many that a life of defensive
maladjustments results. This *actual* loss of status with God, however, is an even more potent matter, and has to be remedied. The
satisfaction of frustrated conscience, with discharge of the sense
of guilt, is accomplished variously, sometimes by implicit processes, rationalization, penitential thoughts, prayer, and so on,
usually by witting or unconscious penitential acts, the motivation
of which we can call a *need for punishment*.[11]

The juvenile, weaning himself from stereotype possessed of
more or less "divine" sanction, is apt to find himself in a peculiar
relationship with the parent of the same sex. So generally is this
the case that the moral systems pertaining to guilt and self-
punishment are commonly referred to an entity called "Oedipus
guilt." There has been postulated a primal horde in which there
occurred a parricidal crime, with succeeding appearance of a
feeling of guilt, perhaps with expectancy of a similar fate on the
part of the sons. The parricidal guilt has been supposed to be

[11] The feeling of guilt and its discharge by the doing of penance is no
matter of religious denomination. Even the proud "atheist" in our culture
feels guilt and arranges his own punishment. Having lifted himself to the
very self-apotheosis by tugging on his intellectual bootstraps, he preserves
his consciousness of distinguished superiority by resolving the suppressed
crime against the unescapable God of infancy in thoroughly childish magical
penitential activity—the "meaning" of which is ignored or rationalized.
Successfully or unsuccessfully, in complete or in imperfect dissociation, we
carry as a system within the self—a system concerned with judging of
"good" and "bad"—this childish integration of irrational quasi-ethical valuations and apportionings of propitiation, *unless* in the juvenile or a later
period we develop insight into our moral or superego system. It is a
dynamism which, fed on the new source of conflict that is presented in
sexual adjustment, becomes in a remarkable number of people *the* distorting
and destroying influence in adolescence. It carries with it maladjustive activities without number and the doing of penance, elaborate and magical. It
even "arranges"—to speak for the moment anthropomorphically—the penal
incarceration of its happy carrier, in all too many cases.
In fact, one of the distinguished psychoanalysts, Franz Alexander, has
founded a theory of law and of criminology on observations of this kind;
see *The Criminal and His Judge;* New York: Nervous and Mental Disease
Publications, 1931. It seems scarcely necessary to state that this generalization
is poorly warranted in the field of criminology alone, much less as a general
theory of public law. I shall recur presently to the topic of criminological
theory.

"transmitted" and to appear in each individual as the root of the Oedipus fear, in turn to be discharged by a penitential castration, fortunately more or less symbolic. I would first comment on this doctrine of the transmission of memories or other paleopsychisms. The notion seems to be either that there are transmitted in the germ-plasm some fossils of the mental life of bygone ages, or that this very bygone mental life still exists at least in outline, making up "the racial unconscious" of which we are but buds, protuberances, or whatnot. Many of the paleopsychic fossils that were in good standing a few years ago have been found to be wholly explicable by an appeal to the concept of infantile experience, a much more acceptable hypothesis than is that of the racial unconscious. The so-called Oedipus guilt seems equally understandable by an appeal to the infancy and childhood experiences that include individuals vested with authority.[12]

One acquires only with difficulty a correct appreciation of the separateness of himself and "external reality," even as it is rather difficult to develop a correct appreciation of the indissoluble connection between oneself and some parts of external reality. Even in the fullness of mature years, most people fail to distinguish between the personal characteristics of any particular bill collector, and certain unpleasant features of bills, as such. The child, then, may perhaps be expected to discriminate poorly in distributing unpleasant characterizations having origin in the loss of satisfaction experienced at the time of the primitive mother-child symbiosis. Such negative valuations will scarcely tend to segregate upon the person most closely identified with the satisfaction of needs. In the case of the boy, they tend very forcibly to segregate around the father. In most girls, they come finally to characterize the mother—rather contradictory to the expectation from the satisfaction of infantile needs. The primitive mother sentiment is in each case the same; then comes the same

[12] This is not the case when the "Oedipus complex" is conceived to be a specific drive—hereditary or otherwise—against the specific blood-father, a notion alike contradictory to common sense and facts available in primitive culture. See, for example, Bronislaw Malinowski, *The Father in Primitive Psychology;* New York: Norton, 1927; *The Sexual Life of Savages in Northwestern Melanesia;* New York: Liveright, 1929. See also the controversial writings in his discussion with Ernest Jones on the nature of the Oedipus factor in the *Internat. J. Psycho-Analysis.*

differentiation of the mother as more and more of a person, and less and less of God. Certainly, at this stage, the tendency is to segregate "bad" impressions upon some figure other than the mother, and the significant other figure is generally the father. In the case of the girl, however, there comes ultimately to be an extra link in the chain of processes, owing to the working of the factor of empathy, a new aspect of which must now concern us.

Empathy seems to function in childhood to produce a linkage of male to male and of female to female. The son comes to be to the father, and the father to the son, a sort of personality-extension quite different from the linkage continuing between the mother and son. Similarly, there arises this new sort of linkage of the mother and daughter. I surmise that there enter into these phenomena culture elements in the shape of traditional attitudes of the man as to woman and of the woman as to man, these being empathetically prehended by the child. However that may be, the factor seems to show as an unwitting prehension by the man of his son, and by the mother of her daughter, such that the actual behavior, expressive and other, of the father to the son and of the mother to the daughter is more direct and authoritative than it is in the other cases. While I deal here with a matter on which data are as yet little more than suspected, I venture the opinion that distressing aspects of reality are most forced upon the young child by the parent of the same sex; and that it is thus that the other parent comes to enjoy a more prolonged approximation to the old all-satisfying divinity. This seems to be the origin of the so-called Oedipus and Electra situations—valid as patterns in many, if not all, cultures, but in no sense hereditary endowments.

It thus comes about that, in the partition of positive and negative feelings between the parents, the son becomes more antipathetic to the father and the daughter to the mother. When the sex-linked parent is oversensitive to the growing antipathy of the juvenile, the vicious situations above delineated are prone to ensue, and the fullest manifestations of so-called Oedipus hatred and guilt make appearance.

Let us now concern ourselves with the various maladjustive dynamisms, considered individually—depending, as usual, on the student's acumen to insure a synoptic view of the era. The

juvenile era is peculiarly the time for the appearance of compensatory programs apt to be carried on thenceforth throughout
life. Possibly because juveniles are good judges of the "eternal
values" in this culture, athletic compensations are greatly cultivated, at least among boys. No matter how much trouble the
boy is having in his classes, if he is becoming a good rough-and-
tumble fighter or a good pitcher, he is apt to secure a large
measure of self-esteem from his playmates and from someone in
the home, and to receive the warm regard of some of the older
boys or younger teachers. It is thus built into a number of people
during the juvenile era that if they are good sportsmen—and into
a still larger number that if they are any sort of sportsmen—
many shortcomings in other lines will be overlooked. The compensatory overdependence on athletic prowess thus nurtured is
often continued to the senium, without any very direct disapproval from anyone. It is conventional to consider athletic
achievements to be related to masculinity, and they therefore
facilitate a beginning of adolescent socialization with the opposite
sex. Unfortunately they come often to be a compensation for
dissatisfactions and inadequacies in the sexual sphere, and a mark
of continued adolescent attitude throughout life. The athlete
often fails in midadolescence when sexual activity of the frank
kind should make appearance.

Parents occupied with other children or with other interests
often encourage the juvenile to study, at least by giving him
every opportunity in the way of time and place, and perhaps by
frankly encouraging his being out of sight. Sometimes, too, in
the school and on the athletic field he receives further encouragement toward this course, being taught that it is best for him not
to be "under foot." These juveniles are thus encouraged to keep
out of the way of others, but are not provided with a constructive program. They generally continue the childhood recourse to fantasy and to daydreams in lieu of other activities.
Many of them discover that they are under no more pressing
necessity than that of killing time, and that time can be eliminated with minimum effort by going to the movies, where one
has but to keep the eyes open; the images presented and their
immediate associative trimmings do the work, no constructive
thinking being required, for the plots are as old as the hills and

interest is attached to the little details of novelty that the producer may have "thought up" to justify the dreary rehash. A superficial sort of life process is adopted by these juveniles and from them come the typical inadequate childishly compensatory folk who never quite get around to doing anything because they have never had to develop any special urge, and their motivation is drained off in the earlier types of satisfaction.

These juveniles tend to escape from the socializing urges by the development of fantastic compensatory illusions of others in much the same way as does the psychopath by developing fantastic depreciatory illusions. From childhood the psychopath has been warped out of any correct appraisal of himself and others. In the juvenile who is facilitated in drifting into compensatory substitutions, we have a beginning of socialization, the development of fairly correct appraisals of himself and of others; thereafter a discharge of the socializing urges (and most other urges) by the childhood method of daydreams and mild amusements. The daydreamer crosses the line into adolescence not armed with improved prehensions of his own and of other selves, but, instead, filled with pleasing fantasies of prowess, charm, and wit. Not only does he tend in general to avoid the tests of crude reality, but now that interpersonal intimacy is a necessity, he is likely to drift in an extremely unfortunate direction. He may seek out friends on the basis of woefully fantastic appraisals of the other fellow as an embodiment of heroic tradition or other "movie stuff"—with succeeding disappointments. He may then, or *de novo*, abandon a real socialization by discharging the tendency in purely fantastic "friendship with" a "movie star" or other inaccessible and unwitting object. These compensatory processes may ultimately lead him to "correspond" with the remote object, but even in the letters—which may, for that matter, never be mailed—the "depth of the feeling" is not clearly expressed. This is one of the most ominous of the preludes to adolescent disasters.

Another somewhat more blessed form of compensatory personality developed in the juvenile era is that of the "student." In particular, juveniles handicapped by physical inferiorities, but also many others who are not able to earn esteem at athletics, find that they can avoid a good deal of the criticism and contempt of other juveniles by cultivating their intellectual abilities. Since they immediately distinguish themselves in the field of particular interest of their teachers, they are usually given strong encouragement in the school. The encouragement of intellectual superiority is so much the spirit of the time that even though there be one of the parents who recognizes the one-sided character of such a growth, he can usually be brought into line by the other parent, the aunts, and others. Or else, owing to the so-called Oedipus antipathy, his disfavor of the studiousness can be converted into an added stimulus by the juvenile himself. These young folk often become grand students and discharge their socializing tendencies in a childlike adjustment with elder teachers, and with such select few of their compeers as are compensating in the same fashion. While this, too, is an unfortunate deviation of the socializing tendencies, and poor preparation for the coming of adolescence, it is a sort of existence that can be eked out indefinitely within the walls of a university.

The role of processes properly referable to sublimation in the juvenile life is somewhat obscure. The element of social approbation becomes newly important in this era, and all growth of tendencies from their childhood status toward accommodation to the standards of the group, when unwitting, might be considered to be, by definition, sublimatory. Many instances of self-modification in unwitting pursuit of group approbation are certainly of this character. On the other hand, there are instances that are not of this character and that are instead maladjustive processes of more or less evil omen for the personality. Juveniles as a class are unkind to underprivileged compeers. While in the early years of this era actual demonstrations of superiority in skill, strength, and the like are the more effective factors in establishing status, this presently gives over to the growing respect for caste marks. The latter part of the era comes to be the very heyday of snobbery and crass social discrimination. Social inequalities are fabricated from all sorts of expansions of the juvenile selves, including the trappings of power and position that parents seem so happy to hang on their offspring. The "outs" are given barbarous demonstrations of the value of being "in" with the privileged group, and find themselves the butt of scandal-mongering, defamation, and the cruelest of malicious mischief. Perhaps largely by virtue of home training, the members of the "in" group become expert at making much ado about nothing, propitiating the elect, and flogging the fallen. The juvenile is taught that the most vile accusations may be flung at the outsider, without any warrant for the opprobrium other than the social inferiority. He learns also that the most obvious viciousness of the elect is not only not to be discussed critically, but is best applauded. If he comes from a home in which there has been a good deal of fairly consistent harping on "justice," a few unmerited punishments for faults committed by one of the elect, coupled with the necessity of grinning and bearing it in order to "stand in," go far to distort his prehensions of the world in the direction of the grossest social opportunism. If he is one of those whose parents move about the country or otherwise prevent his remaining for long in the same school, he finds himself, in each new class, confronted with a fairly highly organized social system, into which he must force his amalgamation if he is not to be ostracized and made the butt of the displacement processes soon to concern us. The role of the stranger to the juvenile group is apt to become highly unpleasant, unless the "new" boy is extraordinarily competent and self-reliant. Some more crafty members usually take him up, divest him of the protecting illusions associated with lack of personal familiarity, and then "put him where he belongs."

Of the legion of defensive processes that make appearance in unfortunate juveniles, I shall discuss but one group. From earlier experience, often accentuated by a teacher thus maladjusted, some juveniles find relief from distressing situations of reduced self-esteem, from anxiety, and from conflict and the feeling of guilt by recourse to the "transference of blame" dynamism. This is particularly common in juveniles showing the psychopathic deviation above discussed, since their formulations of their own and other selves are highly fantastic, their character rudimentary, and their conscience highly developed from innumerable violations of parental prohibitions. In such a juvenile, it is very easy to come to believe that his socially unfortunate position is the fault of other people. When, whether in a psychopath or another, this tendency to transfer blame appears thus early in the evolution of personality, it eventuates in an individual alert to anything which could be interpreted as unfriendly to him and competent at so rationalizing interpersonal events as to show that others are handicapping him, harming him, or denying him opportunity. These juveniles are apt to fall in with similarly paranoid companions and thereby learn more and more perfect ways of rationalizing the world's doings in explanation of their own more or less vaguely perceived inadequacies. This is the only form of direct socializing activity that can be expected among those suffering this maladjustment and, needless to say, it is a very poor foundation for the modification of social tendencies which is to appear in adolescence. Either in situations integrated by powerful tendencies requiring interpersonal intimacy, or in those characterized by conflict and the feeling of guilt, the transference of blame dynamism requires the integrating of strong antipathetic attitudes, sentiments of hatred. It then becomes essential to the person thus maladjusted that there be a supply of personal objects capable of being blamed and hated. It is both remarkable and fortunate, however, that much of human value is accomplished by many prevailingly paranoid individuals, who have insured themselves a few "really worthwhile" objects of hatred. We shall come shortly to discovering that these objects may be of but tenuous reality.

Almost all instances of virtuosity arising from antipathetic tendencies are found to depend on the displacement of a hostile or aggressive tendency from a personal object susceptible of direct action (that is, a person in a primary relationship with the subject-individual) to some other persons who stand in the relationship of a secondary group. This may occur as a more or less direct and healthy growth of tendency, or as an accompaniment of suppression, repression, or dissociation. In the first case, it is often an adjustive sublimation of hatred. In the others, it usually arises from a discomforting stereotype, some few characteristics of which are elaborated into the object-group of an antipathetic sentiment. The people constituting this more or less real group are subjected to behavior and thought that drain off the tendency of the stereotype in a fashion more or less satisfactory to the individual.[13] If the secondary tendency-system is

[13] The tendencies and the experience going to form the original stereotype are usually multiple. In the new, expanded integration the character-

still somewhat repugnant to the self, it is relatively easily rationalized by an appeal to some principle by which the refracted
hatred becomes transmuted into "love of humanity" and the resulting behavior the "combatting" of this or that "evil." [14] In
many cases, however, the secondary tendency-system is one
whose manifestations are socially acceptable and require no
"apology to the self." We might thus find, for example, coming
forth from a complex hostile to an elder brother a useful sublimation, at the expense only of the practical vanishment of recollection of the brother as a real, contemporary person. In all
these more complicated cases, however, the original object-
individual, and, for that matter, the object-individuals making up
the secondary group, have to be avoided or dealt with in primary
relations only in a highly unrealistic fashion. If either the original
or some of the secondary object-individuals are integrated into
any relatively simple situation with the subject-individual, the displacement may fail and the whole body of processes resolve into
those of a paranoid situation.

We have touched here on the processes subtending secondary
groups generally, and must look more closely at this conception
of situations including people-merely-believed-in. School entrance, with its new give-and-take with compeers and the urge to
accommodate oneself to the social situation, brings also a great
expansion of relevance of this mediate kind. The juveniles learn
of strange places and peoples. Formal instruction and informal
discussion teach, for example, of the Chinese, people who doubtless inhabit the alleged region of China. Reproductions of photo-
graphs and examples of handiwork give them fully as much reality as that previously awarded to the figures of the religious
mythology. There is a good deal of information on the peculiar
characteristics of the Chinese and of Chinese life. There is not
much emphasis on the essential humanity of these "foreigners,"

----

istics of the group might be *entirely identical* with those prehended in the
source of the original stereotype. In successful use of these dynamics, however, for obvious reasons *only some* features of the underlying stereotype
appear in the secondary-object-group; the original stereotype is thus more
easily kept submerged in that the prinicpal tendencies involved in it are
satisfied vicariously.

[14] See, in this connection, "Case B" (Chapter VII) in Harold D. Lasswell,
Psychopathology and Politics; Chicago: Univ. of Chicago Press, 1930.

nor on the resemblances of their life to ours. It may never have
occurred to the teacher that the Oriental is much more like than
unlike everyone else. In fact, she probably has some curious
superstitions about these yellow brethren that would come as an
unpleasant surprise to an anthropologist. The pupil combines the
information and misinformation—interpreted on the basis of his
previous experience—with a measure of personal fantasy. The
result is *a sentiment the object of which is an hypothetical (person or) group of people*, integrated around a tendency-system
that may be a derivative of curiosity, the general biological seeking of information. If he has continued thus far in a state of
approximate mental health, and has had no personal experience
with anyone allegedly Chinese, this will probably be the case. If
he has had personal experience, the sentiment will include data
on the known Chinaman, more or less generalized as universal
characteristics of the inhabitants of China. If, on the other hand,
he is the host of tendency-systems that are difficult to keep
suppressed, or that are dissociated, the sentiment about the
Chinese may come rather miraculously to exteriorize the unacceptable personal tendencies. They have been displaced upon
hypothetical Chinese very much as motives are projected on
others in primary relationships. The healthy juvenile, if he is not
too busy, and is interested, seeks information about the Chinese.
The morbid juvenile, in the case of whom "the Chinese" now
manifest a dissociated tendency, notices only the information
that supports the distortion.

    This utilization of a secondary group for the satisfaction of
tendencies denied direct representation in the self becomes a
major characteristic of many warped personalities. It has been a
prominent feature of our Western culture and is in many sections still *de rigueur*. The steps are fairly obvious from detractive
rationalization of the neighbors, through imputing to the underprivileged all the vices disowned by the self, to the most lurid
propaganda-fed prejudices about other national and related
political groups. In one section of America the colored folk are
used collectively as the embodiment of the more contemned of
personal tendencies of the whites. While a "fine sense of justice"
often exempts a particular colored person from the secondary
group sentiment against the Negro, this exemption is usually

uncertain, apt at any moment to fail, for the displacement of unpleasant tendencies is enfeebled by direct relationship with a
member of the carrier group. Moreover, there is generally a
strong tendency to encourage any sensually present representative of the group to behavior of the type demanded by the
sentiment, thus to insure the vicarious satisfactions of all the
tendencies involved. A colored boy has to be lynched, now and
then, for assaulting a white woman; this gives "them" a lesson
about restraining their ferocious sexual impulses—with which all
good girls are familiarized by their parents. The enormous number of mulattoes among us seems never to function as data pointing to noticeably ungoverned sexual tendencies on the part of the
whites.[15] In another section of America the Asiatic carries the
curse; elsewhere, the Catholics, the Jews, the Irish. The red In-
dians were once extremely bad people. The Germans are but beginning to convalesce from their duty in this connection.

These morbid utilizations of secondary group relations, particularly in maladjustment to unsatisfactory personal experience,
are the great danger of the juvenile era of personality growth.
Once well established, this living in considerable part through
situations including more or less wholly fantastic "theys" per-
petuates itself as the major pattern of the personality, and leads
to existence varying from complete futility to very real doing of
evil. The experience provided on the one hand by parental
milieu, and on the other in and out of the schoolroom, should
synthesize into tendencies and processes suited to the situations
which one is to meet in the real world. Unfortunately, the
schoolroom experience is provided in large measure by persons
engaged in such work because of their own difficulties and the
satisfaction that comes to their needs from the peculiar quasi-
parental role in which they stand with juveniles. Teachers by and
large provide a rich field for the study of mental processes none
too adjustive. Their method of selection, the processes making
up their own training, and the measures of reward held out for
them—all these have their place in the general problem.

---

[15] I presume that good people "know" that these mixed-bloods arose—and
continue to arise abundantly—from the seduction by colored girls of white
youths, generally after getting them drunk. I have never heard of such an
event, but lack of events has nothing to do with prejudice manipulation.

Education, in addition to its contribution to one's acquaintance with physical, social, institutional, and personal realities, should certainly be inspired to contribute to the successful elaboration of the juvenile personality. In the first place, the schoolroom experience to which the pupils are subjected should include sorts [of people] calculated to make use of the character factor, when present, and to assist the juvenile in finally bringing his conscience at least to an adolescent level on its path to adulthood.[16] Juveniles should scarcely be trained to outstrip the mores. It is not good for one to be too much in advance of the general cultural level before he has passed the adolescent period. On the other hand, we certainly should not hesitate to detach the young from archaic codes that are clearly destructive of successful living in the modern world.

And of all things, we should not adopt repressive measures to the juvenile's experiments in novel ethical formulations. When we really know why a thing is "wrong," we should be able to deal with it rationally and without emotional prohibition. If we "feel" that it is "wrong," wisdom might not be vouchsafed us, preventing our investigation with the aid of the youth. The stereotype of Christianity, I recall, is reported to have remarked on the advantages to accrue from "becoming as little children." Regardless of any reward in the Other World, it seems safe to assume that one is not harmed by attempting to understand the nature of one's moral ideas. If this procedure is started early enough, one is apt to lead an exemplary life and to be blessed with children who do one honor, and one's fellows good.

On the basis of our current knowledge, we may conclude that under a good educational system, the juvenile would have very little pondering about God, very little to do with dogmas, very little cause for cultivating ritualistic and penitential misuses of activity, and very little need for displacing on strangers and secondary groups a body of negative moral values and personally disapproved tendencies. On the other hand, he would have a very great interest in attempting to foresee injuries to himself and to others that might result from various adjustive and maladjustive social activities, and thus would learn to live and let

[16] Very important experiments in this field are appearing—for example, the North Shore Country Day School of Winnetka, Illinois.

live, excepting for excellent cause. This, I believe, is the way the juvenile socialization should go if it were directed solely to bringing the person to the threshold of adolescence with minimum warp and with maximum remaining ability to profit by civilizing influences. This particular phase of personality growth, the juvenile era, seems to me to be the most important one of all, for children cross its threshold with little but pseudo-religio-ethico-magical notions; the broadening influence of the juvenile period affects some greater or lesser modification of these notions; and this in turn determines inversely the limitations which forever after will be imposed upon the individual by processes referable to his so-called conscience or superego. Once adolescent, he can escape these limitations only by a careful readjustment on much the same lines as those suggested as the educational ideal for the juvenile; and adolescence is the time of dire effects from superego processes. We shall come presently to the matter of developing insight into them, by way of which the mistrained individual, with great effort, may sometimes be enabled to rid himself of his "old man of the sea."

Before leaving this era, it might be well to note that there are occasional successful growths of personality through the juvenile era, despite the prevailing state of our culture. Some people come to preadolescence with well-integrated personalities. Some fewer proceed finally to the psychobiological status of adult.[17] Also, quite a proportion of people who might, from all that has been presented thus far, be expected to fail miserably, do in fact proceed to a very considerable measure of success in living in our culture, however immature their personalities may seem to the psychobiologist, and however much greater their success might have been had they not encountered insuperable evil influences

---

[17] It is perhaps unfortunate that we cannot recruit our experts in the solution of juvenile and other educational problems from this class. It seems that even among psychiatrists dealing with juveniles there is not always to be found insight that has come as a by-product of personal success in this era. The psychoanalytic movement, to which we have every reason to refer a great part of our effective insight into personality problems, for a long time clung to the doctrine of a "latency period," a mythology only beginning to dissolve in the recent work on the "analysis of the ego." Childhood situations and sexual problems appearing in adolescence are generally better understood than are situations pertaining to authority and the dissociations and displacements connected with conflict, guilt, and anxiety processes.

in the course of growth. Consideration of this group brings us to a manifestation of the character factor that is potent in preservation of personality in the face of great handicaps. I refer here to the *idealization of the self as the person one shall presently come to be*, the formulation within awareness of an intended role from increasingly realistic prehensions of personal abilities and limitations. While a great many children on the threshold of the juvenile era have esteemed fantasies as to their role when grown up, these "ambitions" vary greatly in origin, structure, and durability under adversity. The idealization under discussion is not apt to appear in verbal formulation of a particularized goal but rather in an implicit assurance of ultimate worthy achievement that colors thoughts about the self and other selves, and emphasizes the future as prepotent over current disappointments and misfortunes. Many situational factors that would otherwise warp the growth are so reduced in relevance by this integration including future opportunity that the personality growth is in large measure protected. Needless to say, this idealization cannot work miracles, but, acting as a powerful tendency-system, it does create situations that under otherwise identical personal circumstances would not occur.

CHAPTER
VI
——————

Preadolescence

PHENOMENA related to the maturation of the somatic apparatus biologically referable to procreation mark the passing of the juvenile era and the arrival of an epoch of profound revaluations and redefinitions of the self and the world. Unlike earlier augmentations to personality, the course of this development may be followed without great dependence on inferences, for the subject-individual is better equipped for the communication of his conscious experience. He has incorporated into his social activity many of the cultural patterns of his language, and approximated much of the conventional ideology of the self. Again, there is developing a tendency-system that requires *personal interaction* of a peculiarly intimate sort, increasing the relevance of other people in the total situations through which he will thenceforth progress. A great impetus is given to the *consensual validation* of his behavior and thought, and all that is subsumed in adaptive culture tends rapidly to become significant. The study of personal dynamics is thus considerably facilitated in adolescence.

The adolescent is concerned with achieving a dependable body of relationships of his personality with certain highly relevant others who make up a series of total situations. Objectively considered, he is called upon to effect a synthesis of his own individuality into a series of more complex situations, the vector sum of which—by the end of adolescence—comes to be the social whole. The measure of success in this individual-social synthesis is established by two factors: the personality as the resultant of innate potentialities and experience in the earlier stages of development, dynamically coupled with the opportunities presented by the environing personal milieu. Success produces adult personalities, fully competent in group life in the given culture complex. Failure continues the personality in a more or less unsocialized living, often tending *against* the group. The importance of this epoch for consideration from any of the humanistic viewpoints applied to subject-individuals in any culture complex would be difficult to exaggerate. Adolescence in our branch of the Western civilization is of extreme significance, both for the psychopathology of the individual and for the more general considerations embodied in the social sciences.

The culture complex within which the personality has to reach its maturity must always focus in adolescence, but the importance of adolescence for the welfare of the individual varies widely among these complexes. Cultures may be said to differ in a genetic sense in much the same way as do personalities. Some insight into the problems of the individual at each genetic level may be derived from considering civilizations as marked by related levels of elaboration. Just as the personality is definable as a relatively enduring configuration of the tendency-systems embodied in the individual, so culture complexes have their individual "complexion" which is not only relatively enduring, but also dynamically characterized, a vector addition. As the individual may be brought to grow without inclusion of some major tendency-system within his self-conscious system, so too a culture may develop with no adaptations directly subserving certain tendency-systems in its carriers, its people. Personal manifestation of these tendency-systems for which adaptive culture is lacking falls in the region of the mysterious, giving rise to a body of mores, and to a theocratic caste concerned with the elaboration and administration of a religion. If now we classify cultures on the basis of stages of personality growth—thereby attempting a genetic anthropology—the suggestion appears that, in several aspects at least, our offshoot of Western culture is an *early juvenile culture* in rather active elaboration, such that in some few urban communities it is more advanced, and in some few rural communities it is at the level of late childhood. In the latter, it has retrogressed somewhat from its general level at the time of translation from Europe.

There is an hierarchy of values in the life of man, full perspective on which can scarcely be obtained, but some ordering of which can be made from this sort of comparison of individuals and cultures. Infancy demands security on the level of air, food, warmth, and activity. The major requirements are physico-chemical. The values of a culture on this level may be called *economic*. All else is referable to sleep, the condition transcending consciousness, and may be expected to appear only in processes relatively little influenced by the requirement of consensual validity. Dreams and fantasies, implicit activity tending to resolve situations integrated by less evolved tendency-systems, and impulsive acts, rituals, and the like are referred to the transcendental regions guaranteed by the primitive dependency relations to the mothering one, coupled with the resumptions of relatively complete satisfactions in sleep. In other words, adaptive culture of the infantile type ends with providing for the securities demanded by the infant; all other situations are integrated with inclusions from a religious culture. Authority relationships will be absolute. Group activities will be established on patterns sanctioned by the particular theocratic authorities. Preadolescent, adolescent, and adult intimacies and coöperations —including the sexual—will be hedged about with taboos and rituals elaborated theocratically and supervised under threat of divine intervention to punish violations. While the adaptive culture may be included in the field of theocratic authority, in this field—and in this field only—individual freedom of thought and action will tend to become conspicuous, and fortunate innovations will be more and more sought after, as the culture-complex manifests growth.

There would presently appear additions to the adaptive culture of the general pattern of facilitations for the satisfaction of the tendencies to exercise the muscular and the sensory abilities. Thus there will be differentiated, from the general region of the transcendental, the group of values that we may term the *esthetic*. Games, contests in physical skill, and later spectacles will tend gradually to escape from theocratic supervision to a secular status. Decoration, the creation of beauty, first directed toward sacred objects, will gradually spread over the commonplace. Personal beauty will become a matter for contemplation and even for cultivation.

Curiosity tendencies would next tend to escape from the

region of the theocratically absolute, the religious culture. New values would thus be added, for which we may well use Edouard Spranger's term, the *theoretic*. It will now be proper to investigate and undertake to formulate the realities of the economic (physiochemical) and the esthetic world, excepting that this quest must not invade the province of religion, and, in particular, that of the nature of man himself. The investigation of the physical construction of the human body may be expected to come very late in this progress, excepting in cannibalistic societies. In the latter, the divinity will hedge only the members of the tribe itself. In others, we may expect that strange incuriosity in the face of the obvious that reflects the intervention of absolute taboos. It will continue to cover the field of group life— juvenile, preadolescent, adolescent, and adult—which will be operated by ritual and rigid dogmas.

There would follow culture-complexes in which adaptive culture provides for the sociality tendencies that we have studied in the juvenile era. The added values may be called the *social*. The religious culture will now be of the type of current nationalism, with varying degrees of divine sanctions. Patriotic and various other dogmas will control interpersonal relationships in the theocratically interpreted interest of God, the Nation, or the Greater Number.

Provisions next appear in the adaptive culture for primary group solidarity on the basis of the tendencies shortly to be discussed as isophilic. The manipulation of other concrete people becomes more or less free from transcendental restraints. The added values may be called the *political*. Only the relations of the two sexes, including manifestations of the sexual tendencies, will continue to be under theocratic supervision. In the process of growth beyond this stage, we may regard the added values as the *humanistic*. Beyond this, we may envisage a culture elaboration in which the religious is completely replaced by the adaptive. The new values in this hypothetic complex we may call the *anthropognostic* (from the Greek *man*, plus *understanding*).

It is important to note that at each subordinate level religious values must fill the gap between the personality equipment and the adaptive culture, and that the young must be given special instruction in the formal religious culture, lest evolving tendencies for which satisfaction is not available flow over into individual initiative or coöperative behavior dangerous to the carrier or the group. This teaching of the taboos and dogmas becomes more and more urgent as the culture increases in elaboration, for each major step endangers the province of the theocratic authority, and facilitates the expansion of adaptive in contradistinction to religious culture. It is not solely the privilege of the ruling class that resists this expansion. It seems to be natural to award reverence in some close relation to reputed endurance, and to distrust the new and the strange. A dogma reputed to have come down unchanged through the centuries carries with it a certain accumulation of approvals from succeeding generations that have done obeisance before it, and to question it is tantamount to claiming superiority to the great men of the past. Moreover, those who have achieved a measure of generally admitted success in the struggle for group accommodation and contentment in the religion-ridden culture are tired enough and old enough by the time that they have reached a position of authority, to be thoroughly conservative in their attitude toward innovation. If also they are parents, they have enough domestic troubles to render them very sensitive to "young upstarts." A theocracy is generally a gerontocracy, and all old men know that youth is very rash.

Each adolescent in our culture ceases for a while this learning of religious culture and begins an emancipation from the more archaic patterns. While the fate of the experimentation that ensues is all but foreordained, it represents each individual's attempt to add to the culture adaptive of man to man. The individual between the appearance of the intimacy-urge and that of the genital sex drives has a unique opportunity for this sort of achievement. The "other fellow" now means a great deal to one, and one has not yet encountered the knottiest of interpersonal problems. The epoch of adolescence seems to me to be of extreme interest both for psychopathology and for the social sciences generally, in so far as the latter make real their pertinence to human behavior and thought. There are about us innumerable data of this kind, every one a unique experiment. The adolescent personality is in most respects decidedly more complex at its midpoint than is the adult. I shall make no more attempt to present the wealth of processes actually to be encountered in adolescents, than have I the innumerable more or less significant experiences that individuals undergo in the preceding eras of development. I must restrict myself to discussing only those aspects of the epoch that stand in most conspicuous relation to the failures of personality growth, *whether the result of personality warp in preceding stages of development or the limitation imposed by the content of adaptive culture available to the adolescent.* Moreover, being one of those living in and within the culture, I can offer but little more than suggestions regarding this second group of factors which assumes such great relevance in the adolescent epoch, the elucidation of which, however, must await comparative studies in personality growth.

I shall systemize the presentation by dividing the epoch into three phases—namely, preadolescence, from the appearance of an urge to true interpersonal intimacy through physiological puberty; midadolescence, from the appearance of sexual desire tending to integrate a situation of interpersonal intimacy with a representative of the other sex; and late adolescence, from the patterning of sexual behavior to the consummation of adulthood. I shall simplify the consideration by disregarding the somewhat disparate course of personality growth in girls, the age-chronology and events of which are not closely parallel with those in the boy under our culture.[1] Before proceeding, I must comment on an unfortunate usage in regard to preadolescence, one perhaps in a measure the result of psychoanalytic generalizations. We frequently encounter references to this phase as "the homosexual stage" either of "libido development" or of personality. *Isophilic* [2]

---

[1] In Chapter VIII, an attempt is made to remedy the one-sided presentation by a discussion of female adolescence. The ontogenetic psychobiology of woman is not as well understood as is that of man. In all cultures there are to be found significant differences. I venture some distance in delineation of man by reason of acquaintance with pathological material. Comparative studies, by which checks may be imposed on the general and the specific in adolescent personality evolution, and particularly on the growth of sexual tendencies—to which I largely devote Chapter VII—are in their infancy. There is but another manifestation of the juvenile character of our culture: the laboratory of the world is open to us, but we are constrained to maintain our caste superiority, a "trait" at its height just before the adolescent upheaval in the individual.

[2] Literally, "to like equal(s)." Discussion of the nomenclature of sexuality, erogeny, and intimacy in general is postponed to the next chapter.

personal interests characterize preadolescence; homoerotic tendencies may be or become an important tributary of these interests; and in the latter case, homosexual behavior and thought may be an outcome. Sexual, I urge, pertains to the genital apparatus, its type of sentience, and activities directly pertaining to it. Any wider use leads to gross oversimplifications, contradictions, or both. It has been amply demonstrated that one can expand the concept of sexuality to the point at which it engulfs the individual and the culture. In a civilization maladaptive to the sexual motivations, there is generally sufficient personal frustration in this field to energize a rich sexual fantasy with almost any symbols. Evolution of the culture adaptive to sex does not seem, however, to be best facilitated by mistaking everything else for sexual values.[3]

The boy enters into the epoch of adolescence at the time that he first experiences tendencies making for intimate relations with some one or two other boys of similar age.[4] Some one particular person becomes of peculiarly distinguished interest, a new type of sentiment is developed, and there is a new development within the sentiment of self. It is no longer enough that the other one contribute reflections favorable to one's self-esteem. It becomes more important to contribute to the self-esteem of the other, and one's own pleasure becomes secondary to the satisfaction at causing pleasure to the friend. There is an augmented tendency to identification with favorable attributes of the other boy. The two, who are never so happy as when they are together, unwittingly but assiduously cultivate each other's characteristics, develop identical or complementary interests, and so alter their social values that they come to be in more or less complete

3 This notwithstanding, I would venture that it is to Freud's earlier writings, in which "the ego" was certainly all but overlooked, that we owe not only the initiation of creative thought in revaluing sexual attitudes and prejudices, but in very fact the great progress in realization of psychopathology, the social sciences, and the normative arts. The change was coming before Freud—but it had been coming a very long time before Freud. And the inertia it was to encounter is by no manner of means to be charged against Freud's so-called pan-sexualism.

4 We shall first consider the case of the boy who, having come through the juvenile era without serious personality warp, finds himself with access to other boys of comparable age, and with free time to spend with them. We shall presently consider the case of the boy who by reason of isolated home, or similarly, is cut off from easy access during the preadolescent development.

agreement one with the other. Peculiarities of the home life of the one tend to lose their further effectiveness because they fall into unfavorable comparison with similar factors in the home life of the other. Mutual "suggestion" becomes potent. In other words, the two personalities tend to become closely knit to each other.

The individual up to this time may have lived and participated in a society of compeers in which he had very few playmates excepting girls. The parental influences may have coöperated to make him much nearer the average behavior type of a girl than of a boy. But with the coming of preadolescence his interest swings inevitably toward an individual of his own sex. He is not happy unless he has a boy with whom to associate, and if none but girls are available he will attach himself to the one of the girls who deviates to the greatest extent toward a masculine habit of life. In general, however, his former liking or indifference for girls is now converted into an active antagonistic feeling, such that almost any boy does much better as a playmate than the previously most esteemed girl. If he is forced by circumstance to play with the tomboy, he demands of her a parallel negative feeling toward other girls, and a more or less active shunning of their participation in play.

The close personal nature of the new interest transmutes the juvenile ideals to a new center in *people as intimates*. Abstract groups now require personal embodiments. Concrete groups lose the differentiation of their members into family and similar classifications. There is not a loss of personal differentiation; Tom is still a carrier of values different from those of Dick. But the values that remain are values functioning with increasing directness. The boys of the school class become much more a *significant unity* than their individual differentiation would seem to justify. Their individual definitions begin to be recast in terms of the school class. Family prestige, trappings of wealth, the deference of teacher to parental caste—all these sink from attention in the distribution of personal valuation. The widest "social distance" between two families may be transcended in the unity of the boy and his chum. If extrinsic factors tend to separate the two, the unit tends to escape from this pressure. When factors intrinsic in the two personalities are opposed in tendency, the influence of the group surrounding the chums is often more potent than that of the formative agencies behind the discrepancies.

Each two-group exteriorizes its new bipartite personality as a body of behavior nucleated in a conscious formulation of an idealized object of intimacy. The drive for concrete representation usually centers this ideal in the person of some member of the immediate environment, often a particularly well-equipped boy in the same school class or neighborhood. The embodiment of the ideal, however, is subject to a demand for performance. It is not enough for the preadolescent that this or that attribute is hypostatized; it must be concretely demonstrated. Given a satisfactory person, the two-group, without loss of its intimate interpersonal relation, finds new outlet for the intimacy urge in a more complex relationship of its members with the third boy approximating their new ideals. The problem of personal loyalty in intimate relations arises. The affectional bonds of the new boy generally already include a fourth—his chum. A four-part arrangement of intimacy is even more of a problem. Moreover, the new boy is peculiarly admirable, not only to the original two-group, and to his chum, but in all likelihood to other boys in the environment. The complexity of individual integrations rapidly resolves itself into membership in a larger group made up of two-groups focused in the leader. The chums now take comparable or complementary parts in the activity of a social unit, the more or less organized *gang*, the first autonomous societal process into and within which the boys' personalities are integrated as part of a whole.

Secondary group accidentals, which may have all but overshadowed the juvenile so that his self-consciousness centered largely in himself as embodying a family or heroic myth in competition with other complex representations, are sloughed off in these intimacy integrations of preadolescence. But the primary differentials of the boy's personality remain in varied measures conspicuous. The warp of his personality from the average may be so great that he cannot find anyone of comparable age with whom he can establish chumship. Or his "inner" difficulties, concealed by juvenile "social" devices, come to the front in the processes of intimacy and arouse such negative attitudes in the chum as to destroy intimacy. He proceeds a little way and with-draws to try with some other boy. He may or may not have ultimate fortune.

So, too, in the gang organization, some of the chums, mea-surably successful as a two-group, discover in the larger associa-tion demands for coöperation to which one or both cannot accede. They disintegrate the two-group from the larger unit, or the two-group itself is disintegrated and new chums sought. The personality functions in the gang as it has grown to function. If the boy is psychopathic, his availability for socialization is about nil, for an emphatic *realization* of the group is required. If he has an intense antagonism toward his father, displaced on all figures of authority, the gang leader may become its object, and the outcome is then a vector sum of the personality tendencies called into action on both sides.

Both the two-group and the gang show "superpersonal" re-ality in that the individuals concerned manifest the incorporation into their personalities as potent values of *behavior patterns and standards satisfactory to the group.* The prime motive of the individual is no longer the furthering of individualized causes by all manner of techniques, but is the securing of direct satisfac-tions in furthering the group causes, often in behavior divergent from the preexisting personal patterns. Devotion, allegiance, and loyalty to one's group and the group-members become a more or less powerful system of tendencies in the personality. This new tendency-system, the maturation of which initiates pre-adolescence, and the satisfaction of which requires interpersonal intimacy, is in a nuclear fashion the basis of social processes. Preadolescents present to the student a social world in miniature —an isophilic world, it is true, but one in which rudimentary in-stances of almost everything social may be found.

The significance of two-group and gang for the growth of personality is very great. *Every individual tendency that meets with group acceptance is powerfully reinforced.* Every conflict brought by a member into the intimate interchange of preado-lescent socialization tends thereon to a resolution. One or another element of the conflict may be powerfully reinforced. The op-posing tendency, too, may be discharged by group action, may be sublimated as a result of new social values cooperative with a change in the dynamic balance, or may be developed by new experience toward a rational integration free from conflict. There are conflicts that bar the carrier from the group, and conflicts the group resolution of which were perhaps better unresolved, but, regardless of a leveling of personality values toward an average, the gang sociality develops its members in the general direction of increased mental health. And the nearer the preadolescent approximated to healthy personality growth up to this era, the less of mediocre stereotyping he is apt to undergo in the new relationships.

Personalities tend in one sense to confluence in the intimate group. The attributes of the chum that are integrated into the total situation of the boy function vicariously for a time, but often reappear as modified attributes dynamically copied into the boy. But there are many personality differentials that are not thus unified, and interpersonal conflict situations are by no means a rarity between chums and between gang members. Juveniles do not enter into intimate give-and-take with instant success. Preadolescents find plenty of chance for manifesting "human nature." Violations of personal "property right," rivalries in all fields, resistances to manipulation for the "common good"—especially when it is diametrically contrary to one's wishes—struggles for personal supremacy, for relative approval, likes and dislikes released by fatigue or boredom, sadistic aggressions—all these and many another disintegrative force have to be vanquished by the intimacy-need, frequently with the skillful aid of the leader. Internecine motivation has to be avoided, and the processes that serve in this connection run the gamut from coercion, rigid disciplinary steps, administration of more or less primitive justice, to skilled accommodation of divergent tendencies into *ways of mutual functioning that will work.* The creation of competitive or actual combat situations with other groups is useful in the discharge of tensions among the members, in increasing the group solidarity by augmenting its prestige, and in organizing the leadership. Under a skilled hand, the preadolescent gang may develop astonishing organization, with graded duties, responsibilities, powers and prerogatives, rituals, creeds, and even *magnae chartae.*

A high degree of actual organization, however, whether it be in part explicit in stabilized, almost institutionalized, forms, or instead merely implicit in the form of a "strong" leadership, can occur only in groups composed of members manifesting a high degree of intimacy. In other words, the freedom of integrating situations energized by the new interpersonal drive is the measure of gang organization. Powerful tendencies conflicting with the interpersonal drive weaken or suspend its manifestation. The "weak" or low-order gang is made up of individuals who are securing some measure of satisfaction for the intimacy drive without much "pooling of personality," without their integration into a powerful interpersonal situation with strong group loyalty and powerful group opinion. Some of these boys are not much warped, and effect intimacy in the two-group, but the larger integrations are too feebly motivated to weld the chums into more than a shifting allegiance to the gang spirit. The case of the boy incapable of even two-group intimacy is most unfortunate; he is denied an important factor in the growth of his personality. If he participates in group activities it is generally as one of an aggregation, like the class performances in the last years of the juvenile era, not as a member of an autonomous social unit.

A living of this first stage of adolescence is necessary for the socialization of the personality, particularly in our culture. The preadolescent social organization, growing *in medias res* of the transition phenomena which escape solution in the home and the school, even if its behavior is hard on property and even persons, is always an experiment in culture adaptive to the features of the environing situation that impinge on the members. Unfortunate boys in unfortunate situations may come to unfortunate solutions; on occasion a "bad" gang may suborn a "good" boy unfortunately exposed to its influences. If this occurs, it may be charged off somewhat to deficiency in the victim's character-factor, and still more to poor management on the part of relevant adults. By and large, the chum and gang phenomenon must be recognized as one of our most hopeful tools.[5]

[5] There are several studies on this subject that should be pursued by the student: W. R. Boorman, *Developing Personality in Boys;* New York: Macmillan, 1929; Paul H. Furfey, *The Gang Age;* New York: Macmillan, 1926; H. W. Gibson, *Boyology;* New York: Assn. Press, 1916; William Healy, *Mental Conflicts and Misconduct;* Boston: Little, Brown, 1917; L. A. Pechstein and A. L. McGregor, *Psychology of the Junior High School*

The initiation of preadolescence is accomplished by a drive making for situations of intimacy. Maturation of the body causes this to be followed more or less closely by the appearance of definitely sexual tendencies. What was a powerful drive before is now greatly augmented. Because of the chum and gang solidarity, the community, sympathy, and contagion of ideals and interests, and because of the superpersonal power of the social unit for the abolition of more feeble inhibitory tendencies, the real chums and the more closely-knit gangs begin to manifest processes of a decidedly sexual character. Some of the boys become pubescent before others; some of them discover the pleasure of genital manipulation sooner than others; none of them can very well escape the knowledge as soon as experience comes to them that the genitals constitute a remarkably pleasure-giving part of the anatomy. Fantasies, fables, and actual facts about the genitals become common property, and individual and collective genital manipulation, once begun, is apt to spread rather rapidly among the members. Coöperative or mutual sexual behavior is quite frequently an important part of the gang life. So important is this factor that in the boy in whom powerful inhibitions as to the genital region have been inculcated, his prudishness may destroy the possibility of his further growth with the gang.

A curious cadre of socialization in connection with sexual freedom appears in gangs themselves. Sometimes individuals who are powerfully inhibited in the genital field, and who therefore cannot enter into the communal sexual play, are able to maintain, because of their other abilities (socially available traits), a measure of intimate association in the gang notwithstanding the "distance" created by their nonparticipation in the more definitely sexual gang behavior. The boy who is too firmly inhibited

Pupil; Boston: Houghton Mifflin, 1924; J. J. B. Morgan, *The Psychology of the Unadjusted School Child;* New York: Macmillan, 1924; M. V. O'Shea, *Social Development and Education;* Boston: Houghton Mifflin, 1909; I. A. Puffer, *The Boy and His Gang;* Boston: Houghton Mifflin, 1912; Clifford R. Shaw, *The Jack-Roller;* Chicago: Univ. of Chicago Press, 1930; John Slawson, *The Delinquent Boy;* Boston: Badger, 1926; W. I. Thomas, *The Unadjusted Girl;* Boston: Little, Brown, 1924; W. I. Thomas and D. S. Thomas, *The Child in America;* New York: Knopf, 1928; Fred M. Thrasher, *The Gang; A Study of 1,313 Gangs in Chicago;* Chicago: Univ. of Chicago Press, 1927; Miriam Van Waters, *Youth in Conflict;* New York: Republic Pub. Co., 1925.

to coöperate in communal sexual behavior, yet is able to maintain sufficient status in a high-order gang by reason of athletic or other abilities, is in need of a strong character factor. Lacking this, the drive of sex and the drive of the gang toward sexual behavior push him to degrees of compliance at the verbal level at least, without his being able to rectify his conflict. This compromise may be the beginning in the gang of clear-cut maladjustive proceedings in regard to sex which are to color their subsequent life. On the other hand, feeble and poorly constructed inhibitions tend to disappear in the socialized sex behavior of the gang. This comes about both because of the power of social forces in altering individual personalities subjected to them and also because of the great power incorporated in the sex drives. Many boys, who, if they were to go on without enfeeblement of their inhibitions and without developing rationalized escapes for their impulses, would eventuate in inadaptability for later marital adjustment, if not in severe mental illness, find in the superpersonal power of the gang society a real curative influence.

In the case of boys who are not specially endowed with attributes available at the gang level, and whose inhibitions as to sexual play resist these impulses, there generally results a rapid exclusion from any gang thus characterized, with accessory behavior calculated to make them regard themselves as "outsiders." These outsiders are sometimes fortunate in finding a number of the comparably inhibited, who none the less have considerable effective social urge, and who—barring the common sexual behavior—can engage in gang activity. They thus find a "suitable" gang and are safely incorporated into its community of interest and behavior. Their "suitable" gang is probably much less firmly knit than was the one from which they were excluded. In gangs inhibited as to community sexual behavior, the sexual tendencies may still function as a powerful integrating influence in energizing rituals, "secret" signs and acts, and the like.

There is a belief traditional among some students of human nature to the effect that these manifestations of gang life are deleterious. One finds among some psychiatrists a tacit if not an expressed belief that gang cultivation of sexual pleasures is most unfortunate. Appropriately enough, such students rarely discover that mutual masturbation often becomes a competitive game and that frank homosexual procedures are by no means uncommon in gangs. I have had opportunity to study one community in regard to the alleged evil consequences of these factors and can contribute something perhaps a little more than prejudice to the matter of gang "sexuality." In this community—a fair-sized village of the Middle East—a large number of the early adolescents participated in overt homosexual activities during the gang age. Most of them progressed thereafter without let or hindrance to the customary heteroerotic interest in later adolescence. Some of the few boys in this community who were excluded from the gangs as a result of their powerful inhibitions, who missed participation in community homosexual play, did not progress to satisfactory heterosexual development. Judged by objective showing, there resulted a proportion of maladjustive sexual processes per capita very much greater in the nongang boys than in the gang alumni.[6] The experience of crude community sexual activity, such as that often occurring in groups the potent leadership of which is exercised by boys comparatively free from personality warp, has not, in any case in my experience, seemed to be other than a healthy influence in the development of personality—this notwithstanding learned prejudice to the contrary. We shall come later in this chapter to consider the distortions of personality, particularly as to the growth of socialized erogeny and sexuality, that are the usual outcome of gang exclusion or the preadolescent participation in mere aggregations of other badly warped boys.

Dissertations about adolescence inform one that puberty ushers in very rapid and elaborate changes in the soma; that with this goes a singular expansion of the mental life; that peculiarities of adolescence are explainable by the combination of overrapid physical growth and overrapid increase in mental scope—all of which may be true, but is not the whole story. Preadolescence seems always to begin some time before the puberty changes have made their appearance and continues to a time well past this somatological landmark, how far past being varied among individuals. Sooner or later, perhaps many months after puberty, there comes a rather rapid change in the character of impulses in

---

[6] In considering these data in connection with the discussion making up the next chapter, it may be noted that *of some actively homosexual individuals from this community*, while I have good reason for believing *some came from both groups*, those that have led lives *obviously maladjustive* in regard to homoerotic tendencies are of nongang origin.

the growing boy, in the sense that he experiences an increase in fantasy about adult folk and a marked diminution in the satisfaction derived from his chum and the gang attachments. Hero worship on a new level begins to displace the reality of the gang and its standards. The chum is no longer as satisfactory as are fantastic individuals built up by contemplating certain late adolescent or adult personalities in the environment or in the literature—which has now become of some importance. The isophilic, or actually homosexual, socialization loses its importance, and instead it becomes important that one should adapt oneself to the pattern of heteroerotic interests manifested by the hero. It begins to be important to be thought by others to have intimate association with some certain girl. Woman, who had previously been anything from a matter of indifference to a matter of actual hostility, is now elevated into a certain quasi-importance. The impulses making for interest in securing the esteem and submission of the girl grow to be prime causes of behavior.[7] The initial objects of this interest are often girls chronologically much nearer adult than is the boy—sometimes the older sister of a friend. Fairly young schoolteachers may serve, or even the young mother of another schoolboy. The transition from this admiration of the more mature woman to girls of the boy's age-group is usually quite prompt, often being assisted by the object of the "puppy love."

The variation in age-chronology of the change from the isophilic sociality toward interest in girls is marked.[8] This implies

[7] For reasons which need not now detain us, I consider that each individual shows, at the appropriate stage of development, a definite *heteroerotic* drive. I do not share the opinion popular among alleged authorities on "homosexuality" to the effect that there can be an innately determined absence of the heteroerotic drive, or an inborn obligate "homosexuality." Any effective insight into certain of the grave distortions of life in our civilization requires that postnatal experience be given great weight in explaining the failure of many to manifest heterosexual activity, and discounts heavily the hereditary factors postulated by many authorities. We will recur to this subject in the next chapter.

[8] Paul H. Furfey has worked out a scale for determining what he calls the *developmental age*, a coefficient intimately related to the growth under discussion. See "Some Preliminary Results on the Nature of Developmental Age," *School and Society* (1926) 23:183–184; *The Measurement of Developmental Age;* Washington: Catholic Educational Press, 1927; "Developmental Age," *Amer. J. Psychiatry* (1928) 85:149–157.

a measurable type of maturity quite distinct from either growth in intelligence or gross body growth. The chronology of the stages in developmental age is rather widely varied, rate of development in this sense being probably a complex function. The developmental age is a highly significant factor in socialization and group formation, perhaps our best objectively determinable clue as to the individual in that connection. In each gang, there may be one or more boys in whom the developmental processes do not parallel in speed the average, but instead lag behind. These boys are not "ready" for the change to heteroerotic interests when it makes its appearance in their particular gang, and unless they have the good fortune of finding others similarly retarded with whom to fraternize, they are forced by the social pressure of the gang to retire from group life, to adopt group life in a chronologically younger gang, or to engage in spurious heterosexual gestures. In the last mentioned case, since the preadolescent attitude toward women is not mere indifference but includes also some measure of negative feeling, the gestures toward the girl are prone to yield results not at all encouraging to continued effort, and perhaps quite unfortunate to one's self-esteem. In the case of these boys, the factors next to be discussed are of peculiar moment.

To every adolescent on the threshold of heteroerotic interest, there apply potent factors derived from the previous experience with members of the other sex, adult, adolescent, and juvenile. In boys, the mother's influence is of incalculably great importance. Some phases of this matter have already concerned us. Let us consider in particular the preadolescent situation of the boy who has been tied to the mother as a substitute for her disappointment with her mate. A classical source for the deviation under discussion is the somewhat homoerotic divorcee who has one child, a son, and who secures her principal pleasure in life from discussing with other unhappy women the fatuous character of men, from whose unholy embrace she has succeeded in extricating herself. In these boys, often reared in almost exclusively feminine environment and sometimes tediously instructed as to the general worthlessness of the male, with the coming of preadolescence and its negative feeling-tones regarding the other sex, there is very much the same phenomenology as in other boys. When, however, their compeers progress to the threshold of midadolescence, these boys begin to diverge from the average. If their experience has not delayed the process of physiological maturation—their developmental age is equivalent to that of the other boys—the heteroerotic drives appear at the same time, but the initial impulses making for interest in older women are generally continued, often accentuated by disappointments in girls. The "puppy-love" phenomena meet either with direct rebuff by the amusement of the love-object, or, when encouraged by a pathological woman, carry but little satisfaction, and fade from a position of central importance. If the heteroerotic impulses focus on a frankly incestuous object, the mother or an aunt, then either the object finally recoils when unable longer to deceive herself as to the nature of the impulse, or a woefully maladjustive life is initiated for the boy.

Let us digress to consider the nature of the rebuff secured from girls by boys not actually inspired by erotic interest, but activated toward the other sex by social pressure. In some cases, for reasons that should be evident, the boy chooses for his object the most masculine of the girls. He proceeds toward her conquest. Being less fully masculine than his compeers, he none the less uses exaggerated (because consciously adopted and fraudulent) aggressiveness. Regardless of the more or less ubiquitous interest of girls of this age in boys, this girl is "put on her mettle," and in all likelihood roundly defeats the boy, even in a physical encounter, without due regard for spectators. In other cases, armed with experience of innumerable innuendoes about "bad girls" from the mother, the boy proceeds to the acquaintance of a girl conspicuous by her excessive "goodness." Thereafter, an escape from boredom means a retreat from heterosexual efforts. In yet other cases, he proceeds, guided by an intuition of the situation, toward an apparently really suitable girl, actually one motivated by homoerotic interest in other girls and the corresponding aversion for boy society. She encourages his attentions, for they increase her prestige among girls—they satisfy status-seeking—but, under cover of an apparent acquiescence, she makes him the object of sadistic aggressions replete with feminine finesse, so that he is baffled, hurt, and taught to think twice before again exposing himself to any woman.

If the individual concerned in this inadequately motivated effort to conform to the gang pressure is one who has already suffered serious genital or sexual inhibitions, from which he has made but a partial escape through the instrumentality of the gang life, these rebuffs are of no small moment in the personality growth. There is some considerable body of data that suggests that even the development of somatic factors is retarded in many cases by the influence of experiential factors of the type of these genital and sexual inhibitions. We therefore expect and find a considerable number of boys who suffer great damage as they progress rather belatedly to the threshold of midadolescence; in fact, they constitute a large proportion among schizophrenic males.

One unfortunate course that appears as preadolescent maladjustment to a persistent (unresolved) sexual situation of any sort is a recourse to compensatory daydreaming. Many of the individuals who have not succeeded in stumbling along into heteroerotic interests begin the development of sexual fantasies. This is peculiarly detrimental not alone because it discharges the most important group of impulses making for interpersonal intimacy, but because it is profoundly enfeebling to the dreamer's self-regard. Fantasy was a satisfactory tool in childhood. If one could not find playmates one was able to do fairly well by fantasying them. While one did not secure the experience that one should have had, still one could get on and presently when opportunity appeared the somewhat warped personality could slowly be brought into a fair degree of approximation to the average. Even during preadolescence many lone individuals derive enough from constructive fantasy to carry them on into something like typical, even though belated, development. But fantasy can but very rarely take the place of realities for the boy on the threshold of midadolescence; there are few who have experience that can be thus worked over. Compensatory fantasy to drain off the frankly sexual motivations has to be elaborate and usually associated with autosexual procedures of some kind. Very elaborate fantasy cannot be carried on in intimate contact with others. Innumerable discrepancies and points of conflict arise between the inner processes and the events having external personal reference. People are apt to interrogate one about how things are going, and this carries with it the question of how much of one's fantasy one can "get away with." The boy engaged in sexual daydreaming is easily embarrassed by such questions, and so comes to avoid people who might ask questions. He tends to seclude himself, thereby further reducing the already small chances of fortunate experience. His loneliness increases the necessity for fantasy, and there is thus created a vicious circle, accentuated by a growing consciousness of inadequacy, guilt, and shame. Usually he has good cause for believing himself suspected of masturbation, and frequently that he shows signs of its "ravages."

The character of the fantasies developed at this time often pertains to the other sex. I might perhaps best picture the course of these events by referring to a series that is rather common in the history of those later to become schizophrenic. The boy has not been able to go on as have his compeers in the pursuit of the heterosexual object. He compensates for his failure by fantasy and masturbation. He finds one day on leaving the movies that he has "fallen in love" with the heroine. To fall in love with an unknown woman whose picture one sees on the silver screen is decidedly a fantastic business. But the student must not overlook the very real, unfantastic force of this situation. These boys become desperately in love, more desperately than it is possible to be in love with a real person. For in this fantastic love affair there are no rebuffs, one is not required to accommodate oneself to another, there are no unpleasant disillusionments, one can plunge into the business of "loving," can outdo his more realistic fellows, can exceed anything to be found in the cold reality on earth. The boy generally makes some tentative gestures toward seeing how his "great love" is received by his environment. As it is more or less natural for everyone of this age to be at least feebly interested in the movies and since other boys see the moving pictures of this particular individual, know her name and have opinions about her, he can discuss his beloved rather briefly, excepting as to her "true" relation to himself. He can make considerable appearance of socialized interest while he is actually feeding his fantasy. He must not mention how madly he is in love with the actress, how many of his hours of nights are spent wakefully fantasying about her; but he can talk about her quite a bit. He cannot allege that he is having the sort of affairs with her that certain of the boys begin to allege they are having. He fantasies all that to himself, but if he starts telling anybody about it, reality begins to be unpleasant. It thus comes about that as this fantasy of love with the movie actress grows more and more frankly sexual, he must reduce more and more his actual social contacts, for other boys are becoming very frank about demonstrations of sexual prowess, and are more and more inquisitive as to his. The fantastic love affair comes to be in more ways than one a disaster to socialization—an event the import of which may be most ominous.

Not only does this "production" of a fantastic love-object involve the boy in an almost inevitable breach of socialization, but this recourse to a purely fictitious object of the other sex may mask from the victim the fact that he is entertaining all but frank incestuous wishes, the screen of an homoerotic motivation that will presently result in severe and destructive conflict.

All in all, any persistent sexual fantasy occurring after the maturation of the genital apparatus in puberty must be viewed as definitely dangerous to the mental health of the individual. While actual adjustive efforts in this as in other fields probably proceed from or arise in constructive fantasy, these preadjustive reveries are brief and their utility is demonstrated in the succeeding sexual activity. Sexual daydreaming becomes definitely dangerous as soon as its content becomes incommunicable to the chum. When it occurs in an individual not socialized to the extent of having a chum, it is one of the most destructive of the manifestations of autoerotic arrest, leading generally to a paranoid personality, if not to schizophrenia, frequently with suicide.

Before terminating this sketch of preadolescence, I must develop somewhat the topic of the isolated boy and his modified course toward maturity. Three special cases of isolation call for comment. The first and most unfortunate is that of boys who, because of serious deviation of personality growth, are excluded from gangs and chumships. Those whose progress was fair into the juvenile era are one class. One of these boys is usually clearly conscious of his "difference" from the other boys, of his being an "outsider," of his being distrusted, if not despised, by the "regular fellows." Often, he has earned a nickname cruelly indicative of the most conspicuous social manifestation of his limitation. The drive toward integrating isophilic situations is not diminished by unfortunate experiences, and this boy is usually deflected by its distorted manifestations from whatever of successful activity he may have shown in the juvenile era. His self-respect is gravely impaired. His authority-attitudes are upset. His schoolwork suffers. If he can he becomes loosely associated with some other "failures," often under quasi-leadership of an older, badly beaten boy. In this "crowd," which possesses but vestiges of the true social organization of the gang, cooperation is reduced to the level of "hooky" playing, general truancy, and the like. It may be that the boy is so unhappy that he submits to manipulation for criminal purposes. It may be that, while he is incapable of submitting himself thus far, he is glad to participate in activities clearly damaging to those who "belong." Learning his rudiments of social action from others who can but observe its superficial manifestations, rather than participate in it, he may grow a crop of definitely antisocial ideals, achieving a truly criminal plan of life. The tenuous returns from the "crowd" association, shot through with malicious discharges of hatred engendered by defeats at "really belonging," may then urge him to try for a completeness in himself. He may then approximate the ideal of the lone wolf, living thereafter in bitter isolation with his hand against all groups and all group living.

This isolation resulting from unassimilable personality is a continuation of the juvenile failure in the case of the obsessional boy and the psychopath. The urge to intimacy and the genital sexuality come to both, but there is no possibility of adjustive action in either case. The substitutions of the obsessional boy are extremely unsatisfactory to his compeers, and he is compelled to work out his needs for friendships by maladjustive integrations with individuals much his inferior in status, or with those so considerably his senior as to look on him as a somewhat peculiar but intelligent younger brother. He is not apt to secure any experience that would contribute to the growth of the sexual tendencies away from an autoerotic level, and his inhibitions are so strong that both the implicit and the explicit sexual activity have to occur exterior to consciousness. Witting self-masturbation is almost never used for the discharge of his sexual tensions. They have to secure release in sleep, by unwitting "accidents" amounting often to masturbation, or by the intervention of others. The sufferer of psychopathic personality receives from the maturations underlying adolescence merely a great many more impulses to entangle himself in frustrations, and now comes rapidly to justify the use of Partridge's term, the *sociopath*.[9] By the time the genital sexuality is clearly manifested, he has usually begun his course through so-called correctional institutions, reform schools, and so forth.

The second case is the isolation brought to the boy by misfortune of sociogeographic location. Death of a parent or other cause may operate to remove a family group, including a boy approaching the preadolescent growth, from a "good" to a "bad" neighborhood, from, say, a satisfactory suburban area to one of severe social disintegration.[10] If the boy has not been provided with the early experience that conserves and develops the character factor, then he "adjusts" to the new environment in much the same fashion as the feebly inhibited boy does to the gang pressure. He merely sinks from a conformity at a superior social level to one at a lower level. If, however, he incorporates a strong character factor, a large part of the personal environment continues irrelevant to him. He is incapable of manifesting many of the integrations and activities that characterize the new area. He does not "mix" with the boys of his new neighborhood or school. Not only is he not "one of the fellows," but the "fellows" themselves are discomforted by him. They discover that, however much he is attracted to them and they to him, no matter how readily he undertakes to be one with them, he has a singular—and a perhaps damnably admirable—inability to coöperate in some of the gang behavior. Whether he becomes a detached leader or an utter stranger none the less respected, or again the peculiar enemy of the gang, these outcomes, and various grades and shades of combinations, are determined by vector summation of his personality assets and liabilities and the effective tendency-integration of the boys' groups. His personality growth in significant ways approximates that of our third class of isolation, and the steps may be extrapolated from its consideration.

[9] *Loc. cit. supra.*
[10] See, for example, Clifford Shaw, *Delinquency Areas;* Chicago: Univ. of Chicago Press, 1929.

The third class of isolation is primarily geographical. The only preadolescent in a sparsely settled rural community is a classical example. This boy may secure some socialization of the ordinary preadolescent type in the hours of the country school. On the whole, however, the inaccessibility of his home—and the ignorance of his family of the significant needs of this era of growth—tend to separate him from gang life, if not from having a chum. This boy always suffers a prolongation of the adolescent epoch. He usually takes on superficial behavioral patterns of preternatural maturity, for the elders are much more attractive to any preadolescent than are juveniles and children. But this early "aging" is specious. The working out of isophilic tendencies is not satisfactory and is spread over years of experimentation—usually with caution learned by disappointing, if not actually painful, experience. Fantasy processes and the personification of subhuman objects are called on. Loyalty is developed to abstract ideals, more or less concretely embodied in fanciful figures, rather than to concrete groups. The capacity for sympathy becomes peculiarly differentiated because of the elaboration of its underlying tendencies in loneliness, among fanciful objects. From this background, there may come individuals who *finally* mature a personality that stands out well above the average level of achievement, the more in that the carrier comes to integrate interpersonal situations in which he is more of a participant observer than a unit merged in unthinking coöperation. The force of public opinion on such a personality may remain relatively unimportant. In our culture, there are roles for which the training of isolation and slow completion of preadolescence is by no means disqualifying.

On the other hand, the isolated boy, safe from the gang stereotypy that in some measure produces mediocrity, lacks the practice that ensues in unthinking accommodation of oneself to others with whom one has sympathy. His interpersonal relations are not easy, and, despite the effort entailed, tend often to superficiality. Possessed of capacity for intimacy of extraordinary depth, his experience of fraudulent folk may early drive him into a skepticism about people that is extremely annoying to more socialized personalities.

Besides this recrudescent self-isolation as an escape from painful results of one's social inexpertness, there is another factor destructive to the growth of the preadolescent personality constituted by the frankly sexual tendencies. Particularly in our culture, until very recently characterized by an almost psychotic dissociation of sex from life—and by corresponding symptomatic graft and preying on credulity by pimps, panders, "evangelists," and "specialists for men"—the solidarity of chumship and gang life is needed to effect some release of the preadolescent from sexual taboos. The idealized figures of the isolated boy's world can have but his own experience with sexual and antisexual motivations, and sexual behavior with subhuman playmates cannot liquidate the inhibition and feeling of guilt about sex. The drive for sexual gratification, once experienced, is generally insuperable. The dreary story of self-immolation in the name of "willpower" with which to overcome the "solitary vice" is peculiarly the story of the boy isolated in fact or in principle. The chapter of our civilization that deals with taboos against masturbation is the part of human history that best teaches the destructive power of ideas as personal embodiment of cultural entities—in this case, an idea enjoying close kinship with God.

Male Adolescence

ADOLESCENCE is that period of the individual's life during which he develops or attempts to develop techniques for living intimately with others. It is the epoch during which the individual achieves or tries to achieve full membership in his particular community, enjoying its permissive and its facilitating aspects, and successfully adapting himself to its prohibitions and restrictions. Beginning near the age of nine, adolescence all but always reaches into the twenties, and frequently to the end of life. Initiated by the coming of the urge to intimacy, and beginning of preadolescence, it progresses through collaborations with members of one's sex, through the full awakening of the sexual impulses, through midadolescence, the era of patterning of the sexual behavior, and late adolescence, the era in which the individual seeks his place in the world as shaped by his needs for interpersonal relations. One becomes adult when one achieves a thoroughly satisfactory interpersonal integration, particularly in the field of sexual situations. This achievement, in our culture, is one second in magnitude only to the much more swift and relatively unhampered procedure of being born.

Interpersonal relations are matters of ultimate importance in life. One may survive and surmount almost any other sublethal difficulties. Success in intimacies with another, however, requires a personality that is comparatively free from limitations or deviations of growth. One individual, at least, in any two- or three-group must approximate to mental health, or the collaborative actions of the group will fall short of complete resolution of the situational complexes encountered in the course of the group life.

Incidents of stress or the accumulation of interpersonal tensions finally destroy the imperfect social integrations, often with more or less of a resulting conviction on the part of the members that human collaboration is an unattainable ideal, and that society is essentially a predatory, a mercilessly competitive, or a nonsensical, aggregation that has occurred without rhyme or reason—purely by chance. We shall presently call in question this notion and its rich progeny of social doctrines.

In the meanwhile, we must sketch the course of growth of interpersonal relations as it tends to occur in the epoch under consideration. It is well to note that the relation of the growing young with persons removed from their own personality-growth era is no longer our principal concern. We have now to be primarily interested in relations between persons not only of similar developmental stage, but of similar social status.[1] The typical intimate interpersonal relations of preadolescence subtend two boys probably of different families. With the coming of the change after puberty, the typical interpersonal relation takes some time appearing, but tends more and more definitely, as growth progresses, to become one between a young man and a young woman of comparable personality development and status. If this is finally and fully achieved, we discover that the individual has passed through adolescence and is a young adult. Of the years that follow puberty, however, several may be spent in patterning various social behavior units, and many in getting into shape to enter into full intimacies, including sexual situations. Because the disorders of sexual adjustment are ruinous to other development, we must devote considerable attention to the patterning of this form of behavior.

Before we can proceed further into this subject, however, we must, like the adolescent subjects of our study, make revaluations and redefinitions in the interest of a more realistic understanding of the processes and the situations concerned. There being little

[1] Interpersonal relations that I would regard as of healthy import in mid and in late adolescence cannot exist in the situation created by a parent and child, nor even—other than most exceptionally—in the situation including a nephew with an aunt or uncle of about his age. In this latter type of situation, elements of status tend to be vitiating, in addition to the complications by intrafamily appreciation of the close blood relation with one of the parents.

or none of our culture adaptive to the sexual tendencies, they remain for the most part in the realm of the mysterious—if not still in the region of religious damnation. The study of personality cannot proceed without a preliminary clarification of the ideational confluence and confusion that obscure these phenomena. We have therefore first to attack the problem of the terminology of intimacy, of erogeny, and of sexuality.

We shall refer to the phenomena that arise before the awakening of the genital sexuality, and that continue thenceforth to show as the need for personal intimacy, by two terms derived from the Greek word meaning *fond of*. Adding the prefix derived from the Greek word for *equal*, we shall adopt *isophilic* as a term by which to refer to the preference for individuals approximately equal in general characteristics of personality. By adding the prefix derived from the Greek term for *stranger*, we form the term *xenophilic* with which to refer to the preference for intimacy with individuals signally different in general personality characteristics from those of the subject-individual. We have encountered the isophilic tendency in discussing preadolescence, and shall come presently to the much more complex xenophilic tendencies.

In Chapter IV, we encountered somewhat of the meaning of the zones of interaction between the individual and the environment, and touched on *erogeny*, the securing of pleasure-giving sentience by manipulations of these various zones.[2] We have given a rough classification of personality on the basis of prepotency of zones, in which there is implied a classification of erotism. We have now to consider erogeny from the standpoint of *environmental agency*, classifying it, on this basis, under three rubrics: autoerotism, homoerotism, and heteroerotism. This introduces an expansion of its meaning, such that we now come to realize that erogeny includes the securing of pleasure-giving sentience directly from the interaction zones *and mediately* by the prehension of pleasure given to another. A discussion of autoerotic interests may make this more clear.

---

[2] From this limited subjective viewpoint, the zones of interaction may be called—as, for example, in the psychoanalytic writings—the *erogenous zones*. I trust that by now the student is aware of their wider-than-subjective importance.

The occurrence of *autoerotic* interests implies desire to secure one or more of the various forms of pleasant sentience derivative from the zones of interaction of one's own body. Behavior in response to autoerotic interest might be directed to the excitation of one's own genitals, *autosexual* activity.[3] This, however, need not be by way of self-manipulation. A situation objectively appraised as one of normal sexual intercourse of a man with a woman may be and often in fact is, for one or the other party if not for both, one of autosexual behavior rather than of heterosexual. Self-masturbation, the manual (and related) manipulation of the genitals, is therefore but one form of autosexual behavior, and but one of many forms of activity in response to autoerotic interests.[4]

The conception of *homoerotic* and *heteroerotic* interests similarly refers to the desire to secure pleasure, but now by prehension of the pleasure of another derived from the manipulation, by the subject-individual, of some zone of interaction of the object-individual's body. The homoerotic interest manifests as inclination to the pleasure-giving manipulation of another person of the same sex; the heteroerotic, one of the other sex. *Homosexual* behavior is then the manipulation of the genitals of a member of the same sex, for the pleasure experienced in his enjoyment. *Heterosexual* behavior is the manipulation of the genitals of one of the other sex, for the satisfaction derived by prehension of the other's pleasure. In the homoerotic and the heteroerotic interests we see, obviously, much more elaborated interpersonal tendency-systems than in the autoerotic.

The nuclear problem of erogeny that characterizes midadolescence is the patterning of the *sexual* habits. This statement must be understood to imply that there continues to be all the other forms of pleasure-giving behavior and thought, all the

---

[3] Pleasure-giving sentience arising directly or mediately (by reflection) from the genital zone is *sexual*, just as that from the mouth is oral, and that from the lower end of the alimentary tract, anal.

[4] Finger- and tongue-sucking, nail-biting, and the like are instances of behavior in response to autoerotic interest centering in these cases in the oral zone. They are *not* autosexual, for the pleasure-giving sentience does not arise in the genital zone. We shall come presently to consider interpersonal behavior specifically in the one field, and will discover much the same possibilities for comparison as in the case of the genital.

other fields of erogeny, to which is now added the genital. There has always been a distinctive character to sentience arising from the region of the genitals, but the pubertal change greatly accentuates this difference, and the sexual then becomes entirely unlike any other type of pleasure.[5] The newly matured genital dynamism, like all the other dynamisms concerned with the biological functional activity of the organism, requires the discharge of the energy partitioned to it, and creates its appropriate "psychological necessity"—sexual desire, or *lust*—for the integration of situations suitable to its satisfaction. It inspires play, revery, and more elaborated activities to this end. If it is denied any satisfaction, the tension of accumulating lust can finally suspend any other integrating tendency—excepting physicochemical hunger and acute oxygen need. Its power is so great that it can be used to energize almost unbelievably complicated processes.[6] At the same time, the successful utilization of the processes of compensation and sublimation for the complete satisfaction of the sexual motivations is impossible.

The satisfaction of lust in the male requires fairly frequent physiological activity of the somatic apparatus for the ejaculation of the seminal fluid, the biophysicochemical embodiment of the interactions characteristic of the genital zone.[7] This necessary ejaculation of the spermatic fluid is of the same order of events

[5] There is no objection to calling the prepubertal genital sentience *phallic*, after the fashion of the psychoanalysts. It must, however, be observed that in this presentation we do not follow the doctrine of "displacement of partial impulses upon the genitals," with resulting "progression from the phallic to the genital stage." Correspondingly, a "continuation at the phallic stage" after puberty has no meaning in our terminology. The changes by which sexual sentience comes to arise from much the same zone that previously gave rise to phallic sentience are primarily rather abrupt changes in the integrator dynamisms, the result of somatic maturation. As already suggested, personality factors, experience, may and probably do delay somatic maturation—or, conceivably, speed it up. They are not the maturation, and only confusion comes from the notion that erogeny is displaced on the body, as hair might be moved by skin-grafting.

[6] The prehension of this fact as a precipitate of personal experience has been a factor in gaining support for the less admirable speculations of the less conservative psychoanalysts.

[7] The female seems to require only occasional incidents of the physiological activity subsumed in orgasm. I doubt, however, if the prevailing opinion is correct, which suggests that these orgasms may be missing for years on end. On the other hand, it is very frequently the case that women fail of orgasm in sexual intercourse with men.

as is respiration and the taking of food. No action of merely implicit character can take its place. If there is successful inhibition of explicit sexual activity during the waking life, it will occur in states of reduced consciousness. Moreover, so distinctive is the pleasure arising in the organismic acme of sexual activity that once consciously experienced, it cannot be excluded from recall except by the dissociation of this very powerful system of tendencies, with great danger to the personality integration unless ample satisfactions of the dissociated component are provided —as, for example, in major hysteria.

It must be noted, however, that strong inhibitory tendencies can greatly delay the initial consciousness of orgasm. Many women of the passing generation seem never to have been aware of it. The boy entering midadolescence cannot fail to have seminal ejaculations, but he can have them in sleep without any waking recall of the attending dream experience. This continues to be for some time the rule in the case of boys so morbidly virtuous that they have been isolated from intimacies including verbal sexual activity. These nocturnal emissions are often the cause of parental excitement, the results of which are sometimes thoroughly bad for the growing boy. One learns, for example, of parents who inform the boy that this must not happen again. Others say nothing definite, but make quite clear that they are agitated about the event. Worry about "night losses" is thus encouraged, a major addition to the complex of sexual sin. As the harassed youth is quite apt to have no recollection of the dream events associated with the "pollution," and less than no realization of the inevitable nature of seminal ejaculations, he may become so disturbed that his sleep cycle is upset and a state of chronic fatigue induced.[8]

The customary course of elaboration of the sexual tendencies begins with autosexual experience. Whether self-masturbation is learned from the example of an older individual, from a compeer, by experimentation on the basis of verbal information, or quite by accident in the course of some nonsexual behavior, it is certain to be important for at least a brief period. The initial orgasm may be regarded as anything from the most remarkably

[8] The discussion of sleep, rest, and fatigue must be postponed to Chapter IX.

pleasant experience of life to something terrible that has happened to one.[9] The somatic apparatus concerned in the expression of lust, in the growth of sexual excitement to the climax, in the orgasm, and in detumescence, is remarkably complicated. All three of the integrator dynamisms are involved, the neo-encephalic chiefly as a result of cultural influences and inhibitory and facilitating experience acquired in regard of the genitals. Moreover, a considerable part of the genital apparatus is common to the urine-excreting function. These two major biological activities require quite different and in part mutually exclusive patterns of neuromuscular inhibition and stimulation. The penis has both the circulation of blood and lymph concerned with the maintenance of tissue health, and the circulation concerned in the engorgement of the spongy erectile tissue. The latter is controlled by facilitation or retardation of the venous return to the general circulation of the organ, delicately through the instrumentality of a neuromuscular unit that is responsive to activity of the sexual tendencies. Other things being equal, the degree of engorgement of the penis, flaccid or erect, is an index of the unhampered sexual motivation in the existing total situation. It is not uncommon for the preadolescent, newly acquainted with the orgasm, to undergo recurrent prolonged erections of the penis. This is often the source of much embarrassment, and sometimes, of much worry as to abnormality or disease. In part

[9] The fear that serious damage has been done as an interpretation of the first experience of this kind is by no means uncommon. The only frequent similarly episodic phenomenon including sensations increasing to a maximum with spasmodic motor discharge is sneezing. Obviously a process for dislodging obstructing or irritating material from the upper air-passages, sneezing has none the less taken on at least four remarkable relationships to human erogeny. In snuff-taking, it was cultivated in its own right. In so far as it is referable to certain osmic (smell) phenomena, it often serves as the channel of expression of dissociated systems including factors giving genital, fecal, or other odors exaggerated negative values. See a report on the analysis of a psychogenetic "hay fever" by Ernest E. Hadley. By strange virtue of possessing erectile tissue in the turbinal processes—thus resembling the penis and the clitoris—the nose sometimes comes to participate in sexual excitement and in phenomena associated with the oestrus cycle in women. At these times there comes to be turbinal congestion, often with increased nasal secretion and sneezing, perhaps from obstruction to sinus drainage. And finally, perhaps by combination of factors from all the other three, sneezing occurs as a sort of precocious orgasm in some folk when they fantasy the preferred sexual relations with a peculiarly desirable object.

because the erect member exposes much more of its sensitive surface to contacts—and perhaps also undergoes during erection an enhancement of sensitivity per unit of surface area—these prolonged erections are attended by considerable sexual excitement arising from the local irritation. The boy therefore experiences desire, however undifferentiated may be his awareness of it, and is correspondingly distracted from his other interests and activities. Masturbation or some other procedure for relief is almost automatic, corresponding rather closely at this stage to the play by which the newly developed abilities of the infant and child are exercised and their energy dissipated.[10] If there are inhibitions that interfere with this exercise of the newly elaborated sexual abilities, various complications of the physiological components may arise and provide a basis for hypochondriacal preoccupations that are far from healthy.

Sooner or later, all boys secure lucid, if frequently highly incorrect, information about the sex act as commonly practiced in the less warped part of the human race. They commonly correlate this disastrously with the fact of their existence as individuals; in other words, they are shocked by the idea that sexual behavior must have been manifested between their parents in order that they might be born, and they do something with the distress which is thus caused them by the information. If one wishes to understand the evolution of any individual human

[10] Unlike finger- or thumb-sucking, "infantile masturbation," and the like, these physiological discharges of the sexual apparatus cannot be hampered by mechanical and related devices. If they could, we may be certain that grave mental disturbances would follow promptly. As it is, however, symbolic representations active in sleep suffice for setting off the orgasm, when the waking life is too inhibited to afford relief.

The double function of parts of the urogenital tract underlies various more or less morbid interchanges of the activity of orgasm, and that of micturition. Enuresis, prolonged incontinence of the urine—almost always an indication of serious personality warp—may occur at puberty, or, having existed into adolescence, may rapidly cease after the experience of sexual excitement and orgasm. In acute schizophrenic states, urgency of urination often appears as a phenomenon of sexual excitement, and the act of micturating seems often to take the place of the orgasm. In states of comparative mental health, on the other hand, situational factors that stir perhaps dissociated sexual tendencies often interfere with micturition. Thus the near presence of a person actually suitable as a sex object—however consciously unaware the subject may be of this suitability—often makes it difficult to relax the bladder sphincter.

personality it is well to know what the subject did about this information. If he accepted it as a matter of fact, as something which had not previously come to his attention but which none the less might be accepted as true—just, for example, as the fact that a cat of his acquaintance has had kittens must, by the very nature of things, indicate that the cat was previously in sexual congress with another cat—he has probably been fortunate in the elaboration of his personality to this stage and may have no great difficulty stumbling through the mid and late adolescent periods to adulthood. If, on the other hand, the discovery of parental intercourse comes to him as a profound shock, as an extremely revolting datum, if he is unable to think of it without a feeling of illness, shame, or horror, then one will in all likelihood discover in him that the mother sentiment has not been developed properly; that it is of a too primitive character and too dominant for the proper growth of sexual habits. One often finds that it is around this time that the individual is able for the first time to make something of his previous knowledge of sexual relations between the parents. While he has apparently gotten along pretty well thus far despite their indiscretion in having intercourse in his presence or within the range of his sense organs, this previous experience now begins to be noxious and to exert a markedly distorting effect on his development. I mention this to emphasize that a too literal acceptance of the notion of "traumatic experience" and of "childhood fixations" does not contribute to the understanding of personality problems.[11]

It comes about in the case of a good many boys that their initial experience in sexual coöperation with a woman involves one who is considerably removed from mental health, and the contact comes to be a handicap in the midadolescent patterning. In the "good old days," it was rather common experience that if one, of course quite unconscious of purpose, went with one's chum for a walk at the right time in certain streets of the com-

[11] The primitive genital phobia mentioned earlier is a factor of another order. Its manifestations are both more obscure and far more extensive. Thus, it may have potent influence on sexual behavior in preadolescence, often in the curious facilitation of mutual or cooperative sexual behavior *without* self-masturbatory behavior. The boy can manipulate another boy's genitals, and is quite willing to be manipulated, but will not masturbate himself.

monwealth, or in front of certain houses of the village, a more or less buxom, quite peculiarly attractive lady of comparative maturity could be encountered, by whose inviting manner one was put somewhat at unconventional ease, and with whom one could make a real beginning of that which everyone seemed to enjoy surreptitiously, and become acquainted with the mysteries of sex in a simple and direct fashion. Thanks to plentiful and well-marshaled reform influences, and to our progressive organization of vice and crime, only a few are able to make their debut in this fashion nowadays; the great majority coming in contact with the streetwalker, the dance hall girl, and their ilk—the principal distributors of venereal disease—and being seduced in a less friendly and hygienically satisfactory fashion, for money, by a pimp's orders, or for malice only. The effects of the seduction by the practiced and accomplished, rather self-respecting prostitute of old have seemed in my experience to be singularly lacking in evil consequences.[12]

For the last few generations, however, the initial heterosexual experience has been the point of departure for courses varied from states of moderate mental health to the inception of grave mental disorder, the latter in a significant number of people. The contribution of this even to the permanent warp of personality is, in my experience, far greater than has been emphasized elsewhere. One can see in any clinic for venereal diseases plentiful evidence of the train of events that follows the contracting of one of these maladies. A great deal that is most unfortunate

[12] I recall no individual who has come to grave mental disorder in any direct relation to his having been inveigled into the somewhat maternal embraces of a person definitely accepting herself as an "honest" prostitute. I must deplore any appearance of enmity to progress and therefore should perhaps refrain from any statement as to the case of a good many of the boys who are "picked up" by streetwalkers, or, for that matter, by fellow high or business school students who are all but in very fact streetwalkers. Progress we certainly have where reform has been vigorously applied, for there is now so intimate a liaison between the sex business, the liquor and narcotic drug business, and the business of racketeering and other crime, that only the wholly unsophisticated and the entirely reckless take chances with "easy" women casually encountered. Most youth is unsophisticated, regardless of a veneer of worldliness. As business must be run at a profit, and the reckless seldom have much to lose, the cost to the young of the organization for supplying forbidden "pleasures" is very great.

happens in a personality which on the threshold of midadolescence receives such an extreme rebuff.[13] And the evil of infection with these diseases, immeasurably great though it is, is probably rather insignificant when compared with the evil done already warped personalities by the direct contact with human degradation to which they come in their efforts at manly satisfaction of the sexual drives. For the too well-reared youth does not seek an equal-status situation for his plunge into sexuality. He would not lead a nice girl astray, and seeks the experience at a lower stratum. Existence in a lower social level, however, does not necessitate that its denizens shall be mentally ill. No girl approximating a state of mental health will integrate herself into a situation of sexual intimacy with one of these virtue-ridden boys, who would express contempt for her if she were yielding. His search will therefore lead him to someone to whom his contempt is a matter of comparative indifference. This often means that his personality is irrelevant in the "sexual act" that is contemplated; that it is his purse, or his family's purse, or something of that sort that matters. His plunge into heterosexual performances is thus devoid of heterosexual motivation, and the experience is generally far from pleasant. It may be that he prehends the hostility of the woman and finds himself utterly impotent. It may be that he instead proceeds to the very moment of introitus, only to have precocious orgasm. It may be that he develops a satisfactory erection but is all but anesthetic and goes on stolidly

[13] It would be a very great contribution to mental hygiene if one could suppress the spread of venereal disease among adolescents. Here too, I may have overstepped the bounds of virtue, for some of the admittedly good are bitterly opposed to the dissemination of information about venereal prophylaxis. If I recall aright it was a distinguished urologist who undertook the establishing of prophylactic clinics in the city of Baltimore, and thereby discovered his ungodliness—at the hands of a fellow practitioner, the latter, an enemy of prostitution, being a gynecologist.

The U.S. Public Health Service has made a good beginning in a long-term campaign against the evil of venereal disease, and several states have enacted laws calculated to further this work. Clinics and hospitals have been made available to sufferers. But as long as sex is a thing of darkness and shame, as long as the Complex of Sexual Sin is one of our most cherished cultural depravities, the infection of adolescents with syphilis—the cause of innumerable forms of disability, including *dementia paralytica* (syphilitic disintegration of brain tissue, until recently incurable and almost certainly rapidly fatal, now curable in some cases by methods that carry very real risk to life)—will continue on much the same large scale as today.

to no end. The actually antagonistic woman becomes furious at this stage and finally repels him. It may be that his degradation is more frankly invited, and that he is offered dangerously attractive opportunities for revolting perversities, from the very start. And he is fortunate if the escapade ends with his departure from the immediate situation, without receiving attention from some other members of the coterie of graft and vice with which he has made contact.

Roadhouses and dance halls are a considerable source of unfortunate experience for the youth pursuing heterosexual initiation. If the patronage of unattached males is cultivated, there are usually provided a considerable number of hostesses to entertain the guests—at maximum profit to the house. To the sexual advances made to these women one or two sorts of responses are usual. Either assurance of satisfaction "later" are offered until the guest's money has been expended—whereupon he may be asked to wait outside, while the hostess is "trying," unsuccessfully, to get away; or, where steady patronage is more important to the management, he is given "satisfaction" as expeditiously as may be —frequently by a perverted practice; almost invariably in a fashion that makes recollection of the experience unpleasant.

In contrast to these rather ugly events, we must notice the considerable emancipation from sexual taboos on the part of current adolescent girls, and consider the effects of the resulting sexual freedom. At the levels of its manifestation, this movement is removing the stigma of sin from premarital intercourse, and thus sparing the participants from much of the evil associated with the passing situation. Many of the participants, however, cannot escape the traditional elements incorporated in their superego processes, and therefore enter the sexual acts maladjustively in an overemotional or a cynical fashion, from which the experience necessary for mental health is not obtained. The strength of the sexual urges couples with the support of the group example to break down the feeble inhibitions in the comparatively healthy personalities and facilitates the unsuccessful patterning of behavior. Were healthy growth of personality to the adolescent epoch generally the case, there would then be little sexual disorder in our younger folk. For the already badly warped and strongly inhibited, however, these easy sexual intimacies are but more complicated instances of the processes that we have considered in segregation from gang sexual behavior.

The passing sexual culture is perhaps most characterized by the romantic sentimentalizing of feminine virtue. The new departure seems, on the other hand, to overvalue the merely sexual, as contrasted with human intimacy. The notion that any woman is declassed who would have sexual intercourse with a man, before having married him—or at least someone—implying therefore the vital importance to the woman of possessing an at least legally nominal husband, has entailed much evil. The swing of the cultural pendulum to the notion that a man's chief value to a woman lies in his sexual abilities seems to be rather an excess in the other direction. Certainly it brings to an increasing proportion of the more warped of our young men an early discouragement of the heterosexual patterning, and a turning to the autoerotic or the homoerotic types of interest.

Among the considerable and socially important body of people who show an extensive deviation from the pursuit of the biologically ordained heterosexual object, and who, by reason of rebuff, or implicit acceptance of rebuff, or because of other situational factors, come to an autoerotic or homoerotic *modus vivendi*, there are always to be found special problems arising from their sexual peculiarity that reduce the chances of successful living and mental health. The proportion of such people who achieve adulthood is even smaller than is the current average. The proportion who remain in the midadolescent uncertainty of patterning is conspicuous and socially very important. Those who progress into the late adolescence of seeking satisfaction in using a patterned sexual behavior are numerous, but much less important socially. The number who show a regressive return to an unpatterned early-adolescent sexuality is large. I suppose that in this last mentioned group one could place a rather astonishing percentage of individuals.[14]

A comparative few of those whose interests continue to be

[14] I used to think that it was only by failure of the midadolescent patterning of sexual behavior that there arose the processes making up the schizophrenic illness. It has become evident to me that one must go further back than that—the people who have classical difficulties in midadolescence are perhaps already beyond recourse to schizophrenic illnesses, unless they fall into peculiarly difficult situations.

autoerotic work out a way of life in which they discharge their
sexual motivation by masturbatory procedures, having adjusted
their ideals in such a fashion that they can rationalize this as a
purposive deviation from conventional life, for their good. It is
by no means easy to identify these latter and one does not ordinarily encounter adequate data on them. They have a singular
advantage in avoiding intimate interpersonal relations and at the
same time an ability to be rather remarkable phenomena within
the social fabric. Put in the language of the street, they are not
"really human." They show a certain cold, calculating appraisal
of their fellows, frequently coupled with a rather remarkable
technique for dealing with these fellow men and women. The
intimacy urge may be well worked out, and techniques for dealing with members of the other sex carried to a high level of
achievement, in all fields other than that of sexual intercourse.

On the other hand, continued autoerotic interests are by no
means incompatible with genital competence in relations to the
same or the other sex, and there are numerous instances of this
sort of autosexuality. It may be said that only when the fantasy
accompanying self-masturbation is of greater value to the personality than can be any interpersonal reality, does the individual
commonly fail to discover the autosexual utilization of other
people as tools.[15] The psychopathologist encounters innumerable
husbands who masturbate through the instrumentality of the
wives' vaginas, and feel very much more adult in this performance than would they about using their hand. Their performance is undoubtedly nearer to the adult than would be self-
masturbation; but they have none the less failed to develop
heterosexual interests, however fully their other erotic interests
may have come to include collaboration with the other sex.[16]
The deficiency often arises from failure in elaborating the

[15] The exception being the rationally determined patterned masturbator
just discussed, and he avoids these uses of others by reason of expediency.

[16] Considering only the most significant three of the zones of interaction,
with the element of collaborative (reflected) pleasure, and observing that
we deal in a given personality with *a permutation* of these six terms, one
comes to the rather staggering realization that there must be not less than
720 personally typical erogenic modes, including in the purely autoerotic
not less than six. This may serve to point the absurdity of lumping persons
under the popular rubrics of "autoerotic" (or "narcissistic"), "homosexual,"
and "heterosexual."

nuclear sentiment of the other sex, which arises by differentiation from the primitive mother sentiment, with corresponding deviation in the sentiment of self (as a differentiation of the early sentiment of the same sex). These processes should become more clear as we develop the topic of homosexual patterning.

Among those who prove incapable of achieving the biologically ordained heterosexual goal are a great many to whom the mother has continued to be of excessive significance, overshadowing or coloring strongly all prehensions of other women. This handicap is perhaps most vividly illustrated in the case of the woman who has married for spite a man whom she soon comes to loathe, yet with whom the peculiarities of her personality, or economic factors, or other cause, force her to live. When a son is born of such a union, he is generally sacrificed to the mother's unsatisfied erotic tendencies, and he becomes tied to her by the sort of intimacy so remarkably symbolized by Von Stuck in his painting "Die Sphinx." Whether he comes finally to rebel, hates her, and goes through life destroying as much as he can of that which arouses the mother-stereotype, or instead goes on being her child-lover, the result is most unfortunate as to his growth in personality. It is almost certain that he will not proceed in erotic development past interest in his own sex.[17]

The variety of extraordinary relationships that comes to subtend mothers and sons in the current American culture is as amazing as it is wonderful. The emancipation of woman, not alone from the roles of chattel and sentimentalized toy, but from all

[17] It is my purpose in the latter part of this chapter to develop enough of the implications of homoerotic interest and homosexual and related behavior to make these terms scientifically meaningful to the student of personality. The current usages are often quite vacuous, except for fringes of religious or ethical meaning. One often encounters in current psychiatric records and writings references to an individual as "a homosexual," or to "a history of homosexuality." Sixty years ago, this index to something obscure might have been useful. In current life, it is apt to be even less useful than is a notation of the individual's alleged religious affiliations; we know better than to guess much about his living from the latter, while the former still leads the unsophisticated to a great many almost wholly erroneous conclusions.

The time may come when homoerotic interests and the behavior to which they lead will shrink to the proportions of merely preadolescent growth phenomena. Anyone who believes that this is their current importance among us, or that the times are progressing toward this end, is very badly informed, indeed.

formulated roles, into a novel independence without corresponding economic and sociopolitical educational facilities, is presenting us with a new sort of family-group that is often very far from benevolent in its effects on the younger members. The change has been gaining momentum for some time, and the passing generation provides a rich material for the study of its psychopathology. Thus one learns that a son has slept to the age of forty-eight in the same bed with his mother, thereafter going to the mental hospital in a schizophrenic illness. Another shared the maternal bed to the age of thirty-eight, then required institutional care—the mother continuing the habit in which he had long acquiesced of supervising the trifles of his life, the overcoat to be worn, when to wear rubber overshoes, and so on. Another reported at the maternal bedside the performances of each evening of his life well into the twenties. Another suffered anxiety attacks at night that required the expulsion of the father from the connubial bed, to make way for the twenty-four-year-old son. Another returned home drunk to be disrobed by the mother. Another did not enjoy any recreation unless the mother was along. And so on and on, all of these situations being considered by the parties concerned as nonsexual, if not nonerotic. The boy entangled in a situation of this sort before puberty has various morbid courses open to him in midadolescence. There may be a great effort to exterminate any consciousness of the sexual drives. This occasionally succeeds after a fashion, and the individual stumbles in a curiously juvenile manner to the threshold of the senium—and then develops an involutional psychosis; one secures a history of nocturnal emissions and diminishing frequency or volume, with less and less consciousness of erections of the penis. The more common outcome of the attempted "psychic castration" is the eruption of incestuous cravings and schizophrenic disorders. Many of these boys make belated acquaintance with sexual behavior with another male, and come to discharge their sexual tensions in more or less unpatterned behavior of this sort, generally with a great deal of conflict. Others of them take the paranoid way out. Few or none of them achieve any competency in intimacy and fill out their warped lives with elaborations of a juvenile sociality in which not other persons but merely other individuals take a limited cooperative role. Alcohol is the only key that some of them find to even self-endurance. A few of them labor mightily for human welfare in unwitting expiation for some dimly prehended violation of Divine Law.

The introduction of the adolescent to sexual behavior is by no means invariably at the hands of his compeers or a member of the other sex. It may be well at this point to consider the more occasional but still fairly common sophisticated introduction to sexual behavior by a much older member of the same sex. The venereal disease evil is probably less important in these cases, but the evil of sexual vulgarization and depravity is sometimes even greater than in the case of seduction by vicious women. Many midadolescents who have not had frank homosexual experience in preadolescence encounter it in midadolescence, often in a thoroughly unfortunate fashion, on the streets or elsewhere. In certain sections of urban culture, sections, for example, where the economic level is very low and the social organization rather fragmentary, such as the West Madison Street district in Chicago commented on by Clifford Shaw, and in sections in which there are many homeless men, almost all the boys are likely to have homosexual experience. This also tends to be the case in groups isolated from women. The more significant cases of vicious homosexual seduction, however, are not the products of these generalized social situations, but—as in the case of the predatory streetwalker—arise from the behavior of a class to whom we shall refer as the *cacocunes,* a class of unhappily homoerotic people having an inexhaustible and thoroughly pernicious interest in unsophisticated youths.

An encounter with an overtly homosexual individual provides the midadolescent with an important experience, the outcome of which may be unfortunate or otherwise. As in the case of everything else that happens to one in life, this event assumes meaning and influences sequent events largely by virtue of the previous personality organization. In the perhaps exceptional case of the boy who has arrived in midadolescence with no material warp of personality and yet without coöperative sexual experience, the undergoing of genital gratification as a result of the encounter is but an added incentive to personality growth. It is a sexually pleasant experience, but one that includes unpleasant features, both as to the other personality involved and much more as to its violation of the traditional and rational elaborations in his personality as to sexual activity. This boy therefore tends, as a result of the fleeting intimacy including genital stimulation, energetically to seek more acceptable sexual collaboration, namely, after the heterosexual pattern.

In the case, however, of another boy, one for example who has been seriously warped by the continued or augmented importance of a more or less primitive attachment to his mother, and who therefore is not susceptible to any marked heterosexual drives because of the attachment to the mother—with rationalizations generally contributed by her in the shape, perhaps, of advice to keep away from "bad" girls, examples of misfortune resulting from dealings with crafty females, and the like—the outcome is quite otherwise. This boy, stimulated genitally, finds in the homosexual situation the satisfaction of the sexual motivation, a singularly pleasing intimacy with another individual, and, by synthesis, a path out of the dilemma in which the growing sexual espects of his personality and the inhibition of the heterosexual development have placed him. In all likelihood he will pursue further sexual satisfactions of much the same kind, and in the end follow in the path of his seducer. Between these two extremes there are many sorts of midadolescents and varieties of effects of this kind of seduction.

There is, unfortunately, a third variety of homosexual contact the outcome of which impresses me as always bad, and the occurrence of which is a considerable evil to the youth concerned. I refer here to anal in contradistinction to genital seduction, particularly by a sadistic pederast—a pernicious deviate by no means uncommon. Aside from actual physical injuries, including occasional grave and sometimes fatal infections arising by damage to the perineum, this sort of experience eventuates in a train of undesirable sequents. It is not a genital experience and therefore does not contribute to the growth of the sexual aspects of personality. It combines with any preexisting anal erotic deviations of the personality, increasing their partition of energy in the fundamental personality systems, perhaps actually establishing a habit of passive pederasty. If the personality is not thus deviated, the experience tends to assume the meaning of an extraordinary aggression, enfeebles self-respect, and contributes powerfully to distrust of one's fellows. The further growth of interpersonal intimacies suffers, and sometimes there is initiated a tendency, this in already sadistic individuals, toward perpetrating similar outrages on the unsuspecting, as a sort of revenge.[18]

However the actual acquaintance may be made, sooner or later every adolescent meets sex; and having met sex, every adolescent finds the world altered. The partly formulated world-view of his earlier years is strangely refracted, and all but the most primitive of the realities he has known and trusted may become shifting uncertainties, the inadequate apperceptions of a child. This upheaval is in part the result of newly-erupted sexual tendencies and desires, but much more a consequent of acceleration of the physiological developmental rate. Maturation is again comparable with that of the earliest years. But the personality, which in infancy prehended events syncretistically against a background becoming differentiated from cosmic participation, is now more or less highly organized, and this often in ways more or less unfortunate to the new growth.

All the defects and inadequacies now complicate the integration of those interpersonal situations newly required for the maintenance of status. The desire for the role of an adult becomes strong. Conformities that were previously ridiculous now appeal to the boy. He is anxious to receive approbation from many to whose valuation of him he was previously indifferent. The self grows rapidly, and often very irregularly. Self-consciousness is the dominating content of the waking hours. Sensitiveness to manifestations of the expanded self may become extreme. The least approval or disapproval of one's remarks may stir powerful pleasure or give severe discomfort. One's clothing becomes important. One's mannerisms must be noticed and modified. One's companions are no longer simply attractive; they now achieve values in accordance with the reception given them by others whose opinions are temporarily very important. The

[18] Physical injuries received in this way, often concealed because of the pervading doctrines of sexual sin, or for shame at the outrage, come frequently in these cases to have great importance in further growth of the personality. They are real "psychic traumata," remembered, usually, all too vividly.

latter, the people newly invested with value as arbiters of inter-personal reference, are older folk. By their fancied approval and disapproval, even the affectional bonds of an isophilic friendship that has survived puberty may be disintegrated in the service of status-pursuit. A great deal of maladjustive dynamics naturally appears.

The *incomprehensibility of the self*, a result of the rapid spread of relevance and the inadequate foundations of previous self-appraisal, requires rationalizing; the expression of "whys and wherefores" is apt to amuse, rather than to impress, the new ar-biters, and thus to discourage confidences, if not, indeed, intro-spection itself. The adolescent may begin the "life behind a mask" that tends to characterize numbers of our urban denizens. The mask, however, requires so much energy for its successful maintenance that personality growth is apt to end with its suc-cessful construction. As the necessities for masking certain moti-vations vary from one to another interpersonal situation, it may be easier to *avoid further integration of the self*, and to develop, from this point onward, specialized accommodations and interests for various groups, without the growth of a synthetic self-consciousness. If the character factor is strong, such a distribu-tion of the self in so-called logic-tight compartments is not likely to occur. If the personality growth has been healthy up to the adolescent resymbolization, it is impossible. But if the charac-ter factor is feeble, and if the personality is already warped, this process by which there come to be almost as many selves as there are important interpersonal relationships—with a juvenile or childhood self as the consistent nucleus—is the customary out-come of midadolescence. Personalities that follow this course are "popular," for they bring to each cause in which their incoördi-nated interest may be centered "the enthusiasm of a child," or the "keen rivalry" of the juvenile. One allegiance does not inter-fere seriously with other loyalties. These adolescents do very well, as long as, and only as long as, the sexual tendencies can be satisfied in a relatively unintimate fashion. They do badly when, in their conformity to the folkways, they undertake durable in-terpersonal relations such as marriage, and particularly parent-hood. The tendency-systems that in the well-integrated personality make for durable situations of interpersonal intimacy are, in these chronically late-adolescent folk, discharged in implicit processes of fantasy of the general type of idealization.

In idealizing, one projects upon another personality a body of desirable characteristics that exist within the self as a stereotype. The process is a utilization of the same dynamism as that which, used to rid oneself of characteristics regarded as unfavorable, gives rise to paranoid transference of blame. At this point I shall digress to reconsider the source of personality warp underlying both paranoid and sentimentalist attitudes in interpersonal relations. The drive for intimacy and affectional linkage with another is naturally influenced by the pre-existing organization of personality, and of the self. From early infancy, there has been a series of relations involving other people; first, the infant-God relationship; then, the infant-mother; then, the child-mother and the child-father; perhaps then the child-sibling relationships, and so forth. The whole body of human tendencies has been manifested through sentiments elaborated with these various other persons as objects, or as sources of the sentiment of self. The pursuit of satisfactions and the even more fundamental avoidance of discomfort, through the periods of growth, has always been intimately associated with one or another of these sentiments.[19] If now these developmental sentiments have not undergone

[19] It appears that experience always modifies those tendencies of the organism that gave rise to the activity underlying the experience itself. Only in states of regression does this effect disappear. The matter under discussion is one of great importance for theoretic psychobiology. The notion is something as follows: Given a coherent personal experience, the organization of sentiments and stereotypes proceeds in such fashion that the outgrown ones are relatively impotent, most of the included tendencies—as modified by experience secured—being satisfied through the activity of the current personality organization. Whenever, however, the experience connected with some sentiment is incoherent, there is apt to be a disintegration of the sentiment, owing to tensional states arising from unsatisfied tendencies included in it. The related stereotype, however—in a sense the related historic development of the sentiment of self—remains, and frequently retains considerable power, at least as a potential nexus of tendencies, in turn tending to become active.

The activity of the stereotype is manifested as a tendency to *re-establish a sentiment of the same dynamic type* as the one previously experienced, of which it is a memorial element. The current treatment of idealization is then to be understood to imply that previous disappointments and frustrations of sentiment have led to a self-organization that includes powerful stereotypes that take such precedent over a new situation as to *project into*

growth, but have instead disintegrated under the force of incoherent experience, without the intervention of grief or related
phenomena, their potent stereotypes energize fantasy processes,
and tend to integrate situations with perhaps very nearly irrelevant people. If the *object-pattern* of a stereotype is very far
removed from the characteristics of people encountered in reality,
its reecphoriation as a sentiment fixed on another personal object
is improbable, and its activity tends to work out in fantasy and
ritual concerning some cultural entity incorporated from the
available folklore.[20] If, however, the object-pattern of the stereotype is not very far removed in some of its characteristics from
those of people encountered in reality, its reecphoriation is apt to
take place as a sentiment of the old sort applying to an object-
individual perhaps utterly unsuited for an integration of this
kind. His unsuitability is submerged by the projected characterization, which permits prehension of his perhaps single characteristic common to the object-pattern of the stereotype, and
otherwise invests him with features whose sudden revelation would
certainly astonish him. Only gradually, however, does the personal
reality escape from the idealization thrust upon it, and the unwitting victim of the projection stands forth a sadly disappointing person. In the meanwhile, some more valid interpersonal relations involving him have probably occurred and the total
situation has become very complex. Its resolution is often impossible, and its disintegration is sometimes prevented by other
cultural entities—for example, the folkways, mores, and legal
enactments pertaining to marriage.

There come to be many family groups in which the personalities of the parents have become all but submerged, for each
other, in shifting idealizations, positively or negatively affectionate, through life-courses of unnumbered disappointments of
ill-founded attachments, hopes, and dreams. These folk live as it
were in a world peopled with unstable patterns of folklore, a fairy

---

it the older pattern, and reactivate (reecphoriate) an old, perhaps very
immature, sentiment with a new object-individual.

[20] The folklore itself has arisen in effective fantasy—that is, in processes
that have proven quasi-adjustive of tendencies for which rational action in
resolution of related situations has not been found. In other words, it is a
part of the religious culture, filling gaps in the culture adaptive to the
needs of the people.

scene in which the roles of others can undergo the most remarkable metamorphoses as a result of trifling actions, yet whose
idealized roles are able to deny the most obvious evidence to the
contrary. The children of this sort of home evolve the universal
human tendencies, but, the older they grow, the more their sentiments find merely cultural objects. The parent-child relationships come to be almost exclusively of this type. The parental
influence on each child distorts what might otherwise be far
more realistic in the relations of siblings. Out of this situation
there comes a personality whose sentiment formations reflect the
traditional dualistic character of the folkways.[21] All object-individuals are one or another of some certain few cultural patterns;
that is, the individual personality to whom any sentiment is applied is lost as anything more than the carrier of a system of
fantasy. Such a world of people as mere culture-carriers can
work with spectacular success only so long as the mores prohibit
individual variation in interpersonal intimacies. Positive and
negative (paranoid) idealization is *the only way* to deal with individuals as culture-carriers. One "loves" a complex of "traits"
which is for all practical purposes embodied in one's mate; one
suppresses conscious consideration of defects in the submerged
person—preferably one conserves energy required for this continued suppression by a further idealization, awarding the submerged person of one's mate not only the particular culture-
pattern that is "loved," but a measure of manifestations of a
more inclusive negatively valued culture-pattern, the Devil,
heredity, or human nature. To the latter "object," one "hates."
It is all quite simple, after the fashion of the minds from whom
the folklore arose. And, since its origin is human and the structure is that universal in fantasy processes, the folklore is always
satisfactory—so long as there is no better folklore, and no one
who, from genius or "insanity," insists on providing at least as
good an alternative. Also since one learns rather slowly, taking
a long time to equal the stores of knowledge of one's parents,
who learned rather slowly from their parents, in regressive series
into the shadows of prehistory, since many of one's "original"
ideas are confuted by authority and even by personal experience;
for good and many reasons, the established "things that every-

[21] Which, I surmise, is a projection, on the scale of the universe, of the
Me–Not-me antithesis learned in late infancy.

body knows" are dangerous to tamper with. And while genius must perhaps be tolerated, it must be suspect at every turn; and "insanity" is a horror.

We are breaking the mold of sentimentally idealizing people as carriers of sterotyped culture-patterns, but scrutiny of the multiple determinations of this break with the past is scarcely relevant to this presentation. It is enough that the great reservoir of syncretistic prehensions, the culture in which we have had our being, is being explored with the analytic tools provided in the evolutionary conception of personality, the observational-comparative techniques of the biological sciences, and the study of the mental life of persons among persons. The findings, to date, are scarcely more than provocative. But the results of the changing attitude to the individual are providing new data in painful abundance. The adolescent, who in simpler days succeeded or failed in his final evolution with appropriately stereotyped results, is now the prophet of the new era—and in his "showing the ways" aproximates the Irish stallion who "galloped madly in all directions." In part because it is the peculiar problem of adolescence, and in part because it has been a focus of priestly and other folk-fantasy, the adolescent of today is transvaluating sex in a fashion that seems but little short of evangelical. I fear that we are too sophisticated to elevate the phallus again to the Godhead, and a religion of sexual freedom—and one, at that, without venereal disease prophylaxis—is perhaps only another religion, and one the fine frenzy of which passes all too soon to bring comfort to old age and the ugly. Also, since the most destructive factor in the evolution of sexual tendencies is the primitive genital phobia that has been built into many of the current (and near-future) crop of adolescents, I fear that the New Freedom is for many but a mental disorder, attended by disintegration of personality rather than by wider integration into the world of people. After which expression of "gloomy conservatism," I can do no better than to proceed into the psychopathology of adolescence.[22]

Historically, psychiatry has been a field peculiarly afflicted by

[22] *Note by Committee on Sullivan Publications:* The material which follows was included in Sullivan's *Schizophrenia as a Human Process,* with Introduction and Commentaries by Helen Swick Perry; New York: Norton, 1962; pp. 321-351.

bad thinking and premature hypothetic formulation. Of many reasons for this, I will touch upon two. The facts of mental illness have often been seen through the aberrating medium of patho-physiological preconceptions—brain pathology and the like, endocrine disorders being perhaps the most recent. And the physician has been carried into the recondite field of mind without training in the technologies suiting him to his enterprise, and with training tending definitely to disqualify him for perceiving the data on which he should base his conclusion. Especially in the field of the schizophrenic phenomena, there has been a pandemic of formulating on limited if not actually irrelevant basic data, with singularly bad hypotheses, some of the most vicious features of which have been incorporated into persisting psychiatric astigmatisms.

Now, therefore, being about to take up discussion of the origin of schizophrenic processes, I find myself not alone confronted by entrenched erroneous conceptions supported by many adherents, but also embarrassed by the fact that I, too, have a formulation—a premature formulation, beyond doubt.[23] It seems to me that there is evident a certain course of sequents and consequents that make up the reality of this type of personality disaster; and I wish now to present some of the facts, as I see them, on the nature of anteceding conflicts from which many—perhaps "predisposed"—adolescents progress into this very grave form of mental disorder.

There was admitted, one day, to the most disturbed ward of the hospital a nineteen-year-old patient. He was brought to the hospital in a patrol wagon, in the custody of several police and attendants. I was told that he had become disorderly in his home

[23] While some several thousand of my fellows have flowed through the field of my attention, only some two hundred of them, seemingly fruitful sources of information, have been made the subjects of approximately scientific study. In all humility, I must relate that it is on the data of some seventy-five patients suffering undoubtedly schizophrenic processes, and of a hundred fifty persons in whom the outcropping of schizophrenic processes seemed more than ordinarily probable—on such few data from this field of incalculable vastness I have proceeded to a formulation. How diligently I have sought for negative instances destructive to my formulation, I am scarcely the one to judge. The controls to be derived from comparative studies—the consideration of adolescence and adolescent mental disorder in cultures other than ours—have not been available to me.

the preceding evening, and had broken some windows. That morning he had been seen by a neurologist and diagnosed as a case of dementia praecox, paranoid type. I saw him a few minutes after he had reached the ward—he was engaged in arguing with a group of attendants as to whether he should be disrobed and put to bed. When I entered the situation, he assumed a distinctly hostile, superior, and somewhat sardonic attitude toward me. After some formalities, I reduced the number of people present to himself and me, and touched upon several points of his life history with him. The result of our fifteen-minute talk is in many ways expressive of the points that I wish to discuss.

He said that he must, if we wished to help him, immediately be sent home to his father—that he would have been all right had it not been for two vile characters who had been in the house last night, and that he would not have known what they were plotting if it were not for his acquaintance with the language of the underworld. He went on to say that everything was all right until two months ago, when, through the carelessness of one of "those people," he had learned of the plot. He remarked that these people, who by their carelessness had permitted him to stumble upon something of importance, had arranged a fight between him and another young man at Miami Beach, but that he had been fortunate enough to defeat the youngster, adding that a young man like himself had no chance. "They wouldn't give a fellow like me a chance." I asked him what he meant by saying "a fellow like me"—what it was that he felt distinguished him from most people—and he did not produce anything of importance. I reiterated that he had said "They wouldn't give a fellow like me a chance," adding that I could not see wherein he was very different from most nineteen-year-olds, that if anything, he seemed to have some things in his favor—and he said something which indicated that he more or less agreed. The long and short of it seemed to be that there was nothing peculiarly remarkable excepting that he had stumbled upon this profoundly significant information. I remarked that quite often adolescents who were far from satisfied with themselves came to believe that they had discovered something of the utmost importance. He said he knew what was meant by adolescence, that he understood the term meant the period after puberty. I said to him, "Yes, the period in which one discovers sex and attempts to do something with it." He looked interested. I might add that in the course of these few remarks he had lost most of the antagonistic mask and signs of poorly concealed fear. We went on from there by my remarking that I supposed, as seemed always to be the case with people of his age who were brought to a mental hospital, that there was some difficulty confronting him in the field of sex, whereupon he said, "No, I have never been interested in anything but women." I said, "Oh, is that so?" He said, "Yes." I said, "Well, have you had sexual relations?" He said, "Yes, but only with women." I said, "Is it that you wish to emphasize to me that you have not had homosexual affairs?" He said, "Never—I hate it." I said, "Well, then you have come in contact with it?" He said, "Oh yes, in my theatre work I have seen a great deal of it, but I have never had anything to do with it. Whenever anyone approached me in that way I have loathed it because it was so . . . ," pausing, "so unnatural and so dirty." I said, "Well, I suppose you have had some actual experience with it, though, have you not?" He replied, "Never—only with women. Whenever a person has approached me that way I have—loathed it—I have had a strong impulse to hit him in the face. I wanted to knock him down." I said, "Well—I would interpret such a feeling as reflecting a pretty strong interest in it on your part"; by this time I seemed to be talking more or less to myself, thereby providing him with a way of absorbing the intelligence without too strong an urge for impressing me. He said nothing about it, showed no signs of particular distress. He had settled himself in bed, free from any conspicuous tensions. I added some general comments on the social situation created by one's admission as a patient into a mental hospital, on the character of misunderstandings, illusions, and delusions that young schizophrenics are prone to develop in such a situation, and on my hope that he would cling to the belief that he was in the hands of friends and well-meaning, however stupid, people. Having received some measure of assurance from him as to the last point, I took my departure.[24]

[24] While I deem it irrelevant to this presentation, I am constrained to present three additional facts concerning this patient. Firstly, nothing of the procedure of being brought to the hospital, or admitted thereto, or in the events immediately preliminary to my interview with him, had any reason-

It is difficult to avoid a conclusion from a long series of data similar in character to that of this patient. This young man is typical of a large proportion of my patients in acute schizophrenic disorders, in that, as soon as the topic of sex is introduced, he finds himself called upon to protest as to the normality of his sexual interests. He projects upon me, in response to my neutral remark to the effect that all adolescents have somewhat of a problem in the matter of sex, his own suspicion that his sexual interest focuses on members of his own sex. He finds himself suspected of homoerotic interests as soon as the topic of sex appears in the conversation. His activity in resolution of this situation, his overstressing of normal direction of sexual interest, expresses the conflict which he cannot escape—namely, the knowledge that his sexual tendencies include other than women as objects, and the opposing ethical appraisal of this condition as bad, wrong, and shameful, and destructive to the regard of others.

To illustrate the other important group of problems also culminating in acute schizophrenic illnesses, I will present in outline the case of another patient, this one a six-foot-three youth of eighteen. This young man came in the custody of two attendants from a general hospital at which he had been under observation because of suspected *encephalitis lethargica* ("sleeping sickness"). I saw him immediately on admission, finding him very morose and forbidding in his attitude. He was quite willing to state that he was sick, but "of course" there was not any reason for his being sent to a mental hospital, as nothing ailed his mind. His trouble was not of the mind but of the belly; his bowels didn't work, and things were not any longer all there in his belly. It was not difficult to learn that this state had come about by his wearing himself out masturbating. He had masturbated so long and so much that things inside were worn out, gone. I remarked, "In other words, you masturbated until you could no longer have the ejaculation?" He said very simply that this was the case,

____

able implication of knowledge or belief that he might be entertaining homoerotic interests. Secondly, he *had actually*, by clumsy and doubtlessly only vaguely conscious arrangement, secured himself the active attention of an homosexually inclined boy, some months before, and had engaged in behavior showing distinct homoerotic interests on his part. Thirdly, the patient has continued in a severe schizophrenic condition for over two years.

adding that on the occasion on which he had found that he was "through," could not bring himself to orgasm, a change had come over him. He said that thereafter he had gone into the kitchen, eaten his dinner, and then sat around staring at his mother and making noises with his mouth. These annoyed her, and they had sent him to a hospital. As a matter of fact, the family had been so disconcerted by his peculiar behavior and threatening attitude that they had called in a neurologist. This patient proved quite amenable to treatment and made a rather prompt social recovery.[25] He was not permitted to collaborate in intensive study of the underlying problems, and relapsed into a quite paranoid episode after about a year at large. When returned to the hospital, he again recovered—this time with the acquisition of some considerable insight—and remained comfortably employed for some three years. I then saw him on one occasion. He consulted me because he was growing tense and somewhat apprehensive because the woman (considerably his senior) with whom he was having sexual intercourse was urging him to marry her. Our conversation aided him in becoming satisfied with his decision to go slow in taking this step, and the discomfort diminished.

This young man had at one stage of his illness a phenomenon of great importance in many early schizophrenic disorders—namely, a dream of frankly incestuous content. It is not uncommon for those progressing into these grave disturbances to encounter in sleep or other states of reduced consciousness, profoundly disturbing outcroppings of sexual desire for the mother. They dream of having intercourse with her, of being on the verge of it, of palpating her genitals, or something similar. I have known patients to make violent efforts at suicide by immediate reason of the recurrence of such a dream. One is apt to find that the sexual dreams and fantasies that these preschizophrenic youths have been experiencing for months or years before the acute disturbance have pertained to an *unidentified* representative of the other sex. The paradigm is the dream of sexual inter-

[25] The conception of *social recovery* is one used in mental hospital practice to refer to the reintegration of personality to the degree that permits of conventional behavior in the hospital situation, without known remedy of the underlying problems.

course with a woman whose body is clearly revealed, but whose face is not at all clear. Or intercourse is had with "some girl," perhaps seemingly a different one in each dream—although often the girl is continually a stranger, and one poorly remarked as to recognizable characteristics. From what has already been said regarding the obstruction of growth of sexual tendencies by too intimate a linkage with the mother, it might be suspected that these quasi-heterosexual dreams are not all that they seem. We learn that they may mark a course that culminates in a schizophrenic illness, in which there is intense conflict over homoerotic interests; and they are not uncommon in individuals presently to adopt maladjustive homosexual habits. In fact, it is not uncommon for the dream-life to show a gradual or abrupt change from intercourse with unidentified women to sexual relations with someone who turns out to be, if not in fact clearly of the same sex as that of the dreamer, at least a sexually confused, perhaps hermaphroditic, individual.

From my material, in which negative instances are conspicuously absent, I am forced to the conclusion that schizophrenic illnesses in the male are intimately related as a sequent to unfortunate prolongation of the attachment of the son and the mother. That schizophrenic disorders are but one of the possible outcomes of persisting immature attitudes subtending the mother and son relationship must be evident. The failure of growth of heterosexual interests with persistence of autoerotic or homoerotic interests in adolescence, is the general formula. The factors that determine a schizophrenic outcome may be clarified by a discussion on the one hand of the situations to which I shall refer as homosexual cravings and acute masturbation conflict—often immediate precursors of grave psychosis—and of the various homoerotic and autoerotic procedures, on the other.

By the term *homosexual cravings*, I refer not to homoerotic interest, nor to desire for homosexual activity, but to a very disturbing form of conflict arising from vague to clear consciousness of a desire to engage in the genital stimulation of other persons of the same sex, when the self is in violent opposition to this tendency. Homosexual cravings may appear very insidiously in a personality unaware of homoerotic interests, or very dramatically in one morbidly certain of heteroerotic interests. Thus, an adolescent of the graphically isolated type may quite unwittingly arrange opportunities for sexual activity with another of the same sex, and become aware of the meaning of the situation only when it succeeds *or* fails. In the latter case, the frustration is so acute that he cannot longer remain unmindful of his wish, and conflict immediately appears. In the former, the shock of finding himself cooperative is the initial phenomenon of conflict. In the defensively heterosexual individual,[26] the last mentioned denouement may occur, or the subversive desire may gain expression in remembered dreams or in behavior in states of reduced consciousness—for example, alcoholic intoxication, or light sleep. In any case, the appearance within awareness of the homoerotic interest stirs such violent self-reproach that a dissociation or a vigorous defensive process results. If the self is able to dissociate the abhorrent system, the personality continues thereafter to be in grave danger of panic with succeeding schizophrenia, unless the sexual tensions are being drained off by some collateral procedure such as frequent masturbation or more or less definitely autosexual intercourse with women. Moreover, under cover of the dissociation, experience in any case continues to be integrated into the dissociated system, and its partition of energy in the personality to grow.

After the appearance of homosexual cravings, the individual finds himself much distracted, with reduced "power of concentration" owing to interference with his other interests, and corresponding impairment of efficiency in his routine life. The sexual tendencies, whether still accessible to awareness or existing in complete dissociation from the self-consciousness, tend to integrate interpersonal situations in which the abhorrent behavior might occur, and create relevance and strong (positive or negative) interest in suitable people and their views and behavior in keeping with the tendencies. The opposing tendencies within the self tend to integrate situations and to determine relevance and interest in sexually unattractive people and in personal acts and utterances strongly opposed to homosexual procedures. Both sorts of situations tend to be integrated, with more or less complete blocking of satisfaction to their group of tendencies. The

---

[26] The full meaning of this description will become apparent in our discussion below of the resistant homosexual and the bisexual individuals.

accumulation of sexual or other erotic tension increases the power of the related tendencies and an accidental encounter with a person particularly suitable for the sexual behavior generally precipitates an acute disturbance. Not uncommonly this denouement is facilitated by the subject-individual's preternatural naiveté, by which he is led to attempting the integration of an interpersonal situation favorable to the self (that is, favorable to the dissociating system opposed to the erotic strivings) with a person equally conflictful or defensive toward complementary sexual desires. In either case, it is but a matter of time and the flow of events until the victim finds himself being swept towards an abhorrent consummation. If panic does not supervene, a grave defensive process such as the paranoid state may now appear, or the individual may adopt a course of occasional lapses into the contemned satisfactions, with remorse or increasing desperation thereafter.

It might be thought that the outcropping of homosexual cravings could occur only in those without experience in sexual behavior with others of their own sex. It would seem that all those who had passed through the gang sexuality would be insured from these grave eventualities. There are, however, important exceptions to these generalizations. The preadolescent who is estopped from the growth of heteroerotic interests, and who is engaged in frank homosexual performances, comes ultimately to the time when most of his one-time partners have outgrown his type of interest. He now experiences instead of the social sanction of his behavior—which disintegrated or dissociated any earlier inhibitions he brought from the juvenile era—a slowly increasing influx of unfavorable reflections from the other boys. He may continue the sexual and other erotic satisfaction by associating himself with younger boys and progress along the line of a more or less maladjusted homosexual life. If he is an otherwise rather well-developed personality, and is fortunate, he may secure himself a homosexual mate of appropriate status and work out a satisfactory mode of life. But many such boys encounter crisis situations in which a sexual integration leads to great embarrassment, with the appearance in consciousness of a tendency opposed to the homoerotic gratification, that has been growing up to this time in a state of dissociation. And others find themselves in situations in which affectional ties of great importance to the self are increasingly jeopardized by manifestations of the homosexual tendencies. In either case, the sex-condemnatory system may gain expression in some state of reduced consciousness—for example, in a very impressive dream. There may come a night in the course of which the boy awakens in terror from a dream in which a Voice has uttered a warning, couched usually in general ethical terms, that puts an end to comfortable sexual behavior. These sudden reintegrations of tendencies opposed to homosexual activity in turn set up the situation of homosexual cravings, with consequences similar to those above indicated. That the outcome in these individuals who have had earlier overt experience is somewhat less ominous than is the case in its absence is not only theoretically to be expected, but actually the case both in the paranoid developments and in those who undergo schizophrenic disorders.[27]

In those who have grown past puberty without any direct contact with mutual genital interests, one often finds dissociation of some of the erotic tendencies, usually including the sexual. There is apt to be delayed pubescence in these boys, and their personality warp is often of the type that culminates in homo-erotic interests. The primitive genital phobia may have been an important factor in their deviation, or there may have been dissociation of the genital (phobic) or other erotic tendencies in late childhood or the juvenile era. One may learn, for example, of an instance when the boy, as a juvenile, reported to one of his parents some sexually motivated behavior of an older boy, some vulgarism heard or seen around school, or some precocious experimentation, with a reception of the data so painful that the related interest was excluded from the self.[28] As the sexual ten-

[27] Some considerable number of these people, on the appearance of the *craving* situation, adopt a modified course of interpersonal relations, discontinuing all overt homosexual acts and becoming mildly paranoid toward all members of the same sex, carry on a vigorous (juvenile) social life with women, and often finally marry a daughter-equivalent, with whom there is sufficient potency to insure offspring—a very gratifying demonstration of virility.

[28] Perhaps an example will point toward the important dynamic summation and cancellation arising from sentiments and stereotypes concerned in this sort of ethical learning. A boy a little over five years of age for the first time observed his father's penis, semi-erect, and hastened to the mother

sions increase, there come nocturnal emissions with or without remembered dreams, and an involuntary reactivation and interest in data previously acquired and currently available as to sexual matters. There may be consideration of "trying masturbation to see what it is really like," and other conscious preoccupations with sexual topics—even discussions, when started by another boy. But actual behavior is delayed, on various pretexts, and enough unwillingness displayed to discourage opportunities for mutual performances. When finally autosexual behavior begins, there is much self-condemnation, and efforts to augment the "will-power" against it. Not only does this fail, but the boy generally experiences incidents in which he finds himself remarkably free from conflict and self-reproach in satisfying the sexual tendencies. In retrospect he is disconcerted at realizing how "depraved" he can be in states of sexual excitement. He may suffer great self-reproach and make extreme efforts to lift himself from the degradation, seeking aid from the church or the family doctor. Spartan habits of life may be adopted. Physical exertion may become the only serious matter in life.[29] The diet may be modified. Sleep may be interfered with. Everything is done to insure the sexually-inhibitory system within the self from dissociation or suppression by incidents of sexual excitement, with the ensuing appalling abandon to sexual sin. A stream of evil consequences comes to attach to the sexual acts, aiding thereby the suppression of the system. "Weakness," loss of mental ability, aches and pains here and there, but especially in the re-

---

and maiden (maternal) aunt with the report that "Daddy has a great big dickey, and it's made of wood." The information proved extremely disconcerting to the auditors, and his interest in other people's penes was dissociated. Within six months, however, he, in company of some men, witnessed coitus of a bull and a cow, and reported this interesting event to the self-same audience, with a notably different reception. The aunt's reaction of shocked virtue proved amusing to the mother, who refused to be chagrined. The juvenile then prehended several personal facts, including the unwisdom of discussing such events with women. The dissociation was lifted, it now being necessary merely to suppress behavior (including speech) about such things when in the women's company.

[29] One of these boys—who became pubescent at the age of seventeen and a half years—remarked to me, after his fourth schizophrenic episode before the age of twenty, that he thought some of the boys "expressed themselves in athletics" (his chosen course), while others, the unfortunate minority for some reasons unable to use this method, "expressed themselves in sex."

gion of the spinal cord—everything to the proverbial growth of hair in the palms of the hands—come to serve the self in the contest with sexuality. The traditions of damage by masturbation exist widespread in the medical profession, the clergy, and among parents. Masturbation is alleged to lead to enfeeblement of the body and of the mind, to "insanity," and to physical disease. The troubled adolescent who seeks help in overcoming sexual impulses can always find someone to supply these lurid details.[30] His failure in control of the sexual impulses then brings increasing results.

The boy who has been led to expect some determinate evil consequence from masturbation, but who cannot control the impulse to the extent of suppressing the behavior, progresses into a sad state. Under cover of what appearance of complacency he is able to muster, he seeks in every personal contact the feared confirmation of the damage he believes to be ensuing. His chagrin at being the victim of his own penis increases, and his self-respect is so gravely reduced that he grows more and more subject to embarrassment. Blushing, shiftiness of gaze, even sudden impediments of speech, contribute to his humiliation. Social coöperation becomes most painful to him and he tends to seclude himself, or to develop screen-activities more or less unwittingly directed to the distraction of attention from his extreme self-contempt. His awareness is often occupied with pessimistic sexual reveries,

[30] The student should appreciate that there is a considerable part of the population in which there has been no great problem in handling masturbation, for the good reason that it did not occur to anybody that the individuals concerned might have such a problem; thus there was no particular puritanic interference with their lives, and they progressed from masturbation to more satisfying sexual performances without any stress. This is the normal course of events in dogs, horses, apes, and men who are not suffering too much from unfortunate social intervention. Many of these more fortunate people later encounter the traditions in common speech, in smoking car discussion of sexual topics, and the like. They are prone to develop secondary convictions about masturbation based in part on their own superiority and in part on actual facts, and come to regard and to talk about it as childish. Their influence, however, is relatively innocuous unless they chance to be psychiatrists or doting uncles, and has little to do with the path of destruction that ensues from chronic masturbation. Sometimes, however, the patient—or the nephew—who "knows" that his continued masturbation is enfeebling his body, being pooh-poohed by these well-meaning ones who have "put away childish things," thus acquires a new conviction of evil in the form of a belief that he is interfering with his maturation.

and these tend often to focus in some part of the somatic schematization of the self. If he has been caused to anticipate mental enfeeblement, he is apt to evolve not alone symptoms to be explained as the effects of preoccupation, but also aches and pains in the head and neck. The inability to "concentrate" in routine work and the incapacity to integrate a satisfactory sleep-situation combine to produce chronic fatigue, and the picture of so-called neurasthenia appears.[31] If he has been led to anticipate bodily evils perhaps from the loss of semen, these tend to be represented in his gloomy ruminations, and an hypochondriacal state may supervene. The coenesthesia, the influx of sentience arising in the viscera, that forms an important element in the backgrounding of personal reality, is affected. Attention swings gradually to particular items in this flow of sentience, and the interest fixed in the region concerned begins to disturb the somatic functional activity. Phenomena which should continue to be of the character of local physiological action are elevated into focal consciousness, and made part of the total integration, subject to influence from situational factors that should normally have no connection with them. The somatic unity is strangely disturbed so that the stomach, for example, may be required, in addition to its activity in dealing with part of our physicochemical food intake, to function in some relation to a quite different universe of communal existence—namely, the symbolic-social and cultural. It is integrated more or less specifically (as symbolically schematized) into situations in which not foodstuffs but perceived and fancied aspects of interpersonal situations are concerned. It is stimulated and inhibited in relation to the digestion of social contexts. The gastric secretion of hydrochloric acid tends now to be excessive and wholly unutilized in the depraved "digestion." The hyperacidity gives rise to symptoms from irritation of the already hyperesthetic nerve-endings, and the coenesthetic influx becomes peculiarly rich in the very data that have been made prepotent. The musculature of the stomach tends to become hypertonic, and spasm of the pylorus is added to the sources of discomfort and gloomy rumination. Pain, burning sensations, excessive and often peculiar appetite, epigastric distress before or after eating, "heart-

[31] The meaning of this chronic fatigue and the neurasthenic picture will become more clear after the discussion of sleep, in Chapter IX.

burn," anorexia, and even vomiting—all these confirm the sufferer in the conviction of bodily ruin. A vicious circle is established, with increasing detachment of the sufferer from more externally conditioned events, and an increasing partition of energy to fantasy processes. The doctor to whom this boy is sent may or may not discover the "functional" nature of the trouble. If he does not, a gastric ulcer is suspected and perhaps "discovered." If he does, he is apt to have little to offer the patient, and often prescribes antacids, and other more or less active drugs—with novel increments to the difficulty. Or dietary nuisances may be adopted, and the youth from thenceforth strives increasingly to bolster his self-respect by vanquishing the singular difficulties that he encounters in getting the right things to eat—becoming a burden to himself and everyone else who gives him a meal, additional to the misfortune implied in being important chiefly as a person who has diminished gastric capacity.[32]

This hypochondriacal interference with bodily function is especially apt to focus in the genital apparatus itself. The pessimistic revery centers on the offending organ and a variety of urological and genitourinary symptoms appear. These may be anything from rumination on the discovery of hitherto unnoted anatomical peculiarities—such as the customary discrepancy in size of the two divisions of the scrotum—to delusion formations and hallucinated symptoms amounting to schizophrenia. Frequently, the overattention to the genitals begins in an unimpressive manner, and the boy is treated by his advisor as merely uninformed. He is told that nothing is the matter with him, that he is perfectly normal. This does not help in solving his masturbation conflict, and he either seeks a new advisor or develops more symptoms with which to harass the first. Not infrequently he secures some treatment, even if it is only a suspensory ban-

---

[32] The pylorus seems generally to mark, in the somatic schematization of the self, the end of the *upper part* of the alimentary tract. The oral erotic type of personality usually unwittingly "draws the line" in symptom formation at this point. He is preeminently the victim of "diseases"—and their "treatment"—of the mouth, nose and throat, and stomach. He contributes much to the specialities of dentistry, rhinology, and laryngology—including tonsil-removing—and gastroenterology. He may involve the lungs or the heart as an extension, but he seldom gets below the stomach unless he proceeds directly to the genital tract in order *to screen* more or less clearly prehended oral desires.

dage, the wearing of which makes consciousness of the genitals even more acute. Occasionally, he is given intensive treatment for something or other allegedly physically wrong with him. He may undergo an operation for the repair of a perhaps authentic varicocele, or of a patulous inguinal ring. He may be urethroscoped or even cystoscoped—an experience not immediately to be forgotten. It may be found that his verumontanum is congested, and deep urethral instillations may be made. And his prostate may be examined, to the extent of massage—quite a destructive experience, especially if any excess of erogeny attaches to the anal region. Or again, his complaints of *night losses,* or *losses at stool,* or *a drop that follows urination,* or of *peculiar sensations* in the scrotum, groin, or perineum—any or all of these may be diagnosed as "sexual neurasthenia"—and everything from electrical claptrap and "violet rays," to firm counsel to buck up, forget it, or get himself a woman, is prescribed in its treatment. If he is extraordinarily unfortunate, he consults a quack "specialist for men," and from thenceforth is treated for money only, with liberal cultivation of new symptoms, so that he can always be "re-feed" whenever he seems to have more money. In any case, it is rather certain that he has *not* presented to his advisor an understandable account of his trouble, for the excellent reason that he does not have full access to the data concerned.[33] And in any case, he will follow one of three courses: a progression to grave mental disorder; a settled hypochondriacal state, itself a rather serious mental disorder;[34] or a marked improvement when an all too frequently quite accidental event of interpersonal re-

[33] It would be a great mistake to assume from these comments that *all* "functional" (that is, nonorganic) genitourinary complaints of adolescents are concomitants of masturbation conflict. The fundamental thesis of this presentation emphasizes that *no phenomenon of total activity can be stripped of its personal embodiment and translated directly into causative factors.* There are no personality phenomena that always mean a particular thing. It is true that these hypochondriacal complaints centering in the genitals *often* arise as sequents in a conflict over masturbation. They occasionally arise from quite different sexual sources. They *may* arise in the course of an apparently normal heterosexual life.

[34] The more or less stable hypochondriacal sexual maladjustments that contribute so much to the income of quacks and the like may be closely related to defense reactions by projection of blame. We encounter many individuals who progress from hypochondriasis to paranoid state, and some who show a sort of alternation of the two states to such effect that they are chronically either paranoid *or* hypochondriac.

lations starts him toward a more adjustive solution of his sexual problem.

Many youths in the grip of severe conflict between the sexual drives and tendencies opposed to masturbation never establish a situation of mutual confidence with another person. Some of them attempt it, and find themselves in so anomalous a position that they give up hope of securing assistance. Thus, the boys in high or preparatory school may be given a lecture on sex hygiene, with the suggestion that all those who wish may confer with the professor in private. Unless the lecturer has created an impression of most extraordinary sympathy, the really harassed pupils go nowhere near him. Not uncommonly, however, some of the more intelligent pupils do seek him out and attempt to convey to him their formulation of the problem. All too often they have the attitude of "knowing it all," of dispensing pearls of wisdom to the ignorant. A boy who has, for reasons susceptible of discovery, come to suppose that erections of his penis constitute that which is called masturbation, then "learns" a body of confusions that adds quite remarkably to his troubles—without the helpful advisor having any suspicion that they have been discussing barely related topics in using a common term. Or the boy finds that the advisor's thirst for intimate data repels him, and, despite the best of intentions, claims problems that have little reality and avoids any frankness. Or yet again, he plunges desperately into confidences that are for discoverable reason intensely interesting to the advisor, only to meet rebuff and upbraiding, to be bathed in ethical whey that nourishes the conflict, or to find that his confidant's interest is expended as soon as the spicy details are exhausted and that the interview is being terminated with banal assurances and some haste to get on to the next boy.[35] The expectation that a youth who is suffering a severe masturbation conflict will be so facile at confidence as to be intelligently frank in the initial interview with a stranger is at best rather fantastic, while the optimism that leads a counselor to give advice in a situation thus uncertainly adumbrated is but another demon-

[35] We are not concerned here with the well-organized teaching of sex information in the grammar school. The feasibility of this highly desirable instruction has already been demonstrated. Also, the unwisdom of abbreviated and poorly managed courses of this kind is well known to the psychopathologist.

stration of the low regard in which personality is held by that great majority who have not enough personal insight to know that problems of living transcend matters of gossip or preaching.

In the adolescents who manifest these genital hypochondriases, we often encounter the so-called *castration fear* or anxiety. By this term, we refer to a particular component of personality that has arisen from some more or less specific experience sequence in childhood or early in the juvenile era. It may be that a parent or someone else in authority over the child has enforced his disapproval of genital manipulation by a direct threat to the effect that if the behavior is continued, the penis will be cut off, perhaps pointing the threat by exhibiting the instrument to be used —for example, a pair of scissors. Or it may be that some intercurrent misfortune is coincident with a situation in which the child is enjoying the forbidden pleasure, and the two become confluent. Thus, an attack of earache coming on after the child has retired and engaged in some genital stimulation, *known to be severely disapproved* (sinful) may have the effect of a punishment for the sin, and become dynamically as effective as a direct threat of amputation of the penis. Finally, a stream of unfortunate events may become associated with the genital pleasure, and lead the child on some occasion to wish that the offending member did not exist. This thought, however, represents a complex fantasy of change in the somatic representations of the self, and usually one that the child has been taught to regard as also "sinful." It brings with it threats of evil that would flow from the "remedy." There is now a secondary conflict, and confusion of the self-integration, with fear of a magical tendency of the injury to occur as punishment for the prohibited genital manipulation.[36] If any of these influences add to the self enough energy to dissociate the then relatively feeble impulses making for genital stimulation, there is apt to be no recrudescence of the problem until preadolescence. In the meanwhile, the memorial ele-

[36] These rather obscure processes, as they are revealed in individual personalities, are closely related to the category next preceding—in turn related to the direct threat of "castrating," that is, amputating the penis. The religious culture built into the personality is the link from act to fear. It is another manifestation of the effect of inculcating the doctrines of crime and punishment, sin and penitential act, from which comes the generalization of the need for punishment.

ments of the actual events are overlaid with the details of life, and, in common with all reflections to the self that have given pain, tend to fail of ready recall—in fact, frequently to exist in the repressed quasi-mythological condition. When now in adolescence the genital sexuality makes appearance and conflict supervenes, these earlier relatively inaccessible deviations may manifest in the service of the opposing tendencies as an undue fear of evil consequences to flow from masturbatory or other sexual behavior, and a deepening hypochondriasis.[37]

An occasional outcome of all these sorts of adolescent conflict is *suicide*. Besides the self-destruction that may terminate the graver mental disorders, there also occur instances in which the act is not preceded by serious disorder of social behavior. Some adolescents are so baffled in their attempt to subjugate the interest in autoerotic satisfactions that they destroy themselves almost as if in revenge on the offending part of the somatic equipment. The paralysis of interest in others and in future possibilities of the self has progressed in them to the point that life has become colorless and wholly unattractive. Their deaths may therefore be classed as quasi-rational, in contradistinction to those of the depressed and the schizophrenic youth. The probability of self-destruction is always rather high in the course of the manic-depressive depression—particularly in the stage of convalescence.[38] Deaths resulting from personal acts in the course of schizophrenic disorders are often the result of misadventure. The

[37] The conception of castration fear has been overgeneralized, as have those of compensation, sublimation, and the defense reactions. The enthusiasts for this interpretation reason somewhat as follows: The penis is all-important; therefore, any reverse or reduction in self-esteem leads to a feeling of castration, and all the nonpleasant emotions are but manifestations of "the castration complex," or castration fear, anxiety, and so on. I do not wish to minimize the importance of the penis as a factor in personality; a medium-sized man with a small penis is generally very different, in his attitude to others, from a medium-sized man with a large penis—everything else being equal. But the notion that the penis can be equated to or made to exceed in importance anything or everything else in the male personality is absurd. The interpreting of any derogatory or aggressive behavior as castrative does not seem to be particularly illuminating. In fact, all this sort of universalizing "reasoning" reminds one of the "henid" of Weininger, or the grammatic definition reported in one of the "Boner" series: All sentences are either abstract *or cement*.

[38] The greater number of suicides at all ages is to be referrd to this disorder. Deep depression in a personality characterized by more or less cyclic

sufferer ends his life quite incidentally to some fantastic procedure for the remedy of his distress—to be reborn, to protect
others from some delusional contamination, to save the world,
to demonstrate omnipotence, and the like. Psychopathic and
other badly warped adolescents sometimes "use" the threat of
suicide as a tool for insuring attention from others, and occasionally die as a result of "accidental" misjudgment—too great a
dose of poison, too long a delay in calling for help, and so forth.
These latter, in particular, manifest the tendency that is called the
wish for death.[39] This complex motivation that manifests superficially as a desire for death, or even in facilitation of self-
destructive impulses, is far from having a unitary source. *Passim*,
the disturbances of the somatic schematization connected with
this motivation tend frequently to concentrate about the head in
the form of recurrent headaches, migraine, and neuralgias.

Consideration of suicide takes us to the contemplation of religious interpretations of the observed growth of personality by
the long-circuiting of tendency-systems. *Hope*, which we may
define as the integration in a total situation of more or less probable but contingent factors subsisting in the future, carries many
people through severe disappointments and states of temporary
thwarting to belated success or old age without despair. The
religious cultures which have sprung up from time to time have
included formulae in this connection, very frequently offering,
as matter for integration in one's curent situation, factors not of
a mere earthly future but of a transcendental Future Life, to be

---

mood swings should always indicate great care in this particular, to be
redoubled as the patient improves and seems to be fairly near his average
state. A great many of these patients have destroyed themselves in the course
of the first "visit" home from the mental hospital.

[39] Freud, in *Beyond the Pleasure Principle*, and in his subsequent writings,
has developed a conception of "death instincts" that are universally distributed in people, and opposed to the "life instincts." This is part of the so-
called metapsychological formulation, the philosophy of Freud. Like all
other philosophies, it is insusceptible of rigorous demonstration, and may be
considered to be valid for its formulator and some others of related life experience. I do not recommend its wide adoption. The student is certain to
have difficulty enough preventing premature crystallizations of his own
opinions in some universalizations of terms. For a discussion of the wish for
death, see, for example, Ernest E. Hadley, "Vertigo and the Death Wish,"
J. Nervous and Mental Disaese (1927) 65:131-148; and perhaps *ibid.*, "Presidential Address of the Washington Psychopathological Society," *Psychoanalytic Review* (1928) 15:384-392.

experienced only after this one is finished—often to be gained only by approval of the priestly caste. These doctrines have served to render the prehended real *rational*, and have been a great boon to those who live by the exploitation of the socially underprivileged, who are taught to seek their reward for unhappy compliance here, in the shimmering expanses of the Other World. Unfortunately, whenever manpower has come to be valuable to the Elite, there has had to be added to these doctrines a restraint calculated to overcome a certain urgency of the particularly thwarted about reaching the realms of bliss.[40] Interest in the Future State comes easily to denizens of any social order of extreme inequality of opportunity, if the greater number have no means for prehending the real inequalities of personal abilities and opportunities, or have no means of communicating these prehensions from one to another. When, however, the adaptive culture available to the most unfortunate caste has grown to the point at which many of its denizens become aware of these individual variations in personal ability and in the opportunities provided, then, if the social fabric is to be preserved in its grossly discriminative state by dependence on a Future State and related dogmata, some universal tendency system that cannot be entirely restrained has to be legislated out of bounds. The underprivileged then obviously fail to live up to the rules, and are open to censure and punishment. Merely secular law can scarcely serve in this connection, for the more enlightened masses at least vaguely surmise that secular authority vests in their collective submission. The law that disqualifies a part of human nature must therefore be transcendentally sanctioned; it must be an addition to the mores, as such inculcated into most people within the family-group; and it must be wholly exterior to the social criticism that begins in the juvenile era. The tendency

[40] Saint Augustine, I believe, made it against the rules in the Western culture for one to hasten his translation from this vale of woes. Psychopathologically considered, suicide, while always antibiological, was rational and pseudo-adjustive up to the time of this religious enactment (dogma). It would be interesting to trace the cultural processes that fixed the time which Western Europeans were required thus to forego the privilege of expediting their receipt of the Heavenly reward. Now that the religious culture is deliquescing and the Hereafter is losing value along with the other dogmata, current adolescent suicides are not at all in the class of the pre-Augustinian flights to eternal bliss, and must be regarded as irrational and nonadjustive.

systems that have been subjected to this dogmatic thwarting in our culture are numerous, but by far the most powerful of them is that manifesting in sexual behavior.[41]

The adolescent of bygone generations often came promptly to be "religious." He accepted the entrenched regulations of life perforce. One could not but interpret one's own peculiarities as Satanic—good reason for seeking to learn the rules by which to live through the years in this cruel world accumulating as much merit as might be toward the blessed future. Sexual asceticism was the greatest good, and both organized and informal opportunities for its achievement were provided. Once one had turned from the lure of the flesh, one could live quietly in a considerable measure of sanctified intimacy with a group of kindred souls. Or one could take to a dignified paranoid state and go about a slow "psychical castration." If schizophrenic phenomena appeared, this did not necessarily disable one: quite a few opportunities for utilizing this eccentricity were provided in the business of evangelism. Moreover, one might, if needs be, found an eccentric religion and often secure the necessary disciples. If there was some skidding on the slippery path to superhuman chastity and other fantastic virtues, these could be charged off as temporary gains in the losing battle waged against the good by the Evil One. The sweet odor of sanctity could best be appreciated in the ecstasy of repentance for Sin. The noble rhetoric of those whose duty it was "to be cruel to be kind" was so powerful that a multitude of little prophets interpreted the Almighty Ones to their followers, without uncertainty as to the accuracy or completeness of their information. Sex without issue was Sin; and as sex is inescapable in youth, issue was abundant. And the wheels

[41] I would not wish to be interpreted as holding that the structure of the mores has arisen by *deliberate acts* of theocrats or others aware of the dynamics with which they operate. Far from it; the mores have arisen as the implemented fantasies of religious leaders, generally highly rationalized in the faiths that they professed. These fantasies, being those of people of more or less related cultural backgrounds, have been acceptable to the followers— if the latter did not *know better;* that is, have culture actually adaptive to life in the particulars concerned. That those fantasies have functioned to promote achievement, and to work extreme cruelty, are alike beside the point. The day is still far beyond the scope of the writer's imagination when there will be no mores, no religious cultures, but only adaptive ways of doing things.

of the growing industries, and the guns of the growing states, and the coffers of the budding capitalists, made use of such issue.

The Renaissance, the rapid growth of physical sciences and technologies, and the dissemination of literateness, were some of the factors that hastened the flowering of the religions of nationalism that had been growing parasitically on the religions of the Other Worlds. Education in mundane things, even today in its infancy, nonetheless accomplished some realization of secondary group relationships. It interlocked in this effect with the rapidly expanding systems of transportation and communication. Concentrations of population in urban centers functioned to accelerate the dissolution of many superstitions of various primary groups. The ascetic ideal grew increasingly absurd, and the ideal of the brotherhood of man moved off even further beyond the horizon. Disillusionment became the spirit of the times. Superstitions that had at least the virtue of wide acceptance were destroyed in wholesale. The claptrap of statecraft was offered in their place. But the nationalist theocrats were puny specimens in contrast with the great of old who manifested but ephemeral glory here, in their tedious proconsulate for the Transcendental Ones. It became increasingly difficult to conceal from the now verbal masses the shallow and shortsighted self-seeking of most representatives of the State. The ministration to the common weal was observed very frequently to lead to personal profit. Even the mighty rhetoric, automatic acceptance of which seems all too human, was degraded in political bickerings for preferment—the successful achievement of which often led to so immediate a profit-taking that it violated public decorum. Money, now regarded by some psychoanalysts as a transubstantiation of the infant's meconium, and Power, similarly regarded as the castration of the father, became the matters of importance. The Western culture had progressed into late childhood, and the adolescent must look to earthly preferments instead of treasures in Heaven. The socialization of men, the collaboration of compeers, the integration of enduring and benevolent intimacies—for these even the religious culture was becoming tenuous. Those who could find their way through the jungle along the footpaths adaptive to money or power might fare passing well. But those who turned aside from these pursuits and sought a fairly human life risked their necks amid eldritch wonders of crumbling faiths matted together with a swiftly-growing fungus of laws and short-lived institutions exuded by antisocial statesmen in the protection of special privilege. Individualism and National Independence were the watchwords. The Great War taught many adolescents the futility of the new religions of individualism and nationalism, even as it gave birth to a rival to the growing international faith, capitalism, in the shape of the communistic dogmata. The theocrats of the two have ever since waged war under warrant of the noble rhetoric, to which not alone the most underprivileged, but most of the Elite, still attend devoutly.[42]

At the level of least social privilege where hunger, squalor, pariah-hood, abysmal ignorance, and often disease combine to emphasize the consciousness of utter inferiority, there are born some infants who embody exceptional abilities. Some of these not only survive but come to adolescence. If their personalities are not already so warped that they might well be dead, or accident has not lifted them somewhat above their expectations, these youths generally find themselves confronted with the alternatives of grave mental disorder or crime. Compulsory education and the less estimable of the public prints equip them to rebel against their apparent fate. Their intelligence and experience dissipate notions of preferment in Church, State, scientific or learned pursuits. They readily discover that in commerce or industry they can "get ahead" only by patiently accommodating themselves for an indefinite but certainly long period to the pattern of the moron. They readily infer that there is no ultimate necessity for

[42] The panic of 1929 and the slough that followed it pointed to something so radically wrong in all that had gone before, that the religious culture of the Western World at the time of this writing survives almost wholly by human inertia and the necessity to fill the gaps in our grasp on life. The Chief Executive and other exalted American theocrats counsel patience while the "economic pendulum" slowly swings back to "American normalcy"—allegedly a *natural* cyclic phenomenon—while striving with might and main to *do something* that will give their creeds new "face" by temporarily extricating the people from their misery. Some little lasting good will doubtless come out of the political expediency, but it is to be hoped by the thoughtful that something more than emergency patchwork will take place. Encouragement may be found in the increasingly vocal dissatisfaction of a few of the great industrial leaders. When the most privileged in our world of money and power perceive the inadequacy of our current religions, fundamental remedies should be near.

the extreme hardships that they encounter—that in fact these inequalities that deny them any opportunity to enjoy the exercise of their abilities are ordained by nothing more august than a group of men in the stupidly selfish exercise of power. If they express their grievances by merely verbal behavior, they come promptly to discover that one's voice does not carry if one has neither money nor power. And if they act more directly, they violate the all-pervading web of laws, and are apt to find that they have forfeited even the little security the State grants to "the least of its subjects." Never sympathetic toward the myth of Justice, such a one has long since learned that even the Established Elite must sometimes resort to the highest courts to protect their rights and privileges. It seems also that status or money are often needed to energize even the first cogs of this machinery of protection, so God-like in its leisurely indifference and arbitrariness, so punily human in many of its personifications. At the same time, such a one is taught that there is nothing to insure one from being seized upon by this machinery of Criminal Justice. This is a part of evil chance that inheres in one's lack of status. It is quite impossible to live within the letter of the Law, which no one any longer knows in its entirety and which everyone is by definition made to know. And there are generally instances to be observed of *highly selective*, mean, partisan, and criminal interventions of this machinery to wreak unmerited hardship on some unfortunate compeers. Aware that one cannot without fortunate accident "earn" enough by legitimate activity to "pay" those whose income derives from providing a roof over one's head, heat in cold weather, and food, it is not strange that the underprivileged adolescent of superior ability often chooses to be exploited by organized crime. Here he finds opportunity for the competitive pursuit of status, for he is at last opposed to compeers in the established order. Here he can fraternize intimately with some kindred souls. And even the sexual tendencies may often be dealt with somewhat more satisfactorily than was the case before he embarked on his "career." [43]

[43] A chapter entitled "The Working of Welfare" survived the fourth revision of this book. Its elimination should not endanger the thesis that the personal embodiments of law and other alleged welfare institutions with whom people enter into primary (direct) relationship mean more to most of the denizens of the culture than do the more abstract entities that these

Crime, generally definable as the willful violation of any law that is alleged to protect the public, assumes the proportions of a special problem in relation to adolescence. According to the archaic dogmata from which one Law proceeds, a person grows from irresponsible infancy to some point at which he achieves free will, knowledge of all the laws, the capacity to intend public damage, the ability to know and judge the nature and consequences of one's acts, and an exquisite discrimination as to the difference between right and wrong. Before this marvelous point has been achieved, one cannot *intend* an act to the extent required for the perpetration of most full-fledged crimes. But all citizens achieve this point at one and the same particular *chronological* age, excepting one be "insane," "mentally incompetent," or "of unsound mind." As the student may surmise, the psychobiologist has a certain difficulty in this field; he cannot find anything but dogma in the entity, free will; he is certain that only a small proportion of the citizens are capable of learning the more coherent of the laws, much less the vast body of statutes and similar ordinances that are in fact the Law; he has not previously granted much importance to the business of "intending" within awareness; he has come to view almost all intentions as good rationalizations that seemed chiefly to obscure from the self all that might be judged unworthy in the effective motivation of one's behavior and thought.[44]

The psychobiologist, by arduous self-searching, comparative studies, and inferences from phenomena that have seemed to occur while he slept, has come to some insight into the "nature"

---

agents more or less imperfectly make manifest. As long as the personnel of law enforcement and other welfare work is recruited without regard for the nuclear fact that these agents should *work primarily in the extraordinarily difficult field of interpersonal relations, for benevolent ends*, the excogitation of laws and philanthropies will be somewhat futile. Once more than merely verbal acknowledgment of this nuclear fact has been achieved, the problem of training this personnel for its function may receive some measure of the attention that it warrants.

[44] At this point one may well notice that the criminal law finds it convenient in some cases to *presume* the criminal intention. The wisdom beyond Solomon that each juror manifests in judging these matters of intention is all the more spectacular in that *negligence* (to have the proper good intentions?) may in some cases establish the occurrence of crime rather than accident—for example, reckless driving of an automobile. And negligence, too, may be presumed, under some statutes.

and purpose of some of his own actions in emotionally toned interpersonal situations, to such effect that he is able to predict the consequences that might flow from them. When he turns to the general public—and particularly to the underprivileged sections of it—the *assumption* of this difficult achievement is glaringly ridiculous. Obviously "the nature and consequences of one's acts" must be something quite different from insight into one's motivation in a total situation. Being ubiquitous, by assumption, it may be "common sense" appreciation of the "physical" characterization of certain behavior, regarded objectively—for example, fatal consequences flowing from a hole in the heart caused by the impact and trajectory of a bullet fired from a gun. Or, again, death of a cow as a consequence of the burning of a wax replica of the cow by someone who has made a compact with the devil, as objectively manifested by an anesthetic spot on his body. Or, again, recovery of health as a consequence of the administration by a doctor of an inert remedy to a sick person. The psychobiologist has been trained to suspect common sense when it passes beyond the field of sensory observation, and to scrutinize the presuppositions on which supposed observations are made by intelligent individuals. He may recall with faint amusement some of the notable "observations" made by students of the Watsonian Behaviorism, when it was young. And, finally, he has come to believe that the discrimination of "right" and "wrong" by anyone is generally nothing more than the manifestation of his training in infancy and childhood, as it has survived the later stages of personality growth, and remains effective in the superego aspects of the personality. For that matter, he recalls many instances from his study of personalities in which evil has been wrought without violating any law. And if he has worked with prisoners, he knows other instances when crime was committed without any evil having been done anyone. His respect for the jurist who works good with this incredible implement of the Law is therefore very great. His expectations regarding the "consequences" to a personality from becoming involved in the criminal law, cannot but be guarded. And if he has been called to assist in the enforcement of the law as an expert witness in the trial of someone accused of a crime, he may well extend his pessimism as to "consequences" of a criminal "act" to include all those who are

concerned with the legal processes arising from it, including the public present as visitors in court or as readers of the more sensational newspapers.

The young science of psychobiology and the somewhat older science of biology alike teach the impossibility of securing data susceptible of consensual validation by the study of an *act* torn from its situational context—including the acting organism. The act is of indefinable scope and meaning when it is abstracted from its place in reality, and made the subject of cogitation, as an entity. When, therefore, the State in its business of promoting and protecting the common weal deals with the acts of certain people without regard for the persons concerned or the cultural and other factors potent in the growth and manifestation of any and all personalities, when it neglects to teach parents the content of each year's crop of legislation, produced by the uninformed and irresponsible representatives of its people in legislature assembled, when it prosecutes and convicts people for violating laws created after they have passed out of the eras of formal instruction, when it functions in its law enforcement through persons largely without training in the rudiments of human nature—awarding to all sorts of prevailing superstitions and prejudices a like place in the administration of justice; under these circumstances the psychopathologist can scarcely be filled with enthusiasm even for the "remedies" of "treatment" in place of punishment for criminals, of psychiatric commissions to "advise" the courts, of "examination and recommendations in regard to disposition" of all persons convicted of felonies, and the like. To him, it then would seem that there is not very much hope left for those caught up in the web of the criminal law—or in the business of its practical enforcement—for it is a fantastic structure like the world of a mistrained juvenile who seeks to solve social situations by threatening to black the eye of his compeer if not given his own way about everything, regardless of anyone or anything. To succeed for long in this rudimentary method of social control, one would have to be ubiquitous and omnipotent, unthinking, and wholly ruthless. While many agents of the State may secretly aspire to these qualifications, it is probably impossible to turn back the stream of human progress so far that any people will crystallize such an attitude as their

State. And, if it happened, this apotheosis of arbitrary social control would scarcely waste its substance and encumber itself with an intricate web of verbally expressed Laws, the administration of which had to find its way through a maze of purely verbal behavior, past and present, the *current meaning* of which had finally to be judged by some weary thinkers sitting on a Supreme Court to adjudicate the more vigorously contested disputes.[45]

History shows that the State has come more and more to discover the spread of damage beyond the persons directly concerned in injurious activities, to the public at large. This is the general formulation by which it establishes the criminal nature of certain "acts." The next step should follow the even more cogent consideration of the spread of causation beyond the persons most directly concerned in the criminal or other injurious behavior, to the culture itself, and the surfaces of stress between its patterns and the personalities of its denizens. The prohibitive-retaliative character of the Law; the pastoral and agrarian, intolerant mythology underlying our way of law-making and its tawdry enforcement; the particularistic vindictiveness of people trained to regard themselves as autonomous entities having "rights" in their own name; and the entrenched *laissez faire* of those who enjoy privilege—these are some of the more formidable difficulties that must be overcome in remedying these aspects of social control. The profligate abandon to exploitation, accidental utilization, or wholly useless wastage, of the human values now within our power to identify seems, however, to be the most fundamental defect of our culture, from which flow most of our other evils. As long as the individual fruits of human evolution are so worthless that they can all be thrown into the same bin to

[45] This discussion should include considerations of the civil law as distinguished from the criminal, of the doctrine of *torts*, personal injuries as opposed to public injuries (crimes), and of the gradually evolving proceedings in *equity*, now fairly widespread in juvenile and domestic relations courts. In courts of equity and in some courts of criminal justice, an effort is made to deal with meaningful situations, rather than with mythological states of universal equality, and so on. I would be remiss, indeed, did I not take occasion to acknowledge the wisdom shown by some of our judges, all the more estimable because of the difficulties which the State (its politicians), the sensation-mongers, and the legitimately evil-doing (therefore very conservative) class combine to place in the way of enlightened judicial initiative.

rot or keep whole, as chance dictates, it can scarcely matter if some good human material is ground up in the machinery of Law. By the time one now becomes politically significant, he has generally worn himself down to the point at which his formula, his trick of making a living, seems to be about the last thing that he can learn. If it is scrapped by the appearance of a better formula, he may find himself impoverished and his family reduced to want, without hope. It is all "up to" him; life is all a competition, if not a conflict, in which tears are not wasted on the loser. In such a society, we can scarcely expect that the conservation of exceptional human abilities and their untrammeled nurture will become a function of the State.[46]

Whatever his place in the social fabric, the adolescent can scarcely fail to discover in his seeking of a way of life that the satisfaction of some of his tendencies is anything but a simple matter. Mores, Law, economic pressures, population concentration and mobility, intercommunication, disintegrative criticism, privilege, privation—above all, the total disintegration of the stable world for which his parents trained him—combine to impress on him the incomprehensibility of life as it goes on around him. He becomes afraid. Moreover, as he seeks to rid himself of fear, he discovers that everyone is afraid, excepting only the stupid. Three paths open before him. His personality organization and his opportunity determine the course that he shall try. He may be able to postpone the plunge, seeking the relative security of the university and the pursuit of knowledge, perhaps having recourse to compensatory dynamics in reducing the stress that he experiences. But this is no panacea, for he now embodies tendencies that cannot be discharged in this way. Maladjustments of severe degree are frequent—psychoneuroses, anxiety states, even major psychoses—among those to whom the Higher Education is principally a delay in meeting life. He may, particularly if he is enabled by a juvenile personality and the opportunity, adopt the

---

[46] The wolf-pack ideal and references to the profligacy of Nature are not to be condemned, if they are not mixed with a damnable "compassion" that preserves a vast body of people from death, without giving them any justification for life. Once a culture outgrows the "struggle for existence" with infrahuman opponents, it doubtless comes to the internecine competitive stage. We seem to be ready to quit this struggle for individual acquisitions for a stage of collaboration in the assembly of enduring values.

ideal of respectability, and recast himself as rapidly as may be to compliance with the conventional hypocrisies and evasions of his class, making up for the loss of self-esteem by overvaluing material augmentations of his self, and draining off dangerous tensions by a surreptitious "double life," gambling, alcoholic overindulgences, or the pursuit of other excitements that are only partly frustrating—all of which dwarf his potentialities to the level of a solid citizen and fix him in the pattern of late adolescence for life. Or he may identify himself directly or secondarily with a kindred group that lives in some degree of disharmony with the prevailing majority, often somewhat stealthily, coming frequently to waste his youth and energy in misdirected revolt against fantastically exaggerated opposition, in pursuit of poorly judged goals, or in the overzealous nurture of illusion based on misapprehension of what he seeks. It used to be that generally the adolescent came finally to "settle down"—an expression all the better in that the process was often a regressive disintegration of interest from the adolescent state. The "settling" process has grown quite uncertain, of late, and many factors suggest that there will be no return to the good old days.

The lack of culture adaptive to the sexual tendencies in particular, has been accentuated recently by the changed role of woman as wife and as member of the family-group (mother). The blanket of secrecy and shame that has covered the field of sexual behavior has always functioned to work evil, both by ingraining vicious attitudes to sex and in concealing remediable disharmonies in marriage. Now the difficulties of married life are greatly augmented, for only a part of the depraved attitudes to sex has been dissipated, and the new factors of personal prestige, intersex conflict, economic interdependence, political franchise, and so on combine with the continuing sexual inhibitions to augment marital maladjustments very greatly. Warped adolescents therefore abound, while the Law and the economic *laissez faire* combine to make it ever more difficult for any adolescents to satisfy their sexual tendencies without violation of the mores and the criminal law. The proportion in each generation who must turn aside from the traditional pattern of marriage and the home must grow rapidly, while the number who are estopped by personality warp from any approximation to the heterosexual pattern becomes larger and larger. It appears that the current situation implies an almost geometrically increasing stress between individuals and this part of the social fabric, with outcome in mental disorder or crime. Since it is the ubiquitous and very powerful sexual tendencies that are concerned, it would seem that some intelligence might well be applied to the revision of our culture, if we are to continue to call ourselves civilized, much less to function as a mighty influence in world affairs.[47]

Before concluding this chapter and passing on to consideration of the typical grave adolescent mental disorder, it is necessary to delineate the forms of behavior and implicit processes prevalent in the satisfaction of erotic tendencies among those who cannot follow the biologically ordained heterosexual path because of their personality warp, and deviate from it homosexually, in violation of the law and the mores, in various degrees unhappily and unfortunately. While this field includes a great variety of situations integrated in fashions varying from full adjustment to very grave maladjustment, the principles concerned can for the most part be demonstrated by consideration of genital, oral, and anal erogeny, and the bisexual, the resistant homosexual, and the pervert type of personality organization. The *bisexual individual* is one whose personality organization permits the integration of situations for the securing of genital satisfactions with members of either sex. Male primates, young stallions, and dogs, besides man, show an inclination to avail themselves of facilities for the discharge of sexual tensions without evidence of any particular negative appetition toward members of their own sex, members of other species, or inanimate objects of more or less suitable surface topography. An autoerotically motivated bisexuality might then be said to be universal among the young of these several species and certainly, as by Stekel, to characterize civilized man. The utility of this generalization, however, is decidedly doubtful. The behavior concerned is perhaps but a special instance of the capacity for integrating situations of remarkable complexity as to the "external" factors involved. The more properly bisexual behavior is not of this sort but of a much more complex pattern

---

[47] *Note by Committee on Sullivan Publications:* This ends the excerpt from this manuscript which was included in Sullivan's *Schizophrenia as a Human Process* (see footnote 22 in this chapter).

—namely, a facultative homoerotic or a facultative heteroerotic addition to the heteroerotic or homoerotic organization, with a perhaps only theoretically impossible literal indifference as to the sex of the partner in intimate genital integrations. Before we leave the autoerotic case, however, we must note the frequent occurrence of persons in whom there is continued utilization of autosexual possibilities with the instrumentality of members of one or another of the sexes, in case of enforced abstinence from the preferred sexual object, and for criminal and other unsocial purposes. Thus there is in most groups a number of individuals who *can* coöperate in quasi-homosexual performances, while customarily enjoying heterosexual relations, just as there are many who engage exclusively in quasi-heterosexual relations while actually incapable of other than autoerotic satisfactions. These imperfectly socialized folk contribute much confusing data to any simple schematization of sexual behavior that takes origin in the direct observation of activity.

Excepting the sexual dynamism be recently discharged, any stimulation of the related somatic equipment, including implicit processes (thoughts, revery) pertaining to it, is provocative of sexual excitement, *provided* that there is not active in the total situation a factor that inhibits this excitement. The latter may be a tendency system active in a situation to which sexual excitement and factors tending to its discharges are highly irrelevant. In this case, the sexual tendencies are temporarily suppressed. On the other hand, the inhibitory factor may be a tendency system specifically opposed to the sexual tendencies particularly concerned, in which case it is not a matter of postponement but one of conscious conflict or some genetically related process. With this principle in mind, we may proceed to the primary distinctions in this field. Firstly, the sexual (genital) satisfaction is most crudely secured by any nonpainful manipulation of the parts concerned, without there being particular relevance in factors characterizing the instrumentality that manipulates. This is autosexuality, often including no major interpersonally directed component tendencies, but also often including tendencies making certain instrumentalities peculiarly satisfactory. Secondly, nothing preventing, cultural and innate factors combine in the growth of the sexual tendencies to such effect that sexual excitement and felt lust come to be greatest only when the situation can be integrated collaboratively (intimately) with a member of the other sex, in such a way that the genitals of each are stimulated in the behavior toward satisfaction. This is complete heterosexuality. Thirdly, by reason of youth and intercurrent interference with the long-circuiting of the interpersonally directed tendencies in the sexual system, there is either a failure to elaborate this system to include relevance for members of the other sex or a powerful inhibition of their relevance, although growth has made collaborative situations the preferred sexual integrations, and they therefore occur in such fashion that the genitals of each partner (of the same sex) are stimulated in the process. This is fully homosexual behavior. The dexterities employed in this last-mentioned category are several, including manual, anal, oral, and other interactions in various combinations.

More or less genuinely interpersonal situations integrated primarily by the sexual tendencies include factors conducive to discharge of some of the other erotic dynamisms, and, barring specific inhibitions, these additional tendencies customarily contribute to the integrations, the resolution of which then includes the additional forms of satisfaction. This gives rise to complex extragenital activity as a preliminary, a concomitant, and a sequel to the sexual activity. Some of these activities usually come to be patterned with the sexual habits and to that extent become characterizing components of the sexual tendency system. Situations integrated by the sexual system then generally include the securing of the other pleasures, which may none the less be pursued without inclusion of the sexual system, at other times. The other zones concerned in this sort of confluence interact along with the genital zone, but do not thereby become genital, nor suffer "drainage" of their tendency-system or of their pleasure-giving character into the sexual. The addition of their unique sentience to that taking origin in the sexual apparatus may make a particular sort of integration much more greatly to be desired than is any other one that occurs in the pursuit of sexual satisfaction. This is, in fact, a considerable part of the process of sexual growth. But, on the other hand, the socialized personality secures some pleasure from prehending the satisfaction of the partner from the stimulation of the extragenital zones, and this experience is also tributary to growth, to the discrimination of persons for integration into situations, and to the durability of interpersonal intimacies.

While the synchronous stimulation of genital zones in the biologically ordained coitus is to be taken to be the essence of sexual adaptation, not only is the preliminary, concomitant, and subsequent interaction of other zones customary, but also almost any zone may be engaged directly with the genitals of the partner in primarily sexual relations. The partner is given sexual pleasures while the other secures some other form of pleasure. If the situation is one of true interpersonal intimacy, there is also the securing by prehension of *mediate* pleasure of the corresponding extragenital zone by the partner, and of mediate sexual pleasure by the other—whose genitals may be excluded from direct interaction by reason of inhibition, accident, or conscious design. In these latter cases, the problem arises of distinguishing nonsexual erotism pursued in its own right from *erotism in combination with lust* aroused by prehension, implicit participation in the sexual excitement of the partner. This complicates the interpretation of so-called abnormal procedures in sexuality, but is a necessary step to an understanding both of the practices and of the conflicts that arise from opposition to the related desires.

It might be supposed that the probably universal tendency to view and perhaps to palpate the interesting variety of genitals—exaggerated in our culture by a prudish emphasis added to native curiosity—is always coincident with an impulse to integrate a sexual situation. Not uncommonly, however, one encounters warped personalities in whom the impulse that accompanies the seeing, handling, or even fantasying of the genitals of a person of the more interesting sex is sadistic, tending to action to harm or destroy the organs—loosely, *to castrate* the partner. The manifestations of these hateful impulses vary from defensive fears lest genital damage or disease befall the other, through ambitions to deflower as many young folk as possible—often with concomitant implantation of disturbing notions—and the bringing together of the inexperienced and the depraved, to the dissemination of evil doctrines, genital fears, and venereal diseases, and direct physical violence to the partner. The addition of this sadistic motivation in its milder grades to the tendency-complex integrating a more or less sexual situation may be difficult to discover, the more in that clear consciousness of the malicious attitude is unusual. Its presence, or that of the complementary masochistic motivation,[48] is not to be overlooked in the study of personality as characterized in interpersonal relation, and, in particular, in prevailingly sexual integrations.

In the study of quasi and real extragenital sexual erogeny, we must first be concerned with the primordial oral dynamism. A general term, *stomixis*,[49] may be used to cover all sorts of behavior of this kind, regardless of degree of interpersonal intimacy, and without prejudice as to sex of participants, or as to the presence or absence of sadomasochistic components in one or both. While various of these practices are doubtless of extreme antiquity, they are peculiarly a concomitant of civilized living. Regardless of other factors they are directly related to the need for release of surplus energy in the oral dynamism, and these surpluses are chiefly a resultant of diminished requirements for oral dexterity in the nourishing of the body. The use of concentrated foodstuffs all but ready for swallowing without preliminary extraction by biting, chewing, cutting, gnawing, grinding, licking,

[48] It is uncertain whether sadistic tendencies exist without the masochistic, and vice versa. Certainly, some of the more obviously masochistic individuals —persons to whom no pleasure is greatly to be valued if it is unattended by distress or pain—show on study a capacity for "unintended" refined cruelty to the objects of their personal interest. It seems quite probable, at this juncture, that we shall find that these sorts of overvaluation, positive or negative, of noxious experience arise from a common root. In other words, the surmise is that markedly sadistic individuals tend also to integrate situations making for their own injury; and markedly masochistic, for the injury of others.

[49] The nomenclature here developed departs fundamentally from some of that now more or less widely current. The vagueness of meaning in the older terms prohibits their use in an attempt at exact formulation in this field. *Stomixis* refers to appositions in the sexual act of the oral and the genital zones; *parastomixis*, to behavior in which the oral zone is used in exciting (and satisfying) lust-confluent nongenital zones—often as preliminaries to behavior involving the genitals; and *synstomixis*, to synchronous oral-genital stimulation of both partners. The male concerned in these procedures may be *phaledotic* or *thorodotic*, the former sometimes resulting from peculiar beliefs as to loss of the semen, or from sadistic components. The partner, male or female, may be *phaleleptic* or *thorophagic*, in the former there being a refusal of the semen, from similar peculiar beliefs about it, with or without resultant disgust reactions, or from sadistic components. When the genitals of a woman are concerned in these procedures, she may be *cysthodotic* or *cystholeptic*.

sucking, or tearing, leaves a great deal of energy to be dissipated in some other way. The biting of fingernails, pencils, cigars, and pipes; the chewing of "gum," tobacco, and the like; gnawing of the lips, fingers, moustache, and so on; grinding of the molar surfaces; licking of lips and teeth; sucking the teeth, pipe, cigarettes, and so on; elaborate oral mannerisms, whistling, humming, pointless speech, and the like—all manifest the current widespread need for oral behavior. Yet compared with the proportion of people who show exaggerated oral erotism, recourse to direct stomixic performances in sexual integrations is very infrequent, and first contact with these procedures is often literally disgusting, stirring the biological avoidance reaction to disagreeable substances put into the mouth, by reason of negative valuation that has come to be attached to the genitals. The distinction between the function of ingestion and the oral activities concerned in the dissipation of excessive energy is not by any means automatic in most people, and, regardless of the ease with which particular forms of the latter become habitual, there is apt to be a revulsion against the oral manipulation of extraordinary objects—all the more the case when the object is one toward which one has acquired a strong negative attitude as regards even digital manipulation. At the same time, even the ingestion function is fairly readily habituated to substances that are of disagreeable taste, and many people eat surreptitiously substances that are socially tabooed, while finding some approved foodstuffs repulsive. The study of food-prejudices and feeding-peculiarities as characteristics of personality has shed considerable light on the symbolic import to the self of the oral zone of interaction, and on the great part of the self that is organized around tendencies definitely associated with the oral dynamism. From these data and the study of infant and childhood behavior, it is to be surmised that, if geometric factors permitted, infants would often engage in autostomixis and that once discovered, this behavior would become a habit very hard to "break." Observations of young honey-bears, one of the few animals having facile access of mouth to penis, tend to confirm this, and there is recorded an instance of schizophrenic disorder occurring immediately after postpubertal growth had destroyed a boy's ability to engage in

this form of play.[50] The double factor of oral and phallic erot-
icism concerned may be very powerful in persons of the accentuated oral type, whereas, if the oral dynamism were completely
discharged in the work of securing nourishment, autostomixis
would tend to recur only in case there was either no other way
of discharging the genital dynamism, or no other procedure that
gave pleasure approximating that arising from oral manipulation.
Autostomixis being impossible for most infants and children,
marked confluence of erotisms from the two zones is not apt to
occur until much later, although fantasies of this type would
seem occasionally to have been entertained from early in life.
When the possibility of stomixis occurs to the persons after the
intimacy image has become manifest, the tendency to engage in
this sort of behavior may be strong, and then situational factors
—including relevant past experience, which may reach back to
the circumstances of weaning—determine the outcome in overt
phaleleptic behavior, its resistance with active pursuit of the
phaledotic role, severe conflict—often with extreme disgust reactions—or defensive or dissociative processes. Entities of the
general character of the Complex of Sexual Sin may be suppressed as to phalelepsis, but still prevent thorophagosis, the
sperm being in these circumstances regarded as disgusting, dangerous, or poisonous. In more fully developed stomixis, the seminal fluid, on the other hand, may tend to be a magic embodiment of values imparted to the partner, and otherwise highly
desirable. In those of marked and erotic deviation who none the
less engage habitually in stomixis, the sperm and the prehended
sexual satisfaction may be much more valued than is the oral
satisfaction, in which case the quicker the partner's orgasm, the
better. In others, a precocious orgasm may be disappointing because it prevents confliction of the oral energy discharge. In personalities in whom the homosexual role is very repugnant to the
self, but stomixic tendencies cannot be dissociated, a combination
of phaledotic and cystholeptic fantasies or even overt behavior
may be substituted with some preservation of self-esteem.

[50] See, in this connection, Curt Richter, "Some Observations on the Self-
Stimulation Habits of Young Wild Animals," *Arch. Neurology and
Psychiatry* (1925) 13:724-728.

The anal extremity of the alimentary canal is another important extragenital zone that may be involved in quasi and real sexual erogeny. For these procedures, we shall use the general term *pugisma*, again without reference to sex, degree of intimacy, or sadomasochistic components.[51] Kempf has presented valuable data on the facultative use of the anal orifice and rectum in lieu of vulva and vagina by rhesus monkeys in captivity,[52] and the rudimentary data available to us as to human sexual behavior in other culture-complexes suggests that these procedures are widespread, and sometimes all but fully sanctioned by the mores.[53] The proportion of young folk who encounter proctochresic approaches and partial and complete pugismic behavior seems to be rather large, in part because of the relaxation of inhibitions to homosexual behavior that occurs in light sleep and other reductions of the level of consciousness. The initial experience may be anything from unqualifiedly painful to highly pleasant. While it is perhaps true that the former is apt to be the case only in those suffering local disease or anomaly, the latter occurs in but the restricted case of those already markedly deviated toward the anal type of personality. To these, the experience of proctodotic pugisma constitutes an activation of interest in securing its repetition, and fixes a confluent tendency to integrate situations in which it is likely to occur. The anal type of person, having undergone this confluence of erotisms as a result of real or fancied performances,[54] tends thereafter, according to the vector addition of situational factors to an outcome in patterned proctodotic-

[51] The particularizations in this connection are: the phaleleptic (*proctodotic*) and the phaledotic (*proctochresic*); certain rare situations of the male proctodotic and a woman; the parastomixic deviant, proctolichsis, and —by reason of intimate neurological connection of the ano-rectal region and the inner, upper, aspects of the thighs and perineum—the so-called interfemoral intercourse, often a factor in increasing the energy partition to the anal zone.

[52] Edward J. Kempf, "The Social and the Sexual Behavior of Infrahuman Primates," *Psychoanalytic Review* (1917) 4:127–154.

[53] Pugismic procedures between individuals of dissimilar sex in one culture may be compromises for the drainage of homoerotic motivation. On the other hand, they may be merely the most satisfactory sexual method discovered by a fully heterosexual couple.

[54] The use of instrumentalities for the satisfaction of anal erotism includes syringe tips, enemata, and so on. The confluence with sexual pleasure, however, is not a direct or necessary accompaniment of autoanal play. It, too, requires the intervention of "inner" processes or externally conditioned

phaleleptic behavior, in its resistance with active pursuit of the proctochresic role, in several conflict—often with chronic disorder of the bowel function—or in defensive or dissociative processes.

The zones constituting the beginning and the end of the alimentary tract are factually orifices, ordinarily schematized—as is the vulva—as openings into the body. Their margins and junctions of mucous membrane and skin, and their sensory neural equipment are both abundant and exquisitely discriminative. The only other somatic organization that approaches to their sensitiveness and at the same time permits of some approximation of metric suitability for phalelepsis is that of the hands. They, too, are used in quasi and real extragenital sexual performances, contributing a pleasure arising from the exercise of manual dexterity, and one usually including a measure of confluence from autosexual procedures in preadolescence. A tendency to masturbatory performances is often evidenced as a preliminary, concomitant, or sequel to some other sexual behavior, and it may be the prevailing motivation. Resort is often had to it in situations in which other behavior is impractical or undesirable, and in some warped personalities it is the only behavior permitted or tolerated by the self. Imperfect sexual integrations are often resolved by these procedures when other sexual behavior is suppressed—for example, in dealing with but slightly attractive strangers with whom chance has permitted an integration involving the genital zone. The hands are schematized as less closely identified with the self than are the genital, anal, and oral zones, and their utilization is thus less personal.

It is evident, then, that there are some nineteen sexual or quasi-sexual roles open to a man, and some seventeen to a woman, without recourse to less common forms of erotic confluence.[55] Homoerotic males may integrate situations for one of ten kinds of activity; homoerotic women, eight. In the heteroerotic integration,

experience, but topographical and neurological factors contribute considerably to the probability of confluence.

[55] The tribatic performances of women, and the so-called interfemoral intercourses have not been discussed in the text, but are included in these figures. Double role occurs in synstomixis and in mutual masturbation, in all three situations, male and female homoerotic, and heteroerotic. The doubling of role alters the factor of passivity next mentioned; there is a continuance of appraisal by actual sex in the mutual performances.

each partner may take one of nine roles. But some of the activities seem generally to be experienced as more passive than the corresponding behavior of the partner, and this is often coupled with a consciousness of "femininity" of the part. These roles may be repugnant to the self by reason of a general defense to any submission tendencies, in which case they will be avoided excepting where mutual performances are feasible. The latter thus comes to require analysis as to real intimacy—mutuality of prehension and direct satisfaction—and as to the preservation of prestige, often, but not invariably, prohibitive of great intimacy.

Notes on Female
Adolescence

A COMPREHENSIVE STUDY OF female adolescence would of necessity include much repetition of the two preceding chapters. There are many points of similarity in the development of the two sexes. It will suffice, however, to outline these points, devoting the greater portion of the chapter to detailed consideration of the differences in development. The changes brought about in the girl approaching adolescence in many respects might be said to differ but slightly from those in the boy, later showing a gradual divergence. The preadolescent girl also normally chooses a chum, becomes a member of a gang, and has a period of hero-worship, usually for an older woman. Largely through her gang activities, she acquires sex knowledge and undergoes sexual experiences of an homo- or autoerotic nature. In all the important aspects of these things her reactions do not vary greatly from those of the boy, and failure to become incorporated in group life brings similiar types of tragedies. There is a marked difference, however, between the interests of the two groups; in the girl group there is less emphasis on athletic activities, and the preoccupation with sex does not limit itself to the sexual act but takes on more widely biological significance in connection with menstruation and pregnancy. Often, therefore, the girl group engaging in sexual activities finds satisfaction in curiosity about anatomy, and may miss entirely the discovery of orgasm. Notwithstanding the increase in athletic training of girls in recent years, activities involving physical prowess lack the intense emotional value for the female in contrast with that for the male.

Demands for the maintenance of prestige in the group life make it necessary for the girl to supplant part of her activities with interest in the other sex; that is, it becomes essential to "have dates" and to be seen with boys. This progresses ideally to the point of developing embryonic feelings of affection for friendly boys, finally leading to the choice of one particular boy as a love-object. If everything goes well, the final goal is a satisfactory, stable partnership with one of the other sex. It must not be inferred that the successful progression of the female through the adolescent period runs a course identical to that of the male, even though the end goal might be taken to be comparable. Considered in terms of personality and life interest, the end results are far apart. The female must be viewed as possessing different points of physiology, under different social pressures, and distinguished by peculiar psychic and emotional characteristics resulting therefrom.

During the period of midadolescence—that era when we expect clear-cut differentiation in the development of the two sexes—the girl's immediate environment begins to take on new significance, especially in regard to parental influence. Parents whose lives reflect definite signs of misguiding easily discharge their own defects in overprotection and overguidance. At this stage the mother may feel that her daughter's sex education has been neglected and takes steps to set this aright. The results of these added complications, performed in the name of safeguarding the girl's future happiness, are, to a great extent, dependent upon the degree of normality in the love life of the mother. In such cases, the overanxious, suspicious mother constitutes a fairly frequent problem. Her attitude may be expressed briefly as follows: "All boys are creatures possessed of dangerous animal instincts. All girls are their natural victims and must be protected from them. My daughter is innocent and must therefore be carefully safeguarded." Such an attitude reflects a certain repugnance to frank discussion of the matter and leads the mother to adopting a policy of spying and prohibition. The girl may have led a life of comparative freedom up to the beginning of adolescence, but now suddenly finds her goings and comings a matter of close supervision. She hears vague mention of "bad boys," perhaps a hint about the general lack of self-control of the male, or she may have instilled into her a sense of duty in uplifting boys and keeping

them "clean." She comes to feel that to be touched by a boy is the first step toward further intimacies, and a casual kiss is to be regarded as a serious matter. When such liberties are permitted, the girl may find the matter a subject for worry, may even go so far as to consider herself as "ruined." The tentative efforts she makes toward a normal development are thwarted by the impressions conveyed in the mother's attitude, and the girl later seeks refuge in the preadolescent situation, arriving finally at the unhappy state in which it is better to have no contact with boys whatsoever lest she become "damaged goods."

As an extreme example of parental interference with a normal development of the adolescent girl, one may refer to the mother who is frankly suspicious of the motives of any boy showing interest in her daughter. This mother's attitude is often one of disgust for all things physical. In her own marital relations her lot is that of stoical resignation. Toward her husband she behaves as if she belongs to a "pure order of beings," and she regards marriage as a concession to the unfortunate "animal nature" of the male—or at best, justified for purposes of procreation only. By direct and indirect insinuations and questions, she succeeds in keeping sex the uppermost matter, probably the inevitable outcome of any contact with the male. To this the girl reacts by defiance, by promiscuity, or by complete retreat, depending on her characteristic make-up.

Another type of mother may interfere in a more insidious fashion. Uniformly, among instances of this sort with which I have become familiar, the woman shows strong, unrecognized homosexual trends, was married to preserve her prestige, and is not only frigid with her husband but actually "despises" him. As the daughter's adolescence draws nigh, such a woman may begin active participation in the girl's little affairs, seeking thereby the solution for her own unhappiness. It becomes essential for her daughter to be popular—the number of boys paying attention is to the mother a matter of personal pride. Detailed descriptions of each evening are required of the girl, and by this the mother practically dictates the future conduct and behavior. She performs these "duties" as an aid to the development of her child; the real motivation does not become apparent until her daughter shows a distinct fondness for some particular boy. Then her jealousy becomes active and often leads her to attempt to terminate the affair. Sometimes this is done by subtle criticism of the boy, more often by actual ridicule. The girl so dominated is all but invariably unable to make free choice; if she is ever to marry it must be to a man of her mother's choosing. If she does marry— this probably because the mother would feel "disgraced" otherwise—the husband is usually a man with definite homosexual trends, as this arrangement enables the mother to retain the greater portion of her daughter's affection. She may even go so far as to become personally interested in any friends who call, cultivating a technique of winning them away from the girl. Instead of reacting to this with anger leading to a break from the domination, the girl feels herself to be inadequate to cope with the mother's greater sophistication and suffers a serious blow to her self-esteem.

Contrary to a prevalent belief, the mother who offers little supervision of her adolescent daughter is the one who does the minimum of harm. Not only is this the case when it results from a satisfactory solution of her own difficulties, but also it is the case with all situations of apparent indifference. When permitted to exercise her own judgment, the girl has but to learn the ways of the social group in which she moves, and is freed of the necessity of making her life compatible with the added complications resulting from too close supervision.

Not alone do mothers present problems; the father likewise contributes to complicating the life of his adolescent daughter. If the early father-daughter attachment has not been successfully resolved before adolescence, the father remains a person of great importance in the emotional life of the girl. Frequently his own unhappiness leads to a morbid interest in the affairs of his child. If he continues to cultivate the attachment, the girl may find it impossible to become interested in any other man. She prefers the "pure love and protective care" of her father to the vicissitudes of another life. The parents of the girl are more apt to come into contact with her escorts than is the case with the parents of the boy, and, as a result, the interference of the father in the life of the girl has more direct effect. Paternal jealousy may interfere with any attempted emancipation; for example, the father strives to protect her from "unprincipled" boys, offering objections to this and that one, seeking at last to make the choice for her—again usually one possessing strong homosexual components. Should the father's homosexual tendencies—either latent or overt—dominate the situation, he then seeks to cultivate in the girl an interest for the boys who attract him, perhaps actually joining her group, not to protect her but to compete with her. Still further, he may not trust her with any male escort, openly entering into competition, himself escorting her to parties and dances.

If the father's sexual drive is powerful, he may suspect all boys of "crude sexual motives" and adopt a "watchdog" attitude toward his daughter's activities, literally seeking to discourage any boy who makes his appearance. While apparently seeking to shield the girl from harm, he is actively thwarting any effort she makes toward securing a satisfactory love-object. Situations similar to the following one, recently reported to me, are not infrequent: The indignant father walks out on the dance floor and separates the daughter from her partner, because the boy was seen to rub his cheek against hers.

Besides these direct interferences, it must be remarked that so powerful are the childhood attachments to parents that, even in cases where the daughter's attitude toward the father is predominantly one of hate, she may choose a mate similar in personality to the father.

Even with intelligent foresight on the part of one or both parents, serious traumatic experiences can come to the adolescent girl, with no clearly evident signs of earlier warping.

Inexperienced gropings towards adulthood often meet with catastrophe in the social order if not in the home. In the present era, premarital sexual activity for girls is strongly taboo. In spite of the development of "tolerance" in the last fifteen years, the penalty for transgression of this taboo, when discovered, is relatively great, amounting at times to social and economic ostracism. A definite number of girls (psychopaths) violate this taboo deliberately. Also a smaller number, after their teens, violate the taboo deliberately and with a measure of understanding. We shall now consider the role of the sensitive, highly "moral," average girl who, by accident or otherwise—chiefly because she was swept into the event emotionally, perhaps sometimes from curiosity—violates her own standards and from the resulting conflict suffers a serious traumatic experience in the shape of anxiety as to social disapproval. Should such a situation, through ignorance or by accident, result in pregnancy, the blow is still more severe. Seldom does such a girl find understanding at home, society offers her very little sympathy, and she is confronted by the choice of illegitimate pregnancy, a premature and often unsuitable marriage making for no future happiness, or abortion. If the experience contained love elements on the part of both participants, the end result may not be wholly destructive to her developing personality, notwithstanding more immediate steps to solution. Any beneficial results, however, are usually negated because of too rigid training in the home coupled with the seriousness of having violated one of the most esteemed social taboos. If the sexual experience was one of casual moment, it is the girl who suffers more because of the possible consequences. Often she expects to find love and is bitterly hurt when she realizes that she was but a "passing fancy." Seduction of a young girl by an older man results in disaster because of the early daughter-father attachment, the element of transiency, and the girl's disillusionment following the absence of any kindness and protection from the man. These severe rebuffs are not to be taken as in themselves leading to serious mental disorder. It is to their depredation on self-esteem and to their effects in feeding new fuel to homosexual cravings and masturbation conflicts that one must look for explanation of their contribution toward the graver mental disorders—for example, the serious schizophrenic psychoses. This again is true in the case of men; there is, however, a factor of special import in women constituted by the menstrual periodicity.

Menstruation is in itself a normal biological function, but frequently plays an important role in psychopathology. As a normal function it should create little disturbance, but as a symbol of sexual awakening and approaching womanhood, it attracts unto itself pathological attitudes and symptom formations. In the case of the girl handicapped by an infantile uterus or similar malformation, the onset of menstruation actually initiates a course of periodic invalidism. This accounts for but a small part of menstrual "trouble." Menstruation has earned the sobriquet of "being unwell" and "a curse" for quite other reasons. The discomfort attending menstruation is to a surprising degree due to psychic factors; the physical discomfort varies in individuals, and chronologically different symptoms appear in each. Increased irritability, emotional instability, and slight loss of energy are prevalent. Acute malaise, severe pain, headaches, nausea, and vomiting, even complete prostration, may occur without demonstrable organic cause. To a great extent such symptoms are conversion phenomena—in other words, expression in somatic symptoms of emotional states. Owing to the close connection of menstruation with the awakening sex life and approaching womanhood, it is a peculiarly suitable focus for neurotic manifestations. For example, if sex is associated in the girl's mind with disgust, menstruation, as a symbol of sex, will be disgusting. The resentment of menstruation by certain women may be attributed to strong feelings of revolt against the role of the female. Psychoanalyses of menstrual nauseas, headaches, and cramps often reveal such factors as contributing to their causation. A wealth of superstition has been built around menstruation, to the end that it has come to be regarded as a period of legitimate, partial invalidism. The use of the disability mechanisms may vary, according to the type of girl, all the way from conscious malingering—for example, the girl who takes her day or two off from work each month on the plea of cramps—to the actual, although physically determined, incapacitation of the woman who unconsciously hails this time as a period in which she can regress to invalidism and a need for care.

Not only does menstruation attract unto itself conversion symptoms, but owing to its evidential value in relation to pregnancy, it may also become the focus of morbid fears. At this point it might be well to consider a few of the events with which it becomes closely associated. Nearly all mothers, even those most averse to discussing sexual matters with their children, feel it their duty to impart some information on the subject to the growing daughter. The self-conscious, sexually unoriented woman—and this description applies to a shockingly large number of mothers—finds the occasion a trying one, and may postpone the interview with the girl until menstruation has actually occurred. Anything of benefit that might arise from the encounter usually miscarries from the woman's embarrassment. The girl has, as a rule, acquired some knowledge of menstruation elsewhere, and the situation that is created only serves to stir reactions of unpleasantness in relation to the menstrual period. Some mothers may go so far as to take this opportunity to fortify the daughter's morals. A patient reports the following experience, during the mother's attempt to acquaint her with facts about menstruation: "Now you must be careful, for now you can become pregnant, and if you ever do, I'll kill you. I won't have any disgrace around here." Less harsh mothers manage to convey much the same sentiment in milder terms. So menstruation in the mind of the developing girl is apt to become associated with the idea, "I am now likely to do terrible things which will disgrace me for life." Infrequent menses often serve as justification for the mother's conviction that her daughter is developing tuberculosis, or is "going into a decline." She regards the girl with too frequent menstruation as dying of anemia or requiring surgical intervention. In either case, on the pretext that terrible consequences might ensue, the girl is brought to the doctor, and through such ordeals there arise in her mind grave doubts and fears as to regularity. The fact that absence of menstruation is one of the signs of pregnancy facilitates the development of morbid concern. Early childhood notions are revived, such as that of impregnation by kissing or touching. If the periods are too frequent, the girl may conclude that she has brought harm to herself through masturbation. Sometimes the girl fears she has brought on her menses prematurely, this having been the case with several patients in whom menstruation began at eleven. The irregularity of the early months of menses may form a basis for much apprehension. For that matter, it is quite possible that the irregularity is often the result of morbid fears. If the girl has reason to fear pregnancy, psychic factors may produce delayed menses. The unconscious wish for pregnancy, coupled with guilt and need for punishment, perhaps reinforced by a desire to punish the boy, can sometimes influence the somatic picture to the point of producing symptoms of pregnancy. Among the inadequately informed, delayed menses are a sure sign of pregnancy, even in situations which forbid such a possibility. Perhaps the anxiety may express itself in the fear of having become impregnated from a toilet seat, a kiss, or a dancing contact. One cannot but surmise that emotional states are capable of influencing regularity of menses.[1]

[1] In tracing causes and effects, we are delaing with complex situations involving the interaction of emotional factors and somatic conditions, and the placing of the latter in either of the former categories requires much more extensive data than are now available.

The subject of sex in general, especially the consciousness of instinct drives, is less clearly understood by girls than by boys, notwithstanding the experience ensuing from menstruation. In outlining the similarities of development of the two sexes, it was shown that sex curiosity and the undergoing of some sexually tinged event constitute the principal parallels. The number of girls escaping such knowledge, however, is very great. Workers engaged in the taking of sex histories of married women will corroborate the fact that the absence of the experience of orgasm in a supposedly normal sex life appears frequently. In many cases the experience is completely unallotted to the sex life of the female. Since sexual sensations are more vague and less consciously realized than is the case with the genital manipulation with the male, these procedures must be recognized to have a somewhat different role. It is a prevalent belief among the laity—and even among the profession—that masturbation has no place in the sex life of the adolescent girl. This has the fortunate effect that the girl is less an object of quack literature on the subject than is the boy; rarely does she fall into the hands of a reformer bent on impressing her with the "dangers of the vice." She may even progress through the masturbatory period completely unaware of the occurrences, more especially when there is no conscious manipulation of the genitals—for example, when pleasurable sensations are experienced from pressing the thighs together. Thus we find that a woman who was for many years frigid with her husband experiences a distinct bodily thrill when pressing her thighs together and "thinking some exalted thought about God." This she attributed to religious ecstasy; not until insight was gained from a psychotic illness did she associate the procedure with sex.

It must not be taken to mean that only conscious realization of her masturbation produces conflict in the adolescent girl; some echo of childhood warnings and threats may contribute to a vague sense of guilt about a new bodily feeling. Not too clearly formulated worry may appear in the shape of complaints, blushing, and a feeling of fatigue. Even a leucorrhea may be the subject for worry. A treatment of these symptoms without understanding of the underlying cause may aggravate the condition; to advise extended periods of rest for the abnormally tired individual opens the way for increased daydreaming. Likewise, local treatment for leucorrhea which is psychogenically determined does not diminish the conflict already existing. New conflict appears in connection with the pleasure of local stimulation. Thus in a young patient heavily burdened with feelings of guilt about sexual fantasies, the prescribing of a douche precipitated acute panic accompanied by fear of contamination.

In the individual not heavily emotionally handicapped, who eventually works her way through the difficulties of adolescence, a period of frank or unwitting masturbation may occur without conflict. The fact that girls are less exposed to distorted information on the subject is an aid to more unwarped progress. If, however, something occurs to thwart her successful evolution and an autoerotic adjustment takes precedence, conflict usually becomes evident. This is true whether or not the activity is fully conscious and despite the absence of distorted information. Certainly it is clearer in the case of the girl than of the boy that conflict arises not wholly from masturbation itself, but in part because of its symbolic representation in the personality—namely, the fear of failing to succeed in interpersonal adjustments.

The daydreams of adolescent girls are predominantly more erotic than are those of the boy. They exist in close connection with masturbation but are not necessarily accompanied by manipulation. Girls are less frequently given opportunity for sublimation in a career; even when they are trained for earning, rarely does the occupation hold a lifelong significance. Well formulated, or half consciously, in either case she plans to continue this—stenography or whatnot—only until she is married. Matters of sex assume great moment in her life, being appointed first place in her daydreams—for in the normal, ambitions grow out of constructive fantasy. Thus she attempts to carry out in reality the longed-for popularity with males.

Serious consequences can result from an overpreoccupation with fantasy in lieu of contact with reality. This may come about in several ways. For instance, in overcoming parental restraint, the adolescent girl is pushed to the necessity of carrying out her wishes in daydreaming; she may be laboring under a father- or mother-fixation and this too serves its purpose in her prevailing fantasy life. In these situations lies an important factor for development of serious mental disorder; and the disorder of prime importance in adolescence is schizophrenia.

Pathological daydreaming in girls proceeds rather typically as follows: A boy who in certain respects approaches the ideal mate enters her environment; assuming that the pathological day-dreamer already feels inadequate in carrying her wishes out in reality, she none the less succeeds in noting everything of vital importance in the boy's attitude. She finds him friendly in a casual way, and even though his manner is one of indifference, he becomes the focus of her fantasy life. His activities are of much interest, and she may cultivate the acquaintance of people who can give her information about him. Any chance remark of his is carefully treasured. In her fantasies she is loved by him, she may even see herself as his bride, the envy of all her friends. If masturbation has previously been a problem, she suffers from the added sexual excitement and may struggle again with the old conflict. If masturbation conflict has been repressed, she suffers from sleepless nights and restlessness. The boy is usually unaware of her interest; he may be puzzled by her shyness and self-consciousness in his presence. If he is led to making active overtures, her reaction is one of flight. However, if he remains indifferent, the fantasy life of the girl continues until tensions accumulate to the point of precipitating some overt behavior. While in the less deviated, continued indifference of a love-object leads to his replacement by a new interest, with easy rationalization for failure with the first, these pathological dreamers, on the other hand, begin to lose touch with reality and to believe in their fantasies. Thus the girl may declare her love to the boy, to his great amazement. From the almost inevitable rebuff, the girl is plunged into illness—or into reality.[2] When plunged into illness, the girl may begin to believe herself loved, or married. Such a case is well into mental illness, and fantasies are substituted entirely for reality; the end result is schizophrenia. In some, the love-object may be a person entirely unknown to the girl, someone perhaps in a public position. In a case coming under my supervision, the girl chose one of the orchestra in a theatre. When visiting the place she always sat near the front, hoping that by chance he would glance in her direction. If this occurred, she would be happy for days, con-

[2] The factors entering into a fortunate or unfortunate outcome of these love protestations "out of the blue" are sometimes of great complexity. If the divorcement from reality has been insidious, the rebuff from the astonished love-object almost invariably leads to collapse of the girl's personality.

structing glowing fantasies around the episode. This type of activity may continue for years without a serious break, never being put to the test of reality. The case in point reached the age of twenty-nine before definite illness appeared.

At this point it might be well to ask the question: What are the precipitating factors of a schizophrenic illness in the adolescent girl? The foregoing comments on pathological daydreaming offer a clue in many cases. The rebuff suffered from unsuccessful carrying over of the fantasy into reality may constitute a serious trauma. This trauma does not occur in the realm of the love life; it is more closely connected with the girl's prestige and social approval. In the present day, in most groups, marriage is regarded as the only recognized mark of sexual success for a woman. When no real drive toward a heteroerotic object-love exists, there may occur an artificial forced search for a mate, with an exaggerated interest in the matter. This may result in the fantastic love affair heretofore described. Friendship with an intellectually inferior male may furnish the girl the necessary assurance of social status for which she strives, fulfilling the necessity of being seen with a man but causing her to suffer privately for his inadequacies. If the drive for social prestige pushes her to marriage with such a man, a mental illness may develop therefrom. Often, however, such a girl drifts from inferior to inferior, always with the question as to why she fails to attract a man she can admire, cultivating feelings of inferiority and developing a late schizophrenic disorder. The schizoid personality may find success in a love relation with a man fifteen or twenty years her senior, in which the attitude of the man is primarily that of a father. This relationship may prove a stabilizing influence for years. The unconscious barriers, however, make it impossible for these individuals to form a sexual partnership with an equal. In them the conscious wishes for sexual success are negated by the unconscious drives, and this usually ends in antagonizing the male or in driving him away.

The development of the precipitating factors of a schizophrenic illness form a different picture. Given a girl who finds refuge in fantastic love affairs and avoids contact with suitable males, what circumstances initiate a panic state, so often the beginning of a schizophrenic episode? It has been suggested that a crude rebuff from the man serving as the fantasy object may institute the onset. Back of this, however, is severe conflict over masturbation. The girl seldom brings herself to making an overt move toward the boy until sexual feelings have driven her into acute conflict over ensuing masturbation. A lecture on the "evils" of masturbation may serve as outer stimulus to acute conflict. It may occur, also, where there is no clear evidence of the precipitating factor. For example, the individual who has led an intense fantasy life for some time without definite manipulation may one day experience orgasm. A sudden increment of conflict follows; something has occurred which is beyond her control. Afterward there may be a confused feeling of weakness and thoughts of "losing her mind." Perhaps more important is the case of the girl whose fantastic love affair carries with it definite homoerotic interests, this in conjunction with confidence in some close friend. The love interest of the fantasies may be converted into a closer attachment to the confidante. This attachment affords an outlet for all the desires and wishes she entertains regarding the man with whom she is but slightly acquainted. Only in conjunction with her confidences to the friend can she maintain her fantasies of a real interest in the man; an actual love relation with an approximate equal would constitute too grave a menace to her personality, especially when the sexual elements are clearly conscious. As the attachment progresses, owing to the girl's greater capacity for homoerotic love, a situation not uncommonly develops in which she becomes somewhat conscious of her inclination toward the confidante. This in turn constitutes an even graver menace to her personality. She may then seek a way out by breaking up the attachment. It often happens that she feels suspected of "unnatural impulses," and thinks that she is being talked about and that her confidences to the friend have become common property within the circle in which they move. So complicated a path toward the occurrence of panic over homosexual cravings is not invariable. Some girls are too shy of human contacts ever to develop a confidante. If such a girl comes to think much about some certain friend whose sympathy she craves, the interest gradually appears to her and this is followed by fear that it is becoming apparent in her behavior and that the idealized one is noticing this and disapproves. If the confidante proves to be a girl of the type tending toward overt homosexuality, a situation in which some homoerotic interests predominate may present itself, giving rise to more severe conflict than previously. Since the case in question is that of an individual incapable of any true object relationship—especially when accompanied by sexual activity—the result may transcend a state of severe conflict and end in one of homosexual panic.

Let us now consider the problems of the conflict fundamental to a schizophrenic outcome. There is still much to be learned in this connection, but it is certain that in the schizophrenic female incest fantasies and delusions are very common. Frequently the individual comes to believe that she is pregnant by her father, thus indicating a strong father-fixation. This is sometimes symbolized in an obvious father-substitute, such as God. I am inclined, however, from the deep analysis of a few such patients, to the opinion that an earlier type of problem is the important factor—that is, an early infantile fixation on the mother, at the level described by the psychoanalysts as the "oral stage of libido development." In other words, she sought to establish a love relation similar to that existing between infant and mother. More data from such investigations may reveal that schizophrenic women, as well as men, continue in a state of nonresolution of an early type of infantile attachment to the mother, in turn resymbolized or displaced on the father.

Let us turn now to a consideration of the differences existing in the homosexual activities of girls and of boys. There is a difference in social attitude toward homoerotic interests in the female, just as there is regarding masturbation. It is even thought that homosexual experiences are restricted wholly to the male, although "crushes" between girls are recognized by many people. These intense attachments encounter little social disapproval; in fact, there is almost no attention given the erotic elements accompanying such relationships. An occasional overt homosexual episode may occur, but it is usually attended by severe conflict and seldom leads to establishing a pattern of sexual behavior. At one extreme of the picture, however, there exists the "patterned" homosexual woman who cultivates "masculine" habits and who has adopted a homoerotic *modus vivendi* as a workable adjustment. Owing to the unrecognized significance of much of her activity, there is an easier adaptation to her role than is the case with the male in a similar situation. Frequently she is a woman of successful career. Still further in this category there is the promiscuous homosexual woman who affects "masculine" attire and habits for the sole purpose of seducing women. The fastidiousness and exaggeration of the inversion in these cases affords characteristic evidence that they are engaged in the pursuit of sexual objects, and not in carrying out the role of an adjusted man. They are analogous to the "bitches" in the male, but should not be confused with the individual who falls into a masculine habit of life unwittingly.

Of the between types there are many—for example, the woman whose life history includes an occasional overt episode followed by conscious or unconscious conflict. There are a number who never pass beyond the stage of intense "crushes" for other females. They may never evolve a satisfactory heterosexual adjustment, but struggle continually with the more or less unformulated homoerotic problems. As an instance, there is the woman showing general sexual promiscuity. From the scant data on these cases, it would appear that such women suffer decidedly from unresolved homoerotic inclination although other factors may lead to their promiscuity such as general hatred of the male or revenge for disappointment in some recent or remote love relationship. They frequent "wild parties," cultivate promiscuity with men, sometimes engaging in intercourse with several men in the course of an evening. If limited to one man, they usually engage in the affair among group activity, including at least one other couple. Discovering the attraction of other women for them, they hasten to cite their powers of attraction to men as proof that they "are not homosexual." Perhaps they attribute their diverse interests to being "oversexed." When isolated in groups of females, as in boarding schools and college dormitories, their impulses carry a generally disturbing influence on the atmosphere of the place. When carried over into conscious seduction of younger women, their activities bring much conflict and distress to many latent homosexuals.

We have yet to study the mechanism of homosexuality in women. The inversion of the love interest in men has received much more attention. We have, from psychoanalysis, data which trace the origin of the homosexual component to attachment to the mother with identification with the father. As far as I know, little has been done toward explaining the promiscuous homosexual and there is little that has been contributed to an understanding of the mechanism of any kind of promiscuity. It seems that this behavior must be considered a symptom-formation. If this is the case, there must be recent precipitating factors in addition to the more remote experience incorporated in the deeper layers of the personality. Theoretically, one should be able to resolve the situation by analysis, just as the symptoms of a neurosis can be removed thereby. The difficulty in getting data as well as in effecting the "cure" of the deviations which eventuate in prostitution lie in the lack of interest in the individual concerned in the accomplishment of a change.[3]

Concurrent with incomplete or deviated evolution of the sexual life, we find certain consistent consequents in the personality. Ambitions and life goals not primarily sexual are influenced by the more fundamental peculiarity and a permanently adolescent type of personality is involved. I wish now to consider three sorts of people roughly definable as types of those who are permanently adolescent. I do not here intend to definitely describe a particular group; I shall limit myself to a convenient method of presentation, realizing at the same time that individuals are often combinations of more than one type. For instance, the element of promiscuity and the drive for popularity may occur side by side in the same individual.

We may first consider the individual who, while apparently succeeding in an adjustment on a heterosexual basis, distorts the real object of her interest into a great need for popularity with many boys. This might be classified as the last stage of the gang age. Some women never progress beyond it. To be adored by several men simultaneously becomes a profound necessity. Their affections are withheld to a great extent, while there is an insatiable demand for material and emotional returns from men. If their training has impressed upon them the ideal of fidelity, it is difficult for them to choose a partner in marriage. Always there is the possibility of meeting a more interesting man afterward. If married, they are discontent unless their moral code permits of

---

[3] I incline to the opinion that homosexuality in women is more often psychogenetic in origin than is it organic or constitutional.

certain freedom. Adoration is a necessity, platonic or otherwise. Probably more important in their personality make-up is the narcissistic factor, although homoerotic interests dictate the demand for prestige among other women. Anxiety may be the result in such cases when this prestige is lacking. Invalidism is one of the symptom-formations used by these women when confronted by the passing of their sexual charm.

If the heterosexual adjustment is to be considered as the norm, there remain to be discussed two other types of women who do not achieve adulthood. Rather characteristic of these is the woman who remains on the level of a preadolescent adjustment with its unpatterned homosexual and autoerotic activity—typically the "crush" type. Such an individual may reach chonologic adulthood without the acceptance of a satisfactory sexual adjustment as a part of her personality. She may show the "disgust" reaction to sex, especially in relation to the male. She is uncomfortable with men, but instead of retreating exclusively into fantasy, she clings to the same uncomplicated preadolescent situation which admits of the existence of the male in a nonsexual way only. She succeeds in "floating along" in this fashion for many years without a serious break. She may seek a profession in which she is thrown almost entirely in the company of women—as examples, school teachers, club secretaries, and others. Under social and economic pressures, it may be that some of this type marry. The sexual handicaps in their marital relationship, however, are never overcome. They endure the sex act as part of their wifely "duty," regarding their frigidity as part of their "purity." Sometimes the affection is turned toward another woman, this taking the form of a rather etherealized friendship. Or again, the homoerotic interest may be on a mother-child basis, which denies the existence of any conscious sexual impulses. Sometimes there is unsuccessful "sublimation" of the sex urge, and this leads to severe conflict over masturbation and homosexual cravings. Still there is the necessity of pretending that the sex part of their lives is of no importance. Although this preadolescent adjustment may succeed fairly well for years, with the coming of the involutional period there is forced upon such an individual the realization that time is creeping up on her and that her best years are about to pass. Then there is agitation and despair, often coupled with violent self-reproaches for whatever sexual activity has occurred. A para-noid state may develop therefrom. In general it is the nonaggres-sive type of paranoia, characterized by depression and suspicious attitudes toward the world—a state of mind not necessarily in-compatible with life outside of an institution. As a contrast, ob-sessional personalities may be found among this group character-ized by "purity" as regards the sex life. In them the early childhood tie to the parent has never been outgrown—they rationalize their failures into the high calling of "giving up my life to my mother" or being "unwilling to leave my mother alone."

We may consider the "modern" woman as a third type. She is the individual with a career, whose ambition is to be a "man among men." The modern scene gives more opportunity to such an individual, more tolerance. The woman with the great "inner drive" to be a man, to compete with the male, has always existed. She usually enters the more masculine professions—medicine, law, business. These women are apt to court struggle with prejudice, seeking and aggravating instances of more or less real discrimina-tion against women and deriving inordinate satisfactions there-from. The really intelligent among them achieve a place in the world of masculine affairs, reaping in due time the respect of their male colleagues. The majority, however, become lost in the struggle, and sooner or later develop great bitterness toward men, attributing their failures to being "discriminated against as women." Often they are inferior individuals whose only claim to fame is their revolt against the role of female. Their efforts tend usually to be more easily defeated than is the case with a man of similar mediocre ability because of the pressure of sentiment against them. The factors contributing to the formation of such a personality drive have been extensively discussed in analytic literature. Freud makes an early reference in his "Three Contributions to the Theory of Sex," in which there is offered the hypothesis that the development of female sexuality contains important variations from that of the male in that the center of interest must shift in the pattern from the clitoris to the vagina—the clitoris and the penis having similar likeness, the vagina being the typically female organ. Further light is shed from later writings on the "castra-tion complex" and "penis envy" in women, and the possibility of problems arising in the female as a result of physiological difference receives attention. In brief, the psychic development of woman must undergo an adjustment similar to that in the physiological realm, if she is to attain adulthood.

As the love life of the girl adolescent progresses, her personal ambitions must undergo alteration or be sacrificed. If she marries, a career becomes difficult; if she bears children this is increasingly difficult. The woman showing a strong urge for the masculine role cannot make this adjustment; the motivation of such urge may be the result of her envy of a brother or her feeling that she was a child unwelcome because of her sex. In marriages where the husband is somewhat aware of the woman's desire for a career, a partial concession may be effected. Sometimes the establishment of a free sex life outside marriage serves as a solution. Perhaps there will be established a homosexual union between two women, this serving in lieu of the customary family home. A greater number none the less find no stable sexual partnership. They may become isolated individuals—they may engage in hectic flight from homosexual attachments, finally ending in the promiscuous group heretofore described. The majority of maladjustments go the way of marriage to an inferior male or existence on the verge of some homosexual arrangement. In general, the woman with average training and ability cannot find happiness in fulfilling the urge to "be a man." Neurotic outcomes may manifest themselves in the well known "chip on the shoulder" against all men. A paranoid development would be the typical psychotic outcome. Milder forms of this state find their locus in the religious fanatic reformer, "free thinker" organizations, and the preaching of free love. Because of the relatively tolerant attitude of modern society, many of this group escape the outcome of severe mental disorder. We shall conclude that they suffer from a socially successful maladjustment; that is, they manage a somewhat useful and successful existence but with more pronounced personal stress and unhappiness than come to others nearer the norm.

In closing, I must remark that the subject of female adolescence is not easily exhausted. As was stated at the opening of the chapter, a complete consideration would require a more extensive treatise than is my purpose. Rather the aim has been to point out the importance of the role of parents in the life of the adolescent girl, to suggest the significance of social pressures in the crystallizing of personality difficulties, and to give some idea of the reactions of the girl to these difficulties.

CHAPTER IX

Sleep, Dreams, and Schizophrenia

SLEEP is a well-known but little understood phase of life. Regarded as a negative aspect of activity, it has been made the subject of a number of hypotheses, prevailingly physiological in character. Of these, there are now two or three in reasonably good standing. One refers the phenomenology of sleep to underlying, more or less rhythmical changes in the permeability of neural and related cell-membranes. Our knowledge of vital physicochemistry is rather too elementary to permit of more than suggestive findings toward proof or disproof of this hypothesis. Another, resting on more definite data, finds an at least coincidental change in a fairly recognizable colloidal ingredient of the neural protoplasm. Certain technical devices bring out, in nerve cells, appearances relative to the amount of "Nissel substance" that is present. This substance tends to diminish during periods of wakefulness, and to be restored quite rapidly during sleep. We surmise, therefore, that Nissel substance is a labile colloid, a constituent significantly connected with the functional activity of neoencephalic cells, and that the maintenance of a sufficient supply of it requires periodic intervals of relative inactivity. The third theory is that of central inhibition. It was formulated in the course of Pavlov's study on the spread of inhibitory "conditioned reflexes": "Internal inhibition and sleep are one and the same process . . . Inhibition, according to our analysis, is a partial sleep." [1]

[1] *Lectures on Conditioned Reflexes,* by I. P. Pavlov (translated by W. H. Gantt); New York: International Publishers, 1928. The "conditioned reflex"

In so far as this theory serves to emphasize the total-activity character of sleep, it is in line with the views underlying this presentation. In so far as it makes of sleep a mere neurological phenomenon, it is but a redundancy by which the unknown is "explained" through gymnastics with an unexplained fragment of the unknown.

Sleep is a total *activity* and cannot be explained by an appeal to the more purely organic part of the sleep situation. The processes component in sleep are, in general, of rather low velocity. Many of them are nonessential acquisitions from early training. In other words, the innate tendencies underlying sleep behavior are greatly modified by postnatal experience, just as are any other of the inborn tendencies.

The intelligent handling of infant feeding and sleep has provided a convincing demonstration of the unnecessary character of a body of ritual, conditions, and prerequisites that we find in ourselves in regard of "falling asleep." While many of us have cultivated the seriousness of "going to sleep" to the point that it has become a real ceremony, the modern infant, having escaped training in a basically exaggerated importance in his doing, sleeps when there is nothing more important to do. His sleep, like that of the well-adjusted adult, is interrupted or disturbed by certain intercurrent desires, and by little else. Hunger, sexual excitement, and fear—these are the common factors prohibitive of sleep activity. A great body of sleep disorders of importance to the psychopathologist is related to the last mentioned of the three.[2] Unrecognized sexual desire accounts for some; and a combination of sexual excitement and fear of one's satisfying it by some "un-

is decidedly too complex an entity to be treated in the simplicist style that has become popular in the recent "neurologizing tautology."

[2] Erich Maria Remarque, in *All Quiet on the Western Front;* Boston: Little, Brown, 1929, gives a notable account of the experience of the soldier for long periods under fire. In this book—one, *passim*, of no small psychological importance—he shows that it is by the developing of rationalizations and automatic habitual acts (acquired with the aid of the rationalizations) that the soldiers could proceed to the point where they slept in the midst of bombardments. His discussion sheds a measure of light on the manner in which we alter our reference frames as to Fate, God, and many other things, in adjustive implicit processes including the vanishment of most of our devices for security, and the appearance of events of extreme novelty and most evil portent.

worthy" act accounts for a remarkably large number of instances of insomnia and seriously disturbed sleep.

If, because of persisting maladjustive situations, hunger, sexual excitement, or danger—real or fancied—one is unable to secure sleep, there appears a peculiarly troublesome complication, in that the individual becomes "too tired to sleep" when finally the opportunity is provided. We may assume that this overfatigue is a manifestation of exhaustion of the Nissel substance, which renders the complex total activity needed for the supervening of sleep difficult to achieve. The mental content of such a sufferer is by no means one of active purposive implicit processes, but rather one conspicuously lacking in integration. If an effort is made to "rest," to suppress the more or less random restless movements of the body, and to ignore the sensory input, after a time one recovers to the point that the active integration of the sleep-situation can occur.

Considerable research has been done on the nature of fatigue, with remarkably little in the way of results. I cannot offer anything more than generalities in this connection. It appears, however, that when the energy dissipated in the organism considerably exceeds its usual amount—whether because of an unusually great amount of physical activity, because of much emotional disturbance, or because of "necessary" but "tedious" interpersonal activities—there appear fatigue phenomena, including something indistinguishable from what we have called regression and involving all the functional activities of the organism. As one might expect from the evolutionary hypothesis, this regression first appears in the most highly evolved and complicated organizations in the body—namely, the neoencephalon. Cognitive procedures become uncertain and peculiarly exhausting. Fine adaptations in the motor field become difficult and if they are necessary are very exhausting. The facility of recall of past experiences and the ability to throw these into meaningful and useful association with one's perceived situation are greatly diminished. The utility of one's reference-frames is impaired in a characteristic and important fashion.

To render this last-mentioned factor somewhat more clear, I shall refer to an extraordinary situation in which the effect is more clearly demonstrated—namely, the state of narcosis. Nitrous oxide is peculiarly apt to provide the sort of experience to which I refer, probably because of its insidious but prompt action. During the dream state at the beginning of anesthesia one is apt to experience some thought characterized by an astounding validity. For the first time in one's life there comes an understanding beyond perchance of some more or less important matter. Thus, while losing a tooth, I once discovered the Truth about sensation. The nitrous oxide machine ticked. I noticed that my auditory perception of this ticking was undergoing a series of changes. In the first place it was adapting itself in loudness to the apparently markedly diminishing rhythm of my circulation. And in the second place it was increasing to a point where at its maximum the beat became not only deafening but exceedingly painful. In the valleys of the pulse waves the sound would fade out, and give me opportunity to consider the phenomena. I considered with uncanny clearness, with unprecedented lucidity. I concluded: "Behold, here I have convincing and complete demonstration that the function of the auditory perception apparatus is most intimately related to the flow of food to its cells. It is greatest at the crest of the pulse wave, and when these cells are being intoxicated ever so slightly during the time of minimum arterial pressure, they are no longer capable of functioning against the influence of the anesthetic." In the dream state, this seemed to be a discovery of well-nigh ultimate importance for the physiology of the sense organs, for there was nothing in particular except a sort of cosmic ignorance as a background against which these thoughts could fall in reference. All the relevant information from study, observation, and everyday events was suppressed. There was no reference-frame active excepting the small band of material still holding out against the effects of anesthetic, because of the "set" with which I had fallen asleep. It was a wrench to give up the conviction of great discovery, in the moments after awakening.

There is an intimate relation of the factors concerned in these anesthesia experiences to very important phenomena connected with profound fatigue and privations of sleep. While one is undergoing anesthesia, all the activity systems concerned with interpersonal relations are rather rapidly extinguished. Such is not the case when similar disturbances of recall and reference occur in the course of the waking life. A man becoming profoundly fatigued while engaged in important work suffers this self-same disorder, the attachment of preternatural validity to very imperfect conceptions, with serious impairment of his ability to deal successfully with other persons or to manipulate important inanimate objects.

If the important work on which one is so concentrated as to suspend sleep and permit the development of serious fatigue phenomena chances to be an attempt at resolving a conflict-situation —as it is, for example, in the case of an individual on the verge of schizophrenia—then the psychiatric importance of sleep privation stands out with great clearness. The fact that the preoccupation is one concerning what are to him the gravest matters of his life, insuring extreme interest, confirms the sleeplessness, and his condition passes rapidly from bad to worse, owing to the interference with his appreciation of the relative importance and the personal meaning of events and perceived occurrences. The connection, therefore, of a period of disordered sleep with the onset of a schizophrenic illness is intimate, and of a nature such that one might well believe that an intercurrent "good night's sleep" would often postpone the disaster.

The total situation called sleep may be regarded as a product of integration by a tendency or system of tendencies. Its extraordinarily obscure character is a result in part of the extreme detachment of the sleeper from direct relationships to other people, and in part of the changes in the character of consciousness attendant in each one of us upon the change from sleep to awakeness. Despite this obscurity, an observational study gives us some important clues to the factors relevant in the sleep situation, and to processes concerned in its integration. As we have stated elsewhere, children, in the act of falling asleep, often show a reactivation of some earlier pattern of behavior—for example, thumb-sucking. We may speculate that by such a device, the child dissolves the acquired realization of the self-world disjuncture, again provides for a sort of cosmic wholeness by using a part of itself for the satisfaction of the oral group of desires (now regressed to the root-tendencies), and thus destroys the relevance of the world of more or less detached things and people. Again, we discover, in some late adolescents, a series of events significantly related to such an hypothesis. Some youths, preparing for sleep, show signs of sexual excitement in the form of erection of the penis. Masturbatory procedures having been abandoned as other than infrequent devices for resolution of sexual situations, these adolescents none the less, in the ritual for falling asleep, include as a frequently necessary item a holding of the erect penis in one hand. Manipulation is not necessary; the contact of hand with penis is necessary. Here, too, it is as if there were a return to a "cosmic" self-sufficiency in the sexual field. And when such frank devices for symbolic exclusion of the outer world are not in evidence, one often finds some procedure in the sleep ritual that can be seen to stand in close analogy to them. On the other hand, the individual concerned is not to be expected to "have information" about these exclusory acts. They may be known to occur; quite frequently, however, they are unwitting habitual performances, but very necessary ones.

Many of the acts appearing in sleep rituals that impress the observer as decidedly exterior to our hypothesis are of origin similar to a number of habitual gestures shown in moments of perplexity, during periods of boredom, or at times of unpleasant emotion. David M. Levy, to whom we owe the confirmatory data on the genesis of thumbsucking, and so on, has observed in growing children and juveniles a series of events which gives us an insight into these gestures and obscure acts in the sleep ritual. During nursing, the infant usually engages in certain "accessory movements" with one or both of the upper extremities and perhaps with the lower. These accessory movements tend to be patterned and, wholly or in apparently unrelated parts, to survive as the gestures to which I am referring. Their inclusion in the sleep ritual is thus but a step removed from acts toward direct cosmic completion, and of a wholly analogous utility. The sleeper seems then to proceed to the integration of the sleep situation by procedures of symbolic satisfaction of tendency systems ordinarily tying him to "external" factors.

A study of sleep behavior has also brought to me the convictions that, quite aside from restoration of Nissel substance, sleep is necessary for the maintenance of the waking dissociation of powerful tendency systems, and that its contribution to the success of the dissociative dynamics takes the form of the release and fantastic satisfaction of the dissociated systems in the activity of sleep. Recent additions to one's sleep ritual often seem to be all but consciously intended arrangements for such release and satisfaction. The student will observe the relationship of this hypothesis to the interpersonal acts in states of light sleep, mentioned in the discussion of dissociation. "Talking" in the sleep is of similar explanation, and we will presently find that the explanation also applies to the important group of dream-phenomena.

Sometimes, probably because of increments in the power of the dissociated tendency by events peculiarly relevant to it, in the course of the preceding day, the general unconsciousness of the "meaning" of a performance used in falling asleep may be suspended and awareness restored to the detriment of the sleep situation. The individual may "doze" only to be awakened by an unknown something, and a something that causes his return to full consciousness. He awakens with a start, often preceded by a cry or groan. In the process of awakening, the waking balance between the dissociating and the dissociated systems is restored, even to the point of erasing any recollection. He remembers nothing from the sleep; it may be that he does not remember having been "asleep," and indicates by subsequent action that he regards himself as having been continuously awake, notwithstanding the fact that he may have been observed for some minutes in the throes of a wretched experience in which he has gasped, choked, groaned, or otherwise given more or less clear expression of the keenest misery.

There are individuals in whom the whole course of sleep seems to be rather badly marred by recurrences of such phenomena. There are some who seem to have "bad dreams" in which they suffer keenly—with or without abrupt awakening—without any recollection thereafter. And to some of these there comes a time when the dissociated system, in the altered state of somnolence, makes its presence felt so keenly—frankly, or in crude and terrible symbolism—that sleep becomes for them a thing of terror, to be avoided as long as possible. In the effort to avoid sleep, the sufferer enfeebles himself in the fashion above mentioned, so that the terrors of sleep increase. And then comes a time when the dissociated system becomes the prevailing integrative factor in a situation something like somnambulism—one way of onset of schizophrenia.

Thus, there came to the hospital a clergyman, aged 36, of

excellent family history and with a record of much achievement. He came by transfer from a general hospital to which he had gone for the relief of an intestinal affection which had appeared some six months previously, and had grown in severity. Now there were interesting features of this malady, one known as mucous colitis—so far as I know a physical disorder that is of rather purely "mental" origin, probably one of the special disablements. It had appeared at a time approaching a crisis in his personal affairs, in the course of several years of a maladjustive sex situation. It did not cause him any great pain, but it did get "terribly on his mind," so that he finally was hospitalized for its study and treatment. In the hospital, as elsewhere, he impressed everyone very favorably. But he did not sleep well, and one night "awakened" in a panic of apprehension as to his having been poisoned. He was fully awake, so far as the intern observed, but he was hard to manage and desperately fearful for his life, a prey to rather formless persecutory notions. In the morning, however, he was his old self, delightful and coöperative. Again the following night he awakened in a most disturbed condition, was quite disordered; next day, again comfortable. The next succeeding night saw him so disturbed that he was transferred to the mental hospital. I saw him about noon the next day, after a night in which he had been dissociated, fearful, and definitely hallucinated. He was perfectly clear, a gentleman who was coöperation itself in giving a typically commonplace history of himself and his physical illness. His evasions were of the best traditional character, the troubles of the preceding nights were minimized, and one was encouraged to "pass over" what had been "perhaps a bad dream." The second night, however, after awaking from sleep, he was even more disturbed. A "normal day" succeeded, but he began to look rather strained, and an occasional odd remark appeared in his commonplace account of his commonplace life situation. And that night the disturbing context appeared *before* he fell asleep, and his condition next day was definitely psychotic and so ominous that I insured him a good night's sleep because of the fatigue phenomena that he was showing. The next day was a good one, with but few slips in his vigorous "normality." But he progressed rather rapidly into a definite schizophrenic psychosis. It looked, however, as if he had made a wonderful effort to avoid the eruption of the dissociated system, and that if he could have handled it during sleep, he would have gone on much longer—probably to late middle life. Whence it comes about that unhappy people are devoted to the sleep-producing drugs, and even the psychiatrist is keenly interested in ways and means of safety enforcing sleep during times of stress within the personality.

Before considering the use of chemotherapeutic agents for the remedy of sleep disorders and sleeplessness, let us pay some attention to the "natural" sleep disturbers and sleep protectors, the entities known as dreams. There are those who devote themselves to "demonstrating" that dreams are "reactions," imperfect or otherwise, to "poorly perceived, peripheral or internal stimuli." This formula, as quoted, while perhaps difficult to interpret, may be quite correct; if it means anything, it means a great deal.[3] An individual of my acquaintance once consulted a dentist for the removal of a bicuspid tooth. The dentist "tied on to" the tooth before the nitrous oxide anesthesia was quite complete. The patient reported, on awakening, a dream including a black rock "seen" against an undifferentiated background, and identified in some fashion with his discolored tooth. With the impression of the black rock there had been incorporated an element of angular velocity, rapidly going over into a ride on a B&O Railway express that progressed at great velocity through an interminable curved tunnel. He stood on the glassed-in observation-platform of the train, conversing on a personal subject with his most intimate friend. The angular component of the velocity was opposite in direction to the angular movement applied by the dentist to his tooth. That, "of course," is all there is to the dream—as seen by the amental type of investigator. Tooth; angular movement; dream of angular movement; *hélas!* Some of the "work" done "on" graduate students by anti-Freudian investigators of sleep and dreams is even worse than this nonsensical translation of the

[3] As the somewhat amentalized investigators arrange their "experiments" and interpret their "results," however, they seem to consider that they are disproving the *validity* of the dream as a process of the personality, and reducing it to the somewhat incoördinate, if not actually drunken, activity of a nondescript bunch of neurons either affected with a batlike propensity to activity when all good neurons should be out of commission, or not yet tired enough to stay under the general coverlet of "synaptic disunion."

anesthesia experience. Some of it, however, is "much more scientific," including, for further example, the "facts" that my acquaintant had ridden on a B&O train possessed of an unglazed observation platform on which he had been engulfed in cinders on unexpectedly entering a tunnel. While he had never traveled with his most intimate friend, the fact that the friend was his most intimate friend is a perfectly good "reason" for his dreaming of him—and so on and so forth.

From before the days of the Pharaoh in whose dream came the seven fat and the seven lean kine, in divers places, among divers people, the dream has been granted validity.[4] With the appearance of Freud's *Traumdeutung*,[5] the dream reassumed its role as a fact valid in our modern views of life. Moore [6] approached the problem of the psychoanalytic interpretation of dreams by the road of experience analogous to dreaming, occurring in "anyone accustomed to dozing off in the daytime." He concluded that these hypnagogic and hypnopompic phenomena seemed to confirm the conception of the dream as arising from experiences of the day just passed, and that the content of the dream and dreamlike phenomena might be seen to stand in the same relation to our trends of thought as meaning stands to the incoming sensations of waking life.[7]

In sleep and certain related states in which the total situation is

[4] I shall not digress to comment on the interesting and remarkable dream tales like James Stephens' "Desire" in *Etched in Moonlight;* New York: Macmillan, 1928, those in Thomas de Quincey's *Confessions of an English Opium Eater*, Robert Louis Stevenson's *Across the Plains;* New York: Scribner's, 1892, the wonder of "Kubla Khan" by Samuel Taylor Coleridge—about whom J. L. Lowes has prepared an excellent study of elaborative mental processes, entitled *The Road to Xanadu*—nor even the horse-dream in Dostoievsky's *Crime and Punishment;* although we shall presently discuss both night-stallions and -mares.

[5] A translation of the most recent edition, made by A. A. Brill, is soon to appear.

[6] T. V. Moore, "Hypnotic Analogies," Study II in *Psychological Monographs* (1919) 27:387–400.

[7] The relation of dream-experience to the outcropping of mental disorder has long impressed me. It seems that a formulation bearing not only on the dream content but also on the nature of the sleep situation can be elaborated on the basis of the data thus obtainable. I shall present such a formulation in categorical form, thereafter discussing some factual material connected with it, particularly some at least analogous material provided by the schizophrenic processes.

integrated in a fashion calculated to hold the relevance of events prevailing outside the limits of the body at a minimum, the implicit processes are in part concerned with divesting incoming sentience of its power to disturb the total activity concerned. If it were not for these processes, many "interesting" events would receive their "appropriate" measure of attention and the (sleep) situation would be destroyed. The sentience caused by their impinging on the sleeper's receptors would activate other systems of the personality irrelevant to those active in sleep. Such sentience and the rudimentary "inner" processes connected with it must therefore be dissociated at the most elementary level. Besides this divesting activity, the implicit (sleep) processes are concerned with factors pertaining to the particular total situation that is intercurrent with the temporary total activity of sleep—the situation activity in which was interrupted for securing of the needed "rest."

The first-mentioned group of implicit processes does not ordinarily leave records easily recallable as dreams. The latter group of processes, on the other hand, is attended in part at least by a limited awareness, and is reproducible on awakening as dream experience, in turn showing certain characteristics arising from the factors concerned in maintaining the sleep-situation. By this, I seek to refer the *peculiarity of dream experiences* to a distinctive type of implicit total activity that goes on in sleep. We may assume that those implicit processes which fall within our classification of "reality controlled," many of which are of the type of logical thought, proceed chiefly by means of verbal symbols, each one of which is attended by an elaborate context of meaning.[8] The contexts of meaning, even the most rudimentary, attached to and constituting a part of each verbal symbol, include important references to "outer" realities. We have already deduced some evidence in support of an assumption that the integration of the

[8] We may assume that implicit processes of this order require the functional integration of a considerable part of our cerebral neural equipment, as they deal with a great part of our previous experience. The areas concerned in verbal procedures—speech, auditory interpretation, and writing— the most distinctive of the human equipment, are probably a great part of that to which we refer. To these may be added the apparatus concerned in the association of that mentioned with abstract visual conceptualization and perception.

sleep situation proceeds from an initial detachment of as many as possible of the important tendency systems from situational involvement with "outer" factors, and their satisfaction by ritualistic, fantastic methods. We therefore expect in sleep a deviation from any elaborate verbal operations, in the direction of ever more autistic ("purely personal," cosmically complete) implicit processes. Logical verbal procedures in dreams are certainly rarely reported. In the occasional dream that includes verbal symbols, the processes in which words occur are usually either brief or "nonsensical"; that is, the verbal symbols have not been used in the customary way. There are, however, some data apparently contradictory to this conclusion about verbal processes in sleep.

Some of us have come to know that at times we are capable while sleeping of fairly complex verbal behavior rather well adjusted to a limited field of external reality. Thus sometimes one can make a series of appropriate replies to the remarks of an accustomed person who is trying to arouse one. And when one is quite fatigued and in conversation with an accustomed person, he can drift off into sleep, continuing a fairly logical presentation —usually, however, with rapidly increasing irrelevance to the topic of discussion. But of the first of these activities there is seldom any trace recoverable after awakening, unless one awakens in the actual process of replying to the disturber—a result usually following the presentation of a more complex demand or a sharp emotional note by the disturber. And in the second case, one can seldom recall more than a fragment of the conversation, the fragment immediately preceding the return to full awareness. In other words, in the first case always, and in the second generally, we are concerned with the group of processes concerned with the devaluating of externally conditioned events in the interest of a sleep integration, and not usually with the sort of processes concerned with a total activity interrupted to permit the activity of sleeping. In some cases of conversation carried on into light sleep, the verbal behavior does continue for some brief time to be relevant to the total situation existing at the time the speaker dozed. For that brief time it is objectively related to the pre-existing situation. At the same time the sleeper is apt to begin to dream, from which, for that matter, he may arouse with the conviction that he has continued in alert conversation. If his sleep has been but very brief and of little depth, this is often the case. If he has slept for some minutes, or if he fell deeply asleep, then incongruities in his recalled dream promptly warn him that he has been sleeping.

This sort of dozing during interpersonal activity is of some considerable theoretical importance. I believe that it provides rather convincing factual material in support of the hypothesis that one does not succeed in integrating sleep so long as there are included in his total situation *many* factors of externally conditioned reality. Moreover, without any very convincing data in support of the contention, it is none the less my belief that the depth of sleep is intimately related to the proportion of externally conditioned factors which are included in the total situation integrated at any particular time as sleep. In other words, if the individual enters into the state of sleep with no concurrent unresolved total situation affecting him, then his sleep may be of great profundity. This, as a matter of fact, is a situation scarcely to be anticipated, at least after childhood. Thereafter, one is almost certain to have interrupted his activity in some total situation in order to secure sleep, and the longer one lives the more it is apt to be the case that a number of events may well transpire during any period of time which he has allotted himself for sleep, the occurrence of which events will justify an immediate suspension of sleep activity and a return to more or less adjustive activity in the intercurrent total situation of which the events are expected to form a part. In such cases, the integration of the sleep situation includes "sets" which are to become active upon the appearance in the stream of sentience of signs indicative of the expected important event. I surmise that the more of such sets there are included in the sleep situation the more shallow will be the sleep and, in all probability the less will be its effect in relieving fatigue.[9]

That there is a relative depth of sleep may be accepted without

[9] The conception of the "set" in sleep is one to which some attention must be devoted. The creation of relevance and the dissociation of tendencies which would interfere with the total activity demanded for resolution of a particular situation have been discussed in Chapter III. The notion now before us is something to the effect that the integration of a sleep situation requires a quite massive dissociation, but not a disintegration, of tendency systems. The velocity of total action thus proceeding in dissociation is usually low, but occasionally high. The sleeper occasionally awakens as a result of adjustive fantasy processes, having effected a solution of a problem that had characteristics in common with the concern which was interrupted in order to sleep.

question. That we have yet developed a satisfactory criterion of depth of sleep is much to be questioned.[10] Until a quantitive method for studying the depth of sleep has been devised, we must be content with tentative formulations. I believe that the depth of sleep is a simple correlate of the type of processes involved. In other words, the more nearly the sleep-activity approximates to the primitive, the more profound is the sleep. In the deepest sleep there is nothing other than primitive implicit processes, while in the most shallow sleep there are processes approximating the type of logical thought. Recollection of dreams from the deepest sleep is difficult if not possible because of the characteristics of primitive processes. The dream recalled on abrupt awakening from deep sleep is usually couched in settings and activities perhaps last experienced "in reality" in the latter days of childhood. Its symbolism is that of childhood fantasy. It pertains to a process of a piece with processes common in the dreamer's childhood. Whatever may have been his conscious appraisal of the related situation actually suspended in the securing of rest, the dissociated tendency system has been reduced to an activity at a childhood level. Rather than follow up a train of speculation as to the number of interpersonal problems whose solution is feasible by childhood formulae, I shall undertake to clarify the conception of the symbol as a further contribution to the undertaking of the dream.

In introducing a consideration of the *symbol* I can do no better than to quote from Edward Sapir: "All activities may be thought of as either definitely functional in the immediate sense or as symbolic, or as a blend of the two. . . . Symbols [like shaking one's fist at a person] are primary in that the resemblance of the symbol to what it stands for is still fairly evident. . . . Language is seen to be the most complicated example of . . . a secondary or referential set of symbols. . . ."[11] As I would wish the student to view the symbol, it is a something either primarily or

[10] See, in this connection, the important contributions from the Mellon Institute of Industrial Research, by H. M. Johnson and his associates. It may be "news" to the reader that the inactivity characterizing sleep is one of a highly relative nature, such that "of twenty-two college boys studied. . . , the least motile stirs about once in 25 minutes; the most active, once in 7¾ minutes; the most typical, about once in 13½ minutes."

See, also R. D. Gillespie, *Sleep and the Treatment of Its Disorders;* London: Bailliere, 1929.

[11] "The Status of Linguistics as a Science," *Language* (1929) 5:207-214.

secondarily related *in* the person to something else. In the growth of each personality there is a vast accumulation of symbols, making up in very fact that precipitate of experience to which I so often referred. At what might be called the peak of the inverted pyramid of symbols are the primary symbols of infantile experience, and toward the ever broadening base extended toward the future, the exquisitely meaningful symbolic formulations of abstract conceptions, for the most part verbal. Between the two is a great mass representing the elaboration of unnumbered experiences undergone in total situations of a progressively more complex type of integration. The "full meaning" of any of these symbols, the "something else" for which each stands, is interwoven out of the multiple factors included in the former situations and actions.

The utilization of each symbol is in a fashion dependent upon the availability of processes similar to, if not actually identical with, those concerned in its origin. When I think privately of my "self," I am referring to unnumbered experiences with other people, perhaps recalling none of them at the time, but being possessed of only so much meaning for the word "myself" as there are remaining factors of the previous interpersonal situations readily accessible to my recall. The word, as it "occurs to my mind," is thus susceptible of a decidedly variable spread of meaning, one that may be very small, in states of profound fatigue, extreme distraction, and the like, one, however, the richness of which might occupy days and days of recollection, if opportunity (a suitably integrated situation) were provided. It is thus to be seen that if one considers a particular symbol as to its richness of meaning, one must consider the particular total situation in which it happens to be active—it means a certain part of its entire historic elaboration. This *meant* part of its history is never entirely inconsistent with any other part of its total meaning.[12]

Applying these deductions to the problem of sleep with dreams —recalling that implicit activity, excepting that concerning the

[12] This is one of the important truths underlying the psychoanalytic treatment of personality disorders. The symbol, presented either as a symptom or as a figure in a dream, is led to an activity in the course of which a sufficient body of its "total meaning" is recovered to permit a conscious reintegration of a dissociated system, or a consciously chosen resolution of a persisting situation.

coenesthesis, must be of the character of secondary or referential symbolic sorts—one expects that in the deeper levels of sleep the types of symbols will tend to be of the earlier class, approaching or including the primitive. Regardless of the actual significance of factors integrated into the concurrent total situation that preceded sleep, the implicit processes occurring during sleep will tend to take the form of symbolic performances of the type characteristic of childhood and the early part of the juvenile era. It thus comes about that the content of most verbal behavior in interpersonal relations is not due to inconsistencies inherent in the meaning of verbal symbols, but to the multiple integrations of the situations in which they both originated, and are put to ineffective use.[13] Conversation, on which many throughout their life put the utmost of conscious faith, is only occasionally used to convey accurate or comprehensive information. It is chiefly used as a tool in producing satisfactory situations and in contributing to activity for satisfactory resolution of these. Moreover, in conversation, the words used and their grammatic ordering may be largely subordinate to inflectional and other devices used to create the "impressions" communicated. It is in large part as the result of this impressionistic "misuse" that there arises the vagueness of verbal symbols—so distressing to the compulsive thinker who often, *passim*, is a past master at casting a deceptive screen of words over concrete reality. One's verbal symbols, other than those carefully elaborated as *terms* in abstract formulations, are not inconsistent but generally vague and frequently overlapping. One's use of them may be extremely inconsistent and unconsciously or deliberately fraudulent.

We come thus to the activity of symbols, or to *symbolic processes*, these being recognized to include a great part of the implicit and much of the explicit total activity. The utility of a symbol as a symbol *for* something being determined by its historic evolution in the personality concerned, so its utilization in a particular total action is determined by the inclusion in its his-

---

[13] The development of logical linguistic technique is made the subject of a highly systematic study by C. K. Ogden and I. A. Richards, *The Meaning of Meaning;* New York: Harcourt Brace, 1923 (Introduction by I. P. Postgate, and supplements by B. Malinowski and F. G. Crookshank). Note the relationship of this exquisite referential use of language and the usage discussed hereinafter.

tory of a factor entering into the composition of the processes concerned. Thus, in the deeper levels of sleep, regardless of the multiplicity of factors integrated in the total situation pre-existing the sleep, the total activity in progress toward its resolution during the period of sleep will be symbolic activity in form and process of the type characterizing the sleeper's juvenile years or childhood. Juvenile, childhood, or even late infantile symbols and activities, the former determined by historic identity with "meanings" in the pre-existing total situation, and the latter determined by processes in connection with much earlier "fragments of meaning" in the historic part of the individual—these will go to make up the dream-work. It is from the mutual effects of these two factors that there come the phenomena to which Freud, in the *Traumdeutung*, referred as the "manifest" *versus* the "latent" content of the dream.[14]

Remembered dreams are to be regarded as experience as valid as is any other. They are only very rarely logical and immediately understandable; they are often far indeed from the type of mental content to which the dreamer is accustomed in his waking life, often being couched in symbols from the period of childhood. While there are activities throughout the period of sleep, the occurrence of a dream sufficiently impressive to be recalled is always to be considered as a part of the activity in some situation of real importance to the individual—that is, one including so strong a demand for resolution that it cannot be entirely dissociated during the maintenance of the intercurrent sleep situation. Any strong emotional coloring of the dream is to be considered valid as of the epoch revealed in prevailing symbolism—a criterion not always easy to apply. In general, dream events of a fairly adult character of symbolism accompanied by terror are to be suspected of referring to a really grave life situation. For that matter, any strong unpleasant emotion in a dream is apt to be indicative of serious stress within the personality. When there

---

[14] The "mechanism" of *secondary* elaboration is to be taken very seriously, for any consideration of the dream events after awakening is very apt to lead to the disappearance of bizarre and incongruous incidents, and to a falsified "recollection" much more "reasonable" and commonplace. It is quite possible that the manifestations of this secondary elaboration are peculiarly apt to affect items significant of the activity of dissociated systems within the personality; of this I am not yet certain, nor need it detain us at this point.

occurs a terrible dream garbed in the symbolism of events being currently experienced in the life of the dreamer, we may be certain that the existing personality synthesis is in grave danger of disintegration, often that a schizophrenic psychosis is imminent. It is by no means uncommon for the person who has experienced such a dream to progress rapidly into a state of delusion in which the dream experience is held to have been real, a link in the chain of actual events. This brings me to the presentation of another body of data, the material from some accessible schizophrenic patients. In these data it will appear that the verbal productions refer to a stream of experience strikingly analogous to dream-experience, yet also to a decidedly less recondite meaning-context than that usual in dreams.

Some five years ago we received into the hospital, by transfer from a neighboring institution, a twenty-three-year-old youth who, among other things, confirmed my surmise as to the intimate relations existing between the schizophrenic disorders and the phenomenology of light sleep and dreams. This patient, concerning whom I have made a fairly comprehensive report in one of my studies,[15] is the younger of two boys, children of a Government clerk of retiring disposition, and a dominating, overreligious, overprotective mother. The war provided the elder son with an opportunity for weaning, and he did not return to live at home after the Armistice. The younger, our patient, however, was bitterly treated by Fate. He was in high school at the time of the mobilization. He said, speaking of his mental illness, "The first

---

[15] "Peculiarity of Thought in Schizophrenia," *Amer. J. Psychiatry* (1925) 82:21–86. The case in point is that of G. H., pp. 63–72. In this connection reference should be made to the following case reports. In the paper above named, there are five others: E. K., a catatonic episode in a somewhat defective boy of 19; V. H., a "markedly dilapidated" boy whose schizophrenic illness occurred at 22; S. F., the 18-year-old mentioned in Chapter VII; W. Q., a 23-year-old whose progress was unfavorable, but whose utterances are worthy of study; I. D., a man of 35 when first recognized as ailing, a prolific writer, following his catatonic state, some of the productions of whom are included in the published report. In "Affective Experience in Early Schizophrenia," *Amer. J. Psychiatry* (1927) 83:467–483, there is a brief report of Q. R., a patient whom I first saw when aged 22, in the third year of his illness. In "The Onset of Schizophrenia," *Amer J. Psychiatry* (1927) 84:105–134, there are four rather extended reports. And in "Tentative Criteria of Malignancy in Schizophrenia," *Amer. J. Psychiatry* (1928) 84:759–787, there are five rather brief summaries.

signs were right around the time the war started, here, 1917 [when he was about 17 years old]; sort of lost consciousness, was hazy one night; I was at home, because struck with that fear . . . . in the second or third year of school . . . . couldn't swing all that was on my head, and swung off at a tangent; was really afraid that something terrible had happened, blamed myself for it." His brother had enlisted "the first day war was proclaimed"; he had been away for perhaps six months before the incident of the "haziness." Our patient kept on in school, going on to graduation, but says that "I had carried that fear from that night; fear of something; my feelings were off the track; sort of off-angled, I'd say. I was fond of people before that, and fond of them afterwards, but I dove into work." After graduation, he decided to follow his brother's example, and went to sea as a common sailor. From experience in the case of other patients, I am inclined to believe that this procedure might easily have stabilized our patient to the extent that he might have gone on thereafter without grave psychosis. But this boy developed typhoid fever on the return trip, and was retrieved from the Marine hospital by his mother and nursed through a long convalescence. He thereafter found employment, under the supervision of a distinctly unusual type of man. Our patient was very conscientious, a hard worker, and progressed finally into a position where he was the subboss of the group—a dozen or so young men—and correspondingly the target of their spoofing and so on. He took a railroad trip one day and among the passengers of his train was a woman of easy virtue and ambition for affairs with young men. She succeeded in engaging him in an attempt at sexual intercourse which terminated by *ejaculatio praecox*. Not long after, he felt that his boss was making reflections on his virility, had some persistent ideas to the effect that he was suspected of homosexual desires, became obviously disordered and was moved to a mental hospital. Here he fell under the care of a psychopathic young physician who had some clues to analytic technique, having himself been treated in one of the more advanced institutions. Along with other methods of investigation he took this patient to his room quite often in the evening, for mutual practice on the mandolin. He impressed on the patient the importance of the homosexual factor in his case; the patient passed finally into a panic state and was transferred to us. In the course of a rather long period of care it became evident that at the times when his content was most schizophrenic, his total behavior was strikingly like that of an individual in the act of falling asleep. I paid some attention to the symbolization of his utterances and concluded that they showed at such times a close parallelism with the reported phenomena of dreams.

He improved quite markedly; was taken out against our advice by the family; and promptly relapsed, having a schizophrenic fugue which is rather well described as follows. The patient planned to get a job and earn some money and thereafter visit his married brother, who owed him some money, "but my money ran out, so I went up to Forde [the town where the brother had married, and the place of residence of the brother's father-in-law; the brother himself had moved to the neighboring town of Freda; the patient may have forgotten this] intending to call up my brother and . . . [the father-in-law, "Mr. R," receiving the call, and being already advised of the boy's illness] . . . I was met at the station by . . . four men, there [including Mr. R]. They were . . . four Masons . . . and we went up to the Masonic hall with them . . . and . . . [from there] went to Mr. R's house. I went in a Masonic hall—with this Mr. R . . . I felt in some way there was some connection—I just felt connected with the organization in some way. I always looked up to them in some way; thought a great deal of them. It changed me a good deal . . . since the day . . . the first day it started with Masons . . . when I went up to the Masonic hall, there. As I say, I went up there with Mr. R, and I was very fond of him; he took me in there, and I worked for him [this later, subsequent to the fugue under discussion]. And I . . . sort of married him when I first went there . . . went up in Mason's Hall. He did some things there; I sort of understood them . . . and I went to his home, and there's where I met this girl . . . I couldn't say I had seen her since." It is necessary at this point to interpolate that "this girl" is a peculiarly interesting symbol. At the time of his return to the hospital, he was "married or something to a girl down there." The girl to whom he was thus rather indefinitely linked, however, was not the girl just mentioned, but another one, a friend of his sister-in-law, whom he met in their apartment at Freda, some

short time after the fugue, to which I am coming. The text of
the patient's remarks concerning this and the subsequent "girl"
can scarcely be reproduced in full. Note, however, the following:
"He's [Mr. R] a wonderful man. [Question: "And you think that
you moved your affection from him to this more or less fanciful
girl?"] Yes, sir—I never felt that way toward my brother; but I
felt that way toward Mr. R. The whole thing started when I went
up to the Masonic hall—I sort of looked, or it was, something
sacred—he was a pretty big man in Freda."

Let me digress to indicate here some of the relevant facts. This
boy's father had immemoriably been under the mother's domination and was not even of an impressive build. Mr. R, on the other
hand, is a handsome man of much presence, and a prosperous and
influential citizen. While the boy is all too well accustomed to
oversolicitude, the juvenile type of mothering, and the feebly
peevish carrying out of the mother's policies by the father, he
has had but little experience with a positive, powerful, yet kindly
father-substitute. He arrives in Forde destitute, and far from
mental health. In fact, he so arrives as a result of 'running away'
from the parental situation—on removing him from the hospital,
the mother had brought him into contact with a so-called Christian Scientist; on being urged to pray with this practitioner, the
boy remarked that he did not need assistance in praying, put on
his hat, departed to a neighborhood hotel for the night, and soon
after quietly boarded a vessel and sailed for Savannah. It is not
so extraordinary, therefore, that after he "tried to get a job in
Savannah, and couldn't get a job there, didn't come across any in
the papers . . . and . . . so . . . I didn't have any money . . .
so I went to Forde," and was both efficiently and effectively received by Mr. R; given an opportunity to demonstrate how "bad"
his behavior might be—in the Masonic hall—and thereafter taken
home for the night by the kindly Mr. R; it is not so strange, I
repeat, that he "sort of married" this parent-substitute. To continue the theme: "His wife's father [Mr. R] asked me to stay
with them. . . . They'd met me at the train . . . I went to bed
there—I called her father . . . or called Mr. R up. . . . I thought
I had met her before—right after I'd gone to bed, I suppose. . . .
I woke up and . . . called him upstairs, then, and asked him her
name. That night, I got to feeling bad about piling in there with-

out money; I couldn't get out of the house, so I jumped out of the second-story window. That's when I started hiking down the road. I went to bed there and felt so bad about it [his poverty], and I got up and left. . . . Didn't like the idea, and hiked around Alabama a bit." The story of the fugue itself follows: "When I left Forde and was hiking it, and reached a town named Exter, and was at the railroad station . . . and all these red lights around the station . . . and at that time I imagined it was for my purpose. Red torch light . . . and when I got off the train at the next town . . . a man across the street had one, and I had the notion that if I crossed that line, I would see red . . . and . . . white sand along the road . . . and when I looked across the fields, it looked like water, and I imagined I could see big boats there . . . and the sand glowed red. . . . I wonder if that was real or imaginary." This patient has great difficulty in piecing together the impressions of his return to Forde.

On his return to the hospital, he patched up a fair institutional recovery and presently entered the military service, with a not too uncommon postschizophrenic interest—to wit, aviation. In the army he experienced many schizophrenic phenomena. At one time, he was detailed to a power plant and one day introduced somewhat of a novelty into the firing of a boiler by dousing the coals with gasoline. The resulting expense to the Government was so great that on his recovery from burns, he was made the subject of a psychiatric study and detached from the service. He spent the next month or so at home, intimidated his parents, and was returned to us about four and one-half years after the date of the first admission. While he retained some insight into the fanciful nature of many of his former delusions, he settled down to a rather comfortable state in which his waking hours were largely devoted to religious preoccupation. "I intend to live a Christian life," he stated, "and by all I've read, and the summation of all I've heard—to date—it's the only life to live. I don't say I'm doing all of it. I feel I'm rather more in contact with Satan than with our Lord; but . . . I shall vanquish the Enemy." He seemed to have plentiful reminders of the Tempter, in the shape of auditory and tactile hallucinations. Women galore talked to him; they were of two classes, one of which was good women. They "materialized"—at his times of greatest stress—"out of their voices, first into a sort of spiritual body, but it feels perfectly real when they press against me at night." "Some nights, I have as many as six or seven—women, in bed with me at one time." Questions elicited the information that he was also approached by boys, some of whom occasionally entered his bed. He suffered much from the palpation of an invisible hand, so active that sometimes it brought him to orgasm. While the bedfellows that engaged his attention made no end of amorous advances, he did not have intercourse with them: "I believe that it would be more of a destructive force than a good force—sex—outside of God's way of giving it to man, and that is in the relation of man to woman in wedlock. There's no real satisfaction outside of this. Because anything else isn't God's way, and so it isn't any real satisfaction. The whole world is in a period of oversexuality. The War did it. Sex really isn't very much, and should not have any attention—except for bearing children." It might be illuminating to quote his remarks anent a period of stress, in which, I surmise, he was "in grave danger" of masturbating. "The voices became terrible; I heard dozens of them—and then came the voice of a preacher, babbling. I don't mean babbling, but more a chanting, you know. And it went on and on; couldn't make much out of it. And then there was a great—like a great congregation, saying all together 'He has broken his vow'; like a congregation making a response, you know." He came to regard his principal activity as constituting a closer and closer approximation to his "Christian ideals," but, oddly enough, was so pestered by his "colleagues on the ward" who read every one of his thoughts instantly by telepathy, that he purposely avoided all social contact. The student may perceive, in this telepathic publicity, an excellent aid in maintaining the "purity" of one's "mind."

The schizophrenic fugue is an episode in the life of the individual during which he manifests processes resembling those of somnambulism (sleepwalking) but significantly different from them. He is not possessed of his "normal" waking consciousness, yet engages in extensive behavior, often passing days in the peculiar state, and usually, but not always, "going away" and perhaps returning to the place at which the fugue began.

The difference of the schizophrenic fugue from a prolonged somnambulistic episode reflects a fundamental difference between schizophrenia and hysteria. It is chiefly a dissimilarity in regard of the involvement of the self. In hysteria, the self is either dissociated *in toto*, as in the case of multiple personality, some mediumship, and the like, or is completely detached from awareness of the meaning of the symptoms constituted by the quasi-autonomous activity of the dissociated system. In schizophrenia, the self is never displaced *in toto*, and never detached from unpleasant awareness of the personal (rather than merely organic) reference of the system active in dissociation. The hysteric may suffer, but only as one suffers a somatic distress. The schizophrenic suffers *as a person* in relation to real or fancied others. Be he ever so violent in repudiating a personal source of his hallucinations, they are experienced in a fashion meaningful to him. These differences are fundamental; there is no such disintegration between the self and the autonomous dissociated systems in schizophrenia as there always is in hysteria. So too, in the more or less massive quasi-automatisms of the schizophrenic fugue, the self is not asleep, but is conscious and fully aware of *personal factors* in the total actions.

In the fugue, the self is involved, but the consciousness is not of the type to which I would refer as fully developed. Paradoxically, there may be conscious involvement of the self without that degree of integration to which we may apply the term *self-consciousness* in its usual sense. I can perhaps best illustrate both the fugue and the diminution of self-consciousness by reference to a not too uncommon sort of dream. One of my colleagues in the course of coming to understand himself underwent a nightmare perhaps the most typical of this sort of experience of any that I know. This young man, one of the most talented in dealing with disturbed patients, and one who had come to a belated realization of the homoerotic tendencies in his personality, was at that time engaged to a woman whom later he married. He had come, however, in dealing with his mental content, to look temporarily upon a homosexual *modus vivendi* as a possible, perhaps to be desired, consummation of some of his tendencies. He dreamed one night somewhat as follows: He stood on a plot of lush green grassland. It was most beautiful and agreeable. He had observed incidentally that it was at the lower level before a huge concrete dam that towered far above toward the zenith. As he was enjoying himself, to his astonishment, a band of water appeared between his plot of land and the foot of the dam. As he watched this, it widened. At the same time, astonishment gave way to fear increasing toward terror. Synchronously, someone far above on the top of the dam called to him. [His associations place the person as his fiancée.] He struggled with himself; he was in panic; he wished to go to her—to be on the solid concrete monolith. He leaped over the widening band of water—he found himself, even as he was making the wild effort to jump the broad band of water, leaping from the edge of his bed into a pool of moonlight on his bedroom floor. The crash did him some injury, but it was some time before he could rid himself sufficiently of fear, and "recover sufficient touch with reality" to discover his hurts, calm himself, and return to sleep. The self is abundantly evident in this dream. The self-consciousness, as an approving reference-system concerned in our appraisals of personal reality, however, was slow in full recovery from the dream-situation. In the schizophrenic fugue, the state of awareness throughout is very like that of the moments following the "awakening" of the dreamer, varying only in the sense of greater reduction at such time as the patient is "wholly out of touch with reality" (generally in panic) or engaged in very troubled "sleep."

Events of schizophrenic fugue are by no means invariably incidents in the course of a subacute psychosis, nor are they in all other cases phenomena to be followed by continued psychotic behavior. In a considerable number of individuals, the schizophrenic fugue is followed by years of merely eccentric living, with or without grave psychosis in middle life. It appears that the processes making up the fugue may in many cases actually function in remedying otherwise hopeless total situations, just as do many of the processes that are usually maladjustive. I shall illustrate this from the history of another patient, received into the hospital at the age of 23, not because of "psychosis" but because a mental hygiene clinic had felt that his treatment as an outpatient was inadvisable. He said that he was "nervous," and entered treatment voluntarily. He was quiet and passively coöperative for a few days, but most uncommunicative. Under routine, and the customary interviews for determining his "mental status," he seemed to improve somewhat, being less restless and less anxious in facial expressions. He stated that he felt worse in the mornings. It developed that, having been reared in an unusually narrow religious atmosphere, he had since about 16 years of age suffered a good deal of conflict in regard of sex, and had had many more or less vague apprehensions of physical disorder as the result of masturbation. His childhood had been lonely, as the parents had not been companionable with him and could find no children who were "good enough for me to play with." Attendance at Sunday School extends backwards beyond his ability to recall, and school began at six. He was not allowed to join the Boy Scouts; needless to say, he was prevented from entering any gang. He dropped out in the second year of high school, because he feared he would not make the grade. At this time, he was very self-conscious, felt his eyes were weak, and had difficulty in looking at people. He had begun to practice masturbation around 14, being taught by a colored boy. Nocturnal emissions began as his conflict over masturbation took form. He mentioned the emissions to his mother, who assured him that they were bad for him, and "must not occur"! When about 18, he read some alleged medical books designed for home consumption, and learned that any and all kinds of sexual activity are injurious, but that, for the sake of future generations, an individual must occasionally sacrifice himself. Self-consciousness was given as a sign or symptom of masturbation; he thus came to "know" what was his trouble. He consulted a doctor, "confessed all," and was circumcised. No benefit ensued. His family moved often, on Their Master's business, from town to town. As he tells the story, when he was about 20, they moved to a fairly large city, Sidney, and there he got on fairly well. On the next move, he came to live in a much smaller city, began to have "stomach trouble" and consulted several physicians. One of them hospitalized the patient and made a diagnostic study, thereafter advising him to masturbate once a week and forget his troubles. Four months later, the family moved again, and the boy had his "first love affair." His sister outgeneraled him on this matter and he was again in a doctor's office. The physician advised him to have sexual intercourse. He did not follow this advice, "got worse," and went to another doctor who referred him to the mental clinic.

In the hospital he was rather restless and suspicious that we would "try to prove me insane," and retain him. He had much to express concerning his bad health and unpleasant anticipation in this connection, particularly as to the evil result from his continued nocturnal emissions. He resisted the notion that there were mental aspects of his troubled state and was much annoyed because he did not receive vigorous (physical) medical treatment. I saw him first on this twenty-first day under care, and on that occasion, a staff conference, he said in part the following: "I have thought that the Mental Clinic sent me here as a result of more or less of a misunderstanding. Because a doctor sent me to them, they thought that it was something mental—they thought that I was weak-minded, or something like that—it was easy for them to find something the matter with me. — — — —[16] I know that there is nothing wrong with my mind, as far as thinking is concerned—reasoning, or anything of that kind." He was asked if the fact that he had failed for years to escape conflict about his sex impulses impressed him as pertaining to this "mind." To this he replied in the negative. His statement of complaint was, "Extreme nervousness, self-consciousness, and a feeling it will affect my body and organs; sleeplessness, bad dreams; I believe that those things are my troubles, mostly." He was anxious to secure something "to keep my mind occupied with"; hard work might be the thing. He felt that if he secured a job among strange people (strangers) he would get over his "nervousness, sometimes, self-consciousness . . . I can't look at people right in the face." Asked as to the worst of his anticipations, he replied, "I thought that maybe I might go crazy from it—I thought that there was some weakness, something physical—thought that it might kill me. I also thought that I might get the grit and get over it." A question was asked as to how he had avoided depression, and to this somewhat recondite interrogation he made a significant reply: "Tried to kick it off like my father told me to; he said that it was 'will power' to shake it off." In what way had he been shaking it off? "I have been trying to forget it. . . . When I am feeling bad, I always work harder than usual."

[16] In reporting verbatim conversations, the series of dots (. . .) is used to indicate that matter has been excluded at this point; the series of dashes (— —) is used to indicate pauses in conversation. The quoted matter presented is not always in the exact order of its production. Rearrangement of matter has been made in the interest of clearness of context.

There is, in this material, the conventional nothing-wrong-with-my-mind motif by which individuals strive to protect themselves from the fear of insanity, in turn a manifestation of Divine retribution and a spur to the dissociation or suppression of sexual motivations, sexual thoughts, and sexual behavior. The patient is promising, in this connection, because of his insight into this situation, reflected in the qualification, "as far as my thinking is concerned." If he insisted entirely on the physical-basis-of-the-difficulty, then we would find ourselves confronted by the additional problem of attacking and breaking down this defensive formation, before we could come to grips with the troublesome conflict. The organization of experience within the self may be such that any yielding of the defensive formula, physical-basis-etc., is perceived as entailing an immediate success of the sexual motivation, the feared "insanity." In this latter case our procedure has to take into account the advisability of the patient's "being much worse before he is better." In the patient under discussion, for reasons already clear in the history of his "ethical" training, the escape of the sexual motivation—for reasons not yet obvious—is to be both "crazing" and lethal. As is often the case, this poor kid has been instructed to "develop will power," "get the grit," and so on, in the fashion to which the deliberately blind are eternally recurring.[17]

The patient under discussion, continuing to "feel terrible," to wish to leave the hospital, and to keep everything but symptoms to himself, was finally called upon to answer a somewhat searching interrogation. In the course of three hours of questioning, the following was elicited: The boy, consciously, detests his mother and loves his father. She, he at times believes, has put a spell on him that makes it impossible for him to stop masturbating. His older sister has always been taught to dominate him. The only time since his sixteenth year that he has been approximately comfortable was a period during which her "wildness" and running around with the "worst kind" of men was occasioning the parents much worry. He has been "in love" with several girls—

[17] This reminds me of an ancient "psychiatric" practice of dispensary doctors, recounted by E. Mayo: "In these 'nut' cases you do a Wassermann; if it is negative, you tell the patient to buck up. If he doesn't buck up, you commit him to a hospital." Of all sad words and so forth that one encounters in the history of unhappy folk, the saddest seem to be "forget it."

invariably decidedly younger than himself, except (at about the age of 13) a movie heroine that he knew only on the screen. He has never made any advances to any of the "love objects." He started masturbating the year after the "love" of the movie heroine. The next "love" is reported as follows: "After I left school, I was working all the time. I sort of fell in love with a girl then, in the Sunday School. She was eleven years old. I fell in love with her but I never, hardly ever, talked to her. She was only eleven years old, and I used to think that I was going to wait for her to grow up. That girl has been in my mind for years. I never talked much to her. I was sort of terribly scared; if anyone would mention her name I would feel funny, I would get red or white in the face. I don't know what made me that way, unless it was these losses. I wonder if it would have affected me—there wasn't anything sexual or about sexual intercourse—and I never thought about her when I was masturbating. I remember how bad I used to be then, nervous." Now follows the account of the fugue in this case. "I went away from home while still working there . . . I had to go to work at six o'clock at night. I was in trouble with this nervousness. You see, I was also studying designing but never seemed to make any headway; seemed that when I would try to study I would get exhausted . . . couldn't get up any ambition— and it would make me mad, sometimes . . . sometimes I would stop my work and masturbate, and I would feel bad over that. Well, I went in and punched the clock, and got a notion that I wasn't going to stay, and walked out, walked out the railroad track—kept going all night—forty-three miles, altogether. I don't know what I was thinking; I seemed to be against the people at home for some reason or other. I guess I was not altogether what you would call in my right mind. That evening I was just like I had been a lot of other times; when anybody would look at me, it would seem to grate on my nerves; something wouldn't let me look at the men. I remember that night before I left the house my mother gave me fifty cents and I was sore over that. Also some quarreling around home worried me. Well, I walked along the railroad all the way to Chase and remember walking along narrow streets there, with old-fashioned gas lamps, and on out into the country on the pike toward Bolling [the State Capital]. I imagined things on the way, I remember. I thought my mother had put poison in my food, or something. You know how things get on your nerves. — — — — I slept in a buggy seat all day. Felt kinda spooky but didn't feel any real fear. Next morning I saw a farmer and — — got a job. — — Then I got real sick; it was a real sickness to my stomach; thought I was going to die. I felt real bad, so I told him I was too sick to work. He didn't seem to believe it much. I was real bashful and self-conscious and couldn't look up at him. — — So I left there and started walking around the mountains, looking for another job—looking for another job up in the sand pits or at the stonecrusher. I was going to get a job there; I must have been half out of my head. — — A man took me back to town in his car — — he took me to the house but I slept out in his garage. Next morning I was real sick—I think I vomited a lot, I don't remember. Thought then I was going to die. Then we went up to the house of the boss of a factory, there, to get a job. He wasn't at home, or something; I don't remember. I found a railroad track going out of there to Chase; thought I would go for home. So I started on the track—got to another town, and I went into the telegraph office to send a telegram home. I remember when I left this farmer's, I walked around in some rather strange town, I don't know what it was, now—I remember walking along the pavement, and having fears that it would come up and hit me. The pavement looked strange. I went in a store and got some ice cream and cakes, and there was a blind man sitting across from me and I gave him some cakes—then went down the tracks. Well, this telegraph operator must have been reading a description of me in the papers—I had been away from home for a week and a half or two—and he said to wait, that he was going home himself—then he must have phoned my father, for he came and took me home."

We have now considered a general theory of sleep and dreams, unpleasant dreams in general, a "nightmare" with a terminal "somnambulistic act" and difficulty in reintegrating the usual self-consciousness, a schizophrenic fugue occurring in the course of a subacute psychosis, and one preceded and followed by a less conspicuously maladjustive condition. I wish now to follow up this development of the topic of sleep, dreams, and schizophrenia by comment on a patient who finally suffered a schizophrenic dissociation late in a life characterized by rather successful compensatory satisfaction of the sexual tendencies; his psychosis, how-ever, so gravely endangered his life that a chemotherapeutic agent was required to suppress his conflict. As a preface to this report, I shall refer briefly to an earlier attempt at interfering by phar-macodynamic means in schizophrenic situations in which the patient was at a standstill.

There are many chemical substances which, when introduced into the body, produce marked disturbances of the integrator dynamisms. Some years ago it occurred to me that since many individuals come to an impasse in their schizophrenic illness, such that the rate of change of condition becomes very low and there is neither positive nor negative progress but only a sort of very tense standing still, it might be an excellent maneuver to disorder the integrating systems, and thus artificially to alter the type of total situation that the individual is integrating. Now, atropine is a powerful alkaloid, the taking of which is attended by much dis-turbance of the autonomic (paleoencephalic) nervous system. While the drug is remarkably powerful, its effects are such that the lethal dose, the quantity that leads to fatal poisoning, is very large. It may be given—if there is no idiosyncrasy—to the point at which not only the older but likewise the "new" nervous system is much affected. In large doses, it brings about such dis-turbances of the neoencephalon that the subject becomes deliri-ous, and—as had been demonstrated in its use for the eradication of addiction to morphine—this state of delirium may be extended safely over a matter of many hours. We therefore tried atropine on some schizophrenic patients in whom all progress seemed at a complete standstill.

Under dosage of atropine such that consciousness was not affected, and the patient merely experienced phenomena in the field of the autonomic system—dryness of the throat, flushing of the skin, and so on—there was no more effect than that seen in schizophrenic individuals confronted by any new variety of ominous "inner" experience—such as, for example, an attack of appendicitis, or an operation for the "removal of foci of infec-tion," or the intraspinal injection of horse serum, or any other of the astounding "treatments" that every now and then undergo some vogue. When, however, the dosage was pushed to the produc-tion of delirium, we secured some remarkable results. The impasse was abolished. The state of the patient, after the treatment, was a distinctly new one, in which processes making for recovery were observed in each one of the three individuals on whom the method was tried. Unfortunately, atropine is not primarily an intoxicant of the cerebrum, and its other effects are both marked and troublesome in the extreme. A search for the ideal delirifacient has not been productive, to date, and our attempts at chemotherapeutics have taken another track. Before discussing this, I wish to remark on the phenomena reported by two of the patients who underwent atropine intoxication—the third proved to be a defective with a marked speech defect. In the period following the sensory nuisances occasioned by atropine, there appeared a prolonged and elaborated dream in which a particular person—in one case, the traditional Chinaman—entered into this and that kind of a situation, all of which, however, were of one character— represented one type of interpersonal relation concerning the subject. This dream sequence was extraordinary, not like anything the subject had previously experienced in sleep. It was very vivid and as readily recalled as are the details of a short and terrible nightmare. In one of the two patients who came under treatment by a talented colleague of mine, the material of the atropine dream served as a key to the elucidation of his personality problems. In the other patient, also, the dream material seemed to be of a particularly meaningful kind, and one from which one might expect results in psychotherapy. I was unable, however, to follow developments in his case.

There was admitted to the hospital some years ago a gentleman fifty-one years of age, in the throes of a very severe acute schizophrenic panic. The history of the illness was somewhat as follows: The only boy in a group of three, two older sisters; none married. The mother died many years ago and the father about one year before the patient's illness. A normal gestation; both infancy and childhood normal. Very bright and learned well. Of a happy disposition, conscientious and unselfish. In his first position, he remained seven years, and in the second, 17 years—to the onset of illness. "Many responsibilities fell on me" at the time of his father's death. During the early days of acute symptoms, he received a telegram announcing the death of the aunt (Clara, *vide infra*) who had cared for him as a child.

Five days prior to his admission, he wrote to his sisters a letter including the following: "I feel that my days as a teacher are numbered. I feel very weak but am trying my best to get better, to conquer the spirit or have the spirit conquer. How is Aunt Clara and her sickness—better I hope—I hope she may fully recover." On the preceding day, he had started a letter to the members of the special school of which he was principal and treasurer. Two days before admission, he made a start at writing one to his directors. He wrote many pages of seemingly meaningless material. One of them is headed "How things are bound up together. Many kinds of men and beasts." Thereafter follows a string of integers, from 1 to 100; another by twos from 2 to 112; another by threes from 3 to 82, an error which leads the line to end with 100; another by fours, to 100; and another by fives to 100. Another page is covered by lines made up of repetitions of "last," "lad," "sad," and again "lad." After two nights during which he did not sleep but instead paced the floor, he was found to be suffering hallucinations of the barking of dogs, crying of babies, and of automobiles moving in special relation to him. He believed people were watching him, that the physician called by his friends was writing to the neighbors, asking them to watch him. He believed the telegram of his aunt's death was a fake. He expressed bitter self-recriminations, saying that he was a liar, a slouch, no good, a glutton, and even accused himself of having estranged his landlady from her husband—an entirely erroneous notion.

On admission he was found to be in very fair physical condition, somewhat arteriosclerotic. He was at times blocked in his speech, being seemingly unable to express himself. He asked how his sexual energies could be controlled, and inquired as to the advisability of castration, and so on. That night, he became much disturbed, much excited, noisy, and at times actively antagonistic. The next morning, he was quieter but seemed rather disoriented and actively hallucinated. He appealed to various staff physicians to be operated upon for the control of his "sex energies," made many references to his "bestial nature." His excitement was continuous, greater at night, and he progressed into a state of physical exhaustion. He said, "My passions run toward the organs of reproduction," and recounted how since childhood he had experienced a recurring dream, perhaps once or twice a month, in which he sees a beautiful stallion. In the dream he glories in its grace of form, its motion, gallops and rhythm. It is his desire to ride the horse or drive it. Then his "feelings became base," he gives way to a desire to finger the sexual organs of the horse, at which junction he has pollution. Not only does he dream of horses, but his thoughts during the daytime continually revert to them. His life has been one of struggle to overcome this tendency. The greater the effort he has made, the greater is his desire and thought about horses. He says that he is beastly, morbid, and inhuman in these desires. It has been largely because of constant thoughts of a horse that he has felt himself unable to marry. People now believe him to be a prostitute or that he maintains a house of prostitution. While describing his difficulties, he is very tense. He believes that he is under a spell, that he is hypnotized—perhaps by the physician who was called early in the acute illness.[18] His productivity was shortly greatly reduced by incoherence, perseveration, and blushing. He insisted on going nude "to purge myself of sin," was destructive, resistive, but also most affectionate to attendants. His feeding was a great problem; artificial feedings were regurgitated.

By the thirteenth day under care, the patient's physical condition was most grave, our therapeutic armamentarium seemed exhausted, and I had recourse for the first time to ethyl alcohol as a chemotherapeutic agent for the relief of a schizophrenic impasse. It seemed that the patient was shortly to die of exhaustion unless we could interfere with the violent conflict-situation including his

---

[18] I am indebted to my friend and one-time associate Dr. Paul J. Ewerhardt, for this account of the patient's productions shortly after admission. As his condition progressed rapidly downward, he was not coherent on the fourth day of hospital care, on which I first saw him. He was brought to my office but refused to enter, immediately identifying in it "the presence of Satan." I was astonished not so much by the character of identification as by the speed of its achievement, as I was quite certain that he could scarcely have seen me before his vigorous opposition to coming in. It later developed that he had noticed my bronze statuette, Men's Stallion, and that this had been the sign of the Evil One.

The symbolism of the horse, stallion, gelding, or mare, is of great importance in many individuals. See, for example, the final paragraph on page 130, report of case 75, *Amer. J. Psychiatry* (1927) 84:105–134. Also, a forthcoming study, "The Symbolism of the Horse," by Ernest E. Hadley and the writer.

highly organized ideals and the sexual cravings. Atropine was out of the question because of his grave physical condition. Ethyl alcohol is well known to possess relatively low toxicity and is peculiarly suited to the purpose in this case because of its rather specific effect on more recently acquired or highly elaborated functional activities. While perhaps a general protoplasmic poison, the rather specifically inverse relation of the effect of alcohol to the recency of habit-acquisition should, it seemed, render it of almost unique utility in such a situation as that with which we had to contend. The results quite justified my optimism. Improvement became apparent almost at once and he went on to discharge as "recovered" about four months subsequent to admission. It developed, incidentally, that the "hypnotic spell" which he believed to have initiated his illness had been cast upon him by an attractive and persuasive book canvasser. He has been occupied successfully with his former duties for some several years past.

The history of the use of liquors containing ethyl alcohol is coterminous with the recorded history of the human race. Elliott Smith presumes that it "began with the storing of the life-giving barley" and that it has played a very real role in the history of civilization "not merely in provoking jollity or degradation, in promoting friendship and geniality, or in exciting discord and criminal irresponsibility, but also in the ritual of almost every religion." [19] The distribution of the present use of alcoholic beverages is well nigh universal among the known inhabited regions, and the degree of its use is everywhere widely varied among individuals. It behooves one, therefore, to give some measure of thought to ethyl alcohol, not only as an evil, nor yet as a chemotherapeutic agent for practical use at a particular stage in some few cases of schizophrenic illness, but also as an essential factor in one of the human dynamisms. That the ingestion of alcohol acts to reduce the force of recently acquired inhibitions may be accepted as proven. It reduces the effectiveness of obsessional substitution processes and thus and otherwise brings about that release from morbid inhibitions to which Kraepelin referred. It enfeebles the referential processes by which one attends to the "reactions" of others, and so *simplifies* interpersonal relations. If pushed to excess, alcohol impedes the integration apparatus to such a degree

[19] G. Elliott Smith, *Human History;* New York: Norton, 1929.

that only early childhood and infantile types of total situations are formed. If the intoxication proceeds still further, the somatic apparatus is palsied, and dream-states with twilight activities are manifested until stupor supervenes.

Because of its simplifying effect on interpersonal situations, alcohol is the tool by use of which an indeterminable but great number of adolescent, juvenile, and psychopathic personalities are able to stumble along throughout life. That their stumbling way entails a vast amount of misery for those with whom these unfortunates are closely associated is not a reflection on alcohol; it is a reflection on the general culture that produces them. So, too, with the late paranoid individuals, even those that injure or kill their mates; I doubt if this be a fruit of alcohol, but rather one of our general culture. These folk in many cases would avoid having mates were they left free to develop an individualized life-plan instead of compelled to fit the home-and-family stereotype. To the many young men and women who nowadays marry not for love or for convenience, but as a supreme demonstration of "normality," alcoholic overindulgence is all too little relief from the stress set up by their unrecognized cravings. It does yeoman service for the majority, but its peculiar effectiveness comes from its enfeebling effect on what is in most cases a socially necessary control, the comparatively recently acquired patterns of inhibitions in conformity with usage.

The continued personality integrity preserved by this device is not always endurable, and is frequently anything but admirable, to persons making up the environment; as a result, there is apt to be a social deterioration of the drinker, a "sinking" to strata in which the interpersonal situations are of a less complex order. Since alcoholic intoxication has no effect on the ideal formations themselves, but only on their functional efficiency, the change brought about in the drinker's situation does not represent a satisfactory adjustment, and is in turn complicated by stress. A vicious circle is apt to result, and the personality to suffer seriously. Here, again, accepting as proven some evil effects on the central integrating systems from very severe or from recurrent severe alcoholic intoxications, we are constrained to view the downward course of individuals addicted to alcohol as largely a cultural product. In this connection, the current scene in the

United States of America—in which the attempted enforcement of prohibitory legislation lacking any approximation to a universal approbation is added to the more insidious culture patterns—is one worthy of study as an experiment in the field of individual-social synthesis.

Before concluding the consideration of the influence of alcohol in interpersonal relations, I would recall its mention (*passim* in Chapter VII) as a device for facilitating coöperation in "unworthy" acts, and comment briefly on its occasional relationship to the *onset* of schizophrenic illness.

We received one day as a patient suffering "alcoholic hallucinosis," [20] a man of 32, the only son of a dilapidated, ne'er-do-well, heavily alcoholic (and seriously deteriorated) farmer. The mother of the patient had died, following a long invalidism, some ten years previously. The patient, who was brought to the hospital by his only sister, two years his senior, was the only son. He had left home at the age of sixteen, and come from his country home to a neighboring city where he lived as a boarder in the home of a widow, to whom he rapidly became the eldest addition to her own ten children.

His history, as imperfectly obtained, suggests that he had been of rather average infancy and childhood, an average schoolboy, finishing the eighth grade, thereafter going into a trade. His habits had been exemplary until soon after his mother's death; he began to drink, immediately carrying this to some excess—a condition that has existed ever since. He usually "got drunk" on his "days off." The landlady reported, however, that in the fifteen years he had lived with her, he had been away from home for but two periods, one of six days, and the more than eighteen months of his military service. He had undertaken to enlist in the cavalry,

---

[20] The differentiation of "true" schizophrenic episodes from "alcoholic hallucinosis" is one of the less profitable occupations of the psychiatrist. Bleuler suggests that the latter type of illness does not show "lively somatic hallucinations and affective disturbances," the predominance of which would indicate schizophrenia. The "somatic" experiences to which he refers are largely of sexual origin: The alcoholic rarely *needs* such experiences in the resolution of the situation integrated by his dissociated system. The "affective disturbances" are a feature the validity of which the present writer impugns. Discussion of these questions, as also of many another, is not suitable to this text; they will be included in a forthcoming monograph on schizophrenia.

had been rejected because of visual defect, and was thereafter drafted, served overseas for many months, and was repeatedly in action. The only change noted after the service was a great increase in his smoking of cigarettes.

Shortly before the war, when twenty-six years of age, he married a "very fast woman," with whom he could tolerate life for but six days. He then returned to his foster home, discussed his "attempt and failure at married life" with the landlady, and suppressed further discussion of it. The sister, for example, never knew that he had been married. The wife, incidentally, contracted syphillis from someone else between the date of his giving her up and his sailing for France. Overseas, he had a great friendship with another enlisted man; they came to be inseparable and drank a great deal together. The friendship died out after his return. His wife atempted to renew relations with him, but during her fatal illness, he did not see her. "When he was notified of her death, he said he did not believe that she was dead but that she had the message sent in order to get him to see her in the hospital." He thereafter insisted on the landlady's eldest son accompanying him in his trip to identify the remains.

He was a steady worker, continuing to drink on his "days off" only. He became entangled with another woman, "never more than a prostitute," married, with two children. She had been trying to "vamp" him for years and had succeeded in getting him to buy her a lot of furniture, on the installment plan. He met increasing difficulty in making these payments and "was very much upset over his attachment to this woman." He finally sought the advice of the (foster mother) landlady, and on it, let the furniture go by default and refused to see the woman again.

He was becoming rather more comfortable after having solved his second heterosexual difficulty, when two events occurred, the outcome of which was his admission to a mental hospital. He had to work very hard for about eighteen hours, at the end of which both the patient and the other workmen were greatly fatigued, wet, and cold. A quantity of whiskey was drunk, contrary to rules. The next day was his "day off." He visited another unit of the same concern, one at which he had formerly worked, and there, while drinking, mentioned that the men had drunk while on duty the night before. Thereafter, he went home and slept, being finally awakened by a dream that distressed him profoundly. On going on duty, he felt that he was suspected of having reported to a superior on the violation of the antidrinking rule, and that his co-workers believed that he was a "traitor" and a "bad guy." He saw men congregating in groups and talking, presumably about him. On trivial grounds, he came to believe that he was going to be "bumped off." At the end of two days of this, he refused to leave home and heard neighbors saying, "If we could only get him out of doors, we could get him." He felt that the gang of boys who were accustomed to congregate in the vicinity of his place of employment, and who were very friendly with him and his co-workers, had learned of his fancied "snitching" and were "going to get him." His hallucinosis increased, kept him awake at night, and eight days after the night of overwork, he was received, extremely apprehensive, harassed by threats of injury by "boot-leggers," "men in town," and friends of those on whom he was thought to have "snitched."

In the hospital, he was made to feel secure enough to get a good amount of sleep. Following this, he improved somewhat only to have, after recounting the initiating dream, an acute accentuation of hallucinosis in which his mother and sister were denounced as lewd, and he was made the target of "other vulgar and unpleasant expressions," which he would not recount. After a few interviews, in which, so far as I could judge, he permitted himself to become acquainted with his dissociated tendencies by way of a "bargain with himself" in the shape of full belief in the reality of his persecution, he improved markedly and came to discharge. Under the rather intelligent mothering of his landlady, he "checked up" on the reality of his experiences, came to a degree of insight, spent some two years in convincing himself of his mental soundness, married—this time rather well—and now (five years after the episode) has two children.

The onset of psychosis, as he reported it, was as follows: "I had been very tired after that night, but got pretty rosy and didn't have sense enough to go home to bed when I got off duty. I went to the old place and drank some more with some former cronies. You remember, I had been called as a witness in an inquiry into drinking at that place, before my transfer. I had talked to some of my friends, there, about the drinking of that night before. Then

I went home and slept for hours. I awoke after a dream; never had such a dream—never thought of such a thing before, in my life; I dreamt that X (the landlady's eldest son) and I had a sexual affair." So far as I could discover, this is the only time that a frank homosexual content had made its appearance in the patient's consciousness, in many years past. The close friendship, alcoholic indulgences, and intimate and entirely "ethical" association with very loose women had apparently served for release from a dangerous accumulation of desire connected with the dissociated tendencies.

With this but fleeting consideration of the grave maladjustive processes that may ensue on alcoholic excess, I will refer to another evil of the time—the reckless use of hypnotic drugs by the laity and by overworked or careless physicians. While I have no doubt as to the efficiency of such drugs as paraldehyde and cyclo-barbital in tiding a personality over an emergency, I am equally certain as to vicious contributions to personality failure to be charged to the use of sleep-facilitating drugs. As in the case of ethyl alcohol, so with these chemicals; no contribution to an actual resolution of difficult situations is secured by their use. Not only does their use generally amount to a mere nonadjustive dynamism, but it is complicated by evil aftereffects. In exchange for some relief from fatigue, one suffers a disturbance of functional efficiency in the following day. It is unfortunate that the popular hypnotics are not as unpleasant in their effect on the coenesthesis as is hyocine, for their routine use is indubitably a facilitation of mental disorder. Besides their direct effect in temporizing with troublesome situations, they give rise to a complex sort of habituation showing in certain nonadjustive situations as a belief in the necessity of some particular drug. The chosen chemical is then taken with religious regularity, often in increasing dosage and with noxious effects upon the body, to no more realistic end than would be an obsessive stepping across every second crack in the sidewalk. Such a patient sleeps quite well on four placebo tablets as on his customary twenty grains of barbital, although his suspicions may be aroused by freedom from some accustomed discomfort next day.

The rule should be that props to failing personality syntheses are justifiable in emergency, especially (and perhaps only) when fatigue phenomena are an outstanding feature. The continued use of hypnotics is never justified. In the case of individuals who cannot for some time make a beginning of actual treatment for personality difficulty, devices other than chemotherapeutic agents should be used—for example, the afternoon swim, massage, the wet sheet, and changes in the dietary system—particularly a change in the time of dosage in heavy drinkers of coffee. There is also the problem of the patient who could but *will not* begin effort toward the reorganizing of personality that makes up actual psychiatric treatment. While I hope to shed some light on this problem in a subsequent chapter, I would here remind the psychiatrist that there are plenty of medical practitioners from whom such a patient can secure coöperation in standing still, so that the specialist need not feel himself to be under urgent compulsion to prescribe drugs and placebos.

I cannot leave this subject without comment on the use of the truly *narcotic* habit-forming drugs—in particular, the opium alkaloids—morphine and heroin. Cocaine should be included in this category, the more in that its use often begins the disintegration completed by the more damnable addictions.[21]

There is no room for doubt that narcotic addiction is a personality disorder of the most grave omen. The proportion of those once "in the habit" of using morphine or heroin who are carried to real "cure" is very small, indeed. The proportion of "addicts" who are able to carry on useful living for even a relatively short time after their habituation to the drugs is very small. The proportion of them who preserve their pre-existing personality organization is negligible; almost all of the socially desirable "traits" disintegrate rapidly.[22] To become addicted to these drugs is an extreme misfortune; one of the worst, if not, in very fact, *the* worst,

[21] Cocaine addiction has considerable importance in its own right—for example, as a factor contributing to crimes of violence.

[22] These are my conclusions from some intensive investigation of a material made up of young Americans. Perhaps we should have data on the personal and the social significance of opium addiction in Orientals before drawing any broad conclusions. My "feeling" about the subject, however, is such that I would encourage legislative effort looking toward exacting the death penalty for active proselyting to the drug traffic.

misfortunes that may befall an adolescent. It is not so scandalous—
so appetizing to sensation-mongers and morbid uplifters, and
therefore so profitable to the ever-abundant extortionists—as are
sexual misfortunes. There do not seem to have been more lynch-
ings of drug peddlers than of politicians, policemen, and others
who prey on "immoral practices." Yet, if I had to order, on the
basis of psychopathological data, a scale of evils that could occur
in interpersonal interaction, I would head the list of inevitably
destructive events with narcotic-drug addiction; there would be
a gap between it and homicide for economic gain; and I would
find sexual assault by "foreigners" (for example, a Negro) well
down the list.

With this, I conclude the presentation of personality growth
and disorders likely to mar its course. We shall next consider the
practical application of the insights gained from the ontogenetic
formulation. The life processes tend to an almost infinite diversity
of late adolescent and adult personalities. Among the diversity,
there are some that are fairly distinctive, around which the con-
tinuum of variety might be said to "concentrate." To these, we
may apply the terms *types* and *typical situations*. These will be the
subject of the succeeding chapter, being presented, I trust, to a
student already convinced of the unique character of each life-
situation to which he is introduced by each new person. The
physician, taught by every new experience that nothing generally
applicable is of any great use to the patient who consults him,
none the less systematizes his procedures on the basis of a more
or less conscious schematization of recurrent interpersonal relations in which he is involved in the conduct of his work. His role
is worthy of close study. His success is often a measure of his
capacity to identify himself intelligently with the role of the
patient. This, too, is deserving of reinvestigation.

In every phase of psychopathology and the study of social
welfare, there are before the student two courses from which to
choose. He may give rigid adhesion to a more or less rapidly
acquired system of rationalistic doctrines. Or he may strive always
to preserve an ideational freedom so "unnatural" that it requires
recurrent scrutiny of one's intellectual operations. The above
sketch of sleep, dreams, and schizophrenia—the latter being my
major interest in psychopathology—may point up, better than

many words, my conviction that the student is best served in typi-
fying morbid processes when he secures, not rigid syndromes, but
instead rather vague nuclear conceptions susceptible of growth
with his experience.

CHAPTER
X

Types and Typical
Situations

IN TURNING TO types and typical situations it is my wish that we cease for the time being to concentrate our attention on the individual as a nexus, as the presenting aspect of processes and interrelations of processes partly described in the world of space-time by the life history of the individual personality. For the moment, let us draw out what may be of value in considering the individual after the traditional unitary fashion, in order that a greater meaning may come to inhere in the dynamic conception of the person as he ordinarily takes himself to be, a self-conscious being possessed of knowing, feeling, and impulses to action, of information and beliefs, of means and ends. Even as we do this, we must keep in mind the truism expressed by one of my contemporaries to the effect that man of all creatures is distinguished by the tendency to make ends of his means.[1] In the early years of this century Adolf Meyer well said, "Once for all we should give up the idea of classifying persons as we classify plants. . . . In the process of emancipation from traditional and untenable views of man, an iconoclastic attitude towards all attempts at practical characterology and theories of constitution was probably the only safe pro-

---

[1] H. D. Lasswell, *loc. cit.* The succeeding quotation is from Adolf Meyer, "An Attempt at Analysis of the Neurotic Constitution," *Amer. J. Psychology* (1903) 14:354–367. For the types he then suggested, *vide infra*, this chapter. As a general bibliography to this chapter, reference may be made to Appendix C of the *Proceedings of the Second Colloquium on Personality Investigation*; Baltimore: Johns Hopkins Press, 1930.

cedure." But also, as he continues, "The existence of special types is nevertheless obvious to common sense."

Typology, in so far as it refers to a scientific procedure, must reflect a preoccupation with some major analytic aspects of persons. One of the "traits" which may be said to distinguish man from the subhuman species refers to his capacity for integrating situations of unparalleled complexity. A typology can therefore be erected on the abstract consideration of the integrating dynamisms themselves. In the last analysis this preoccupation is one suited to a specialized physiology. Its author will consider people as they tend to fall into classes by virtue of differences in the autacoid and older neurological dynamisms. Our current term for these differences is perhaps *temperament*.[2] He will also contemplate classification on the basis of difference in the integrative abilities of the neoencephalic and special sensory dynamisms, the former of which will approximate our current divisions on the basis of measurable intelligence factors. Provisionally, this typology will have on the one hand something like the following divisions:

> sanguine,
> choleric,
> sentimental,
> phlegmatic,

and over against these, divisions something like the following:

> [Idiot],
> Imbecile,
> Borderline intellect,
> Normal,
> Superior.

To the combination of these two categories there will be the added subdivisions on the basis of degrees of acuity in and prepotency of "imagery"[3] of the

[2] See, on typology generally, the excellent *Bibliography of Character and Personality;* Cambridge: Sci-Art Publishers, 1927, and the treatise by A. A. Roback, *Psychology of Character;* New York: Harcourt Brace, 1927. In the former, the author lists 3,341 titles.

[3] See, for example, W. Jaensch, *Grundzüge einer Physiologie und Klinik der psychophysischen Persönlichkeit;* Berlin: Springer, 1926. See also the critical studies of H. Klüver: *Genetic Psychology Monographs* (1926) 1:71–230.; *Psychological Bull.* (1928) 25: 69–104; *Proceedings of the Ninth*

visual,

auditory,

tactile,

olfactory,

gustatory, and

other special sensory fields.

Rather than preoccupy himself with integrator dynamisms, the morphologist will undertake to achieve a typology of gross bio-physical organization. After the fashion of Kretschmer [4] he may subdivide men into the *leptosome* and the *pyknic*. The student of disease processes may be astonished to find, as has Draper,[5] that this gross morphology of the body can be correlated with something of potential morbidity. Over against the leptosome he may find that there is a peculiarly high incident of gastric ulcers; over against the pyknic, an extraordinary frequency of gall-bladder disease; and from his study, a third type given to pernicious anemia. It will presently appear that the psychiatrist as a student of total action also discovers that he can divide mankind, some-what uncertainly, into two classes that are also somewhat related to Kretschmer's—namely, the introvert and the extravert.

The biophysical organization being the relatively enduring resultant of communal interchange, we might at this point con-sider a classification on the basis of prepotent zone of interaction, perhaps seeking, with Abraham,[6] people showing organization in analogy to the:

sucking oral,

biting oral,

expulsive anal,

retentive anal.

International Congress of Psychology; 1929, 264; and Psychological Review (1930) 37:441–458.

[4] E. Kretschmer, *Physique and Character* (translated by W. J. H. Sprott); New York: Harcourt Brace, 1925.

[5] George Draper, *Beaumont Foundation Lectures;* Baltimore: Williams & Wilkins, 1928; *Disease and the Man;* New York: Macmillan, 1930.

[6] A partial bibliography of Abraham's writings appears in the somewhat insular "Bibliography on Psychoanalytical Psychiatry: 1893–1926," by John Rickman, *British J. Medical Psychology* (1927) 7:358–374. A comprehensive "Bibliography of Scientific Publications of Dr. Karl Abraham" appears in the *Internat. J. Psycho-Analysis* (1926) 7:182–189. The three papers in point are to be found in the *Internat. J. Psycho-Analysis* 4:400–418; 6:247–258; and 7:214–222.

Passing from preoccupation with the physicochemical and the biophysical levels of our communal existence, the typologist may concern himself with classification on the basis of the cultural factors which have come to be the most conspicuous ingredients of the personality, and on that basis one may set up divisions somewhat along the lines of Spranger's four "fundamental value-directions": [7]

the economic,
the theoretical,
the artistic,
the religious.

Rather than preoccupy himself with valuing processes, the typologist can abstract for classification a prevailing or characterizing attitude of the personality toward the cultural heritage itself, arriving with W. I. Thomas at: [8]

the philistine,
the bohemian,
the creative.

And in touching upon this prevailing attitude, it becomes interesting to analyze further, to discover if there can be found a formula (analogous to the role of special sensations) as to "desires" underlying attitudes, whereon one finds that this great sociologist has organized a system of four "wishes." These are wishes for

new experience,
security,
recognition,
response.

One also finds that Freud has made a dichotomy into the *life instincts* and the *death instincts*.

From all these formulations we learn ways of looking at a subject-individual rather than exclusive distinctions between

[7] E. Spranger, *Types of Men* (translated by Paul J. W. Pigors); New York: Stechert, 1928.

[8] See, for example, the presentation in H. S. Jennings, J. B. Watson, A. Meyer, and W. I. Thomas, *Suggestions of Modern Science Concerning Education;* New York: Macmillan, 1925. There is, fortunately, a reprinting of W. I. Thomas and F. Znaniecki, *The Polish Peasant in Europe and America;* New York: Knopf, 1927. The methodological section of this is fundamental.

species and varieties of individuals. Now the most naive way of viewing individuals divides among three classes: those who interest us and reciprocate with a showing of interest in us, those who interest but are not interested, and those to whom we are indifferent. Even a little reflection on this classification shows its weakness and points to the fact that, of all the world, other people are the most interesting objects known to us. Individual discriminations as to the degree and kind of interest that we "take" in others must concern us, rather than interest or its absence. But equally we are unable to escape a gross classification of people into those to whom we feel sympathy and those toward whom we have antipathy. The third category, those to whom we are indifferent, is clearly a product of sophistication. Before developing more situational typology, I wish to develop the classification in which the principle may be referred to an attitude toward events.

It is to Jung [9] that we owe the popular distinction of man into extravert and introvert. His typology has come to include not only this fundamental distinction but also distinctions on a second basis of reference to four "mental faculties": thinking, feeling, intuition, and sensation. Before the twofold division can be applied to the individual, it must be modified by yet a third factor—namely, the personality manifestations that are conscious and those that are unconscious. Thus, the individual whose principal mental functions are along the line of thinking may manifest himself in his rationalizing activity toward events as, say, an extravert; feeling, intuition, and sensation in his case may be relegated to the unconscious and each in turn from that "region" manifest in processes extraversive or introversive. Hinkle,[10] the foremost exponent of the Jungian viewpoint in America, has brought forth a modification of this typology, in which certain of the combinations to be expected from the multidimensional classification of Jung are eliminated. All in all, however, there seem to be a great many people who cannot be fitted, without violence, to either the parent system or her modification of it.

That there is validity in a division of humanity on the basis of

[9] C. G. Jung, *Psychological Types or the Psychology of Individuation;* New York: Harcourt Brace, 1923.
[10] Beatrice Hinkle, *The Re-creating of the Individual;* New York: Harcourt Brace, 1923.

attitude toward events has impressed a large number of students. There seems to be a more or less perfectly justified dichotomy of actual people between polar or modal types of habitual or enduring "ways" of interacting with events, personal, impersonal, or social. The delineation of the actual difference is the problem. McDougall has surmised, perhaps chiefly as a result of investigating the effect of alcoholic beverages on allegedly introverted people, that the extravert attitude is the primary and that introversion is the manifestation of an autacoid, a hormone. The more of the hormone there is produced in a given organism, the more his attitude diverges from the extravert norm, and the nearer he approaches a wholly abnormal total introversion.[11] There would then be a linear distribution of some sort, and it has been suggested that various "traits" might be found to be directly related to the position in this extravert-introvert scale. On this assumption, tests have been elaborated, purposed to use such entities as suggestibility and negativism, but none of the efforts impresses me as of fundamental importance. Yet it seems to be quite definitely the case that to some people "presenting" events fall into relatively simple relationship with the self, while to others events must be prehended in a *series* of references to the self. People of the latter class manifest an analytic tendency that remains relatively undeveloped in the former. When we find that there is a rather high correlation between classifications so disparate in bases as the crude morphological, that of disease potentialities, and this syncretistic-analytic formulation, one cannot but be impressed by the possible importance of a common factor, or a group of concomitant variables.

Provisionally, the extravert is the one who takes things as they initially impress him, and the introvert the one who subjects them to a more or less extensive series of appraisals on the basis of various valuations to him. The extravert falls into many total situations including others, most of these being relatively simple. The introvert falls into relatively few total situations with people, and of these most may be of great complexity. The extravert personality is capable of manifesting in a unitary fashion various sets of its incorporated tendencies, in total activity for direct satisfaction.

[11] William McDougall, *Outline of Abnormal Psychology;* New York: Scribner's, 1926.

The introvert personality, on the other hand, in integrating an interpersonal situation on the basis of any of its groups of tendencies is but initiating a series of processes leading to much more complex total situations and decidedly less direct satisfaction. From an historic viewpoint, the life experience of the introvert greatly augments the elaboration of the self, and there is a corresponding increase in the capacity for suppressing relevance; that of the extravert may flow by with little evidence of increasing self-awareness, and with a continued naive sensitivity to more purely environmental factors.[12] The extravert continues to live in a world in which everything may be assumed to be understood; the introvert has become impressed with the multidirectional meaning-implications of events. The comment of Piaget[13] concerning understanding between children continues to apply rather closely throughout the social life of the extravert: "If they fail to understand one another, it is because they think that they do understand one another," owing to a continued naive egocentrism. The introvert, on the other hand, has early learned that people not only cannot always read his thoughts aright, but that they have somewhat of a faculty for error in such reading. If he fails to understand or to make himself clear, it is because he has too complex a conception of the individual with whom he is communicating, owing to an overly sophisticated egocentrism. Working with others appeals to the extravert—even though he hopes to be spared much contact with introverted folk; working with others may become so difficult and annoying to the introvert that he as much as possible eliminates them and contents himself with interest in less recondite data, machinery, engineering practice, or natural scientific research.

The possible social and unsocial aspects of extraversion and introversion lead easily into a consideration of persons on the basis of their prevailing attitudes to others:

> social,
> unsocial,
> antisocial,

and to the preferred ordination of them as to others, as *dominant* or *submissive*. The dominant ordination brings with it a classifica-

---

[12] In gross oversimplification, the extravert asks of events, "What now?"; the introvert, "Whence? Why? Whither?"

[13] Jean Piaget, *loc. cit.*

tion of *political types* of which there might be the three attitude-variations: dominant social, dominant unsocial, and dominant antisocial. Similarly, we find the classifications submissive-social, submissive-unsocial, and submissive-antisocial might well apply to students alike of politics and of criminology.

We have touched on the direction of erotic interest in other people, listing the

autoerotic,
homoerotic,
heteroerotic,

and here again we find factors entering into combination with the dominant and the submissive attitudes, and with the social, unsocial, and antisocial trends. In making these combinations, however, we must not lose sight of the nonsexual factors entering into human social organization; the unsocial are by no means solely the autoerotic.[14] There is then to be considered the division on the basis of overt sexual behavior:

the autosexual,
the homosexual,
the bisexual,
the heterosexual, and
the perverted sexual.[15]

In touching on perversions, we enter into the field of the physician-psychiatrist, to whom, as Freud has remarked, deviations of sexual behavior are but presenting symptoms of personality disorder. Again, quoting Meyer, "from the general picture of nervousness we now should attempt to select and discriminate certain types *and especially to define certain names and distinctions.*" [16] This authority distinguishes:

[14] The Thomas "four wishes" is more nearly in line with the complex totality of social life.
See, for a contrary view, J. C. Flügel, "Sexual and Social Sentiments," *British J. Medical Psychology* (1927) 7:139–176.

[15] A group of people in whom sexual satisfaction is secured by some procedure complexly related to the sexual "sensations" themselves; in other words, in whom the sexual tendencies have been seriously warped by inclusion of fetishistic, sadistic, coprophagic, urophagic, necrophilic, urolagnic, or another of a host of symbolic processes but remotely related to the securing of genital, oral, anal, dermal, and other sensory inputs.

[16] Adolf Meyer, *loc. cit.* Italics are mine. The following italicized statement occurs earlier in the article: "*The best medical standard* [of typology] *is that of adequate or efficient function.*" A description of the types enumerated is to be found in the article.

the psychasthenic,
the neurasthenic,
the hypochondriacal,
the hysterical constitution,
the epileptic constitution,

and "of much more importance to alienists are certain types already akin to definite mental derangements":

the unresisting (responding easily
     to fever, to intoxications),
the maniacal-depressive,
the paranoiac,
the deterioration type.

Having presented a classification of constitution emphasizing the unfortunate functional tendencies, I choose next to present the same authority's classification of definitely disordered process-pictures, the Meyerian psychiatric nomenclature.[17]

(1) The *anergastic* set of facts—activity denoting organic loss in the sense of actual tissue destruction; for example, arteriosclerotic dementia.
(2) The *dysergastic* set of facts—implying a disorder of the metabolic support with a remedial (reaction for repair) disturbance of the nervous tissues; for example, delirium in acute or chronic infectious diseases.

The *not primarily organic* set of facts, these in turn including:

(3) The more odd and archaic types, constituting the *para*-group:
   (a) the *parergastic* set of facts, in which scattered or set daydream and fancy-forms involve the general activity.[18]
   (b) the *paranoiac*, in which thew are merely a distortion of the attitude under some dominant systematizing delusion.
(4) The *thymergastic* group, in which there is largely a disorder of the affect (*thymos*, in contrast to *nous*); the phenomena observed in the manic-depressive psychosis.

[17] "In our work in psychopathology we learn to single out frequently recurring combinations of facts, which sometimes occur in pure culture and sometimes in combinations. . . . To obtain an internationally intelligible terminology, [we may start] from a term which would comprehend the whole realm of psychobiological activity. *Ergasia* seems to cover the field. It is derived from the Greek *ergazomai*, to be active, to work. . . . *Ergasia* is the best term for *performance* and *behavior* and psychobiologically integrated activity in general. . . ."
[18] Meyer would use *parergastic* to replace "schizophrenic" because the latter term seems to him too closely identified with the concept of dementia praecox, "a term unduly prejudicial prognostically."

(5) The *merergastic* set of facts, including the "minor psychoses" often called *psychoneuroses* "or very euphemistically and evasively 'neuroses,' although only psychogenically intelligible":

   (a) Nervousness, general and undifferentiated.

   (b) The irritable weakness called *neurasthenia,* probably oftener a disappointment reaction than one due to any physiological "nervous exhaustion."

   (c) *Hypochondriasis.*

   (d) *Anxiety attacks.*

   (e) The *obsessive reactions* and *ruminative tension states* with dependence on the substitution of rituals or false obligations or doubts.

   (f) *Dysmnesic substitutive hysterical disorders,* comprehending the whole group of "hysterical" evasions and substitutions, submersions, or benign dissociations.

   (g) *Convulsive disorders* of *epileptic* and *epileptoid* nature, and their equivalents.

(6) The *defective development* group of facts, the *oligergasias* or oligophrenias, called idiocy to a level of up to two years, imbecility with a level up to seven years, and morons with a level of eight to twelve years in intelligence.

In this classification of the more or less frequently encountered congruent phenomena of mental disorder, we are presented the five groups of factors that must be conceived as conditioning the individual human organism in each total situation. There are: the group of *neurogenic* factors pertaining to the central integrating dynamism; the *organogenic* factors pertaining to the autacoid dynamism, the circulatory dynamism, the eliminatory dynamism, and so on; the *exogenic* conditioning factors, relating to dietetic and climatic influences, and to influences such as those of poisonous substances elaborated within, or absorbed from outside the body; the *psychogenic* factors "which can be referred definitely to specific life-experiences and their memories or associative tendencies, in contrast to" the fifth group; the *constitutional* factors, "inherited or at least ingrained reaction-tendencies or behavior-tendencies, much less modifiable." [19] We shall now return to consideration of the person among persons, seeking what little aid there may be found in a schematization of total situations as they involve the chronologically adult.

[19] The specific names of these factor-groups, and the quoted matter, are from Meyer. At this point attention may be called to the extraordinary utilization of inference by which not only the constitutional but all the

Scheme IV

Interpersonal Situations

Division on the basis of the principal group of tendencies
involved in their integration.

I. Kinship—(partly) characterized by extrinsic durability:
   (1) The group of surviving consanguinous relatives
      (a) mother
      (b) father
      (c) elder siblings
      (d) younger siblings
      (e) other significant relatives
   (2) The personal household
      (a) the spouse
      (b) the eldest child
      (c) intermediate children
      (d) the youngest child
      (e) adventitious members
         (i) husband's mother-in-law or
            wife's father-in-law
         (ii) elder siblings-in-law
         (iii) other relatives, consanguinous or by affinity
         (iv) others, unrelated
   (3) Guardianship, and others.

II. Subrogative—characterized by clientship to one in the status of
   expert:
   (1) economic-financial

---

other groups of factors are lumped under a modified psychogenesis—for
example, in the remarkable document of Georg Groddeck, *The Book of the
It;* New York and Washington: Nervous & Mental Disease Pub. Co., 1928
[Monograph #49]

The eminent neurologist and psychoanalyst, Smith Ely Jelliffe, has repeatedly pointed to the importance of psychopathological consideration for the
interpretation of "organic disease." He has demonstrated most convincingly
the unwisdom of an internal medicine divorced from psychobiological considerations, and has done pioneering work toward the elucidation of situational factors having significant relations to nephritides, tumor formations,
encephalitic symptoms, and other "obviously organic" states. See his "Psychopathology and Organic Disease," *Arch. Neurology and Psychiatry*
(1922) 8:639–651; "The Neuropathology of Bone Disease," *Transactions of
Amer. Neurological Assn.* (1923) 49–419; "Somatic Pathology and Psychopathology at the Encephalitis Crossroads," *J. Nervous and Mental Disease*
(1925) 61:561–586; "The Mental Pictures in Schizophrenia and in Epidemic
Encephalitis," *Amer. J. Psychiatry* (1927) 83:413–465; and "Vigilance, The
Motor Pattern and Inner Meaning in some Schizophrenics' Behavior,"
Psychoanalytic Review (1930) 17:305–330.

    (2) legal
    (3) medical
    (4) scientific
    (5) religious

III. Friendship—characterized principally by a wholly intrinsic durability:
    (1) Of the same sex
        (a) of similar age
        (b) younger
        (c) older
    (2) Of the other sex
        (a) of similar age
        (b) older
        (c) younger
    (3) Mixed—couples

IV. Accommodative: Associateship—characterized by relatively durable adjustments arising from mutuality of ends, or interdependence:
    (1) occupational
    (2) recreational
    (3) other

V. Ordinate—based on relations of super- and subordination; regimentation, and so on:
    (1) (owner—slave)
    (2) liege—vassal
    (3) master—servant
    (4) boss—worker
    (5) worker—boss
    (6) servant—master
    (7) vassal—liege
    (8) slave—owner

VI. Formal—based on tempero-spatial contact, contiguity, coincidence, and so on:
    (1) routine—social
    (2) occupational
    (3) recreational
    (4) other

Each rubric of the above table may be taken to refer to a situation worthy of consideration by reason of distinctive characteristics. Of some of these, volumes have been written.[20] The first

[20] Not only is there a rich and variegated literature on interfamily relationships throughout the psychoanalytic material (see, for example, A. A.

kinship relations are those from which the very buttresses of personality are derived. The relationship of son and mother may or may not grow from an infantile one, through the childhood, the juvenile, and the adolescent eras; arrested development in this field is of profound importance. The daughter-mother relationship has yet another step in the evolution, is perhaps for this reason even more uncertain of successful evolution, but is facilitated by the distribution of tendencies from mother to mother and father.

The relationship of daughter and father may be of the utmost importance in arresting the evolution of personality. That of the son and the father often bulks large in the adolescent epoch. Always the source of the man-pattern in childhood, the father in mismated couples may assume extreme importance as an embodiment of antipathetic valuation. One type of "castration-fear" that can arise is direct, a punishment through or to the mother and in or by the son's genital apparatus, arising from the adolescent re-symbolization of actual sexual interest in the mother, in turn violating the incest formula.[21] In addition there may be formed one of the social configurations variously called "Oedipus complex" and "castration fear," in which the father's antagonism, envy, or jealousy is coupled with the son's "feeling" of sexual sin—culturally acquired.[22] As a result the self becomes formulated either as contemptible and in danger of being so perceived by

Brill, *Psychoanalysis;* Philadelphia: Saunders, 1912; and J. C. Flügel, *The Psychoanalytic Study of the Family;* London: Internat. Psycho-Analytic Press, 1921); massive "anthropological" volumes such as Edward Westermarck's *History of Human Marriage;* London: Macmillan, 1921; and Robert Briffault's *The Mothers;* New York: Macmillan, 1927; and the growing literature of child guidance; but also excellent practical treatises such as *Ideal Marriage: Its Physiology and Technique* by Th. H. Van De Velde (translated by Stella Browne); London: Heinemann, 1928; and even, of late, "handbooks" (for example, Wm. H. Kniffin, *The Business Man and His Bank;* New York: McGraw-Hill, 1930), in which relationships such as the interpersonal factors concerned in maintaining credit with one's banker are discussed.

[21] Which I cannot accept as inborn, nor permit myself to explain on any fanciful *Urhorde* theory, nor yet account for on any *established facts* of infancy and childhood. I consider that there must be such facts to be found, that incest-awe is an ontogenetic acquisition, probably one of the early man-ways. See in this connection an interesting inference by E. E. Hadley, "The Origin of the Incest Taboo," *Psychoanlaytic Review* (1927) 4:298–316.

[22] See, "The Oral Complex," *loc. cit.*

one's contemporaries, or as wickedly unsafe and in need of constant aggressive protection from compeers. Irrationally conciliatory or irrationally hostile attitudes to other males of parallel status, therefore, arise from this kinship relation.

The relationship to elder siblings of the same sex may fail of elaboration into an adult role, and serve as foci for much the same sort of tendency-systems as those just discussed in relation to the father. The peculiar attitudes of the mother and of the father to the eldest son may give rise to peculiarity of attitude to him on the part of all subsequent children. Elder siblings of the other sex may assume appropriate displacement from the configuration of the other parent—for example, the boy's immature sentiment for the mother may be displaced as to its object upon an elder sister, thereby dissociating it from the full force of the incest awe.[23]

The relationship with younger siblings is quite other than that with elder. Again subject to complication by reason of differential parental attitudes, it is apt to include a good deal of the paternal or maternal role. Peculiar and sometimes very important processes may complicate the growth of two boys a few years removed in age as one reaches the period of serious stress in mid-adolescence, when the other is but well into preadolescence. If the elder has been rather "rough" on the younger while the latter was juvenile, the tables may be very effectively turned at this time; the new isophilic solidarity encourages the younger, its none too joyous abandonment by the elder makes him the more melancholy over the "unfeeling" jibes of the "kid brother." The case of two boys or girls who are yet nearer in age may include during preadolescence covert to frank sexual behavior, with or without mild to grave guilt processes. There may also be seductions of a juvenile brother or sister by an adolescent elder, with or without important consequences, dependent in part on early training and in part on the more current parental performances—especially if the event is reported by the younger sibling.

[23] The gradation of incest-guilt in the one step of kinship may be so great that the brother-sister love is only *consciously* wrong, while the son-mother attachment is opposed from the deepest unconscious. The "taboo" on sexual relations between brother and sister may be acquired in preadolescence. It has often to be "taught"; the true incest-awe is generally learned quite unconsciously.

Relationship with aunts and uncles, cousins, and nephews and nieces of approximately parallel age may follow the general rule —namely, that sentiments for members of the closest kinship group may persist for years and affect seriously the growth of corresponding aspects of the adult personality. The love of a girl for an elder brother may complicate her subsequent marital relations to the point of utter failure, even severe mental disorder.

Marriage and other relatively durable interpersonal relations involving sexual adjustment are the test of personality evolution. Their psychopathology is the psychopathology of personality. Every deviation which has thus far concerned us has its exemplification in the mating and mismatings of the person and the spouse. Nearly every type of interpersonal situation can be set up in these legal or extralegal affiliations. We see couples in which the man is in all but fact married to a mother or a daughter, the woman to a father or a son, brother has all but married sister. We see the keenly inferior mated with a person of so much lower or so much higher status that the whole body of the social system is incorporated into a two-group. We see the feminized victim of an infantile mother sentiment mated with the masculinized rebel against an infantile mother sentiment. We see the "ultrafeminine" child-wife victim of surviving childhood sentiment for the father married to the overmasculine doubter of his potency, because of bisexual uncertainty or foreconscious homosexual tendency. We see a variety of "marriages of convenience," with or without occasional procreant contact, in which the *actual* interpersonal sexual intimacy situations are extramarital, enduring or fleeting. We see the marriage determined by the fact that one woman proved resistant to one's sexual charm, and thereby escaped the curse of unmotherliness in the unconsciously homoerotic rake. We see those determined because the man proved fatherly in that he never pressed for sexual satisfactions during the courtship. And we encounter everything from absolute repulsion toward sexual activity, through total frigidity and complete impotence, to a furor of sexuality with increasing anxiety because the sexual object is failing to serve as a cloak for the desired—and feared— object of distorted sexual tendencies. There are many couples in which intimacies are only to be achieved—in one or both members

—by means of fantasies in which other people are substituted for the actual spouse.

Next to the psychopathology of marriage is that of parent-hood. Children can function as everything and anything, from the sublime gifts of Life, the nurture of which is the true fulfill-ment of personality, to mere justification of "sinful" sexuality, a penitential burden for "uncontrollable human nature." [24] In the last-mentioned category, the girl is a more terrible penance than the boy, for she may presently be "ruined" and bring disgrace on the family—somewhat as it should be, since she is the fruit of one's sexual sin—while the boy can at worst only become paretic, otherwise psychotic, or a criminal. Children are anything and everything from slaves, baubles, pets, to treasures to be protected, pampered, and otherwise completely unfitted for the life of human beings. They may be "educated" for anything and every-thing from the clergy to the role of private in the rear rank of the internecine warfare betwen the parents, usually with the aid of their kinfolk. Their "education" may reflect the rigorous training of one of the parents, often softened and confused by the sur-reptitious and inconsistent overcompensatory laxity of the spouse,[25] or a "liberality" amounting to oversolicitous overkind-ness, the *opposite* of the training of the parent, again correspond-ingly complicated by the spouse. The children may have very little place in the lives of one or both parents; they may be the center around which the parental living is wholly oriented. All too generally, they are new tools of the parents turned to the delayed pursuit of lost aims and ambitions. Their relationship seldom approximates that of opportunity for insuring opportun-ity, of tolerant support during the evolution of individual personality.

The eldest child is prone to two misfortunes: He is the first experience in parenthood; and he is the firstborn, and, as such, the

[24] Thanks to our continued savagery regarding illegitimacy and the sancity of wedlock—a religious matter, but also an economic system legally enacted and fought for by "the weaker sex"—a child may still be one of the most terrible blows to one's status.

[25] The factors manifesting in the rigorous "discipline" being among those which lead to the selection of the spouse, the antidote to their manifestation must be morbid and inconsistent.

carrier of a great body of cultural patterns brought with us from the shadows of history. He is apt to have several surviving grandparents, a plethora of uncles and aunts, and, in general, to be the focus of all the prejudice and superstition of two families. If he is a boy, he is apt to grow into morbidly close or morbidly distant relationship with the father. If the firstborn is a girl, there are additional complications from the disappointment of potential hopes, later to be overlaid with undue positive or negative attitudes.

The intermediate children of groups of more than two have decidedly the best chances of successful personality growth. Not only is the production of four children a biological necessity for "full" representation of a stock, but it is an excellent psychobiological rule, for two of them are apt to have a fair measure of developmental opportunity, being neither eldest nor youngest.

The relationship of the youngest child is peculiarly complex. Not only is he the "baby," so far as the mother is concerned, but also he is the baby in so far as all the other siblings enter into his world. While the firstborn may encounter the greatest resistance to his efforts at weaning himself from the child-parent relationship, and must in fact often carry the family as more or less definitely dependent on him for the rest of his life, or make a complete and irreparable breach with them, the youngest is often brought to an accepted role of "the child," and actively continues his dependency, sometimes with great subtlety.

The lone girl in a sib-group of boys, or, even more impressively, the lone boy in a fair-sized family of girls—here, in truth, we encounter complex intersib relationships, often with an extraordinary attitude on the part of the parent of the other sex. The resulting personality is apt to be exceptional in important respects.

In monosexual sib-groups, the parents of whom are none too happily associated, the eldest is apt to feel the increasing disappointment of the parent of the same sex, and the youngest to be warped toward a sexual inversion, to satisfy this growing parental desire. In expressing such crude generalizations, I am doing considerable violence to the *absolute necessity* of studying every situation as it is encountered, and in this particular case, the unconscious inversion of sexual interest in one of the mismated parents may be peculiarly strikingly manifested in the partial or complete inversion of all but the eldest and the youngest child in the group.

Our next grand division, the subrogative relationships, requires attention to the personality factors common in experts, themselves. As a very crude approximation to a most imperfect rule, it may be stated that experts are inclined to a dubious practical socialization. Whether, as some would have it, one becomes an expert in order to escape an especially keen sense of personal insecurity, variously energized, or, as seems more probable, conscious superiority in one line is taken to grant one a certain leeway in other matters, the fact seems to be that experts as a lot are rather difficult people. They live in part in a world of extraordinary preconceptions, a world more scientific in some of its aspects than is that of their clients. They are approached by people who come to them as to allegorical figures, rather than to one having information. If they resist the role thrust on them, their Philistine clients suspect their expertness, and go elsewhere. If they accept it, they find themselves committed to a rather transubstantial sort of living, in which various outworn traditions must be followed while the luminosity of their genuine superiority is expected to suffuse their every notion, including subscription to these archaic folkways. Since one's expert advisors are of *one's choice,* so these new authorities are often required to reflect the most variegated credit on one's judgment, just as in the juvenile era one's parents had to be defensible against any invidious comparisons; the possession of a good office—at the right sort of address—a collection of art-objects, and evidences of patronizing a good tailor may be taken to be necessary accoutrements of the experts of today.[26]

Friendly relations may be viewed with the psychoanalysts as aim-inhibited sexual relations, or as necessary fulfillments of nonsexual tendencies. Both of these views probably have place in explaining this form of relationship. To insist, however, on the exclusively sexual motivations of isosexual men's and women's clubs, societies, lodges, and games is either to expand the con-

[26] It is to be hoped that as we grow in appreciation of the rightful place of knowledge in the conduct of life, we may progress somewhat in the direction of our oft-quoted Greek preceptors.

ception of human bisexuality to an extreme degree, or to ignore relevant facts of human social organization, primitive to civilized, in all levels of which the isosexual society is to be found, complementing the marital relationship. Complex motivations incorporating parent-child factors are to be found in friendship relations in which there is much difference in age or in status. This subject will concern us further in the final chapter.

CHAPTER XI

The Study of Personality

IT HAS BEEN SAID that from those who cannot forget the religion of their adolescence there come two classes of beings: those who are able to follow the olden ways—the priests, who know; and those who are not content—the philosophers, who seek. The philosopher who finds, or who grows weary of searching, becomes a priest. I doubt if students of personality have right to the title of philosopher; I know that the reflective methods of some philosophies lead to nothing of anthropognosis. But equally I know that many a student of personality has grown weary of searching, and has made a religion of what little or nothing he had found. The quest for certainty in the world of personality is an adventure on which all adolescents embark, from which but few travelers return with that contentment born of achievement, and in the course of which many reach the Isle of Circe, and remain.

The physical sciences have one problem of personality in the "personal equation," the limitations of our special senses. The social sciences have many. The workings of personal bias and inexperience are everywhere evident in the brief course that the social sciences have had among us. They share the defective instrumentality to which the physicist long since attended; they are at the great disadvantage that a refining of their instruments means a refining of their selves. This has long been surmised by the psychiatrist, and of late we have been told that only a self-understanding individual can hope to achieve sound understanding of another person. Only to the extent of one's insight into one's self may one hope to achieve insight into another mind; so runs the dictum. Even the interpretation of observable human behavior is measured as to success by the formulated experience of the observer. The interpretation of communicated "intelligence" of things beyond the personal ken of the hearer is one of the fancies with which we justify our relaxations. I have tried to suggest some of the factors that have given us past successes sufficient to save us from despair, and shall now work over the ground in some detail.

The study of individual personalities is a form of social interaction. In the interpretation of written and similar records of the subject-personality, there is a secondary-group interaction. In the accumulation of information about the subject-individual from other individuals, there is always an interpersonal relation with many complexities. Of these, an hypothetical detachment of the observer-personality is the most stupid. No two people have ever talked together with entire freedom of either one from effects of interaction of the other; a trans-Atlantic telephone conversation with a stranger, conducted in an unfamiliar language, and pertaining to a boatload of hogs, would be no exception to this rule. And when, as is so often the case in personality study, the subject-individual on whom a report from a second person is desired by the investigator is a friend or foe, a son or a parent; when the purpose of the investigator as envisaged by the informant may include almost any or all the prevalent value-superstitions, when the very language of the two conversing may be so differently evolved that identical verbal symbols stand in but remote relations of meaning—how all but certain it is that the truth will remain unknown, and that the "detached" investigator will come away only a little more certain of his preconception as to the "facts."

Some years of study have taught me that the most productive informant is at the mercy of the interviewer's experience-limitations and personal bias. And that the interviewer's report, once he is more than a tyro, shows nothing in discontinuity of narrative, of the many occasions on which he has turned away from important clues, garbled the temporal sequence of events, and discouraged the flow of information. One of the first things he learns is the achievement of a specious state of complacency. In this he is at one with all untrained observers of events; "just having been there" is supposed to equip one for testimony as to "what happened." The report of an interview is often unsatisfactory not only by reason of imperfect development of the relevant information, but also by reason of unwitting fraud in the shape of finality and completeness. I have known many "explanations" of personality-disaster to collapse into sheer nonsense on discovery that the "explanatory events" followed the disaster, or occurred in a sequence otherwise divorcing them of their supposed relationship to it.

When, now, it is the personal interview of the investigator and the subject-individual that concerns us, then, indeed, it is the recognition of factors in the interpersonal situation that should be the central problem, and not an "objective observation" of phenomena from the standpoint of an illusory scientific detachment. Freud is again to be credited for "discovering" the age-old fact that, given a chance, personalities interact. His creation of the "mechanism of the *transference*"—and the somewhat later noted "*countertransference*"—has not been a wholly unmixed blessing, however. The still widely-held classification of mankind into those who *do* and those who do *not* (*can* not, it is alleged) "make a transference" is more wonderful than helpful in personality study.[1]

In "transference," we have almost everything of the direct interaction of personalities. The phenomena that characterize it are strange only to a people who are singularly incapable of intimacy. Its direct remedial effect—occasionally noticed, as such, usually related to "curative suggestions" and other accidentals, and often denied—arises in its at least brief provision of that interpersonal situation that is the most needed of all by people of the current scene. The terrible isolation of the many is the peculiar characteristic of our people, the nucleus of their mental disorders.

---

[1] In the older psychoanalytic formula, patients were divided into (1) the *transference neuroses*, the victims of which entered more or less readily into the transference-relationship with the analyst, and (2) the *narcissistic neuroses*—among them, conspicuously, schizophrenia—victims of which "could not" so enter, *because of fixation of their libido on the self*. This is of a piece with the "unpsychological character" of schizophrenic thought; *vide supra.*

The processes which go to maintain an *unnecessary* and harmful isolation of personality from personality have already concerned us. The technique of the personal interview is devised to overcome their effects, and to isolate their manifestation. It is based on an assumption that the subject-individual is more or less willing to enter into some degree of intimacy with the interviewer, although the interview method seems often to be used without attention either to the basic assumption or to its most obvious implications. Thus the practice of the law in "establishing" the validity of reports, in securing "evidence," is theoretically opposed to this assumption; and its interview methods are founded on a philosophy that answers to our definition of religion. The still popular dogma that Truth *is* or is *not* an ingredient in or a characterizing attribute of a given personal report must be rooted out of the student of personality.

There is no epistemological problem about total action; it is always valid. Truth and error, precept and illusion, are attributes pertaining to rational processes (those concerning consensual validity) and to self-consciousness, the social reflection of the personality. The self mediates in most attempts at communicating information. Two people talking together *say* verbal combinations more or less entirely self-consciously. The two personalities integrated into the total situation within which this self-to-self conversation is occurring *communicate* more or less, as it were, *under cover* of the verbal interchange. A penumbra of personality-meaning is attached to the culturally standardized words. It is conveyed from one to another in the measure that there is empathic linkage from similarity of personality. Penumbrae of personality-meaning attach to culturally standardized inflections, gestures, postures, and other *expressive dynamisms* used in and along with the conversation. They convey from one to the other in the same measure.

We can "talk about" this intercommunication of personalities, this real intimacy, in many ways. In the end, however, if we have conveyed information to our auditor, some meaning has been conveyed exterior to our capacity for verbal formulation; the event is not capable of complete objectivation, stenographically, phonographically, kinegraphically, or polygraphically. We have improvised in words, syntax, intonations, postures, and unknown ways culture-patterns that have brought correct "response," in the shape of that which was within us, in the "other" personality. A glance of the eyes, at some certain moment, may have completed a task beyond our power of words. Some day, we may know "all about" the intercommunications of personalities, the exchange of information between people. In the yet again abundant meanwhile, to each student of personality, I council as his first and last study the observation of his own participation in each social situation in which he seeks knowledge of another.

Until one has elaborated his self by the inclusion of complex fictions as to the necessity of objective verification of all conclusions, one is a naive student of human nature. When he has been completely successful in divorcing himself from "subjectivity," he has become a priest—of a religion not yet practiced. The measure of success of the student of personality is found in his ability to formulate the subject-personality sympathetically, subjectively. To achieve this formulation he uses a variety of references to material provided by the subject. When he is finished he has a basis for prediction as to the future course of the subject-personality through more or less clearly hypothecated total situations.

Experience has taught me that personality studies should begin with direct contact with the personality to be studied. All that one has available in his personality becomes effective in a deliberate situation of intimacy with another. One's "first impression" is among the most valuable points of departure that can be conceived. Unfortunately, it is the most in need of refinement of any of the technologies at our disposal. Thus we like or dislike at sight, or even at hearing—over the telephone. The wisdom and weakness of this rapid appraisal of others may perhaps be elucidated by personal reference. For years it has been one of my necessities that I should succeed in selecting from dubious personnel those who could be integrated into total situations with schizophrenic patients, with profit to the latter. While my efforts have been attended by a perhaps remarkable measure of success, there was a certain proportion of frank failures. These failures were incidences of psychopathic personality. In other words, my favorable appraisal of personnel as a result of an hour's conversation had always to be taken contingently subject to demonstration of psychopathic personality in actual performances. I have sought for years for a sign among the phenomena of my first impressions that would act as a clue in separating the psychopathic members from among those who received favorable appraisal as potential members in community life with schizophrenics. I have found nothing.

It behooves the executive to "like" and to "dislike" on the basis of potential success. Such a crude use of the universal tendency requires very much finer differentiation for the student of personality. He cannot aspire to that wisdom at which all things mundane are to be taken without personal valuation. Quite the contrary, he must become as deliberately conscious as possible of the valuations swiftly exteriorized by him on each personality that becomes a subject of study. He needs to develop a social psychology of empathy. I surmise that his first impressions are for every student his nearest approach to another personality; that from the occasion of initial contact to the end of however extended a series of contacts, the drives for interpersonal intimacy and other tendency-systems in himself and his subject will be functioning to restrict and distort the picture. The Stranger comes to us uncatalogued. Our systematizing tendency, especially in these days of innumerable superficial contacts, reduces him to a more or less mediocre bundle of characteristics as soon as familiarity is established.

The social psychology of empathy begins in an appraisal of the roles for which "liked" people on the one hand and "disliked" people on the other are intended by one's personality. It is not enough that the student of personality shall convince himself of a desire to understand his subject. He is required to understand the forces at work within him in integrating the interview-situation. I remarked at the start of the chapter that those who could not escape the need for a religious culture might become seekers. In these times of interpersonal superficialities, the adolescent drive toward intimacy is frequently projected into a life-work of personality study. Unfortunately, all the other tendencies to which the investigator is showing imperfect adjustment come to characterize him in his work. Thus I have known students who sought only subject-individuals who "burnt incense to the self-regard of the investigator." And there are others who do good work only in amassing data on how other people have been carried to a conflict well known to the investigator. He does not study those who have not known this conflict; in general, empathy is negative toward those who have solved it.

Once provided with all that can be extracted from initial impression, the investigator proceeds to integrate a situation in which he is to function in facilitating the other person to formulate verbally as much as possible of a life history and picture of the present personality. The great obstacles to success in this field are several. Of these the most vicious is the preconceptions of the other one communicated from the investigator. The curse of valuations, particularly ethical valuations, is never more significant than in this connection. Every personality has a system of these values, and every other individual who falls into intimate relations with him is driven to more or less unwitting acquiescence to this system. Besides the values incorporated in the self, there are the values, often contradictory, of which the investigator-personality is unaware. Thus in the work with schizophrenics, one comes to appreciate that to the extent that an investigator is in the grip of the mores, to that extent he is inadequate for his purpose. The first principle of training such personnel is the inculcation of a relative view of culture. This may be facilitated by reading, for example, cultural anthropology, such as Malinowski's inquiries into Trobriand Island culture. But mere reading is seldom of any effect other than an increase in the language used in rationalizing. The unique rightness of one's ways is thrown into "interesting" relief against the "superstitions" and "curious primitive ideas" of others, in which one develops a polite interest, often labled "tolerance." "It takes all kinds to make a world" now carries a but tacit "but thank God I am not as these others." To the person blighted by a primitive genital phobia, five years of literary research on the phallic cults of man will not weaken his "feeling" that he is studying the "human passions in their most diabolical manifestations." His sleep may deteriorate from the energizing of his own distorted genitality; he may be "carried away" by "new insights" into behavior. But this means more guilt and an increase in penitential doings, not an emancipation. When he is done, his "findings" will but advertise his foreignness and make clear the specious nature of his tolerance.

The gist of the matter is that self-understanding is not primarily an intellectual achievement. It should ensue in rational formulation. But it is a work primarily of intuition, of grasping the "whole" of a configuration. And, regardless of prejudice against psychoanalysis, the free-associational technique invented by Freud is the only tool that we have for that comprehensive exploration of personality by which unguided intuition can be converted into rational insight. This neither minimizes nor accentuates the fact that both novices and also many self-satisfied analysts have a great deal to learn about personality study. It implies that the method of statement, unsupported by the method of free fantasy, *cannot* provide rational insight—however much the insight of the questioner may assist the intuition of the subject-individual. And that the rational insights of the interviewer *cannot* expend the totality of human personality, be he the most "analyzed" person extant. There is always interaction between interviewer and interviewed, between analyst and analysand, and from it, both *must* invariably *learn* if sound knowledge of the subject-personality is to result. In brief, personality study must be a seeking, never a religious service. With this clearly before the student, I shall offer some views on the schematization of personality study, as a point of departure for the inventive genius of each student. I never hope to conduct such an inquiry to my complete satisfaction: Let the student forever beware of excelling the teacher in self-satisfaction; even as he is now to beware of accepting the following as even an outline of personality study.

There is a great deal in favor of making verbatim records of the initial statement of "the situation" as presented by the subject-individual. Everything that can be recorded of his initial communication about "the trouble" or "the facts" is apt to prove most highly significant. Most of it will require many hours for elucidation. Some of the clues given in the first interview are usually a long time in recurring. The subject-individual—to whom, from henceforth, I shall refer as the *patient*—is "set" to some broadly conceived purpose, on this first occasion. He has not developed a body of subordinate processes involving the investigator, as experienced. His presentation is therefore more general than will be any subsequent discussion. This is peculiarly the case when the patient has sought the interview. It is true, however, of any initial contacts between personalities. The comprehensive recording of these phenomena is but an objectivation of some of the materials entering into one's "first impression" of another. The skill of the investigator must grow toward a noninterfering facilitation of the initial communication. The first great step toward success has been taken if the patient has been *permitted* to say and otherwise express whatever he wanted the investigator to know. Even if the "set" has been one for the creation of deliberate fraud, the story that is actually presented is well worth minute attention.

There is a great advantage for personality students in the possession of fundamental medical training.[2] To inquire into the life-situation of a person without being able to obtain firsthand information as to the sort of somatic apparatus he has to utilize in living, and without being able to appraise relative physiological handicaps and facilitations, is to work under considerable, and sometimes very great, limitations. Moreover, not to investigate personally the physical conditions of the patient is to forego the aid of some factors potent in the building of a sound situation of benevolent intimacy. One should certainly make a *physical inventory* of the patient, not alone to discover the disease-history, the state of physical health, and the constitutional features of the patient, but also to elicit synchronously, by use of a technique modified from that of the Institute for Child Guidance,[3] the important ideology in regard of the body, which is otherwise difficult to obtain. Clues may be obtained from tensions, gestures, and comments of the patient undergoing such an inspection that lead easily to highly significant material, the existence of which may otherwise remain long unsuspected.[4] The act of exposing the

[2] See, in this connection, the latter part of the *Proceedings of the Second Colloquium on Personality Investigation,* previously cited. It may well be that the present standardized medical curricula can be modified for the benefit of those who need medical fundamentals as a part of their training for social engineering or for psychopathology. My present opinion is one favoring a prolonged training culminating in the degree of Doctor of Mental Medicine, or perhaps Doctor of Science, to avoid the medical practice implications.

[3] Discussed by David M. Levy in "A Method of Integrating Physical and Psychiatric Examination," *Amer. J. Psychiatry* (1929) 86:121–195.

[4] The role of physical illnesses in the handicapping of life is important—it is often neglected *in toto. Per contra,* the role of personality factors in organizing the symptoms of physical disorder—so common, for example, in

body to the scrutiny of the physician is in more ways than one an auspicious beginning in the revelation of one's personality. And, *also*, it is an occasion charged with great possibilities of good or evil effect on future progress. A great deal of personality-interchange always characterizes a physical examination, and this should be utilized to the full by the investigator. He should be extremely observant of the patient, of himself, and of the inevitable interplay.

One next considers the patient as an apparatus for functional activity in communal existence in the physicochemical world, inquiring into the zones of interaction, the sensory apparatus and projection fields, the neuromuscular characteristics—coördinations, finer adjustments, strength, endurance, and so on—and the more complex integrative processes more or less measurable by performance and other "mental" tests. One thus concerns himself with the equipment of social tools, proceeding—with educational and occupational history-taking—to elucidate the language-development, and other assets and liabilities in intercommunicative expression and utilization of culture-patterns.

The exteriorization of the self is the next concern. One seeks a comprehensive inventory of the person as objectively manifesting functional activity in communal existence with other people. What does he do as work, play, and in important interim situations? Data on both occupational and recreational opportunities, preferences, successes, and failures are adumbrated. One progresses easily into the accumulation of historic data on parents, significant relatives, teachers, personal family—wife and children, and so on—friends, employers, subordinates, colleagues or associates, and broader issues of the economic, political, racial, and religious type. The use of the life-chart is a considerable aid in final synthesis of much of this and later material.[5] I may choose this point to stress the value of an *accurate chronology* in assem-

incipient schizophrenia; this, besides the traditionally "physical" signs and symptoms of hysteria—is almost as frequently neglected by the medical practitioners of today.

[5] See Adolf Meyer, "The Life Chart and the Obligation of Specific Positive Data in Psychopathological Diagnosis" in *Contributions to Medical and Biological Research, Dedicated to Sir William Osler, in Honour of His Seventieth Birthday, July 12, 1919, by his Pupils and Coworkers;* New York: Hoeber, 1919.

bling any factual data pertaining to a personality. Everything of importance should "date." Important effects of the maladjustive process of retrograde falsification are frequently uncovered by attention to this detail. Gross errors of interpretation are prevented. And a sound philosophy of life is encouraged by the implied dependence on actual emergence of tendencies from coherent innate and experiential sequences.

We come now to the more direct investigation, the formulation of the self or *ego*, of the ideal systems or *superego*, and of the repressed and the totally refracted tendency systems, the *id*.[6] The total situation integrated by the patient and the investigator should now develop toward a more frankly expressed purpose of *discovery*. The first division of the work is a reconnaissance of the self, and exhaustion of the ego. This should be directed to three formulations: the person as *he wishes and has wished to be; as he has suspected and now suspects that he actually is;* and as *his "enemies" have seen and now see him.* These three aspects are fairly comprehensive of the experience incorporated in the self. In eliciting the easily accessible data along the three paths, one encounters innumerable leads toward the foreconscious fringes of awareness, and many clues to processes of which the patient is but vaguely aware. There is, in particular, a running account of new personal contacts, from rudimentary to very close interpersonal relationships. Note should be taken of each new figure in the patient's life, to whom directly or indirectly the patient seems to award significance. These other people should be thrown into correct chronology on the life chart. Aside from "dating" people and events, active interference by the investigator should be kept at a minimum throughout this stage of the work. His business is to note closely the phenomena that are occuring, both the information being produced and omitted, and the manifestations of tendencies operating in the interview-situations. When the data readily available for report are running low, there is a stage reached at which it is well to begin systematic questioning. By sustained inquiry, the characterizations of all the persons of high significance in childhood and the juvenile era should be extracted from the memorial elements available for recall. In the case of each such person, and particularly in that of the parents, any data

[6] The italicized terms are those current in the psychoanalytic literature.

on the people in turn effective in the shaping of *their* personalities
are valuable. The latter are chiefly to be obtained as collateral
information from other sources.

Data from informants varies greatly in value. It is never to be
taken as of the same order of relevance as the patient's reported
experience. But it can fill gaps, especially of the earlier years, and
it can confirm and correct the patient's personal account of
events. One wishes to have collateral information on the people
who have been significant at each genetic stage of the patient.
One strives to concentrate the recollections of each informant by
following particular periods of growth, and attempting to orient
him toward recitals *as if* from the patient's viewpoint at that time.
Needless to say, data on the infantile and childhood eras are
"objective." But in the later eras, friends, siblings, and parents
can report "what he said and did," as well as give their surmises
as to what was going on.

Parents should be treated much after the fashion of patients.
One of them may be quite as "sick" as is the patient, and both of
them are so deeply involved with him in the presenting of difficulties that a detached technique of interview is inappropriate.
Each parent should be permitted to "tell the story" very much as
he will. Only after the required amount of sympathetic listening,
with keen attention not only to information and misinformation,
but also to the processes appearing in the interview-situation,
should the investigator resort to systematic questioning on the
step-by-step plan. Parents should generally be interviewed sepa-
rately—one needs all one can get of the personality of each. It
may be well to check over some dubious points afterwards, with
them together. Their interaction is then quite illuminating, and no
longer endangers a full report.

This is perhaps the place at which to introduce a warning about
the investigator's attitude toward accounts that are but strangely
related to facts, about fraud and deception on the part of informants. The parents are two of the people ultrasignificant in the
personality-growth of the patient. Their demonstrations of complex motivation in dealing with facts in the interview show important phases of their personalities. If one or both of them shows
to the investigator an appraisal of his intelligence that might
offend an anthropoid, this is but a part of a customary inter-

personal activity in regard of "their child." It has an explanation just as human and understandable as are its consequences on the patient. Instead of sustaining his self-esteem by dubious "victory" over the informant, the interviewer should be alert to develop the underlying self-appraisals and motivations manifesting in the distorted reports. A psychopathologist who requires that he be "taken seriously" by everybody with whom he enters into relations is no psychopathologist at all.

One reads in many records of interviews that the subject-individual "admits" this or that. This is all wrong. The method of cross-examination is frequently necessary, but it should never be used, in the fashion of our legal brethren, to secure admissions and to impeach veracity. The good interviewer is mildly astonished when his informant shows strong feeling of negative valuation over a fact. He exteriorizes his principles that facts exist, that they are very useful in understanding the patient, and that they have no more of good-or-bad connotation than have a mechanic's tools. He is free of prejudice, but he is not exhorting others to that freedom; he wants the facts of prejudices that have been of importance, and he discourages by his realistic attitude the interposition of prejudice in the way of his getting the facts.

The general scheme of the collateral interview should sketch the patient as a personality at the beginning of the informant's acquaintance with him, develop significant facts throughout the period—thus keeping in mind the evolutionary course to which the earlier chapters have been devoted, elucidate the actual tendencies integrating the historic interpersonal relations of patient and informant from beginning to end, and, finally, attempt a sketch of the patient's personality as it has grown during the period covered. So far as may be, the data should be "dated," once they are recovered, and people "named." I have found it a good plan to request of every informant a supplementary report, by letter, of anything relevant that may occur to him subsequent to the interview; what few such supplements one receives are apt to be worth having.

With the readily accessible material of the patient's *self* exhausted, with most of the collateral information available, and with a synoptic view of the two bodies of data, one is ready to proceed with the more technical processes of exploration. If the preliminary work has been done in a competent fashion, there is already an extraordinary, often wholly unprecedented, *trust* in the investigator's benevolent purposes, wise tolerance, and broad knowledge of people. A perhaps wholly unaccustomed *security* in intimacy has been experienced. Apropos of some not too significant a set of facts, the investigator—to whom we shall from henceforth refer as the physican—has recourse to that communicational freedom called the *analytic situation*. He points out the incomplete character of the report, and explains the utility of free fantasy in establishing connections with lost memories or faded associations. He emphasizes the vagueness that may characterize the initial fantasies, and begins to strengthen the "set" for actual freedom of communication. The patient is instructed to express in words, sounds, gestures, grimaces, smiles, tears, intonations—in short, *in any suitable way*—as much as possible of whatever comes to mind, in the periods of repose into which he is to relapse as often as possible during the interview. In order to relax the interference of his accustomed waking "sets," he is to abandon any purpose other than that of expressing his "thoughts." He may depend on the physician's attendance on the flow of material, which will be apparently incoherent, often irrelevant, sometimes fraudulent, and at first seemingly immaterial to a degree. The design or pattern of meaning, and the life-processes concerned in the fragments of recollection, will presently appear to the patient. The physician may be able to assist somewhat by an occasional summary of what seems to have been in progress. But, in general, only the patient has the facts, and the physician's skill is useful only in so far as he may recognize *incompleteness of recall*, obscure manifestations of processes that are hindering recall, and the like.

This instruction is best given piecemeal. The patient is instructed to relax vigilant effort at recollection to fill some gap in his memory, and to assume instead an attitude of undirected attention to his mental processes. Useful recall is the rule if too significant a group of facts is not at stake. This experience encourages the patient, to whom, otherwise, the dynamics of free fantasy might seem absurd, esoteric, or actually mysteriously dangerous. Ultimately, however, the unhindered exteriorization of free flowing fantasy is to be required.

At the first occasion either of a dream-fragment occurring in the stream of communication, or of the appearance of a "dream-like thought," *once the self is exhausted* and the analytic situation is adopted, reference is made by the physician to the utility of the dream as an aid in reaching those aspects of one's life-situation which one habitually excludes from the workaday world. I make it a rule to defer all "dream analysis" until a time when free fantasy is suspended by phenomena of resistance. But the *first* dream that occurs after attention has been called to their utility should be recorded with great care. The patient, at the time that dreams are discussed, may well be instructed to develop a habit of recording dreams *immediately upon awakening*, each and every morning. They are to be recorded both in the order of recollection, and with a final note as to their probable order of occurrence, dated, and submitted to the physician at the beginning of each interview. Whether all or none of the dreams serve an obvious purpose during an interview is insignificant; the purpose of the interview is not the demonstration of skills—dream interpretations, or whatever—but the growth of awareness of the patient as to his personality. The primal function of a person *to live as completely as possible* is the source of dependence for results of the interviews. The very act of systematically recording the dream experience may be all that this phase of the patient's life will require for weeks on end. If there is an important situation manifesting in the dream, the stream of fantasy will bring it up. The physician then has the notes against which to check the fantasy-productions—for his own information. Unless the development of the analytic situation is obstructed, he has no cause for active intervention.[7]

From time to time, the interpersonal intimacy of patient and physician is altered. The tendencies integrating the situation vary with personality factors active in either one or both. Because of

[7] Initial dreams, those occurring as the first dream or series of dreams, *after the patient has learned from the physician that the dreams may prove useful,* are rather on a par with the first verbal communication. Dreams that have occurred *before* treatment is undertaken may be important; one asks when discussing sleep and sleep disturbances for any recurrent or vivid dreams that may be recalled. One should, however, use some discretion as to an early reference to the importance of dreams; some patients, urged to record dreams before they are convinced that the physician is "the one for them," may give him little else than dreams.

its purpose to free the patient from handicaps, if for no other reason, the drive to exteriorization deals chiefly with memorial elements charged with considerable emotion. Innumerable frustrations, disappointments, injustices, impositions, mistakes, misunderstandings, misjudgments, reprisals, sadistic aggressions, slights, and slurs—all manner of truncated situations once disintegrated through the instrumentality of emotion and maladjustive processes—are reintegrated in a sort of *as if* drama during the free-fantasy exploration. It is necessary, for free communication of these memorial elements, that *any necessity for rational thinking be avoided*. In other words, the patient must not have to *report* the occurrences to the physician, but instead he must *merely express* the momentary content, without subjective appraisal of its effect on himself, on the other one receiving the communication, or on their interrelationship.

The patient must come to *realize* the role of the physician as an object for the momentary application of any and all interpersonal tendencies that appear in the course of the free fantasy. The physician must facilitate this transient objectivation of tendencies in his person. In this, he encounters the problems called by psychoanalysts the management of the transference. Ideally he should flow easily from object-form to object-form, as dictated by the uncovered tendencies of the patient. The real physician, however, restricts this ideal freedom in at least two ways.

Firstly, he is the actual object of a sentiment formed after the pattern of older sentiment-elaborations from the patient's previous *experience* in relationship with him—from *expectations* based on his reputation, from reading, from fantasy about consulting him, and from the *first impression*. This sentiment acts as more or less of an obstacle to the free objectivation on him of tendencies connected with memories recalled in the fantasy. On the other hand, it is very necessary, for it must bear the brunt of powerful antipathetic tendencies, if the intimacy needed for continued progress in the analysis is to be continued. Otherwise the work is interrupted. Obviously, the contributions that the physician has himself made to this configuration during the preanalytic interviews are the determiners of possible success or certain failure in his work with each patient.

The sentiment of the physician will usually follow one of two patterns. In either one, he is in danger of an exalted idealization amounting practically to a priesthood, if not to the role of a demigod, in the patient's intended current life. Either he comes more or less to be a God-the-father or a God-the-primordial-mother. In my work, it has seemed that the latter is the more promising.[8] But in any case, the degree of *idealization* should be held down, lest it interfere seriously with the freedom of fantasy. The effective restriction of idealization is dependent on the physician's own freedom from personality warp. In so far as he is capable of real intimacy in the situation with the patient, to that extent he can inhibit idealization of the sentiment; the measure of this capacity and its characteristic limitations are readily intuited or empathized by every patient.

The physician must be eternally alert to phenomena within himself arising from the specific differential tendency-system operative in the case of each individual with whom he deals. I do not wish to discuss the occasional unwitting selection of the physician on the basis of a factor actually incapacitating him for productive work with the patient. I have known a paranoid individual to go from one to another psychiatrist until he discovered one that would actually fear him, thereon all but forcing the undertaking of his "treatment." And there are morbidly masochistic patients who will seek until they find a physician so savage that

[8] My conclusions are based on work with male patients suffering schizophrenic and related disorders. I have little or no factual material from which to generalize a rule of preferred "transference type," whether, to use a psychoanalytic expression, there are cases when one should "work with the father-libido instead of the mother-libido."

I surmise that an *All-father belief*, found among some of the most primitive of people, is a commonplace of personality evolution. I believe that this comes about something as follows: *A manlike being is made to serve as the idealized object of the disappointed primitive mother sentiment*, sadly unsatisfied by the mothering ones encountered after the birth of personal consciousness. Each child learns that the male is more capable of carrying a generalization of positive attributes than is the female (*pace*, feminists, I probably refer only to "savages"), and the Good Goddess progresses into masculine habiliments as the All-father who *demands nothing*, but is prior to all lesser gods, in their turn invested with more or less highly anthropomorphic demands, authorities, spleens, venoms, and so forth. The physician who approximates this nondemanding and all-satisfying primitive All-father, otherwise the primitive mother-of-infancy, "works with the mother-libido."

they can enjoy the time misspent with him. These are situations in which the physician is suffering a scotoma, a "mental blind spot" in his personal insight, and is himself in need of personality reorganization. The more general factor to which I am inviting attention manifests as an idealization of some particular patient or patients by the physician. In this process we find again the deflection of a tendency-system from a real object into the energizing of fantasy. The physician, from empathic linkage with the patient, integrates the latter into a situation the resolution of which is impossible because of his technical or other taboos. The frustrated tendency then evolves in a fantastic sentimentalization of the patient, with nonadjustive anxiety "lest he mismanage the case"—often an anticipatory guilt of taboo-violation from breaking of the barriers. Not only is the physician seriously handicapped by this overanxiety in handling the particular patient, but his supply of interest for working with others is depleted—which they are quick to "feel," with disorder of the necessary intimacy-situation.

The second factor restrictive of an ideal use of the physician as a carrier of the patient's tendency-objectivations is the occasional positive action which the former is called upon to take. The physician must now and then intervene in the analytic situation to redirect the flow of fantasy. The old conflicts of tendencies make appearance and the two systems concerned have to be separated into two streams of fantasy. The old rationalizations may continue in higher level fantasy processes that accomplish little toward elucidating the tendency that is being avoided. The old projections of blame and of positive attributes may be hard to disintegrate. And the active repressing of tendencies has to be remedied by picking out of the stream for further development certain vague fancies and "half-remembered dreams" that are the first evidences of escape from complete repression. Dissociated systems must be brought to effective awareness, instead of permitted to drain off in symptomatic acts and in streams of fantasy that are not brought into meaningful relationship with obviously related materials. All in all, the physician, while he interferes as little as possible, plays altogether too directing a role to permit his complete subordination to emotional objectivation. His appreciation of this, coupled with his understanding of the sentiment of which he is the object, gives him the tool needed when an actual antipathetic impasse occurs.

When, perhaps in reactivating a long-dissociated hatred of the father, the patient is so dominated by his hatred, and by the rage born of his unresolved guilt about the hatred, that he devotes himself to a fury "at" the physician, the treatment, and anything else that comes handy, then the physician must intervene in representing the reality of the situation—sometimes also with an indication of means for "working off" some of the excessive emotion. If he does not do his duty in this connection, but instead, for this or that reason, permits the patient to blunder away, blinded by great emotion, he is gravely remiss. Whenever the patient is in the grip of intensely sympathetic or violently antipathetic emotion, he is in no condition to deal unassisted with his fellow man. Quitting the treatment is perhaps but a minor one of the unfortunate performances of a patient unassisted in a period of rage.

Despite these two factors, the principal role of the physician using the free-fantasy technique is that of a keenly observant individual on whom—or in whom—the reactivated tendencies of the patient find temporary object. The procedure of *dream interpretation*, to which one has recourse when necessary, is but a modification of the general role of passivity, and is a handicap rather than a help as soon as it becomes an *active* performance. In brief, one invites the patient to develop a stream of fantasy in elaboration of, or from a beginning in, some dream-recollection. One need not assume that the fantasy will give the latent meaning of the dream-fragment. It often happens that streams of fantasy occurring in response to well-chosen aspects of a given dream will synthesize in the patient's awareness, as the "meaning" of the dream. And it may be that, on the first few occasions of work with dream-fragments, the physician sees a clear pattern in the fantasy-streams, and that he is certain enough of the relevance of the pattern to the patient's temporary difficulties to present a *tentative* formulation. But I would deem it much the better practice always to regard the dream as a meaningful action, and to expect that from fantasy about this action other (and probably closely related) meaningful actions will arise within awareness, rather than to regard the dream as an action capable of exact interpretation. The popular notion that dreams can be "interpreted" without the coöperation of free fantasy of the dreamer is absurd and unfortunate. Such "interpreting" is dangerous—even in the case of the very occasional dream "too obvious to be misunderstood." It is from some such "obvious" dreams that most extraordinary discoveries may be made by careful investigation in free fantasy.[9] The great certainty about dreams is this: Subject to the disintegrative effects of secondary elaboration, the dream is a valid process in furtherance of the general tendencies of the dreamer. One wishes, therefore, that the patient shall note and record all his dreams immediately on awakening. And that, once noted, recorded, ordered, and dated, the dream material receive no further attention until the record is in the physician's hands, and the analytic hour is under way. At best the dream is an extraordinary procedure toward adjustment. Its utilization in personality investigation should be kept thoroughly subordinate to the much more commonplace method of waking fantasy.[10]

As the free fantasy develops, it tends to establish a series of hypotheses. The patient—particularly nowadays, when a "popular" compendium of everything is to be had at the neighborhood drugstore—may have come equipped with more or less fantastic notions of Oedipus complexes, repressions, mother fixations, and a host of very New-Psychological entities. Unless the intimacy-situation has been correctly integrated, he is often moved to interrupt the productive work, to exhibit his knowledge to the physician, or to "best" him at the game of interpretation. "Tell me, Doctor!" recurs as to whether this and that is the "meaning" of particular fragments. Or the patient arrives with a dream-record, prepared to spend the whole hour in discussing this dream, or all dreaming—always at an academic level. And the patient who has come to the physician already experienced in psychoanalysis, at such times must present Dr. Blank's "interpretations," "terrible mistakes," and the like. All this is evidence of an imperfect analytic situation, often the fault of the physician.

There is bound to be a growth of awareness of personal ten-

[9] I have no particular fancy for the notion of "usual meaning" of some frequently-occurring dream figures, such as the snake, the steeple, the old man, and so on. This cataloging of dream-symbolism is another sort of behaviorism; it omits the factor that *gives* meaning, and becomes an "objective" dealing with fragmentary appearance of life.

[10] Especially in working with schizophrenic disorders, the complex relation of the dream needs accentuation. Otherwise, the physician is apt to find that his patient confuses dream with waking perceptions.

dencies; but, from beginning to end, the growth is automatic, after the fashion of all experiencing, and the *patient must naturally do the profiting* from what he produces. Uncertainty precedes certainty both of correctness and of error, and free-fantasy material cannot safely be exempted from the generality that one learns for himself. The physician, when he asks if there has not been an elision in a certain stream of fantasy, must know that neither he nor the patient can "know." The patient must understand that such inquiries are not evidences of the physician's esoteric knowledge, but are products of genuine uncertainty, to be discharged not by answering, but by coöperative investigation —by a continuation of fantasy from the indicated point of departure.

Positive and negative certainties are really foreign to free-fantasy context, for a definite "Yes" at one time is quite as apt to be an equally positive "No" in a succeeding hour, when a differently motivated stream touches on the same event. The plural relevance of recollections of earlier experience is a natural consequence of the ever-increasing differentiation of tendencies. The free-fantasy exploration is not comparable to a hunting for fossil trilobites. It is a wholly dynamic reorganization of processes with but an incidental increase in lucidity of the formulation of the self. The *personality* changes. Not only does it seem entirely possible for most of this change to occur without any immediate awareness of change but, if I mistake not, this is precisely the most fortunate course. The rational formulation of insight *follows* the progress in reorganization and should not be made a goal of the free fantasy itself.[11] The facts of personality have to crystallize out of the substance of fantasy, in which they are but phantasmagorically manifested.

To the student of personality, there may well come the question of how he is to separate a *therapeutic* from a "purely research" interest in the subject-individual. The problem is a pseudological abstraction. It is impossible to do good work toward

[11] Some patients, encouraged to "see" the relations of fantasy material to this or that alleged "mechanism"—and thereby discouraged from potential discoveries of the pluridetermination in the recollected experience—come from "treatment" with a really astonishing obsessional state; the whole gamut of interpersonal relations is displaced by a substitute activity of "psychoanalytic interpreting."

understanding a particular personality without being of benefit *to* that personality. For the student can be certain only of that which is demonstrated as correct by the patient, and any increase in knowledge of one's self is profitable. *Passim,* it is quite possible to do bad work with harm to the patient; but it is difficult to learn much about personality by this route. The investigator as distinguished from the therapist may wish to carry his inquiry "further," to avoid the vitiating effects of intimacy with the subject-individual, or to have recourse only to objectively verifiable procedures. The carrying of inquiry further than the patient will carry it is impossible. The undue weighting of certain material—dream-fragments, for example—disorders the flow of fantasy material and creates a pseudo-importance for processes relatively insignificant. The outcome is not more information but more misinformation.

The specious ideal of nonpersonal intimacy or, rather, of personal nonintimacy in personality investigation is sometimes achieved in the "use" of free fantasy by an obsessional individual possessed of a reasonably high intelligence factor. Such a patient assists at every point in the avoiding of emotional complications. In fact, the freedom of the resulting fantasy is just this freedom from emotional validity needed for real intercommunication. This sort of intellectualized "inquiry" may be very productive— of words, figures of speech, imagery; also of ennui. It has but a complex relation to an interchange of information about the personality and its tendency-systems. In fact, it is somewhat less useful in this connection than is ordinary conversation. It is motivated, usually, by a deeply unconscious hatred-system; it generally functions toward a stultification of the physician-investigator. As to the ideal of an objectively verifiable technique, I can but say that it awaits our exploration of personality. When we have discovered *what* is to be observed and measured, then we may look to making measurements.[12]

There comes finally, in each successful investigation of a personality, a third phase of the work. As I recommended that the

[12] From time to time we experience a new burst of "objectivity" in psychopathology. I hope that this book may lead to some abortions of these efforts, thereby saving the objectivists from the pains of their accouchement. I speak for an extremely interpersonal subjectivity on problems individual, social, and cultural, as the necessary preliminary to sound generalization.

use of free fantasy should be introduced gradually toward the end of the preanalytic inquiry, so I now suggest that the *re-valuational* procedures be encouraged gradually toward the end of productive free fantasy. The question immediately arises as to whether there is such an end.[13] There is a time when free fantasy is productive of highly emotional material clearly relevant to the developmental history of the personality, and there comes a time when such material has "run out," and the free fantasy—now that of a much more unified personality—is concerned with relating recent and current events with newly discovered tendencies.[14] The individual is now concentrated on learning what Frank [15] has called the *management of tensions*, and the integration of situations that accomplish what Hart [16] indicates as the *fulfillment of personality*. In short, we have come to a rapid growth to adulthood in a personality that has been out of tune in various ways for matters of whole evolutionary growth-periods.

Before discussing the adult personality, to the achievement of which therapy at least must apply itself, I wish to traverse the field of the interrupted or incomplete investigation of personality. I have said that no increase in knowledge of the self is harmful. Against this flat statement is the adage to the effect that a little knowledge is a dangerous thing. The current scene gives some color to both views. There is an increase in really human appreciation of man's problems on the part of those to whom preoccupation with general betterment is satisfying. And there is an increase in the conservative and the radical elements of society encouraged by surmise as to the relative nature of ancient values. On the one hand, we find an increasingly numerous body of

---

[13] The physician is frequently called on for a prognostic determination of the "length of the treatment required." The factors which enter into this judgment are literally too numerous to mention, and the theorem of probabilities applies.

[14] One is not to mistake a "cover" or a substitute activity (often shown by obsessional patients) for the evading of repressed or dissociated tendencies as this approach to the end of useful fantasy. The continued pressure of symptoms and symptomatic acts serves readily to distinguish the two.

[15] L. K. Frank, "The Management of Tensions," *Amer. J. Sociology* (1928) 33:705–736.

[16] Hornell Hart, "Family Life and the Fulfillment of Personality," *Amer. J. Psychiatry* (1930) 87:7–17.

workers striving for insights into personal, social, and cultural realities, despite personal limitations by unwitting prejudices and ideals. On the other, we see the timorous souls, cognizant of the new instability, turning to the bulwarking of the old, while the embittered juveniles, encouraged by the defensive attitudes of the Philistines, are having a "grand time" tearing up the surface of things. The creative workers are a promise of what may come. The Philistine and the Bohemian exaggerations, one trusts, are but ephemerae.

The effects on a personality of an incomplete exploration are varied after the manner of the tendencies effective in interpersonal relations. There is the case of the person brought more or less competently to the end of the analytic stage, without attention to the synthesis of adult relationships. He is a fairly numerous species among those who have been "psychoanalyzed." Either he has been weened from a personal dependence on the physician—in which case, in a year or two, he may have effected remarkable growth toward a satisfactory life among people—or he leaves the physician a more or less rabid disciple of the New Knowledge, proselyting where he can, and developing defensive caste-feeling that interferes seriously with his search for intimacy. He may become an analyst, raising in turn his own brood of disciples. The worst that can be said of aggravated examples in this latter class is that in them there has been substituted a paranoid attitude in interpersonal relations for a pre-existing, even less fortunate one.

Somewhat after this kind is the person whose growth toward insight is interrupted in a period of strong antipathetic tendency. He goes forth girt for destroying the enemy, whether he is content with defaming his former physician, with impugning the whole class of personality investigators, or only with criticism of all those dealing with human nature, or whether also he must look for a positive outlet in strengthening some bulwark of popular ignorance; these subsequent developments will reflect the state of his personality at the time of the interruption. If the break comes early, his hatred may show in an aggravated morbidity; he is merely "made much worse" by the physician. If the break comes toward the end of his work with free fantasy—as is sometimes ordained by circumstances exterior to the physician's control—then the patient, after the stormy year or two, may settle down to surpass the technique and skill of the physician—and is apt to progress into genuine creative work of no little merit. These instances must serve to indicate the multiplicity of mixed good and bad results that attend the incomplete personality-inventory.

I shall conclude my sketchy presentation of personality study with a comment on the *exploration of a limited aspect* of the personality. By this, I refer not to the study of part-aspects of personality, such as the study of attitudes, of political behavior, and the like, but to inquiry focused on a more or less clearly delineated tendency-system within a particular person. This can but be a special case of the incomplete personality-study. It is distinguished by the deliberate as contrasted with an unintended incompleteness. From the first hours with the physician—well before the second stage of free-fantasy exploration—the interview situation has been integrated with the limited rather than the general goal. The problems peculiar to it are numerous; the outcome is oftentimes disappointing. As a research procedure, it is to be discouraged—for its result in knowledge of anything is too incomplete for safe generalization. As a palliative measure for difficulties in living, it may often be tolerated, and sometimes recommended. Thus, one frequently encounters personalities showing, in addition to profound warp, the continuing evil consequences from more recent misfortunes; the latter may sometimes be removed or attentuated without recourse to the prolonged series of interviews required for full reorganization of the personality. There are perhaps three modes of this abbreviated inquiry.

Intelligent folk encompassed with the modern strenuosity—lacking the opportunity for intimacy with their self and its ideals, the reflection and mediation required for formulating one's life situation—are frequently greatly benefited by a brief series of interviews with the physician trained in integrating situations of intimacy. Often the patient finds his 'avower' without any help other than the intuited sympathy. In other cases the physician aids a little by exhortation as to the worthiness of the patient's objectives. This is safe only in so far as it expresses in a formula the physician's sound appraisal of the patient. Suggestion, the use of formulae to be accepted *uncritically* by the patient owing to unrecognized factors in the intimacy-situation, is a dangerous practice. If the suggestion is accepted, it merely adds to the already too-complex life-situations. If it is rejected, it carries a negative appraisal of the help that one can derive from those presumed to be useful in personal difficulties.

There is a special case of major suggestion to which I must give a word. This procedure makes use of a subvariety of the sleep-situation, the state of *hypnosis*, characterized variously but chiefly by the passive acceptance of complete subordination to another personality. The patient permits the integration of his personality into the total situation nucleating in the physician. An approach to the infantile relationship to the mother is re-established. It is a situation of great dependency, one far removed from that to which I refer as the intimacy-situation.[17] It may be used in various ways in many people. I would counsel the utmost caution, even in its use for the "quick" recall of an isolated memory. The complaisance of the hypnotized patient is proverbial. But the post-hypnotic integration of the material "so easily" recalled during the trance may be quite another matter. And the utilization of hypnosis for the correction of juvenile and adolescent deviations may finally be proved to require a very complex technique, if indeed it does not prove to be wholly impossible.

Another form of limited exploration proceeds through the first stage of interview into the second, using free fantasy to explore the most characteristically maladjustive processes—for example, to discover important tendencies frequently active in conflict. The third stage of interview, the working out of these tendencies in comfortable forms of activity, then proceeds. As might be expected, this is a ticklish business, especially when it is concerned chiefly with reducing a "censorial conscience." The patient may have powerful tendency-systems existing wholly extraconsciously —such as the primitive genital phobia—in which case work started as a brief inquiry has to be reoriented to a prolonged study, or the end state of the patient is but little better than the first.

[17] The following is quoted from a recent expression of my views on the subject: "Hypnosis is a procedure by which the dissociated systems within a personality are given a degree of freedom from resistance by the self (the dissociating system) [as is the case in sleep]. . . . Hypnosis implies a marked rapport . . . an interpersonal relation of great intensity . . . [involving] aspects of the hypnotist's personality of which . . . he is apt to be completely unaware. . . . If the personality of the hypnotist renders him particularly satisfactory for action in satisfaction of the dissociated systems, then the outcome . . . is apt to be conflict. . . ."

The third form of limited inquiry is one which I have undertaken in the case of some promising patients already suffering incipient schizophrenia or related disorders. The integration of the intimacy situation between patient and physician often cannot proceed in these cases without *mediation*, because of their strong homosexual cravings which may become intolerable, leading to panic, occasionally ending in suicide. The principle is to give them protection by way of the three-group, instead of working with the patient alone. The physician distributes his functions between himself and a clinical assistant, striving thereby to effect a distribution of emotional objectivation such that he can always have a positive balance at his disposal to carry the patient forward. The end achieved is a partial socialization of the subject-personality so that he can live for a while comfortably in a suitable special group. Thereafter, a more thorough investigation may be undertaken.[18]

The study of personality, then, depends on the elevation into awareness of the tendency-systems characterizing the subject-individual. It includes many glimpses of personality-disorder, psychopathology, and from these glimpses we have elaborated the disorder-types mentioned in the preceding chapter. Subject to a considerable margin of error, we become expert at guessing from certain behavior and a little historical data the probable deviations entering into a given morbid personality. The student never knows whether he was mostly right or mostly wrong in these diagnoses of personality disorder until he has actually studied the personality—to the point that the disorders themselves have dis-

[18] A considerable measure of success has been achieved by this technique. It might seem a much simpler procedure to avoid the possibility of panic from homosexual cravings by a *heteropersonal therapy-situation*. This consideration overlooks the basis for intimacy-situations, the tendencies for their integration. The male schizophrenic "gets on with" the woman physician without anything of the tension characteristic of the monosexual group—until he is entirely divorced from reality, comfortably dilapidated or has deluded himself into believing her a man in disguise, then giving way to excitement, perhaps with frank incest fear. So also with the female schizophrenic and the male physician. The outcome of heterosexual therapy of actually schizophrenic adolescents is entirely discouraging. On the other hand, I sometimes send male patients after *stabilization by the mediate technique* to women physicians, with successful outcome. Others do better with men. The poststabilization therapy has to be governed by factors in the personalities concerned.

appeared. From increasing experience, his intuitions of diagnosis become refined. He can reduce the "personal equation" in his interpersonal reaction to an objectively very significant extent. That he can become an instrument of precision has not yet been demonstrated. It does not seem to me to be quite beyond the bounds of possibility, but any great improvement in personality study seems scarcely to be expected until we have made much more extended exploration of the field along the lines thus far indicated. When properly trained students—now very few—have been integrated in a broadly conceived investigation of various personalities existing in some few disparate social situations and culture-complexes, we will be actually on the way.

The Working of
Welfare

AMERICA for long has been characterized by a truly unique interest in individual welfare. The doing of philanthropic acts is our noblest tradition, and one whose hold shows no signs of relaxing. The insuring of personal opportunity has made great progress among us, and those who have profited extravagantly have shown rather uniformly an appreciation of their responsibility, and have given generously to advance the common weal. The new world-power of great wealth has, among us, a rather distinguished record as a new force for good, all the more admirable because it has been achieved somewhat timorously in a world rather obviously greedy, envious, and suspicious. The progress made in the control of disease has fired the popular imagination to some vision of the possible accomplishments that may be expected for well-supported effort for human betterment, and we are becoming tolerant if not actually enthusiastic about the great foundations and the heavily endowed universities.

The growing awareness of unnecessary handicap in life has turned people more and more toward a practical interest in the help to be secured from such movements as that represented by the National Committee for Mental Hygiene, the Institute of Criminal Law and Criminology, the National and the Social Science Research Councils, and the Institute of Human Relations. Personal demand for help in living by way of personality study and other psychiatric techniques has led to an acute problem in the production of competent personnel for utilizing what little we already know of man as a person among persons. An ideal of opportunity-adjustment and social organization is forming, in spite of many obstructive influences.

The amelioration of human misery, for long neglected because it was "everybody's business," is proceeding on provisional lines in a great many directions. Vast funds are being expended in public and private efforts. Associations, funds, clinics, bureaus, schools, hospitals, and sanatoria are in the field. Legislators, police, magistrates, and juvenile and adult courts of several categories make and administer legal regulations. Special and reformatory schools, correctional institutions, penitentiaries, and prisons are in the areas affected. Psychiatric clinics and private and public hospitals for the mentally deviated are finally accorded recognition. The number of people employed in the cure, prevention, amelioration, and segregation of the victims of behavior disorders and handicaps, economic, educational, hygienic, and personal, is becoming enormous.

It is necessary that we attend to the fact that each one of these increasingly numerous agents of welfare or control is a person engaged in looking after other persons, or after some particular attributes of others. Whatever his more or less benevolent warrant, his competence toward achieving the intended goal, his actual influence on the life-course of those with whom he deals, in the last analysis, his every act in private or public welfare, is an interaction of one with another person, and its actual results are of the interpersonal situation, however inspired. Quite apart from their character as ethical, religious, esthetic, social, political, economic, or theoretic-scientific acts of an agent as the symbol of another entity, acts calculated for social welfare or control must be recognized to be events of interpersonal relations, in primary or in secondary group formation. Every such act, in the *practical* application of its meaning to those who are its object, is reducible to primary interaction.[1]

It would then seem obvious that the growth of organized social control and welfare-work must carry with it a great *problem of*

---

[1] It may be that some of the esthetic acts are wholly exempt from this rule. A great addition to the sum total of earthy beauty may well be taken as an exception. The nature of esthetic experience is a question rarely relevant to welfare work, most unfortunately.

CHAPTER
XII

personnel. It would seem that, while we await the great discoveries in personality understanding and the invention of rapid and effective techniques susceptible of truly scientific application to unfortunate people, *the persons* on whose efficiency in functioning we must depend for our attempts at individual guidance and social control must be second only in importance to the plans themselves. I believe that the personnel aspects of much welfare-working are gravely neglected, and that, as a result, a great deal of *misfortune* is caused the ostensible beneficiaries of private and public good works. I am not competent to the task, nor do I feel it incumbent on me, of attempting an assay of the outcome in personality values of any of the current public or private programs, but I know that a good deal of evil is done with the best of primary intentions, and that the evil done without good intentions by many agents clothed with authority intended to do good is very great. This mischief is by no means restricted to the actual functioning of, say, our "reformatories," from which criminologists expect most of the "beneficiaries" to be graduated as confirmed "criminals," or our mental hospitals, which have evolved to replace the archaic "asylum," but which still contribute to the disintegration of many patients; it is a mischief also widespread among private philanthropies, family-welfare organizations, community centers, missions, free employment offices, and so forth. It is widespread in our schools and colleges. It is to be found in the Boards of Aldermen, the State Legislatures, and the Congress of the United States. And of all places, it is prevalent in the relations of Law to its subjects.

There is a Federal Commission now concerning itself with the problem of law enforcement. Though most abundantly be-lawed, the American people are reputed to be strangely lawless, perhaps in this way also distinguished among the peoples of the earth. The Commission will presumably find the facts about this situation. I am told that one of their efforts has already been productive of data most interesting to the student of personality. One useful source of information would be a statistical report of crime; but there seems to be no way of securing even numerical information about crime. Crime, like most personal acts, has a variety of meanings; and for activating of the majestic edifice of the Law it has to "mean" an occurrence known to the police, or to the District Attorney, or to some other agent for *primary* inter-action in enforcing the Law. All sorts of unideal *personal* moti-vations, however, lead to difficulties in the way of even a counting of crimes known to these agents—much less, a cataloging of in-dividual details.

Now, a number of outstanding psychiatrists have been voicing the view that among the things a crime "means" is an act of a person—in other words, much might come from considering the criminal as well as the act violating a law. The American Bar As-sociation has subscribed to this enlightened view and has urged that a psychiatrist be concerned with each trial involving the *degree* of crime called a felony. From another standpoint the per-sonality student may inquire as to the factors of interaction by which *some* of those who thus infract the law are brought to the attention of the law, while most of them go on their more or less belated way unaccessed among the criminal, and therefore presumptively good citizens of the Commonwealth. This might well be a work of supererogation, however, and might better be postponed until we have some information on another aspect of the interaction of agents of law with the subjects of its control. We might study the illegal actions of the police in dealing with people, and vice versa. Better still, since we are now concerning ourselves with law enforcement, we might study the function of the *primary* courts of justice, those held by justices of the peace and police magistrates. The law comes to the man in the street chiefly via the police and these magistrates. His best evidence of its worth for his respect is manifestly the doings of these agents in their dealings with him.

Right-minded people are asked to *obey* the law. The law is in fact founded on a noble fiction about such a right-minded person, the Reasonable Man. The law that has grown on our own soil, that was not imported in the early days of the Republic and ac-climatized to our rural and pioneering society, is the work of representative-legislators, helped out by a truly remarkable body of judicial interpretations—more or less rational attempts at find-ing a meaning in some of the legislative enactments. Legislators are notoriously optimistic as to their law-making functions. When it comes to the executive application of their laws, their optimism often amounts to a Jovian indifference. Our democratic system of representation, far from being a perfect scheme for social control, massively reflects in its pyramid of legislation the promises of satisfaction for momentarily urgent desires of the politically effective population. The legislator, having experienced a fantasy that will perhaps escape the highest court as to its "constitutionality," absolves himself of further responsibility by designating an executive agency. He has "acted in the interest of his constituency and of the country at large," and has given "them" what they wanted. If it "doesn't work," it can be amended, repealed, or permitted to become a dead letter. He is too busy accommodating his political necessities to those of his confreres, giving his support in return for support, to have time for collaborative study of social situations and promising attempts at social remedies; expediency must almost always exercise the guidance.

It is no business of the legislator if "they" whose wish he has fulfilled chance to be a small but highly organized minority and that therefore the enactment was a *legislation of prejudice*, a law to enforce an obsolescent folkway, an attempt by a particular body of Philistines to insure themselves against a particular body of Bohemians. This sort of law is one of our greatest evils, for, once enacted, it is apt to stand, yet cannot be enforced but sporadically. Attempts at its modification or repeal bring the sponsors out in arms, with the best of propaganda at their disposal—for propaganda works on prejudice. It tends to remain on the statutes book, and to be invoked occasionally, although its violation is widespread and habitual. Such laws serve perfectly the ends of those who prey upon others. While the Philistines are relaxed and the Bohemians are growling about legislative stupidity, diehards, sand in the gears of progress, and the like, the petty politicians and other creatures of our indifference to personnel are making use of the "letter of the law" for purposes of subordination, extortion, and the like. These creatures know what anyone else can all too easily discover, that once in the clutches of the machinery of justice, no man—excepting sometimes the political "fixer" properly supplied with funds—can tell the outcome, and that, once exposed to the calumnious publicity easily directed at anyone arraigned "as innocent until proven guilty" of violating almost any of the mores, one has suffered a defamation the evil consequences of which are hard to "live down."

Certainly lawlessness is no private characteristic of those who are not *of* the law, and as long as the police and the magistrates are the relatively irresponsible agents of justice in the matters *most apt* to impinge upon the average man, and these same agents are not even themselves protected from the manipulation of petty politicians, but have often to look solely to these very people for rewards and punishments, we must expect a growing contempt for the law and for legislative activity. For people learn from their personal interaction with the agents of welfare and control, not from the private or legislative fantasies embodied in the welfare plan; and this generality is no more applicable to the "tools" of crooked politicians than is it to well-meaning but stupid agents alike of governmental and of private philanthropies. Personality assassination may be the prerogative of the former, but mayhem by minor agents of Goodness and philanthropy is generalized.[2]

The present scene might be taken to reflect an inborn "trait" of unmanageability, or an evolving "tendency" to crime and communism. I believe, however, that the facts are quite the contrary. Everyone seems to come very easily to respect abstract systems that *work*. Even a rudimentary acquaintance with it leads anyone to unbounded admiration for mathematics; it is a marvelous spectacle of human achievement. Everyone knows that

[2] A great many welfare-workers have learned that their judgment is at the mercy of their impulses. Perhaps the least harmful of these have proceeded to insure their impulses against any awakening! These latter wish to do Good in an impersonal, efficient, and businesslike fashion—as robots dealing with robots. Another group, fairly well mechanized in their allotted field of mercy, are exposed, however, on other sectors, and thus encounter some aspects of "human vileness" against which they are not insured.

A girl, a low-grade moron, who came to the attention of a family-welfare worker because of "unmarried motherhood," so distressed the worker by continued immorality that the latter telephoned one after another of the girl's employers to apprise them about her "loose moral character." The girl finally left town, taking her child with her to grow up in a situation of squalor accentuated by her demonstrated incapacity for "decency." Perhaps this sort of keeping of the public morals is not on a par with the "shaking down" of an unsuspecting user of a subway "convenience" by a police-magistrate-politician combination. It was done in the interest of Goodness, rather than in that of Graft. Yet the boy—fortunately of well-integrated personality—suffered but the loss of his father's one thousand dollars, and the acquisition of a lasting contempt for the social situation that encourages such vampirism.

figures do not lie, no matter how many liars may be good at figures. We become suspicious of the liar's figures because *he* is a liar. I surmise, however, that our disrespect for law is even more deep-rooted than mere suspicion of the users of the law. Not only is the law misused, but it has come to be an unworkable abstraction; it is a thing of the past, extremely in need of revision if it is again to be accepted as good, as an abstraction that works. The path of personality growth leads through respect-for-law. The child and the juvenile develop techniques adjustive to persons actually in authority, and also evolve ideal-systems that are in fact abstract schemes of divine and secular law, the superego aspects of personality. If their experience is consistent, their private legal systems are consistent, and functionally effective. To such people, respect for law is automatic, until they have learned by experience that the law is not to be respected because it is inconsistent or absurd. To the personalities evolved through experience with inconsistent authorities, *injustice* (inconsistent administration of authority) is familiar, and they come to chronological adulthood with deep skepticism about human embodiments of perfection, concrete or abstract. To them the legal fiction of the Reasonable Man—guided doubtless by Social Common Sense [3]—may well seem a ridiculous superstition, scarcely more rational than is a savage's totem.

The Reasonable Man myth does not encounter much difficulty of belief as long as almost all significant people in a given group adhere to the mores. Also, there is then little need for legal enactments. The police powers and primary judiciary functions can be carried on under color of some formula such as "Disturbing the Peace" or "Disorderly Conduct," and insignificant individuals

[3] The philosopher has a World of Common Sense, a construct from consensually verifiable experience of the (quite different) perduring entities of nature. It is in this World, for example, that the sun rises and sets, automobiles and traffic signals function, however uncertainly, and people both exist and express their views to one another. In the expressing of views, however, people often pass out of this metaphysical but very familiar world of common sense, for instance, by referring to Common Sense about interpersonal relations. This is a locution by which they point to their own private rationalizations of those of the mores incorporated in their personalities, of which they have the necessary awareness to talk. Some uncertainty about the precise social *common* sense is to be suspected whenever a speaker has recourse to the expression "of course"—that is, if he is not conscious of a purpose to deceive or prejudice the listener.

who object to some overriding of constitutional or other civil guarantees may be dealt summary justice with impunity. If a malcontent minority threatens to stir up trouble, the representatives of the community can enact a suitable regulation—for example, one drafted for them by the local attorney having the most clients among the influential majority. This is the American folkway, a delightfully Reasonable way of handling divergencies from local behavior-norms, but one whose inadequacies for present urban requirments are beginning to concern even the Philistine lobbies.

Ignorance of law must be assumed to be "no excuse" for a violation, yet no honest lawyer would any longer claim even a superficial familiarity with *all* the laws of his particular state. The Reasonable Man fiction is becoming so rarefied that it is approaching the condition of a religious nebulosity, while the relationship of real men to the body of the laws has grown into a research problem of no mean complexity. The student of personal interaction has now to divide his problems among three categories: those exterior to legal processes; those involving legal processes, but processes somewhat approximating a modern situation—juvenile court cases, cases before courts of domestic relations; and those involving the traditional legal processes, notably those affecting adolescents and adults alleged to have violated the criminal law. In situations within the last-mentioned category, the student of personality must dissociate himself from any factors other than (1) those that have been discovered by the legislators and embodied in law, and (2) those that can be presented *in court* under the somewhat embarrassing "rules of evidence" to the effective satisfaction of a jury of citizen-peers; everything else is irrelevant or immaterial to the administration of criminal justice.

In some states necessarily, and in almost any state if the defendant is possessed of competent friends and other power, the personality of the offender may be granted a noumenal importance—if his offense is such that it cannot be "disposed of" by a magistrate's court. Particularly if he has taken the life of one of his fellows (and has been apprehended), this noumenon of his self must be considered. His *sanity* must be appraised, often by the same jury of citizen-peers. These good peers are guided to an effective opinion on some such recondite basis as "his responsibility at the time of the act," in turn implying "ability to discriminate right from wrong," and "full knowledge of the nature and consequences of his act." If his sanity is not "proven beyond a *reasonable* doubt" as embodied in any resolute one of the citizen-peers, then the penalty provided by law may not be exacted, but instead some other "remedy" must be had.[4] There may be a compromise verdict of the order of "Guilty; Without Capital Punishment," or the outcome may in other ways tend toward the incarceration of the "criminal insane." Experience indicates that the citizen-peers are not beyond finding unqualifiedly "guilty" the most gravely psychotic of transgressors—those who commit "heinous and atrocious crimes." And equally, experience teaches that an "insane criminal," having profited incredibly from a brief sojourn in the mental hospital, is promptly found "sane" by another jury of citizen-peers, and returned thereon to the bosom of the community. I may be thought to cast obloquy herein on the *bona fides* of the "insanity plea" in these connections. On the contrary; I have noted with appropriate "sentiment" the wisdom of citizen-peers in the District of Columbia who, during a newspaper campaign against the distinguished Superintendent of St. Elizabeths Hospital, the Government hospital for the "insane," discharged into their own midst a number of psychotic individuals *actually* a menace to the community. The average felon, even the average murderer, is not nearly so great a menace to society as is the homicidal paranoid individual—who, if he kills, will not kill his mistress' lover, or a competing racketeer, but instead will aim himself at a person of public, and perhaps of actual social, importance. The determination of the presence or absence of paranoid mental disorder is sometimes a task for the competent personality student, with such assistance as he may derive from all available data on the patient's previous life. Such historic data are frequently held to be irrelevant, immaterial, and perhaps actually prejudicial to the proceedings of criminal trials or insanity determinations by jury.[5]

[4] I do not wish to develop the interesting theme of the alienist-physician in his relation to this recondite investigation into "insanity." Some of our state legislatures are attending to the somewhat miraculous character of this jury-determination of defendants' "mental condition" at the time of criminal acts, and procedures have been adopted in some states that are a decidedly important improvement on the traditional practice.

[5] In a recent trial for murder, a committee of psychiatrists were able to secure for consideration, in forming their expert opinions, the previous history of the traverser, by having opinions, *the informants called as witnesses and examined and cross-examined in court.* In the course of this sordid per-

Legislators are not wholly unconscious of the more glaring deficiencies of current procedures under the criminal law, and there is growing concern about dissociating the jury-determination of guilt or innocence from the administration of penalty-provided-by-law. For a long time, there has been reposed in some judges a measure of discretion as to the term and place of punishment; this sometimes in association with a system of election for rather short judicial terms, which results in a certain tempering of discretion with caution by some judges seeking re-election. One cannot always be insensitive to popular prejudice, political expediencies, and the sensational press, if one wishes to go on enjoying the "people's gifts." [6] Now we hear recommendations for commissions to study each convicted felon, to determine the treatment to be meted to him—punishment, psychiatric treatment, permanent segregation, or death. There will devolve on such a commission no little labor in finding the facts relevant to determining the treatment for each of our plentiful crop of felons. Moreover, if their work is to be more than perfunctory, they will be confronted with the same old problem of the personnel who are to interact with the convicts in the accomplishment of the prescribed treatment. [7]

---

formance—in which the mother, brothers, sisters, wife, and boyhood friends and neighbors of the traverser were required to testify to the intimate details of their association with him, despite the often successful efforts of the State's Attorney (an elected official) to impugn their veracity, humiliate them before the packed courtroom, and turn their embarrassment to the semblance of deliberate deception or innate imbecility—the commendable zeal of the officers of the law to secure the hanging of a "Jew" who had shot and killed an outstanding American citizen and distinguished member of the local Bar, supported by the opinions of some of the alienists that the traverser's personality warp (he was a singularly harassed and profoundly "inferior" paranoid psychopath and his victim a gentleman at the opposite pole of social, economic, and self-respecting status) was irrelevant to the "legal establishment of sanity," miscarried to the extent that the jury of citizen-peers assumed the inevitable opprobrium and found him "Guilty; Without Capital Punishment."

[6] Some primitive societies manifest conspicuously a keen envy of wealth and power, the achievement of which is an important goal of most of their members. An anthropological inquiry into this phenomenon might throw some light on the circulation-expanding utility to "yellow" journals of pillorying elected judges, prosecuting attorneys, and chiefs of police, for crime waves, derelictions in duty, and "failure to inspire respect for the Law." The readers of these sheets are the Electors; one might wonder why they seem to enjoy publicity about their own alleged stupidity.

[7] The personnel problem also works to nullify the good embodied in the

Let us consider briefly one of the best instances of this primary interaction in the treatment of objects of public or private welfare, that provided by the mental hospital. In touching on this I shall both be on somewhat familiar ground, and avoid many limiting factors centering in the care of persons guilty of crime, immorality, poverty, illegitimacy, addiction to drink, communism, or other false gods, and persons seen but occasionally for the administration of doles, jobs, or good advice. Moreover, I shall offer but indirect comment on physicians, lawyers, clergymen, and other professional personnel, even though they may spend one of each twenty-four hours in actual interaction with the object of welfare, and exercise "administrative control" over him the other twenty-three.

In general, the persons engaged in nursing and attending directly to patients in a mental hospital are well-meaning folk, even though, denied such work, they might have had to resort to day-laboring; this fact is often apparent. One unfamiliar with human motivation may marvel as to the factors effective in keeping those competent for other work at such jobs, for neither the economic returns nor the social emoluments of the position are attractive— the status conferred by such work is very small. One learns from the promising personnel that they are in the work "because I like it" *and* "didn't have much schooling," "didn't learn a trade," and so on. The apologetic *and* which is the copula of the satisfaction from the work itself with the need for excusing one's being in it carries a wealth of meaning. It tells, for example, that there is "no future" in being an attendant-nurse. It tells that some characteristics of the typical attendant-nurse situation are not appealing to a self-respecting observer: the facts are that a large proportion are "floaters," going from one to another hospital by reason of being "fired," because of unpleasant living conditions, or merely from wanderlust; that many of these floaters are chiefly engaged in drawing pay and allowances, gambling, drinking, or courting sex objects, instead of in interested performance of worthwhile duties; that the admixture of these deteriorant people is so great that the stability of the work itself is affected, for the supervising personnel assumes incompetence, irresponsibility, and

---

parole system, and is not without cogency in the matter of the indeterminate sentence, theoretically a very good innovation.

collusion among the attendant-nurses generally, and being in turn supervised—and relatively incompetent—are quick to discharge blame on the underlings.

Some of the doings of the attendant-nurse in the pursuance of his duty are incomprehensible, not only to him and to his charges but to any competent student of personality. One does it or quits. There isn't any sense to it, and there is no use of trying to modify it, for one's boss has other incomprehensibilities to worry about, and may think that he is being "shown up" or having something "put over on him" if he is questioned about the meaning of the routine. Impossible rules are in force; one finds that these are chiefly for the convenience of one's superiors, in "washing their hands" of trouble, and in "getting rid of" anyone they dislike. "Efficiency," the basis for what little promotion there is, if it is not a pure function of length of employment, is measured by the ability to keep out of trouble, more or less out of sight, and to "stand in" with immediate superiors. Keeping out of trouble, the novice early discovers, means being "one of the crowd." One may not think much of the "crowd" or of some of their sadistic or contemptuous doings, but one doesn't air one's views, nor permit any derogatory facts to percolate through one to a superior. One must avoid even too definite an interest in any phase of one's work, for that might lead to the attention of one of the more remote superiors, and one would then be suspected of "standing in" with him, and thereby come to be an enemy of everyone below his rank—including one's immediate superiors and one's fellows. This, too, is the rule if "classes" are held for one's "education." In the first place, the "instruction" is often quite incomprehensible; in the second, if one takes too much to studying "what it is all about," one is suspected of being dissatisfied with one's lot, and, therefore, of wishing to be better than one's fellows.

The interested observer, uncovering such a lamentably "low morale" in the attendant-nurse, may properly look to the hierarchy of superiors for its source. He then finds that supervising nurses are none too clear on the purpose of treatment, and certainly are uninformed as to its procedures. He finds a battery of more definitely therapeutic personnel: recreational and occupational aides, hydro- and physiotherapeutic aides, dieticians, special nurses. In-

quiry elicits all sorts of practices and all sorts of therapeutic no-
toins from these. Most of them, being rather consciously "in the
dark," are therefore vigorously preserving their "prestige." Beyond, there is the chief nurse and the clinical director. The one
works, through supervising nurses, toward the general welfare of
patients, by means of personnel who are but poorly equipped by
nature and by training. The other works through the chief nurse,
the therapeutic aides, and subordinate physicians, to the same end.
Before the observer can affix blame for the poor morale or stupid
performances on the clinical director, he must consider also the
administrative chief, perhaps the superintendent. And here he finds
an answer, but far from a satisfying one. He finds that he has
reached a focus of lines of indifference, stupidity, and intolerance
that were projected in the primary personnel, but that originate
far beyond the hospital, finally in the good public itself. The superintendent, his chiefs of service, their minions, and the final first line
of interaction with the objects of welfare—all the system reflects
public indifference to the *worker looking after the other fellow.*
The people who can't do much of anything else are good enough
to look after the people who need looking after. One wonders
why we go on with this; why not euthanasia for both groups?

It is reported that some seven million of our fellows are at the
moment "out of work" in the United States. Seven millions of
people, previously able to do something gainful, are in acute need
of economic welfare, well known to be prerequisite to the achievement of other cultural values. Most of these unfortunates, alike
most of those still gainfully employed, have no insight into the
factors responsible for their economic situation. The more learned
among them may refer to the business cycle; the less read, to the
presidential policies. Most of us are suffering some discomfort
from the business depression; we all hope that the return of good
times will be expedited. If it is delayed, the prevailing political
party will certainly suffer at the polls. And very right and proper
this is, not because any political party is likely to have much effect
on prosperity, but because politicians depend for their living on
other people's unsatisfied wishes and discomforts, and enjoy
power chiefly because the public still expects miracles by which
wordy propaganda will be converted into deeds of welfare—to
the elect electorate. As a result of this faith, no man may aspire

to a position of great importance in human welfare, under national, state, or local community governmental auspices, unless he be prepared not only to be a politician and feed propaganda to the hungry, but also to be a politician in dealing with the politicians who legislate the financial sinews by which he must work. So much I offer as my view of a democratic system that is without fundamental respect for human personality.

The best president, governor, director of welfare, state hospital superintendent, commissioner of police, or supervisor of the poor cannot but fail in most of his hopes, as long as he has to depend for his personnel of primary interaction on those who can't do anything else, on relatively incompetent folk of no particular importance to society at large. That a great deal has been accomplished with the personnel now available cannot be gainsaid. But the cost of the achievement is so much greater than is that of equal accomplishment in any other line not involving direct dealing with people's living, that we can scarcely hope to go on in this way. It may be that the economic misfortune now confronting so many will give the necessary impetus to our civic reorientation, and that, before it is forgotten in the next period of prosperity, we shall come to a more sound basis of valuation in things social, and to a trust in the worthiness of welfare-work rather than in the piling of money, bricks, and mortar on a flimsy structure of laws or private plans for disposing of those to whom living has not been a success, through the instrumentality of agents but one step removed from their charges.

Until the indissolubly interpersonal character of social life shall have been perceived as a basic feature of every human personality, and the notion of private good is dissipated as an unworkable fiction, there will continue to be increasing disregard both of anachronistic regulation and of the personal necessity of interest in the general welfare. With a more sound psychobiological view, the cultivation of prejudice and the working of personal advantage by playing on prejudice will be regarded as juvenile and unsuited to man's estate. The cultivation of a broad tolerance coupled with a passion for the facts of personality growth and interaction seems to me to offer the only road out of our present impasse in the management of ourselves among others. Not only does this combination offer the only hope, but the hope that it offers seems to be a great one, by no means too difficult of attainment. It traverses selfishness and self-seeking as they have been known to us, but it does this not by special pleading, or by threat of reward or punishment—here or hereafter— but by erasing them as durable misapprehension inhering in our inattentive growth to an unprecedented level of culture. Just as our forefathers, even though shown that mere distance could be transcended by devices of communication, yet lived for long in the delusion of local cultural superiority, so we, now shown that man can live completely only in indissoluble communal existence with others and with the world of culture, continue briefly to live in the illusion of personal superiority, inattentive to fully human values, and preoccupied with minor attributes of human acts.

Thanks to the Machine, we have that leisure to take stock of our selves which had previously been attained only by the Greeks of the classicial period; thanks to the Machine, we are emancipated from the Greeks' dependence on slavery for this leisure, and from the resulting limitation in perspective. The Machine has thus placed us beyond any people that has been on earth. It behooves us to take stock in time to save our civilization from destruction by the mob violence of unhappy folk ignored too long by those given the leisure to work a remedy. We are not confronted by barbarian hordes. We are not sinking into effete decadence. We are anything but lost to God. We are confronted with unprecedented opportunity to make use of our previously dormant abilities, in the service of a modern, fully human God— the potentialities of human personality.

That the Great Era is to come to us without our effort, or by way of workers in the universities, or through some great genuis for invention, or by new leadership in a novel political scheme— all this is from infantile to preadolescent fantasy. That a new brotherhood of man, with Equality, Freedom, Liberty, Social Democracy, or whatnot for all, is the future state of the Great Society is a regressive retreat from the cold reality of personality differentiation. No one knows the outlines of the future society, and all that is clear is that it will result, if at all, only from a period of creative work in the great laboratory of actual living. The scientific attitude toward all the facts of interpersonal relations is clearly to be our guide in the amassing of the material with which we can rebuild a culture suited to our emancipation from the threat of hunger and the elements, the gift of the physical sciences.

The struggle of the organized church against implications of the new knowledge [8] has prepared the more accessible of the population for a sowing of the seeds of tolerance—unfortunately, the rarest of our possessions. Our course from the cradle onward includes the incorporation of culture-patterns, toward divergencies from which we are apt to feel as unfriendly as do we toward all novel things that we have not made. At the same time, unbiased by definite negative valuations, our curiosity tends toward the investigation of the novel and unexpected, when it is not actually fear-provoking. Something of the but dimly perceived implications of true tolerance is included in a turning of scientific study to interpersonal relations. No act of faith to a dogma of "tolerance" can serve the purpose. The student must *know* rather than merely believe, however evangelically, the factual material in his own personality that is at the bottom of his appraisals of culture-patterns and behavior units that are divergent from his norm; otherwise, he tends to discover nothing of interpersonal reality.

Obviously, then, the sowing of the seeds of tolerance is no simple matter of "popularizing" knowledge or using propaganda. It is an educational procedure that might well begin with the new-born, *if* we had the teachers possessed of the facts that are to be taught. This is clearly the point at which it should begin, if the lush growth of folkways is to be restrained enough to give tolerance a chance of replacing the mores. But the teachers of folkways are, firstly, the parents, and, secondly, the teachers in primary schools. The former are "everybody" and the latter, all too often, are instances of our indifference to personal problems in primary interaction. Teachers have to be "good" people by the time they have left the normal school; they must know something about teaching the age-group with which they will work; other-

[8] The full bitterness of which may be yet to come in America; the Church may be energized by conservative elements to such discontent with leaving to Caesar the things that are Caesar's, that our legislators will be caused to enter upon the statutes a variety of prohibitive laws, calculated to arrest the progress of the universe, or at least the further growth of our acquaintance with it.

wise, they may be almost anything in personality—some of them are actually psychotic. That which they wittingly teach is but a part of that which the pupils learn from them. Parents do not have to be anything but biologically capable of procreation. Foster-parents can dispense even with this requirement. The experience of child-guidance organizations indicates that the remedy of childhood and juvenile behavior problems is a work of retraining the more adult environing people, usually the parents. I shall not comment on the limitations inhering in such a necessity.

It must be in that era of personality growth at which interpersonal intimacy appears as a personal necessity that we should seek our opportunity for sowing our seeds of tolerance with a new humanity. The epoch of adolescence seems to me to be the locus of hope. Preadolescents and adolescents seek assistance and welcome knowledge of people. Children and juveniles seek nothing of us; their "problem" is really the environment's problem in "dealing with" them. Anything done through the parents is accomplished in personalities already beaten into the mold of the past. That which we can accomplish with adolescents is a preface to the future, to parenthood and the second generation. There is a Commission Investigating Social Studies in the Schools, and a National Society for the Study of Education, from the membership of which we may hope for much. There are many organizations concerned with youth as a zone marginal to their interest in children and juveniles, or in the training of parents. I do not know of an organization primarily concerned with the synthesis of personality in adolescence, on which, as a psychopathologist, I must pin my hopes for the Great Society.

The redirection of personality that has occurred in the three past generations of adolescents has brought the more accessible of our people from a world-view that might be called prescientific to one in which many natural-scientific truths are accepted without emotion. The implications of this transition for the guidance of higher education are great; the light shed by it on the processes of cultural evolution is not to be ignored by those interested in more than ephemeral welfare. In particular, this transition forbids a pessimistic outlook on things human, and demonstrates that, however slowly we may wean ourselves from some forms of error, we have the integrative equipment and rational abilities needed for a rapid progression toward truth. Practically, it has raised to the focus of attention in sound welfare-planning the whole matter of culture-building, toward a contribution to which the present text is directed. The adolescent now progresses into a world strange indeed to his grandparents, but one also strange to him. He finds it empty of values corresponding to those which have served previous generations, and is baffled in his search for a stable synthesis of himself and the social whole by the apparently fraudulent character of ethical and religious patterns that have been incorporated within him. To him the ethics of personality as the sublime value is *determinately* lucid, because these values would suit the growth of tendency-systems within him. But he finds no social sanctions deriving from such an ethical system, and only some psychotic or subpsychotic religions— obviously exceptional and abnormal—that attempt to suit his needs. He perceives that his parents contented themselves with muddling through life in the twilight of fading creeds, and he cannot believe that they were quite sincere in their conformities and idealizations. The noise of commercialized pleasure and the dissonances of industrialism seem to him at least more real than the wistful fantasies of heavenly choirs. Hedonism and hard work seem to share a philosophical incompleteness suggestive of the infrahuman; but orthodox morality is not even a respectable chimera beside them. Repressions that seem to have been his parents' chief "hopeful fears" are to him rather banal preoccupations. He plunges, finally, into a midadolescent carnival in which the more grave dissociational processes must serve the tendencies that are not to be satisfied by compensatory "hardness" and the defensive dynamics. The returns of the "new life" to self-respect are of debased coinage, however, and the avoidance of personal "panic" may come to be an all-absorbing effort. In brief, there is not any rational justification for the "show," and the rationalizations worked out by parents and grandparents are tragico-comically inadequate to the world as it is.

It may be that any living thing will strive to live, under any and all sublethal circumstances. If so, we can, if we wish, dispense ourselves of greater than individual problems presenting themselves to us. A fully natural-scientific view of man implies that those who fail improve the race by their failing, and that effort for the succoring of the fallen is an interference to no good end. This scientific formulation, pushed to its full explication, however, indicates that civilizations are in general greatly deviate from the singular ideal tacitly conceived to operate in nature. The cultural-scientific view of man implies that those who succeed best in integrating a consistent body of superpersonal entities go the farthest toward ideal functioning of the human equipment of abilities. Euthanasia, eugenics, sterilization of "the unfit"—these are the tools of natural-scientific cultivation of man. The building of hierarchies of values consistent with the unfolding knowledge of perduring reality—this is the procedure of the psycho-biological *culture* of man. I think that we had best profit from the historic continuity of man, and concentrate our attention on the problems of the second category, so, the facilitation of the adolescent-social synthesis is our most promising field for effort, to which we must turn with scientific technology rather than propaganda and prejudice. From the subject-individuals of such investigations, we may expect both data and also the urgently needed personnel for primary interaction in welfare. The very business of studying personality in its stage of true socialization seems to be the solution of the whole welfare problem; those who find help in the work go on either preoccupied with its justified expansion, as workers in improving human opportunity, or they go on in somewhat less general but none the less ultimately necessary functioning, as the parents of children freed from the present chaotic uncertainty. The way to nurture that genuine respect for human personality needed as the ideal of the Great Society would seem to lie in systematic inquiries as to its conservation and more abundant production—the only *direct* field for which seems to be the epoch of adolescence.

Index